Fuzzy Sets, Decision Making, and Expert Systems

International Series in Management Science/Operations Research

Series Editor:

James P. Ignizio, University of Houston, U.S.A.

Advisory Editors:

Thomas Saaty, University of Pittsburgh, U.S.A.
Katsundo Hitomi, Kyoto University, Japan
H.-J. Zimmermann, RWTH Aachen, West Germany
B.H.P. Rivett, University of Sussex, England

Previously published books in this series:
Zimmermann, H.-J.: *Fuzzy Set Theory—and Its Applications*

Fuzzy Sets, Decision Making, and Expert Systems

H.-J. Zimmermann

Kluwer Academic Publishers
Boston Dordrecht Lancaster

Distributors

for the United States and Canada: Kluwer Academic Publishers, 101 Philip Drive, Assinippi Park, Norwell, MA 02061

for the UK and Ireland: Kluwer Academic Publishers, MTP Press Limited, Falcon House, Queen Square, Lancaster LAI IRN, UK

for all other countries: Kluwer Academic Publishers Group, Distribution Centre, P.O. Box 322, 3300 AH Dordrecht, The Netherlands

Library of Congress Cataloging-in-Publication Data
Zimmermann, H.-J. (Hans-Jürgen), 1934–
Fuzzy sets, decision making and expert systems.
(International series in management science/operations research)
Bibliography: p.
Includes index.
1. Statistical decision. 2. Fuzzy sets. 3. Expert systems (Computer science) I. Title. II. Series.
QA279.4.Z56 1986 511.3'2 86-21502
ISBN 0-89838-149-5

Second Printing 1991.

Contents

Preface

In the two decades since its inception by L. Zadeh, the theory of fuzzy sets has matured into a wide-ranging collection of concepts, models, and techniques for dealing with complex phenomena which do not lend themselves to analysis by classical methods based on probability theory and bivalent logic. Nevertheless, a question which is frequently raised by the skeptics is: Are there, in fact, any significant problem areas in which the use of the theory of fuzzy sets leads to results which could not be obtained by classical methods?

The approximately 5000 publications in this area, which are scattered over many areas such as artificial intelligence, computer science, control engineering, decision making, logic, operations research, pattern recognition, robotics and others, provide an affirmative answer to this question. In spite of the large number of publications, good and comprehensive textbooks which could facilitate the access of newcomers to this area and support teaching were missing until recently.

To help to close this gap and to provide a textbook for courses in fuzzy set theory which can also be used as an introduction to this field, the first volume of this book was published in 1985 [Zimmermann 1985 b]. This volume tried to cover fuzzy set theory and its applications as extensively as possible. Applications could, therefore, only be described to a limited extent and not very detailed.

This second volume concentrates on an area in which fuzzy set theory has been applied very successfully during the last 15 years. In the context of this book it is useful to go back to the original statement of Bellman and Zadeh in 1970 about the role of fuzzy sets in decision analysis that triggered most of the work in this area:

> Much of the decision-making in the real world takes place in an environment in which the goals, the constraints and the consequences of possible actions are not

known precisely. To deal quantitatively with imprecision, we usually employ the concepts and techniques of probability theory and, more particularly, the tools provided by decision theory, control theory and information theory. In so doing, we are tacitly accepting the premise that imprecision – whatever its nature – can be equated with randomness. This, in our view, is a questionable assumption. Specifically, our contention is that there is a need for differentiation between *randomness and fuzziness*, with the latter being a major source of imprecision in many decision processes. By fuzziness, we mean a type of imprecision which is associated with *fuzzy sets*, that is, classes in which there is no sharp transition from membership to nonmembership. For example, the class of *green objects* is a fuzzy set. So are the classes of objects characterized by such commonly used adjectives as large, small, significant, important, serious, simple, accurate, approximate, etc. Actually, in sharp contrast to the notion of a class or a set in mathematics, most of the classes in the real world do not have crisp boundaries which separate those objects which belong to a class from those which do not. In this connection, it is important to note that, in the discourse between humans, fuzzy statements such as "John is *several* inches taller than Jim," "x is *much larger* than y," "Corporation X has a *bright future*," "the stock market has suffered a *sharp decline*," convey information despite the imprecision of the italicized words... [Bellman, Zadeh 1970, B 141]

It is perhaps worth noting that this is a very precise statement—fuzzy set theory has never been an invitation to fuzzy thinking! It is also worth emphasizing that it is not a sweeping statement that in some sense probability theory itself is wrong—only that there are forms of uncertainty where it gives an inappropriate representation.

The basis for all sound decision aids is a good normative and descriptive decision theory. The first three chapters of this book, therefore, focus on the theory of individual and multiperson decision making in crisp and fuzzy environments. Chapters 4 and 5 concentrate on specific decision situations: Mathematical programming, as the search for optimal decisions under constraints, and multicriteria analysis, as one of the most recent and most rapidly growing areas of decision analysis.

The final chapter is dedicated to practical decision making, that is, to EDP-implementations of decision models which aim at improving decision in practise. Two kinds of these systems are of particular relevance: data-based *decision support systems* and knowledge-based *expert systems*.

Decision support systems contain a built-in structure of the problem situation. We have chosen to use the mathematical programming structure to serve as the skeleton of the decision support system described.

Expert systems emerged approximately 20 years ago in artificial intelligence. Their potential for real decision making, however, was not discovered before the beginning of this decade. To a certain extent this is due to the fact that computer technology did not provide sufficiently cheap and efficient hardware before that time.

Expert systems are particularly useful and necessary when the decision situation is not adequately structured to use decision support systems. Being aimed at ill-structured situations in which an expert's knowledge is needed to find at least acceptable solutions, they require particular tools to model and process uncertainties of different kinds. It is obvious that fuzzy set theory is especially suited to this purpose. Chapter 7 offers a number of ways to improve the modelling quality of existing and future expert systems.

Even though this volume is an extension of the first, it is self-contained in the following sense: Chapter 1 includes an introduction to decision making, as well as to the theory of fuzzy sets. More advanced notions, as far as they are needed for this book, are always properly defined and explained before they are used in later chapters. Chapter 6 provides enough background on empirical research to enable the reader to understand why specific models have been chosen. We hope that this book will be useful not only for teaching purposes, but that it will also serve as a guide to scientists and practitioners in decision making who want to make use of fuzzy set theory in order to improve decision making in a broad sense.

I would like to acknowledge the help and encouragement of all my students in Aachen who helped to develop what has become this book. In particular I want to thank Dr. B. Werners who helped to improve the manuscript, to develop examples for the book, and who was always ready to discuss problems with me and to find solutions.

Ms. Grefen typed the manuscript several times without losing her patience, and made it possible for me to meet deadlines that otherwise would have been impossible.

I am especially indebted to Kluwer Academic Publishers for their excellent cooperation and care in preparing this book. In many respects the quality of this book was made possible only by the outstanding services I have enjoyed while preparing this volume for publication!

H.-J. Zimmermann
Aachen, December 1986

Fuzzy Sets, Decision Making, and Expert Systems

1 INTRODUCTION

The Logic of Decisions, Behavioral Decision Theory, and Decision Technology

The term *decision* has been used with many different meanings and in many disciplines. In order to ensure a proper interpretation of the content of this book it might be appropriate and useful to specify clearly what will be meant by "decision," "decision model," "decision theory," and "decision technology" or "decision analysis."

Let us first clarify some more basic notions before we consider the various uses of the word "decision."

The terms *model*, *theory*, and *law* have been used with a variety of meanings, for a number of purposes, and in many different areas of our life. It is, therefore, necessary to define more accurately what we mean by models, theories and laws, to describe their interrelationships, and to indicate their use before we can specify the requirements they have to satisfy and the purposes for which they can be used. To facilitate our task we shall distinguish between definitions that are given and used in the scientific area and definitions and interpretations as they can be found in more application-oriented areas, which we will call "technologies" by contrast to "scientific disciplines". By technologies we mean areas such as operations research, decision analysis, and information processing, even though these areas sometimes call themselves theories (i.e., decision theory) or science (i.e., computer science, management science, etc.). This is by no means a value statement. We only want to indicate that the main goals of these areas are different. While the main purpose of a scientific discipline is to generate knowledge and to come closer to truth without making any value statement, technologies normally try to generate tools for solving problems better and very often by either accepting or building on given value schemes. Let us first turn to the area of scientific inquiry and consider the following quotation concerning the definition of the term *model*: "A possible realization in which all valid sentences of a theory T are satisfied is called a model of T" [Tarski 1953].

Harré [Harré 1967, p. 86] said: "A model, a, of a thing, A, is in one of many possible ways a replica or an analogue of A," and a few years later, "In certain formal sciences such as logic and mathematics a model for, or of a theory is a set of sentences, which can be matched with the sentences in which the theory is expressed, according to some matching rule.... The other meaning of 'model' is that of some real or imagined thing or process, which behaves similarly to some other thing or process, or in some other way than in its behavior is similar to it" [Harré 1972, p. 173]. He sees two major purposes of models in science: (i) Logical—to enable certain inferences, which it would not otherwise be possible to make and (ii) epistemological—to express, and enable us to extend our knowledge of the world. Models according to Harré are used either as a heuristic device to simplify a phenomenon or facilitate its manipulation or an explanatory device whereby a model is a model of the real causal mechanism.

By now two things should have become obvious:

1. There is a very large variety of types of models, which can be classified according to a number of criteria. For our deliberations one classification seems to be particularly important: The interpretation of a model as a "formal model" and the interpretation as a "factual, descriptive model". This corresponds to Rudolph Carnap's distinction between a logical and a descriptive interpretation of a calculus [Carnap 1946]. For him, a logically true interpretation of a model exists if, whenever a sentence implies another in the calculus, in the interpretation whenever the first sentence is true, the second is equally true and whenever a sentence is refutable in the calculus, it is also false in the model. An interpretation is a factual interpretation if it is not a logical interpretation, which means that whether a model is true or false does not depend only on its logical interpretation. It also means that whether a model is true or false does not depend only on its logical consistency; it also depends on the (em-

pirical) relationship of the sentences (axioms of the model) to the properties of the factual system of which the model is supposed to be an image.

2. There is certainly a relationship between a model and a theory. This relationship, however, is seen differently by different scientists and by different scientific disciplines.

   We will now try to specify this relationship because theories, to our mind, are the focal point of all scientific activities. For Harré [Harré 1972, p. 174] "A theory is often nothing but the description and exploitation of some model."

White, eventually, simply points out that "There is a need to logically separate a model and a theory and that they play supporting roles in decision analysis, viz. some theory is needed so that aspects of models can be tested and some model is needed so that the effects of changes can be examined. In particular validation of a model needs a theory" [White 1975, p. 67]. Thus, there seems to be a very intimate relationship between a model and a theory. Both, probably to varying degrees, are based on hypotheses and these hypotheses can be either formal axioms or scientific laws. These scientific laws seem to distinguish between the models and theories in scientific disciplines and the models (sometimes also called theories) in more applied areas: "An experimental law, unlike a theoretical statement, invariably possesses a determinate empirical content which in principle can always be controlled by observational evidence obtained by those procedures [Nagel 1969, p. 83].

These experimental (scientific) laws assert invariance with respect to time and space. The tests to which an hypothesis must be put before it can assert to be a law depend on the philosophical direction of the scientist. Karl Popper, as probably the most prominent representative of "critical rationalism," believes that laws are only testable by the fact of their falsifiability. Popper holds further that a hypothesis is "corroborated" (rather than confirmed) to the degree of the severity of such tests. Such a corroborated hypothesis may be said to have stood up to the test thus far without being eliminated. But the test does not confirm its truth. A good hypothesis in science, therefore, is one which lends itself to the severest test, that is, one which generates the widest range of falsifiable consequences" [Popper 1959].

Let us now turn to areas which we shall call "technologies" rather than "sciences." As already mentioned the main goal of such technologies is to construct tools for better problem solving rather than to generate new knowledge and to come closer to truth.

What, now, is a model in operations research? Most authors using the term *model* take for granted that the reader knows what a model is and what it means. Arrow, for instance, uses the term *model* as a specific part of a theory, when he says "Thus the model of rational choice as built up from pairwise comparisons does not seem to suit well the case of rational behaviour in the described game situation" [Arrow 1951, p. 2]. He presumably refers to the model of rational choice, because the theory he has in mind does not give a very adequate description of the phenomena with which it is concerned, but only provides a highly simplified schema. In the social and behavioral sciences as well as in the technologies it is very common that a certain theory is stated in rather broad and general terms while models, which are sometimes required to perform experiments in order to test the theory, have to be more specific than the theories themselves. "In the language of logicians it would be more appropriate to say that rather than constructing a model they are interested in constructing a quantitative theory to match the intuitive ideas of the original theory" [Suppes 1961, p. 169].

If we consider the size of some of the models used in operations research, containing more than 10,000 variables and thousands of constraints, we can easily see what does not distinguish a theory from a model: it is not the complexity, it is not the size, it is not the language, and it is not even the purpose. In fact there seems to be only a gradual distinction between theory and model. While a theory normally denotes an entire area, it is more comprehensive but less specific than a model (for instance: decision theory, inventory theory, queuing theory, etc.), a model most often refers to a specific context or situation and is meant to be a mapping of a problem, a system or a process. By contrast to a scientific theory, containing scientific laws as hypotheses, a model normally does not assert invariance with respect to time and space but requires modifications whenever the specific context, for which a model was constructed, changes.

In the following we shall not distinguish between models and theories. It seems, however, to be important to mention one possible classification of models according to their character. Scientific theories were already divided into formal theories and factual theories. For models, particularly in the area of the technology in which values and preferences enter our considerations, we will have to distinguish between the following:

1. *Formal models.* Formal models are purely axiomatic systems from which we can derive if-then-statements and their hypotheses are purely fictitious. These models can only be checked for consistency but they can be neither verified nor falsified by empirical arguments.
2. *Factual models.* Factual models include in their basic hypothesis falsifiable assumptions about the object system. Conclusions drawn from these models have a bearing on reality and they, or their basic hypotheses, have to be verified or can be falsified by empirical evidence.

3. *Prescriptive models.* Prescriptive models postulate rules according to which processes have to be performed or which people have to behave. This type of model will not be found in science but it is a common type of model in practice.

The distinction between these three different kinds of models is particularly important when using models: All three kinds of models can look exactly the same but the "value" of their outputs is quite different. It is, therefore, rather dangerous not to realize which type of model is being used because we might take a formal model to be a factual model or a prescriptive model to be a factual model and that can have quite severe consequences for the resulting decisions.

As an example, let us consider Ackoff's model of decision making that describes decision making as a six-phase process [Ackoff 1962]. It is supposed to be a good picture (model) of the real decision making process. Is that a formal, a factual, or a prescriptive model? If it is a formal model, we can not derive from it any conclusion for real decision making. If it is a factual model then it would have to be verified or falsified before we can take it as a description of real decision making. The assertion, however, that decision making proceeds in phases was empirically falsified in 1966 [Witte 1968]. Still, a number of authors stick to this type of model. Do they want to interpret their model as a prescriptive model? This would only be justified, if they could show that, for instance, decision making can be performed more efficiently when done in phases. This, however, has never been shown empirically. Therefore, we can only conclude that authors suggesting a multiphase scheme as a model for decision making take their suggestion as a formal model and do not want to make any statement about reality, or that they are using a falsified, (i.e., invalid and false), factual model.

Let us now turn to the area of decision sciences and analysis. We can find the three kinds of models and theories mentioned above: formal theories, factual theories, and technologies. They differ from each other by their views and goals, by what kind of truth is required, and with respect to their definitions of a "decision." The formal version of decision theory is "prescriptive decision theory," normally called "normative decision theory," "decision logic," "statistical decision theory," or similar. This area constitutes a formal science, normally including utility theory, and considers a decision to be an act of rational choice. This version of decision theory works with closed models—that is, it assumes that all relevant information is given (given that..., find the optimal action!) and therefore does not include the gathering of information or a control or implementation phase after the choice. It is context independent—it considers neither the person of the decision maker, with his abilities and shortcomings, nor the context in which a decision has to be made. Prescriptive (normative) decision theory can be defined as follows:

Definition 1.1

Given the set of feasible actions, A, the set of relevant states, S, the set of resulting events, E, and a (rational) utility function, u—which orders the space of events with respect to their desirability—the *optimal decision under certainty* is the choice of that action which leads to the event with the highest utility, such a decision can be described properly by the quadruple $\{A,S,E,u\}$.

It should be noted that the decision as defined above is nonsymmetrical in the sense that A, S, and E are sets and hence unordered and u is a function which induces an order on E! Figure 1-1 sketches the so-called "basic model of (normative) decision theory," which we shall call the "choice-model" from here on.

The *factual decision theory* is often called "descriptive decision theory," "cognitive decision theory," "behavioral decision theory," or "empirical decision theory." This theory considers problem solving or decision making generally as information processing systems [Newell, Simon 1972]. It works with open models—that is, the information gathering is part of the decision

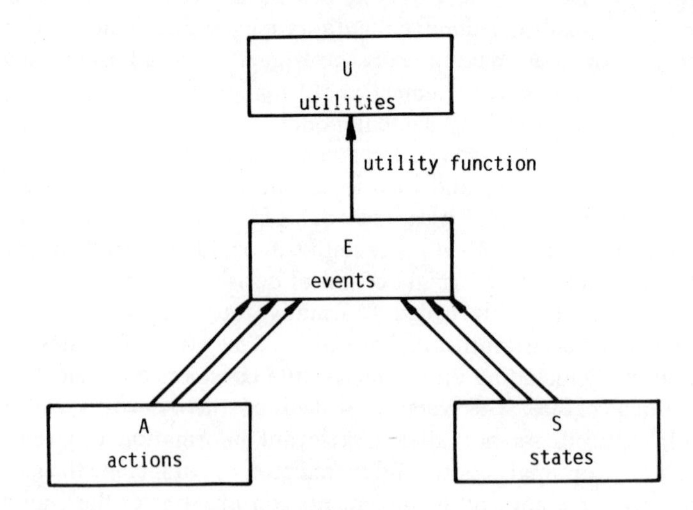

Figure 1-1: Decision as a model of choice.

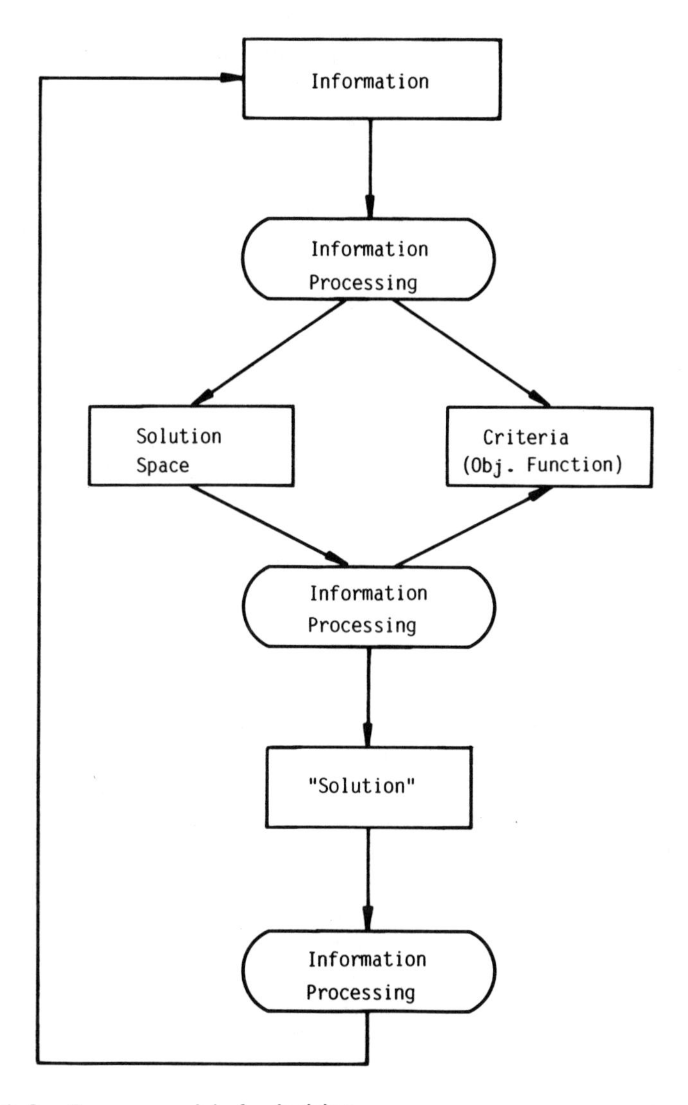

Figure 1-2: Process model of a decision.

process and the sets A, E, S are not regarded as being given. Even the utility function is considered to be developed within the decision process. In this theory, decisions are no longer treated context-free, which means that the human being, as the decision maker, is included in the analysis. Figure 1-2 sketches one possible presentation of this notion of a decision; we shall call it the "process model."

Both types of decision theory assert, in a sense, nomology (validity everywhere and always!) and the truth of their models—the former formal truth, the latter factual truth. Note, however, that in decision technologies such as operations research or decision analysis, models, algorithms, and theories are more means to the end of better problem solving or decision making. Testing of the models is never done context free and for the sake of nomological truth. The effort for testing becomes a relevant factor and has to be compared to possible benefits of the models [Zimmermann 1980].

When we use the term *decision* in the following chapters the interpretation will vary. In some chapters, such as chapters 2 and 3 its connotation in a formal interpretation will be "choice." Chapters 4, 5, and 7 are clearly decision-technology related; chapter 6 will consider some aspects of decisions in a more factual sense.

Optimization, Outranking, Evaluation

Classical normative decision theory and the majority of the models in decision technology take it for granted, that a decision maker wants to maximize utility or another decision criteria and, whereever relevant, assume that he is able to do this. Descriptive decision theory and models in decision technology are less optimistic or more realistic in this respect. They assume only a bounded rationality [Simon 1957, p. 61] of decision makers. That is, they assume satisfying rather than optimizing behavior [Simon 1955, 1956].

Since the end of the sixties there has appeared an increasing concern about the usefulness of the usual notion of a utility function for real decision making. Together with the growth of multi-criteria analysis, there has been increased effort to enrich decision models beyond the strictly optimizing choice model and to render the assumptions about the (mathematical) properties of utility preference functions more realistic. One of the most prominent representatives of this direction is Bernhard Roy. He proposed to substitute for the classical choice model, striving for a complete order of the actions or alternatives, the following classification of types of decisions [Roy 1971, p. 253; 1976, p. 10]: Given a well-defined set of decision alternatives $x \in X$ the decision maker might want to:

α. Select one and only one decision of X, considered to be the "best" (dichotomy).
β. Choose to determine all decisions $x \in X$ that seem "good," reject those

that seem "bad," and require additional analysis for the rest (trichotomy).

γ. Cluster decisions $x \in X$ in an ordered sequence of indifference classes ranging from "best" to "worst" (classification).

If a well-defined scalar-valued utility function exists, all three types of problems can be solved satisfactorily. If the utility or value function is vector valued or if there is more than one criterion as a measure of the desirability of an action, additional assumptions about the aggregating behavior of the decision maker have to be made in order to be able to solve cases α–γ. If one is not able, prepared, or willing, however, to make these additional assumptions, classical approaches of utility theory are not sufficient to offer solutions to the above-mentioned cases.

Roy, therefore, suggested using "outranking" approaches rather than classical decision models. Vincke [1986] describes outranking very clearly as follows: "The principle of outranking relation approach is to work on the set of pairs of decisions (instead of the set of decisions) in order to obtain a binary relation on the set of decisions (instead of a function from this set to the real numbers)." In fact, in an outranking approach the scientist tries to build a relation on the set of decisions (called an *outranking relation*) for modelling only the sure part of the decision maker's preferences, given the available information. In other words, one says that decision *a* outranks decision *b* if the arguments in favor of the preference of *a* over *b* (for all the criteria) are significant and those in favor of the inverse preference are not too strong. The differences among outranking methods consist in the way of formalizing this fuzzy definition.

The outranking relation is in general not complete (there exist pairs (a,b) for which neither *a* outranks *b* nor *b* outranks *a*, nor is it transitive, contrary to the global preference relation obtained in the MAUT (Multi-Attribute Utility Theory). In other words, the outranking relation is poorer than the global preference of the MAUT but is also probably more reliable. Obviously, the exploitation of an outranking relation in order to obtain "the best" decision or in order to rank decisions is much more difficult than in the MAUT.

Outranking is frequently called the European School (by contrast to the American School) in multi-criteria analysis. We shall consider the fuzzy version of this approach in more detail in chapter 5.

Behavioral and descriptive decision theory has also pointed to the fact that for a decision there does not necessarily have to be a variety of actions—the problem often is to make up one's mind to do a certain thing. Often the evaluation of a single project or alternative with respect to a number of criteria (and probably comparing this rating with a given benchmark) can very well be considered as a decision in the sense of the choice model as well as according to the process model.

Summarizing, we can say that the term *decision* has numerous different interpretations. To many of them, fuzzy set theory has been applied. We shall select the most important of these applications and discuss them in chapters 2 to 5.

Basics of Fuzzy Set Theory

In this section we shall give a very brief introduction to fuzzy set theory in order to make this book self-contained. The notions and definitions beyond basic fuzzy set theory that are needed in this volume will be explained in the following chapters whenever they are needed. For further details the reader is refered to Zimmermann [1985b].

In classical normative decision theory the components of the basic model of decision making under certainty are taken to be crisp sets or functions. By *crisp* we mean dichotomous—that is, of the yes-or-no type rather than of the more-or-less type. The set of actions is as precisely defined as the set of possible states (or the state) and the utility function is also assumed to be precise. Vagueness only enters the picture when considering decisions under risk or uncertainty and then this uncertainty concerns the happening of a state or event and not the event itself. This uncertainty is generally modelled by means of probability, no matter whether the decision is to be made once only or frequently.

In descriptive decision theory this precision is no longer assumed; but ambiguity and vagueness is very often modelled only verbally, which usually does not permit the use of powerful mathematical methods for purposes of analysis and computation.

The first publications in fuzzy set theory by Zadeh [1965] and Goguen [1967, 1969] show the intention of the authors to generalize the classical notion of a set and a proposition to accomodate uncertainty in the non-stochastic sense as mentioned above. Zadeh writes:

> The notion of a fuzzy set provides a convenient point of departure for the construction of a conceptual framework which parallels in many respects the framework used in the case of ordinary sets, but is more general than the latter and, potentially, may prove to have a much wider scope of applicability, particularly in the fields of pattern classification and information processing. Essentially, such a framework provides a natural way of dealing with problems in which the source of imprecision is the absence of sharply defined criteria of class membership rather than the presence of random variables. [Zadeh 1965, p. 339]

"Imprecision" here is used in the sense of vagueness rather than lack of knowledge about the value of a parameter as in tolerance analysis. Fuzzy set theory provides a strict mathematical framework (there is nothing fuzzy about fuzzy set theory!) in which vague conceptual phenomena can be precisely and rigorously studied. It can also be considered as a modelling language well suited for situations in which fuzzy relations, criteria, and phenomena exist. Let us now turn to the formal framework of fuzzy set theory:

A classical (crisp) set is normally defined as a collection of elements or objects $x \in X$ which can be finite, countable, or overcountable. Each single element can either belong to or not belong to a set A, $A \subseteq X$. In the former case the statement "x belongs to A" is true, in the latter case this statement is false. Such a classical set can be described in different ways; either one can enumerate (list) the elements that belong to the set, one can describe the set analytically—for instance, by stating conditions for membership ($A = \{x \in X \mid x \leq 5\}$)—or one can define the member elements by using the characteristic function $1/A$, in which $1/A(x) = 1$ indicates membership of x to A and $1/A(x) = 0$ nonmembership. For a fuzzy set the characteristic function allows various degrees of membership for the elements of a given set.

Definition 1.2

If X is a collection of objects denoted generically by x then a *fuzzy set* $\tilde{A}$ in X is a set of ordered pairs:

$$\tilde{A} = \{(x, \mu_{\tilde{A}}(x)) \mid x \in X\}$$

$\mu_{\tilde{A}}$ is the membership function that maps X to the membership space M and $\mu_{\tilde{A}}(x)$ is the grade of membership (also degree of compatibility or degree of truth) of x in $\tilde{A}$. (When M contains only the two points 0 and 1, $\tilde{A}$ is nonfuzzy and $\mu_{\tilde{A}}$ is identical to the characteristic function of a nonfuzzy set.) The range of the membership function is a subset of the nonnegative real numbers whose supremum is finite—extensions are possible [see Zimmermann 1985, ch. 3]. Elements with a zero degree of membership are normally not listed. If

$$\sup_{x \in X} \mu_{\tilde{A}}(x) = 1$$

the fuzzy set $\tilde{A}$ is called normal. As a matter of convenience, we will generally assume that fuzzy sets are normalized.

Example 1.1

A realtor wants to classify the houses he offers to his clients. One indicator of the comfort of a house is the number of bedrooms in it. Let $X = \{1,2,3,4,\ldots,8\}$ be the set of available types of houses described by x = number of bedrooms in a house. Then the fuzzy set "comfortable type of house for a 4-person family" may be described as

$$\tilde{A} = \{(1,.2),(2,.5),(3,.8),(4,1),(5,.7),(6,.3)\}$$

A fuzzy set is obviously a generalization of a classical set and the membership function is a generalization of the characteristic function. Since we are generally referring to a universal (crisp) set X, some elements of a fuzzy set may have the degree of membership zero. Often it is appropriate to consider those elements of the universe that have a nonzero degree of membership in a fuzzy set:

Definition 1.3

The *support* of a fuzzy set $\tilde{A}$, $S(\tilde{A})$, is the crisp set of all $x \in X$ such that $\mu_{\tilde{A}}(x) > 0$.

A more general and even more useful notion is that of an α-level set:

Definition 1.4

The (crisp) set of elements that belong to the fuzzy set $\tilde{A}$ at least to the degree α is called the *α-level set*:

$$A_\alpha = \{x \in X \mid \mu_{\tilde{A}}(x) \geq \alpha\}$$

$$A'_\alpha = \{x \in X \mid \mu_{\tilde{A}}(x) > \alpha\}$$ is called "strong α-level set" or "strong α-cut".

Example 1.2

We refer again to example 1.1 and list possible α-level sets:

$$A_{.2} = \{1,2,3,4,5,6\}$$

$$A_{.5} = \{2,3,4,5\}$$

$$A_{.8} = \{3,4\}$$

$$A_1 = \{4\}$$

The strong α-level set for $\alpha = .8$ is $A'_{.8} = \{4\}$.

Convexity also plays a role in fuzzy set theory. By contrast to classical set theory, however, convexity conditions are defined with reference to the membership function rather than the support of a fuzzy set.

Definition 1.5

A fuzzy set $\tilde{A}$ is *convex* if and only if

$$\mu_{\tilde{A}}(\lambda x_1 + (1 - \lambda)x_2) \geq \min(\mu_{\tilde{A}}(x_1), \mu_{\tilde{A}}(x_2))$$

$$x_1, x_2 \in X, \lambda \in [0,1]$$

Alternatively, a fuzzy set is *convex* if all α-level sets are convex in the classical sense.

One final feature of a fuzzy set which we will use frequently in later chapters is its cardinality or "power" [Zadeh 1981]:

Definition 1.6

For a finite fuzzy set $\tilde{A}$ the *cardinality* $|A'|$ is defined as

$$|\tilde{A}| = \sum_{x \in X} \mu_{\tilde{A}}(x)$$

$$\|\tilde{A}\| = \frac{|\tilde{A}|}{|X|} \quad \text{is called the relative cardinality of } \tilde{A}.$$

Obviously the relative cardinality of a fuzzy set depends on the cardinality of the universe. So one has to choose the same universe if one wants to compare fuzzy sets by their relative cardinality.

The membership function is obviously the crucial component of a fuzzy set. It is therefore not surprising that operations with fuzzy sets are defined via their membership functions. We shall first present those concepts suggested by Zadeh in 1965 [Zadeh 1965, pp. 310]. They constitute a consistent framework for the theory of fuzzy sets. They are, however, not the only possible way to extend classical set theory consistently. Zadeh and other authors have suggested alternative or additional definitions for set theoretic operations; these will be explained as needed in later chapters.

Definition 1.7

The membership function $\mu_{\tilde{C}}$ of the *intersection* $\tilde{C} = \tilde{A} \cap \tilde{B}$ is pointwise defined for all $x \in X$ by

$$\mu_{\tilde{C}}(x) = \min \{\mu_{\tilde{A}}(x), \mu_{\tilde{B}}(x)\}$$

Definition 1.8

The membership function $\mu_{\tilde{D}}$ of the *union* $\tilde{D} = \tilde{A} \cup \tilde{B}$ is pointwise defined for all $x \in X$ by

$$\mu_{\tilde{D}}(x) = \max \{\mu_{\tilde{A}}(x), \mu_{\tilde{B}}(x)\}$$

Definition 1.9

The membership function of the *complement* of a fuzzy set $\tilde{A}$, $\mu_{\complement\tilde{A}}$, is defined by

$$\mu_{\complement\tilde{A}}(x) = 1 - \mu_{\tilde{A}}(x) \qquad x \in X$$

Example 1.3

Let A be the fuzzy set "comfortable type of house for a 4-person family" from example 1.1 and $\tilde{B}$ be the fuzzy set "large type of house" defined as

$$\tilde{B} = \{(3,.2),(4,.4),(5,.6),(6,.8),(7,1),(8,1)\}$$

The intersection $\tilde{C} = \tilde{A} \cap \tilde{B}$ is then

$$\tilde{C} = \{(3,.2),(4,.4),(5,.6),(6,.3)\}$$

The union $\tilde{D} = \tilde{A} \cup \tilde{B}$ is

$$\tilde{D} = \{(1,.2),(2,.5),(3,.8),(4,1),(5,.7),(6,.8),(7,1),(8,1)\}$$

The complement $\complement\tilde{B}$, which might be interpreted as "not large type of house," is

$$\complement\tilde{B} = \{(1,1),(2,1),(3,.8),(4,.6),(5,.4),(6,.2)\}$$

2 INDIVIDUAL DECISION MAKING IN FUZZY ENVIRONMENTS

Symmetrical Models

We shall consider two versions of a decision, the classical choice model of normative decision theory (definition 1.1) and the "evaluation model" described in the first part of chapter 1.

The Fuzzy Choice Model

Let us first consider an example of definition 1.1:

Example 2.1

Let us assume that the board of directors wishes to decide about the optimal dividend. The set of possible actions, A, are the percentages x, $x \geq 0$. The state, S, is defined by the *constraint* $x \leq 6$—that is, for some reasons only dividends not higher than 6% are feasable. For the sake of simplicity let us assume that the resulting events, E, are the different degrees of attractiveness of the shares

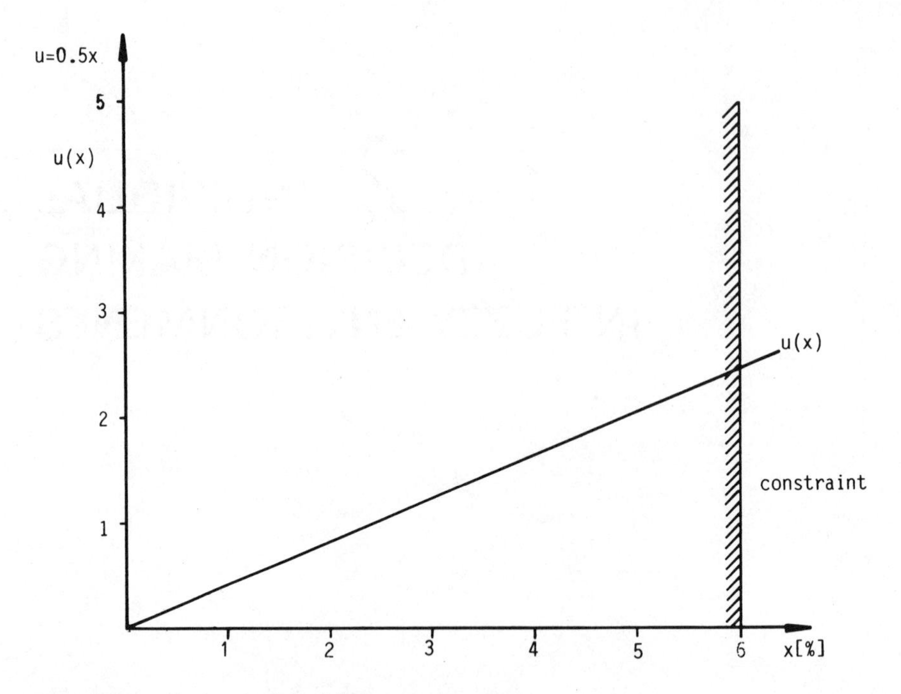

Figure 2-1: A classical decision under certainty.

at the stock-exchange yield after tax. Since the board wants to maximize this attractiveness its utility function (*objective function*), is to maximize $u(x) = \frac{1}{2}x$. Assuming a linear utility function the optimal dividend will obviously be 6%. Figure 2-1 illustrates these relationships.

In 1970 Bellman and Zadeh [1970] considered this classical model of a decision and suggested a model for decision making in a fuzzy environment which has served as a point of departure for most of the authors in fuzzy decision theory. They consider a situation of decision making under certainty, in which the objective function as well as the constraint(s) are fuzzy and argue as follows:

The fuzzy objective function is characterized by its membership function and so are the constraints. Since we want to satisfy (optimize) the objective function as well as the constraints, a decision in a fuzzy environment is defined by analogy to nonfuzzy environments as the selection of activities which simultaneously satisfy objective function(s) *and* constraints. According to the above definition and assuming that the constraints are noninteractive the logical "and" corresponds to the intersection. The decision in a fuzzy environ-

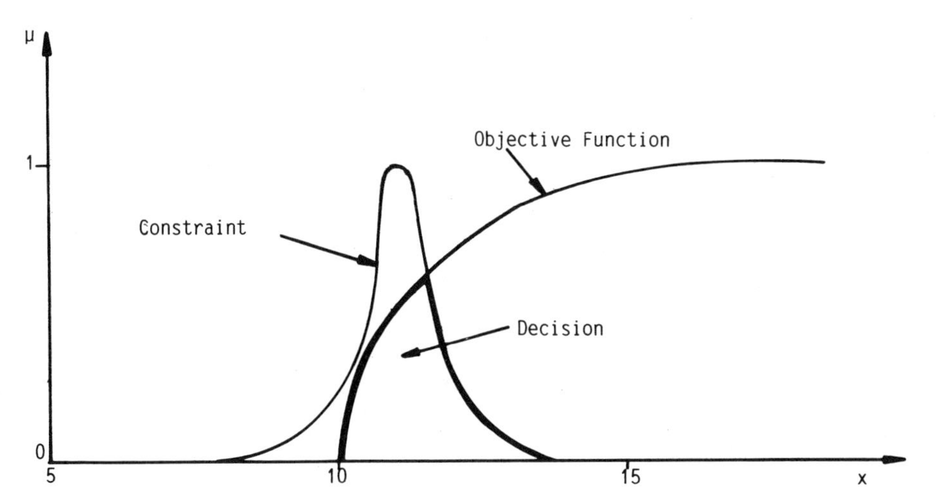

Figure 2-2: A fuzzy decision.

ment can therefore be viewed as the intersection of fuzzy constraints and fuzzy objective function(s). The relationship between constraints and objective functions in a fuzzy environment are therefore fully symmetric, that is, there is no longer a difference between the former and the latter. This concept is illustrated by the following example [Bellman, Zadeh 1970, B 148].

Example 2.2

Objective function x should be substantially larger than 10, and characterized by the membership function

$$\mu_{\tilde{G}}(x) = \begin{cases} 0 & x \leq 10 \\ (1 + (x - 10)^{-2})^{-1} & x > 10 \end{cases}$$

Constraint x should be in the vicinity of 11, and characterized by the membership function

$$\mu_{\tilde{C}}(x) = (1 + (x - 11)^4)^{-1}$$

The membership function $\mu_{\tilde{D}}(x)$ of the decision is then

$$\mu_{\tilde{D}}(x) = \mu_{\tilde{G}}(x) \wedge \mu_{\tilde{C}}(x)$$

$$= \begin{cases} \min\{(1 + (x - 10)^{-2})^{-1}, (1 + (x - 11)^4)^{-1}\} & \text{for } x > 10 \\ 0 & \text{for } x \leq 10. \end{cases}$$

This relation is depicted in figure 2-2. Let us now modify example 2.1 accordingly.

Example 2.3

The board of directors is trying to find the optimal dividend to be paid to the shareholders. For financial reasons it ought to be attractive and for reasons of wage negotiations it should be modest.

The fuzzy set of the objective function "attractive dividends" could for instance be defined by

$$\mu_{\tilde{G}}(x) = \begin{cases} 1 & x \geq 5,8 \\ \dfrac{1}{2100}[-29x^3 + 366x^2 - 877x + 540] & 1 < x < 5,8 \\ 0 & x \leq 1 \end{cases}$$

The fuzzy set (constraint) "modest dividend" could be represented by

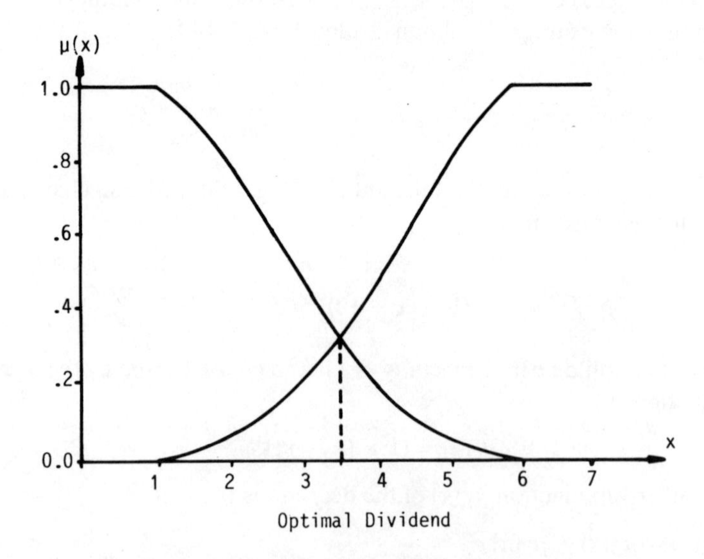

Figure 2-3: Optimal Dividend as Maximizing Decision.

$$\mu_{\tilde{C}}(x) = \begin{cases} 1 & x \leq 1,2 \\ \frac{1}{2100}[29x^3 - 243x^2 + 16x + 2388] & 1,2 < x < 6 \\ 0 & x \geq 6 \end{cases}$$

The fuzzy set "decision" is then characterized by its membership function for all $x \in X$

$$\mu_{\tilde{D}}(X) = \min\{\mu_{\tilde{G}}(x), \mu_{\tilde{C}}(x)\}$$

If the decision maker wants to have a crisp decision proposal, it seems appropriate to suggest to him the dividend that has the highest degree of membership in the fuzzy set "decision." Let us call this the maximizing decision $x_{\max}$ with

$$\mu_{\tilde{D}}(x_{\max}) = \max_x \min\{\mu_{\tilde{G}}(x), \mu_{\tilde{C}}(x)\}$$

Figure 2-3 sketches this situation.

In examples 2.2 and 2.3 the min-operator was used on the basis of the following argument: in the classical (crisp) choice model of a decision the (verbal) linkage between constraints and goals is usually "and." The only well-defined "and" is the "logical and" and this corresponds to the set-theoretic intersection. The intersection of fuzzy sets, however, has so far been modelled or defined by the min-operator. The question arises whether the association "and" – "logical and" – "intersection" – "min-operator" is an appropriate model for decisions.

Bellman and Zadeh [1970, B 150] have already indicated that their interpretation of a decision is more general in a number of ways:

1. The model of the intersection might in certain contexts not be the min-operator but rather the product-operator or others.
2. The intersection might not even be the appropriate model of the "and" and it seems better to talk of the confluence of goals and constraints rather than of the intersection.
3. "In defining a fuzzy decision, $\tilde{D}$, as the intersection—or more generally as the confluence—of the goals and constraints, we are tacitly assuming that all of the goals and constraints that enter into $\tilde{D}$ are, in a sense, of equal importance. There are some situations, however, in which some of the goals and perhaps some of the constraints are of greater importance than others. In such cases, $\tilde{D}$ might be expressed as a convex combination of the goals and the constraints, with the weighting coefficients reflecting the relative importance of the consistent terms" [Bellman, Zadeh 1970, B 150].

The first possible generalization, that is, the use of other operators, is illustrated by the following example.

Example 2.4

An instructor at a university has to decide how to grade written test papers. Let us assume that the problem to be solved in the test was a linear programming problem and that the student was free to solve it either graphically or using the simplex method. The student has done both. The student's performance is expressed—for the graphical solution as well as for the algebraic solution—as the achieved degree of membership in the fuzzy sets "good graphical solution" ($\tilde{G}$) and "good simplex solution" ($\tilde{S}$), respectively. Let us assume that he reaches

$$\mu_{\tilde{G}} = .9 \quad \text{and} \quad \mu_{\tilde{S}} = .7$$

If the grade to be awarded by the instructor corresponds to the degree of membership of the fuzzy set "good solutions of linear programming problems" it would be quite conceivable that his grade $\mu_{\widetilde{LP}}$ could be determined by

$$\mu_{\widetilde{LP}} = \max(\mu_{\tilde{G}}, \mu_{\tilde{S}}) = \max(.9, .7) = .9$$

The second generalization makes it very easy to include the choice model as well as the evaluation model in the notion of a fuzzy decision. In a sense this is already done in example 2.4. Here it can be very well argued, that the task of the instructure is not to *choose* the correct grade but rather to *evaluate* the performance of the student. The evaluation character of decisions will be discussed in more detail in the next section.

The third generalization, concerning the weights of the entering fuzzy sets raises some more basic issues: It was suggested to weight the fuzzy sets by multiplying their membership functions by the assigned weights. This obviously leads to different membership functions. Whether this kind of modification can really be interpreted as a modification of the importance of a fuzzy set or not and whether the type of weighting scheme can be chosen independent of the type of aggregation used has not yet been explored sufficiently [see Dombi 1982]. The weighting also might render the definition of a fuzzy decision nonsymmetrical. Since no restrictions have been formulated with respect to which fuzzy sets can be weighted, it is conceivable that, for instance, weights are only assigned to goals or only to constraints. In this case the symmetry of the decision would tend to disappear. We shall therefore, at the end of the following section, disregard the third kind of generalization when defining the symmetrical model of a decision in fuzzy environments.

The Evaluation Model of a Decision

Fuzziness can occur not only because certain phenomena or relationships are vague (i.e., nondichotomous), but also because of an abundance of information. The former type of fuzziness has been called "intrinsic fuzziness" the latter "informational fuzziness" [Zimmermann, Zysno 1985]. In the choice model of a decision we were mainly concerned with intrinsic vagueness, here we will have to focus attention on informational fuzziness. Zadeh referred to this type of fuzziness in his principle of incompatibility when he wrote: "As the complexity of a system increases, our ability to make precise and yet significant statements about its behavior diminishes until a threshold is reached beyond which precision and significance (or relevance) become almost mutually exclusive characteristics" [Zadeh 1973]. This observation refers to the limited human capability for simultaneous information processing [Newell, Simon 1972]. In day-to-day conversation people use very effectively terms such as "pleasant personality," "comfortable houses," or "credit-worthiness" as labels for sets of objects that could be described uniquely and crisply if a large number of descriptors were used. Since the human information storage and processing capacity is very limited, however, all the necessary descriptors of such a set are not consciously used when communicating with other persons. The description and conception of such a set—which we will call "subjective category"—changes from a crisp set to a set with vague boundaries. The degree of membership of single objects to this set varies gradually. Partitioning such a set appropriately into smaller subsets would certainly decrease the number of descriptors necessary to obtain crisp subsets.

For illustrative purposes we shall use the term "credit-worthiness." This subjective category (one might prefer to think of credit-worthy people) can be subdivided into two major determinants—financial basis and personality—which again are fuzzy but probably less fuzzy than credit-worthiness. By further subdivisions we might end up with a hierarchy of subjective categories and subcategories which in our minds are more completely described, when used, the lower in the hierarchy they appear. Putting it the other way round: the higher in the hierarchy a term appears the fuzzier is its description.

When a credit clerk has to decide about or evaluate the credit-worthiness of a customer he is likely to decompose his decision as shown in figure 2-4. Most of the subcategories are still fuzzy. They can, for instance, be represented by fuzzy sets or fuzzy ratings. In order to arrive at a judgment of credit-worthiness the subcategories (fuzzy sets) would have to be aggregated hierarchically. Verbally the links between the factors would certainly be "and" or "or." If one wants to quantify this process, (i.e., model it formally), the problem arises of how to model these aggregation operations. This problem will be

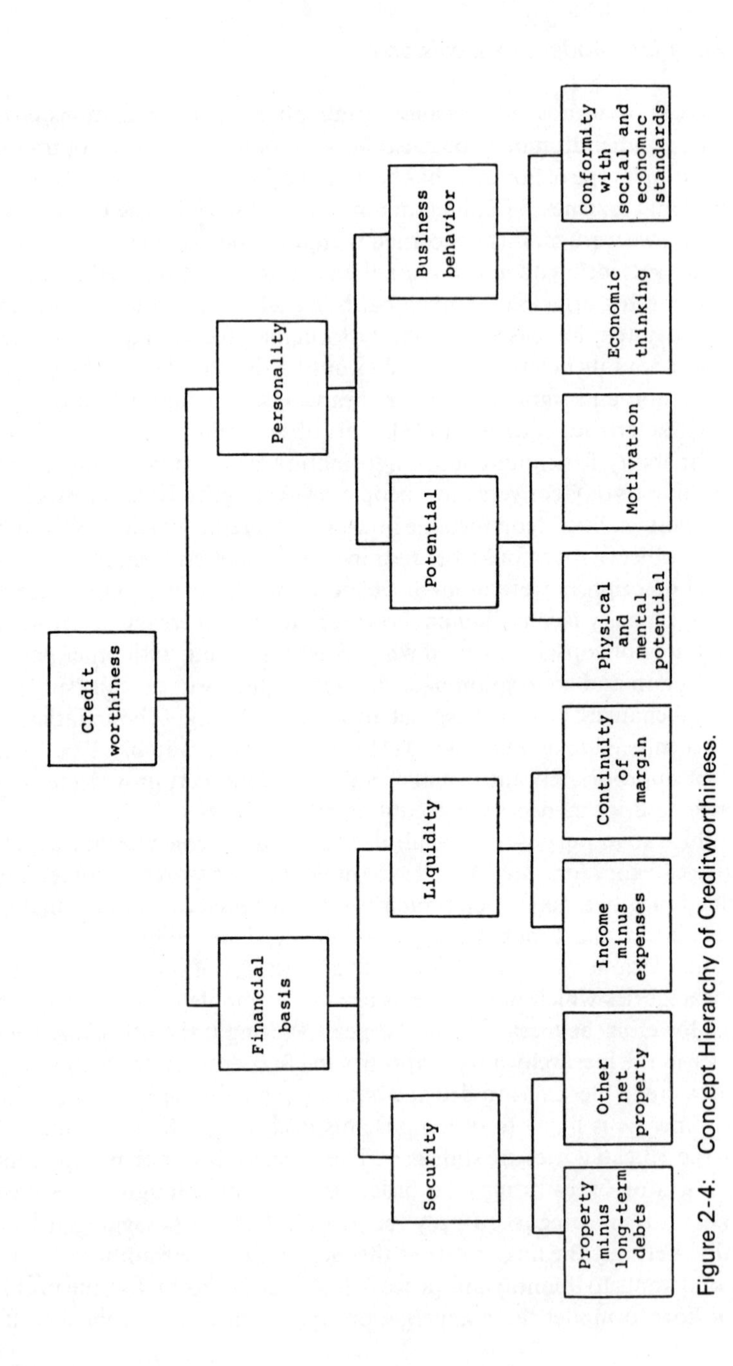

Figure 2-4: Concept Hierarchy of Creditworthiness.

discussed in more detail in chapter 6.

So far, it should have become obvious that the choice model as well as the evaluation model of a decision in a fuzzy environment can be reduced to the model of symmetric aggregation of fuzzy sets, and that a common definition for these types of decisions can be used:

Definition 2.1

Let $\mu_{\tilde{C}_i}$, $i = 1,\ldots,m$, be membership functions of constraints on X, defining the decision space and $\mu_{\tilde{G}_j}, j = 1,\ldots,n$, the membership functions of objective (utility) functions or goals on X. A *decision* is then defined by its membership function

$$\mu_{\tilde{D}} = (\mu_{\tilde{C}_1} * \cdots * \mu_{\tilde{C}_m}) * (\mu_{\tilde{G}_1} * \cdots * \mu_{\tilde{G}_n}) = *_i \mu_{\tilde{C}_i} \star *_j \mu_{\tilde{G}_j}$$

where $\star$, $*$ denote appropriate, possibly context dependent, aggregators (connectives).

Let M be the set of points $x \in X$ for which $\mu_{\tilde{D}}(x)$ attains its maximum, if it exists. Then M is called the *maximizing decision.* If $\mu_{\tilde{D}}(x)$ has a unique maximum at x_M, then the maximizing decision is a uniquely defined crisp decision which can be interpreted as the action that belongs to all fuzzy sets representing either constraints or goals with the highest possible degree of membership (which might be quite low).

Nonsymmetrical Models

The symmetry of the choice model in fuzzy environments rested essentially on the assumption that goals as well as constraints can be modelled as fuzzy sets and that the degree of membership of solutions (actions) to goals and to constraints could be considered comparable. Some authors [Asai et al. 1975] doubt whether this is really true. This line of thought, however, shall not be pursued any further here. We shall rather address the following problem.

What happens, if not all goals and all constraints are fuzzy, that is, can be represented by fuzzy sets? Table 2-1 surveys the types of models that can emerge depending on the situation and the modelling process. Type 1 is the model of definition 1.1 and type 5 is that of definition 2.1. Type 2 is only a special case of type 5. Since the constraints are crisp, the membership functions become the characteristic functions (degrees of membership only 0 or 1), and one seeks to maximize the degree of membership of the (fuzzy) goal over the (crisp) solution space. In the case of several goals, the fuzzy sets representing

Table 2-1: Decision Models

		goal(s) crisp	fuzzy set	fuzzy function
constraints	crisp	1) traditional choice model (non-symmetrical)	2) symmetrical model	3) fuzzy utility non-symmetrical
	fuzzy	4) non-symmetrical model	5) symmetrical model	6) fuzzy utility non-symmetrical

them will have to be aggregated before maximizing the resulting membership function. The reader should realize that models of type 2 and 5 assume a satisfying behavior of the decision maker. Either the fuzzy sets representing the goals can be autonomously defined by the decision maker or they can depend on properties of the solution space. This difference will be discussed in more detail in the framework of mathematical programming in chapter 4. Problems of type 3 and 6 will be discussed in the section on fuzzy utilities. This section will focus on models of type 4.

The basic difference between the models discussed previously and type 4 models is that the decision maker shows an optimizing behavior, as assumed in the classical choice model, but that he is unable or unwilling to describe the solution space crisply. The major problem to be solved is very similar to that in multicriteria analysis: The goal (objective function) induces an order of the events or actions and the (fuzzy) constraints also induce orders in the solution space which might contradict each other. Let us consider a modification of example 2.1 or 2.2.

Example 2.5

The board of directors wants to maximize the dividend after tax. Since corporate tax is supposed to be 50% the objective is to maximize $f(x) = x/2$. The restriction, however, is that the dividend has to be considered as "modest." Figure 2-5 depicts the problem structure.

Obviously the degree $\mu_{\tilde{M}}(x)$ to which the dividend x belongs to the set of "modest dividends" decreases as the value of the objective function increases. A number of ways have been suggested to solve this problem:

1. One could combine (aggregate) the two measures of desirability (objective function and modesty of dividend) into an objective function by using

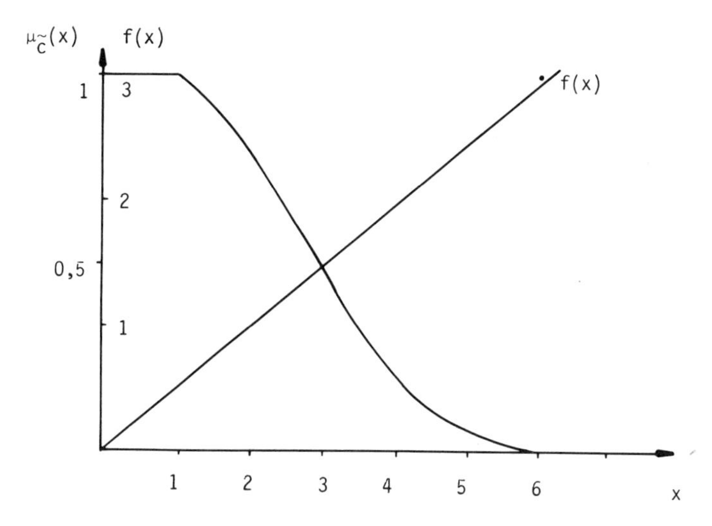

Figure 2-5: Decision with crisp objective function and fuzzy constraint.

scaling factors. In our example one could, for instance, maximize the objective function $\bar{f}(x) = \frac{1}{2}x + a\mu_{\tilde{M}}(x)$, $a > 0$, over the entire solution space ($\mu_{\tilde{M}}(x) > 0$). Obviously the scaling factor a is quite arbitrary and its value can only be justified in a few cases. (One example of such a case is described in Ernst [1982].)

2. One can define and justify a different notion of a decision which allows the existence of crisp objective functions and fuzzy constraints.
3. One can derive an equivalent model in which the objective function can be represented as a fuzzy set, thus reducing the nonsymmetrical model to a symmetrical one, and then determine the maximizing decision according to definition 2.1.

We shall consider approaches 2 and 3 in more detail.

Decision as a set of α-level sets. The basic idea is to determine for each α-level set (definition 1.4), R_α, of the solution space the set of elements for which the objective function $f(x)$ attains the maximum on R_α. Hence, for each α for which $R_\alpha \neq 0$,

$$N(\alpha) = \left\{ x \mid x \in R_\alpha \wedge f(x) = \sup_{x' \in R_\alpha} f(x') \right\} \tag{2.1}$$

An optimal decision is then defined as a fuzzy set $\tilde{D}_{\text{opt}}$ as follows [Orlovsky 1977, Werners 1984].

Definition 2.2

An *optimizing decision* to the problem max $f(x)$ subject to the fuzzy constraint $\tilde{C}$ with the membership function $\mu_{\tilde{C}}(x)$ is defined as the fuzzy set $\tilde{D}_{opt} = \{(f(x), \mu_{opt}(x)), x \in X\}$ with the membership function

$$\mu_{opt}(x) = \begin{cases} \sup\limits_{X \in N(\alpha)} \mu_{\tilde{C}}(x) & \text{for } x \in \bigcup\limits_{\alpha > 0} N(\alpha) \\ 0 & \text{else} \end{cases} \tag{2.2a}$$

$\mu_{opt}(x)$ indicates the degree to which $x \in X$ satisfies the constraints and the optimality condition.

Example 2.5 (continued)

Let us reconsider example 2.5 after a slight modification. The directors want to maximize net yield of the dividend x. They feel restrained, however, by forthcoming union negotiations and therefore by the desire of one of the members of the board of directors to only offer a modest dividend. This modest dividend is assumed to be represented by the fuzzy set $\tilde{C}$ with the membership function

$$\mu_{\tilde{C}}(x) = \begin{cases} 1 - \dfrac{x}{5} & 0 \le x \le 5 \\ 0 & x > 5 \end{cases}$$

Figure 2-6 depicts the situation.

The optimizing decision according to definition 2.2 can now easily be determined:

$$\mu_{opt}(x) = \begin{cases} 1 - \dfrac{x}{5} & \text{for } 0 \le x < 5 \\ 0 & \text{for } x \ge 5 \end{cases}$$

Obviously $\mu_{opt}(x) = \mu_{\tilde{C}}(x)$ for all $x \in \operatorname{supp} \tilde{D}_{opt}$. This is true in general [Orlovsky 1977]. Hence,

$$\mu_{opt}(x) = \begin{cases} \mu_{\tilde{C}}(x) & \text{for } x \in \bigcup\limits_{\alpha > 0} N(\alpha) \\ 0 & \text{else} \end{cases} \tag{2.2b}$$

The fuzzy maximal value of $f(x)$ over $\mu_{\tilde{C}}(x)$ is represented by a fuzzy set in $\mathbb{R}^1$ with the membership function

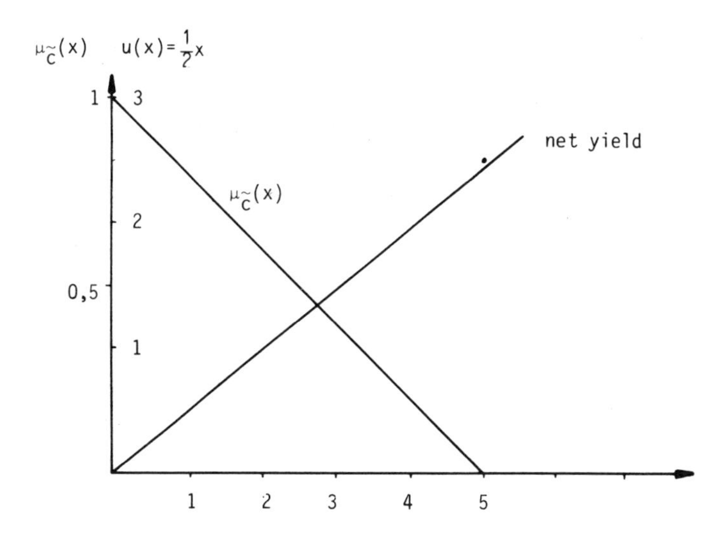

Figure 2-6: Non-symmetrical Decision Model.

$$\mu_f(r) = \begin{cases} \sup\limits_{x \in f^{-1}(r)} \mu_{opt}(x) & \text{for } r \in \mathbb{R}^1 \wedge f^{-1}(r) \neq 0 \\ 0 & \text{else} \end{cases} \tag{2.3}$$

Orlovsky [1977] proves that the membership function $\mu_f(r)$ decreases monotonically over the support of $\mu_f(r)$. He then suggests that a decision maker, in order to determine a crisp solution $x_0 \in X$, has to consider $\mu_{opt}(x_0)$ as well as the value of the objective function for $x_0, f(x_0)$. Since r decreases as $\mu_f(r)$ increases, one first has to choose a pair $\{\mu_f(r_0), r_0\}$ which satisfies the decision maker and then choose an $x_0 \in f^{-1}(r_0)$ with max $\mu_{opt}(x)$. It is obvious that this final decision depends crucially on the preference of the decision maker with respect to r and $\mu_f(r)$, respectively.

For our example $\mu_f(r)$ can again be determined easily:

$$\mu_f(r) = \begin{cases} 1 - \dfrac{2 \cdot r}{5} & \text{for } 0 \leq r \leq 2.5 \\ 0 & \text{else} \end{cases}$$

Which dividend was chosen in this situation would now only depend on the pair, $(r, \mu_f(r))$, with the highest preference of the board of directors.

The transformation of nonsymmetrical into symmetrical decision models (*re. number* 3 *above*): So far the structure of our decision models has remained nonsymmetrical because $\mu_{opt}(x)$ referred to the solution space and $\mu_f(r)$ to the objective function, but the linking of one rating with the other had to be done somehow by the decision maker.

A symmetrical decision model generally requires that the values of the crisp objective function are rated (fuzzily) with respect to the aspiration of the decision maker—that is, the mapping of $f(x)$ onto the interval [0,1], which represents the degree of satisfaction of the decision maker. Suitable suggestions can be found in the literature. Zadeh [1972] suggests the notion of a "maximizing set" which indicates to which degree a solution $x \in X$ approximates the supremum of the function $f(x)$. Zadeh discusses three different cases: positive definite $f(x)$, nondefinite $f(x)$, and negative definite $f(x)$. The maximizing set maps into [0,1] only for the nondefinite case—that is, if $\inf f(x) \leq 0$ and $\sup f(x) \geq 0$ [see Werners 1984, p. 49]. Therefore we shall only consider this case here.

Definition 2.3 [Zadeh 1972]

Let $f(x)$ be a real-valued function for $x \in X$ which is bounded from below by $\inf f(x) \geq 0$ and from above by $\sup f(x) \geq 0$. The *maximizing set* $\tilde{M}(f)$ is then defined by its membership function

$$\mu_{\tilde{M}(f)}(x) = \frac{f(x) - \inf f}{\sup f - \inf f}$$

In definition 2.3 the function $f(x)$, $x \in X$ has to be bounded from above and below, which cannot necessarily be assumed for objective functions in decision problems. We shall, therefore, assume, that function $f(x)$ is possibly unbounded in its domain X but is bounded by the fuzzily defined solution space (constraint) $\tilde{C}$.

Definition 2.4 [Werners 1984, p. 54]

Let $f(x)$ be a real-valued function and $\tilde{C}(x)$ a fuzzy constraint (solution space). If $f(x)$ is bounded on $S(\tilde{C})$ then the *maximizing set over a fuzzy constraint*, $\widetilde{MC}(f)$, is defined by its membership function

$$\mu_{MC}(x) = \begin{cases} 0 & \text{for } f(x) \leq \inf\limits_{S(\tilde{C})} f \\ \dfrac{f(x) - \inf\limits_{S(\tilde{C})} f}{\sup\limits_{S(\tilde{C})} f - \inf\limits_{S(\tilde{C})} f} & \text{for } \inf\limits_{S(\tilde{C})} f < f(x) < \sup\limits_{S(\tilde{C})} f \\ 1 & \text{for } f(x) \geq \sup\limits_{S(\tilde{C})} f \end{cases}$$

The fuzzy set $\widetilde{MC}$ expresses the optimality of values of $f(x)$ and $\mu_{\text{opt}}(x)$, the degree to which values of $f(x)$ can be obtained in the fuzzy solution space $\tilde{C}$. In analogy to definition 2.1, a maximizing decision could now be determined by aggregating μ_{MC} and μ_{opt} and determining the set of points for which the membership function of this aggregated set, $\tilde{D}$, attains its maximum.

Definition 2.5

Let $f(x)$ be a real-valued objective function, bounded over the fuzzy decision space $\tilde{C} = \{(x, \mu_{\tilde{C}}(x) \mid x \in X\}$ by $\inf_{S(\tilde{C})} f(x)$ from below and by $\sup_{S(\tilde{C})} f(x)$ from above. Let $\widetilde{MC}$ be defined as in definition 2.4 and $\mu_{\text{opt}}(x)$ as in definition 2.2. A decision $\tilde{D}$ is then defined by its membership function

$$\mu_{\tilde{D}}(x) = \mu_{\widetilde{MC}}(x) * \mu_{\text{opt}}(x)$$

where $*$ denotes an appropriate, possibly context dependent, aggregator (connective).

Let M be the set of points $x \in X$ for which $\mu_{\tilde{D}}(x)$ attains its maximum, if it exists. Then M is called the *maximizing decision of the nonsymmetrical decision model.*

If $\mu_{\tilde{D}}(x)$ has a unique maximum at x_M then the maximizing decision is a uniquely defined crisp decision which can be interpreted as the action that belongs to the fuzzy constraint and to the fuzzy goal with the highest possible degree of membership.

When comparing definition 2.5 with definition 2.1 three features are noteworthy:

1. In both cases the final definition of a decision is symmetrical in the sense that constraints as well as goals are represented by fuzzy sets. If a decision maker conceives goals as being different in character from constraints, he might express this by choosing an appropriate aggregator $*$ (such as the γ operator [Zimmermann, Zysno 1983]).
2. The degree to which the maximizing decision belongs to the fuzzy set

decision might be quite low in both cases, indicating a "small intersection" of goals and constraints.

3. While in definition 2.1 the fuzzy goals were given without reference to the constraints (solution space), in definition 2.5 fuzzy goals were induced by defining aspirations with reference to the crisp objective function as well as to the fuzzy constraints.

***Example* 2.5** (continued)

The support of the fuzzy constraint for a "modest dividend" is $S(\tilde{C}) = \{x \mid 0 < x < 5\}$. Hence inf and sup of the values of the objective function $f(x) = \frac{1}{2}x$ subject to $S(\tilde{C})$ are determined as

$$\inf_{S(\tilde{C})} f(x) = 0 \quad \text{and} \quad \sup_{S(\tilde{C})} f(x) = 2.5$$

Thus the maximizing set over the fuzzy constraint is defined by the following membership function:

$$\mu_{\widetilde{MC}}(x) = \begin{cases} 0 & x \leq 0 \\ \dfrac{.5 \cdot x}{2.5} & 0 < x < 5 \\ 1 & x \geq 5 \end{cases}$$

The decision $\tilde{D}$ is

$$\begin{aligned} \mu_{\tilde{D}}(x) &= \min\{\mu_{\widetilde{MC}}(x), \mu_{\text{opt}}(x)\} \\ &= \begin{cases} 0 & x \leq 0 \vee x \geq 5 \\ \min\left\{.2x, 1 - \dfrac{x}{5}\right\} & 0 < x < 5 \end{cases} \end{aligned}$$

The maximizing decision is the dividend $x^0 = 2.5$.

Fuzzy Utilities

Let us reconsider the basic model of decision logic as described in definition 1.1. Even though actions, states, or events might also be vaguely described, fuzziness is most likely to be found in the subjective utilities. It is, therefore, not surprising that fuzzy set theory has been applied to utility theory. In most cases this has been done in the context of Multi-Attribute Utility Theory (MAUT), Multi-Objective Decision Making (MODM), Multi-Criteria Decision Making (MCDM), or whatever name has been used for this fashionable area. These approaches will be presented and discussed in chapter 5. Here—in line with definition 1.1—we will restrict ourselves to the consideration of cases with a single utility function, crisply defined actions, and, for the time being, crisply defined states. Although generalizing these models to decision-making models under risk or uncertainty is certainly possible, it is beyond the scope of this book. The interested reader is referred to Luhandjula [1983], Freeling [1980], etc.

Suggested approaches for "fuzzy utilities" under certainty differ primarily in two aspects: (1) whether a discrete or continuous decision space is considered and (2) how fuzziness is formally introduced into utility functions. We shall first consider discrete decision spaces, that is, situations in which there are countable many actions available from which the "optimal" has to be chosen.

Fuzzy Utilities for Discrete Solution Spaces

Two major approaches can be distinguished: The first recognizes the fact that human beings will hardly be able to state their utilities crisply and on a cardinal scale and that a zero-threshold of indifference is a very unrealistic assumption. Utilities are, therefore, modelled as fuzzy sets, often in the framework of linguistic variables [see Zimmermann 1985b, p. 121]. The "fuzzification" of utilities of events, strategies, or projects, of course, does not yet solve the decision problem. The alternatives characterized by their fuzzy utilities now have to be ranked or ordered, which amounts to ranking fuzzy sets. Jain [1977] suggested one way to do this, which, however, was criticized by other authors [Baldwin, Guild 1979] for its lack of discrimination. We shall discuss the ranking of fuzzy sets in great length in chapter 5 where it seems to be more appropriate.

The second approach for discrete solution spaces focusses on the purpose of utilities—that is, the ordering events with respect to their desirability—and hence concentrates on (fuzzy) order relations [see Orlovsky 1978; Zadeh 1977]. What follows will describe these proposals.

The Determination of Efficient (Undominated) Solutions. Orlovsky [1978] addresses the problem of finding a set of efficient solutions that might help the decision maker in his process of choice. Before we consider his approach in more detail let us recall and newly define some notions which we will need in the sequel:

Definition 2.6

Let X, $Y \subseteq \mathbb{R}$ be universal sets then

$$\tilde{R} = \{((x,y), \mu_{\tilde{R}}(x,y)) \mid (x,y) \subseteq X \times Y\}$$

is called a *fuzzy relation on* $X \times Y$.

Definition 2.7

Let X, $Y \subseteq \mathbb{R}$ and

$$\tilde{A} = \{(x, \mu_{\tilde{A}}(x)) \mid x \in X\}$$

$$\tilde{B} = \{(y, \mu_{\tilde{B}}(y)) \mid y \in Y\} \qquad \text{two fuzzy sets.}$$

Then $\tilde{R} = \{((x,y), \mu_{\tilde{R}}(x,y)), (x,y) \in X \times Y\}$ is a *fuzzy relation on* $\tilde{A}$ *and* $\tilde{B}$ iff

$$\mu_{\tilde{R}}(x,y) \leq \mu_{\tilde{A}}(x) \qquad \forall (x,y) \in X \times Y$$

and

$$\mu_{\tilde{R}}(x,y) \leq \mu_{\tilde{B}}(y) \qquad \forall (x,y) \in X \times Y$$

Definition 2.8

Max-min Composition: Let

$$\tilde{R}_1(x,y), (x,y) \subseteq X \times Y \quad \text{and} \quad \tilde{R}_2(y,z) \subseteq Y \times Z$$

be two fuzzy relations. The max-min composition $\tilde{R}_1$ max-min $\tilde{R}_2$ denoted $\tilde{R}_1 \circ \tilde{R}_2$ is then the fuzzy set.

$$\tilde{R}_1 \circ \tilde{R}_2 = \{[(x,z), \max_y \{\min \{\mu_{\tilde{R}_1}(x,y), \mu_{\tilde{R}_2}(y,z)\}\}] \mid x \in X, y \in Y, z \in Z\}$$

$\mu_{\tilde{R}_1 \circ \tilde{R}_2}$ is the membership function of a fuzzy relation.

Example 2.6

Let $\tilde{R}_1(x,y)$ and $\tilde{R}_2(y,z)$ be defined by the following relational matrixes [Kaufmann 1975, p. 62]:

$\tilde{R}_1 =$

	y_1	y_2	y_3	y_4	y_5
x_1	.1	.2	0	1	.7
x_2	.3	.5	0	.2	1
x_3	.8	0	1	.4	.3

$\tilde{R}_2 =$

	z_1	z_2	z_3	z_4
y_1	.9	0	.3	.4
y_2	.2	1	.8	0
y_3	.8	0	.7	1
y_4	.4	.2	.3	0
y_5	0	1	0	.8

We shall compute the min-max-composition $\tilde{R}_1 \circ \tilde{R}_2(x,z)$. We shall show in detail the determination for $x = x_1, z = z_1$ and leave it to the reader to verify the total results shown in the matrix at the end of the detailed computations: we first perform the min-operation in the minor brackets of definition 2.8:

Let $x = x_1, z = z_1$ and $y = y_i, i = 1,\ldots,5$.

$$\min\{\mu_{\tilde{R}_1}(x_1,y_1),\mu_{\tilde{R}_2}(y_1,z_1)\} = \min(.1,.9) = .1$$
$$\min\{\mu_{\tilde{R}_1}(x_1,y_2),\mu_{\tilde{R}_2}(y_2,z_1)\} = \min(.2,.2) = .2$$
$$\min\{\mu_{\tilde{R}_1}(x_1,y_3),\mu_{\tilde{R}_2}(y_3,z_1)\} = \min(0,.8) = 0$$
$$\min\{\mu_{\tilde{R}_1}(x_1,y_4),\mu_{\tilde{R}_2}(y_4,z_1)\} = \min(1,.4) = .4$$
$$\min\{\mu_{\tilde{R}_1}(x_1,y_5),\mu_{\tilde{R}_2}(y_5,z_1)\} = \min(.7,0) = 0$$
$$\mu_{\tilde{R}_1 \circ \tilde{R}_2}(x_1,z_1) = \max\{.1,.2,0,.4,0\} = .4$$

In analogy to the above computation we now determine the grades of membership for all pairs (x_1,z_j), $i = 1,\ldots,3, j = 1,\ldots,4$; and arrive at

$\tilde{R}_1 \circ \tilde{R}_2 =$

	z_1	z_2	z_3	z_4
x_1	.4	.7	.3	.7
x_2	.3	1	.5	.8
x_3	.8	.3	.7	1

In the following we will restrict our considerations on fuzzy relations on $X \times X$.

Definition 2.9

A fuzzy relation $\tilde{R}$ in $X \times X$ is called (max-min) *transitive* iff

$$\tilde{R} \circ \tilde{R} \subseteq \tilde{R}$$

Example 2.7

Let the fuzzy relation $\tilde{R}$ be defined as

$\tilde{R} =$

	x_1	x_2	x_3	x_4
x_1	.2	1	.4	.4
x_2	0	.6	.3	0
x_3	0	1	.3	0
x_4	.1	1	1	.1

Then $\tilde{R} \circ \tilde{R}$ is

	x_1	x_2	x_3	x_4
x_1	.1	.6	.4	.2
x_2	0	.6	.3	0
x_3	0	.6	.3	0
x_4	.1	1	.3	.1

Now one can easily see that $\mu_{\tilde{R} \circ \tilde{R}}(x,y) \leq \mu_{\tilde{R}}(x,y)$ holds for all $x,y \in X$.

Definition 2.10 [Zadeh 1971]

A fuzzy relation $\tilde{R}$ in $X \times X$ is called *reflexive* iff

$$\mu_{\tilde{R}}(x,x) = 1 \, \forall \, x \in X$$

Definition 2.11

A fuzzy relation $\tilde{R}$ in $X \times X$ is called *symmetrical* iff

$$\mu_{\tilde{R}}(x,y) = \mu_{\tilde{R}}(y,x) \, \forall \, x,y \in X$$

$\tilde{R}$ is called *antisymmetrical* iff for $x \neq y$

$$\left.\begin{array}{ll} \text{either} & \mu_{\tilde{R}}(x,y) \neq \mu_{\tilde{R}}(y,x) \\ \text{or} & \mu_{\tilde{R}}(x,y) = \mu_{\tilde{R}}(y,x) = 0 \end{array}\right\} \forall \, x,y \in X$$

[Kaufmann 1975, p. 105].

A relation is called *perfectly antisymmetrical* if, for $x \neq y$, whenever

$$\mu_{\tilde{R}}(x,y) > 0 \quad \text{then} \quad \mu_{\tilde{R}}(y,x) = 0 \qquad \forall \, x,y \in X$$

[Zadeh 1971].

Definition 2.12 [see Zimmermann 1985b, definition 6-20]

A *similarity relation* is a fuzzy relation $\tilde{R}$ that is reflexive, symmetrical, and max-min-transitive.

We shall now turn to fuzzy order relations. Similarity relations and order relations are primarily distinguished with respect to symmetry. Roughly speaking similarity relations are fuzzy relations that are reflexive; max-min-transitive and symmetrical order relations are, however, antisymmetrical. The main purpose of similarity relations is to exhibit the degree of concordance of elements of a set. (A well-known application of similarity relations is clustering.) Order relations, however, aim at structuring and ordering the elements of a set on the basis of, for instance, different utilities assigned to these elements. This order can then be used to choose preferred or even optimal elements from the set under consideration. In the following we shall, therefore, focus attention on order relations.

Definition 2.13

A fuzzy relation in $X \times X$ that is max-min-transitive and reflexive is called *a fuzzy preorder relation.*

Definition 2.14

A fuzzy relation in $X \times X$ that is min-max-transitive, reflexive, and anti-symmetrical is called a *fuzzy order relation.* If the relation is perfectly anti-symmetrical it is called a *perfect fuzzy order relation* [Kaufmann 1975, p. 113]. It is also called a *fuzzy partial-order relation* [Zadeh 1971].

Definition 2.15

A *total fuzzy order relation* [Kaufmann 1975, p. 112] or a *fuzzy linear ordering* [Dubois, Prade 1980, p. 82; Zadeh 1971, p. 177] is a fuzzy order relation such that $\forall x,y \in X$, $x \neq y$ either $\mu_{\tilde{R}}(x,y) > 0$ or $\mu_{\tilde{R}}(y,x) > 0$.

Any α-cut of a fuzzy linear order is a crisp linear order.

Let us now return to the problem considered by Orlovsky [1978]. He assumes that a *fuzzy nonstrict preference relation* $\widetilde{PR} = \{[(x,y),\mu_{\widetilde{PR}}(x,y)]\}$ which is assumed to be reflexive but not necessarily transitive is specified in the given set of alternatives X. Since normally crisp preferences are modelled by pre-orders (reflexive and transitive); $\widetilde{PR}$ requires less consistency of the decision makes than is classically done. The value of $\mu_{\widetilde{PR}}(x,y)$ is interpreted as the degree to which the statement "x is preferred to y" is true.

If $\mu_{\widetilde{PR}}(x,y) \geq 0$ and $\mu_{\widetilde{PR}}(x,y) \geq \mu_{\widetilde{PR}}(y,x)$ for the two alternatives $x,y \in X$, then x and y are considered equivalent (indifferent) to the degree $\mu_{\widetilde{PR}}(y,x)$ and x is considered to be strictly preferred to y to the degree that $\mu_{\widetilde{PR}}(x,y)$ is preferred to $\mu_{\widetilde{PR}}(y,x)$. On the basis of this interpretation two more special relations are defined by Orlovsky [1978].

Definition 2.16

A *fuzzy indifference relation,* $\widetilde{IR}$, is defined as

$$\widetilde{IR} = \{((x,y),\mu_{\widetilde{IR}}(x,y)),x,y \in X\,Y, \mu_{\widetilde{IR}}(x,y)\} = \min\{\mu_{\widetilde{PR}}(x,y),\mu_{\widetilde{PR}}(y,x)\}$$

Definition 2.17

A *fuzzy strict preference relation,* $\widetilde{PRS}$, is defined by its membership function

$$\mu_{\widetilde{PRS}}(x,y) = \begin{cases} \mu_{\widetilde{PR}}(x,y) - \mu_{\widetilde{PR}}(y,x) & \text{for } \mu_{\widetilde{PR}}(x,y) \geq \mu_{\widetilde{PR}}(y,x) \\ 0 & \text{otherwise} \end{cases}$$

$\widetilde{PRS}$ contains only elements (x,y) in which element x strictly dominates y. Each row of the membership matrix of $\widetilde{PRS}$ represents the degree of dominance of the variable, $\bar{x}$, corresponding to this row over all others. The complements of these fuzzy sets, with the membership functions $1 - \mu_{\widetilde{PRS}}(\bar{x},y)$, contain all the elements in which, for a fixed $\bar{x}$, all y are not dominated by $\bar{x}$. If we consider the intersection of all complements of the fuzzy sets corresponding to the rows of $\widetilde{PRS}$, then their intersection contains only elements in which the x are not dominated by any other $x \in X$. Using the min-operator to model the intersection, the membership functions of the set of nondominated elements, $\widetilde{ND}$, is given by

$$\mu_{\widetilde{ND}}(x) = \inf_{y \in X} [1 - \mu_{\widetilde{PRS}}(y,x)] = 1 - \sup_{y \in X} \mu_{\widetilde{PRS}}(y,x) \tag{2.4}$$

$\mu_{\widetilde{ND}}(x)$ can be interpreted as the degree to which x is not dominated by any other $y \in X$.

Orlovsky shows that $\mu_{\widetilde{ND}}(x)$ can be expressed in terms of the original nonstrict preference relations as follows:

$$\mu_{\widetilde{ND}}(x) = 1 - \sup_{y \in X} \max \{\mu_{\widetilde{PR}}(y,x) - \mu_{\widetilde{PR}}(x,y), 0\} \tag{2.5}$$

In analogy to the maximizing sets defined in definitions 2.3 and 2.4 one can now view as most sensible choices for an optimal decision the set of points (solutions) with the highest degree of membership in $\widetilde{ND}$.

Definition 2.18

Let $\widetilde{ND}$ be the fuzzy set of nondominated alternative $x \in X$, then the (crisp) *set of maximally nondominated* alternatives is defined as

$$MND = \{x \mid \mu_{\widetilde{ND}}(x) = \sup_{z \in X} \mu_{\widetilde{ND}}(z), x \in X\}$$

Of particular interest are those sets MND for which $\sup_{z \in X} \mu_{\widetilde{ND}}(z)$ is equal to 1. In this case the elements in MND are not dominated by any other element $x \in X$ and therefore this set is called *set of crisply nondominated elements, CND*.

Let us consider the two following examples from Orlovsky [1978, p. 160]:

Example 2.8a

Let relation $\widetilde{PR}(x_i,x_j)$ be defined as follows:

$\mu_{\widetilde{PR}}(x_i,x_j) =$

	x_1	x_2	x_3	x_4
x_1	1	.5	0	.8
x_2	.1	1	.3	.5
x_3	.3	.6	1	0
x_4	.9	.7	.1	1

This relation is reflexive, not transitive.

Using definition 2.12 we obtain

$\mu_{\widetilde{PRS}}(x_i,x_j) =$

	x_1	x_2	x_3	x_4
x_1	0	.4	0	0
x_2	0	0	0	0
x_3	.3	.3	0	0
x_4	.1	.2	.1	0

According to (2.4) the fuzzy set of nondominated alternatives is

$$\widetilde{ND} = \{(x_1,.7),(x_2,.6),(x_3,.9),(x_4,1)\}$$

Since $\widetilde{ND}$ is a normal fuzzy set ($\sup \mu_{\widetilde{ND}}(x) = 1$) the maximally nondominated alternative is x_4 and this is a crisply nondominated alternative.

Example 2.8b

Let $\widetilde{PR}(x_i,x_j)$ be defined as follows:

$\widetilde{PR}(x_i,x_j) =$

	x_1	x_2	x_3	x_4
x_1	1	.2	.3	.1
x_2	.5	1	.2	.6
x_3	.1	.6	1	.3
x_4	.6	.1	.5	1

This preference relation is not transitive, as the reader might easily verify. The resulting $\widetilde{PRS}$ is

$\mu_{\widetilde{PRS}}(x_i, x_j) =$

	x_1	x_2	x_3	x_4
x_1	0	0	.2	0
x_2	.3	0	0	.5
x_3	0	.4	0	0
x_4	.5	0	.2	0

Using equation (2.4) we obtain

$$\widetilde{ND} = \{(x_1, .5), (x_2, .6), (x_3, .8), (x_4, .5)\}$$

In this case there does not exist a crisply nondominated solution (CND), the set of maximally nondominated alternatives is $MND = \{x_3\}$.

Orlovsky [1978] proofs a number of interesting properties which we shall not consider here. We will only consider the question "when do CND-solutions exist?" because this seems of particular interest to the decision maker: Orlovsky shows that if PR is a finite relation which is reflexive and transitive then the set CND is not empty. To determine an element of CND one only needs to determine $\mu_{\widetilde{PRS}}(x, y)$ and find an $x_1 \in X$ for which $\mu_{\widetilde{PRS}}(x, x_1) = 0$ for any $x \in X$. This is illustrated by the following example [Orlovsky 1978, p. 166]:

Example 2.9

Let $\widetilde{PR}$ be defined by its membership function

$\mu_{\widetilde{PR}}(x_i, x_j) =$

	x_1	x_2	x_3	x_4	x_5
x_1	1	.7	.8	.5	.5
x_2	0	1	.3	0	.2
x_3	0	.7	1	0	.2
x_4	.6	1	.9	1	.6
x_5	0	0	0	0	1

The interested reader can easily verify that this fuzzy relation is reflexive and transitive—that is that

$$\mu_{\widetilde{PR}}(x_i,x_i) = 1$$

and

$$\mu_{\widetilde{PR}}(x_i,x_j) \geq \sup_{z \in X} \min \{\mu_{\widetilde{PR}}(x_i,z), \mu_{\widetilde{PR}}(z,x_j)\}$$

The resulting $\mu_{\widetilde{PRS}}$ is then

$\mu_{\widetilde{PRS}}(x_i,x_j) =$

	x_1	x_2	x_3	x_4	x_5
x_1	0	.7	.8	0	.5
x_2	0	0	0	0	.2
x_3	0	.4	0	0	.2
x_4	.1	1	.9	0	.6
x_5	0	0	0	0	0

Since only x_4 has a column with only zeros in it this is the only element of *CND*. x_4 dominates strictly (to a positive degree) all other elements of $\widetilde{PRS}$ (see row of x_4!).

So far the degree of preference of x over y has still been expressed numerically as a degree of membership in $\widetilde{PR}$. Zadeh [1977] extends this by expressing the degree of preference by terms [see Zimmermann 1985, def. 9-1] of the linguistic variable "strength." A preference relation in this case might look as follows:

$\mu_{\widetilde{PR}}(x_i,x_j) =$ (2.6)

	x_1	x_2	x_3	x_4
x_1	1	not strong	strong	very strong
x_2	0	1	not strong	strong
x_3	0	0	1	not strong
x_4	0	0	0	1

Here "strong," "not strong," etc. are terms of the linguistic variable "strength" (i.e., normalized fuzzy sets).

It is obvious that this type of information requires even less precision of the decision maker when stating his preferences. On the other hand the computational effort in dealing with linguistic preference relations corresponds to that of dealing with type 2 fuzzy sets, which is quite considerable [Zimmermann 1985, p. 50]. Hardly anything has been published so far in this area. The interested reader is referred to Zadeh [1977] for further details.

Fuzzy Utilities for Continuous Decision Spaces

If the decision space is continuous, the approaches described above are no longer applicable. The most straightforward way of applying fuzzy set theory to utility theory is then to interprete the utility function as a fuzzy set. This, however, amounts to viewing the utility function as a crisp membership function, which would reduce our problem to the symmetrical fuzzy choice model defined in definition 2.1. As we have seen, this is certainly a possible approach which assumes some known aspiration levels of the decision maker. It also implies, however, that the decision maker has a crisply defined utility function, which is an assumption that does not seem to be too realistic in general.

Another, probably more realistic, way of applying fuzzy set theory to utility theory is to regard the utility function as a fuzzy function. Such a fuzzy function was defined [see Dubois, Prade 1980, p. 98; Zimmermann 1985b, p. 84] as follows:

Definition 2.19

Let X and Y be universes, $\tilde{P}(Y)$ the set of all fuzzy sets in Y (power set), and

$$\tilde{f}\colon X \to \tilde{P}(Y)\colon x \to \tilde{f}(x)$$

be a mapping, then $\tilde{f}$ is a *fuzzy function* iff

$$\mu_{\tilde{f}(x)}(y) = \mu_{\tilde{R}}(x,y) \qquad \forall (x,y) \in X \times Y$$

where $\mu_{\tilde{R}}(x,y)$ is the membership function of a fuzzy relation. (See Figure 2-7.)

In decision problems we are interested in the event with the highest utility; that is, we search for the maximum of the utility function over the feasable region.

Let us first consider the maximum of an unrestricted function: Traditionally an extremum (maximum or minimum) of a crisp function f over a given domain, D, is attained at a precise point x_0. If the function f happens to be

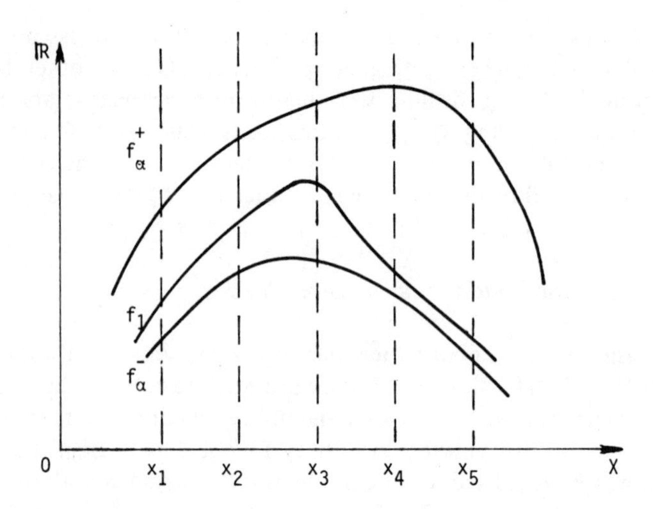

Figure 2-7: Fuzzy Function.

the objective function of a decision model, possibly constrained by a set of other functions, then the point x_0 at which the function attains the optimum is generally called the optimal decision. That is to say, in classical theory there is an almost unique relationship between the extremum of the objective function and the notion of the optimal decision of a decision model.

Since a fuzzy function $\tilde{f}$ maps x to a fuzzy set $\tilde{f}(x)$, say in $\mathbb{R}$, the maximum will generally not be a point in $\mathbb{R}$ but also a fuzzy set, which we shall call the "fuzzy maximum of $\tilde{f}$." A straightforward approach is to define an extended max-operation in analogy to other extended operations [see Zimmermann 1985, ch. 5]. Max and min are increasing operations in $\mathbb{R}$. The maximum or minimum, respectively, of n fuzzy numbers [see Zimmermann 1985, def. 5.3], denoted by $\widetilde{\max}(M_1,\ldots,\tilde{M}_n)$ and $\widetilde{\min}(\tilde{M}_1,\ldots,\tilde{M}_n)$ is again a fuzzy number. Dubois and Prade [1980, p. 58] present rules for computing $\widetilde{\max}$ and $\widetilde{\min}$ and also comment on the properties of $\widetilde{\max}$ and $\widetilde{\min}$. The reader is referred to the foregoing references for further details.

Definition 2.20

Let $\tilde{f}$ be a fuzzy function from X to $\mathbb{R}$, defined over a crisp and finite domain D. The *fuzzy maximum* of $\tilde{f}$ is then defined as

$$\tilde{M} = \widetilde{\max} \tilde{f}(x) = \{(\sup \tilde{f}(x), \mu_{\tilde{M}}(x)) \mid x \in D\}$$

Let $D = \{x_1, \ldots, x_n\}$. Then the membership function of $\widetilde{\max} \tilde{f}(x)$ is given by

$$\mu_{\tilde{M}}(x) = \min_{j=1,\ldots,n} \mu_{\tilde{f}(x_j)}(f(x_j)) \qquad x \in D$$

Example 2.10 [Dubois, Prade 1980, p. 105]

Let $\tilde{f}$ be a fuzzy function from $\mathbb{R}$ to $\mathbb{R}$ such that for any x $\tilde{f}(x)$ is a triangular fuzzy number and let the domain be $D = \{x_1, x_2, x_3, x_4, x_5\}$. Figure 2-7 sketches such a function by showing for the domain D "level-curves" of $\tilde{f}(x)$. In the figure, f_1 is the curve for which $\mu_{\tilde{f}(x)}(f_1(x)) = 1$, and for f_α^+ and f_α^-, respectively,

$$\mu_{\tilde{f}(x)}(f_\alpha^-(x)) = \mu_{\tilde{f}(x)}(f_\alpha^+(x)) = \alpha$$

The triangular fuzzy numbers representing the function $\tilde{f}(x)$ at $x = x_1, x_2, x_3, x_4$, and x_5 are shown in figure 2-8. We can make the following observation: since the level-curves in figure 2-8 are not parallel to each other their maxima are attained at different

$$x_i: \max_{x \in D} f_\alpha^+(x) = f_\alpha^+(x_4),$$

$$\max f_1(x) = f_1(x_3), \text{ and}$$

$$\max f_\alpha^- = f_\alpha^-(x_2)$$

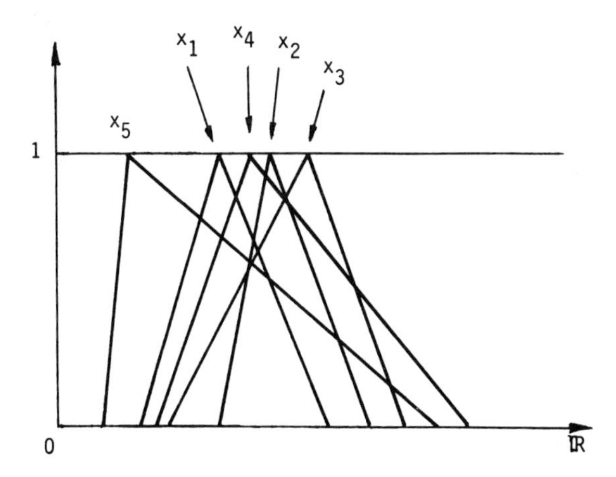

Figure 2-8: Membership functions of fuzzy function at $\{x_1, x_2, x_3, x_4, x_5\}$.

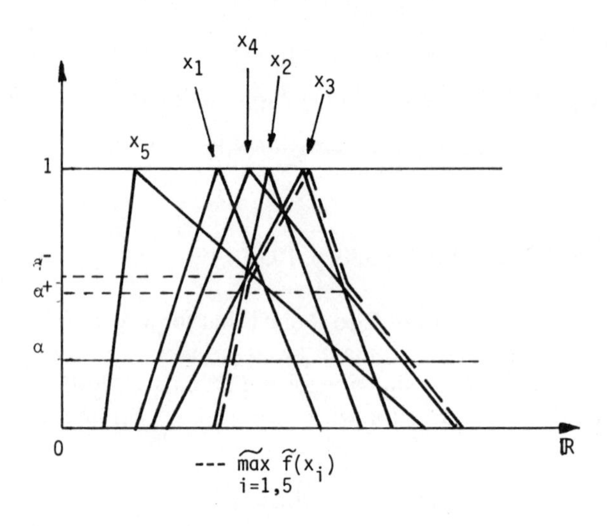

Figure 2-9: The maximum of a fuzzy function.

Thus x_1 and x_5 certainly do not "belong" to the maximum of $\tilde{f}(x)$. We can easily determine the fuzzy set "maximum of $\tilde{f}(x)$" as defined in definition 2.20 by looking at figure 2-8 and observing that

$$\text{for} \begin{cases} \alpha \in [0,\alpha^-] : f_\alpha^-(x_2) \geq f_\alpha^-(x_i)\,\forall i \\ \alpha \in [\alpha^-,1] : f_\alpha^-(x_3) \geq f_\alpha^-(x_i)\,\forall i \\ \alpha \in [\alpha^+,1] : f_\alpha^+(x_3) \geq f_\alpha^+(x_i)\,\forall i \\ \alpha \in [0,\alpha^+] : f_\alpha^+(x_4) \geq f_\alpha^+(x_i)\,\forall i \end{cases}$$

with α^- and α^+ such that $f_\alpha^-(x_2) = f_\alpha^-(x_3)$ and $f_\alpha^+(x_4) = f_\alpha^+(x_3)$, respectively.

The maximum of $\tilde{f}(x)$ is therefore

$$\tilde{M} = \{(x_2,\alpha^-),(x_3,1),(x_4,\alpha^+)\}$$

This set is indicated in figure 2-9 by the dashed line.

Dubois and Prade [1980, p. 101] suggest additional possible interpretations of fuzzy extrema which might be very appropriate in certain situations.

3 MULTI-PERSON DECISION MAKING IN FUZZY ENVIRONMENTS

Basic Models

In chapter 2 we have been concerned with decisions of individuals, that is, an individual decision maker selects a strategy or action among the available or feasable courses of actions. He does this either under certainty—in which case his choice is deterministicly limited by the anonymous "state of nature"—or he makes a decision under risk or uncertainty—in which case the possible courses of action are determined stochastically by the same anonymous world for which no rationality in any sense is assumed.

In multi-person decision making, a decision maker is not alone against the anonymous "nature" or "world"; he interacts with other human beings. According to the type of interaction, three different basic kinds of situations have been identified:

1. Gaming. A game is essentially a conflict situation. There are at least two decision makers whose decisions influence each other's results and whose objective functions are conflicting.

First, with respect to the possible outcomes of a given situation, it is assumed that

> they are well specified and that each individual has a consistent pattern of preferences among them....
>
> Second, the variables which control the possible outcomes are also assumed to be well specified, that is, one can precisely characterize all the variables and all the values which they assume. [Luce, Raiffa 1957, p. 4]

> In summary, then, one formulation of a class of conflicts of interest is this: There are n players each of whom is required to make one choice from a well-defined set of possible choices, and these choices are made without any knowledge as to the choices of the other players. The problem for each player is: what choice should he make in order that his partial influence over the outcomes benefits him most. [Luce, Raiffa 1957, p. 6]

Even though the players are not informed about the moves of the other players it is assumed that they know definitely and completely the utilities characterized by the matrix of outcomes.

2. Team Decisions. Team theory, developed primarily by Marshak and Radner in the early seventies, focusses on a situation in which there is no conflict between the utility functions of the members of a team. So far it resembles very much individual decision making under risk. The difference, however, is, that different information about the state of the environment is received by the different members of the team. This information can be received from the outside world or it can be received from other members of the team. Team theory is concerned with the information system between the members of the team and its repercussions on the actions of the team members and the team as a whole. We shall specify models in more detail in the section on "Fuzzy Team Theory."

3. Group Decision Making. This class of models assumes also a group of individuals with well-specified individual utility functions. By contrast to gaming situations, these utility functions do not have to be in conflict; and, by contrast to the team decision, problem decisions can only be made by the group and not by individual members. The information system between the members is not considered to be relevant and the prime concern is the aggregation of the individual utility functions to group utility functions. Hence, in a certain sense, the group is viewed as an individual decision maker and one tries to derive the utility function of the group from the utility functions of its members.

Fuzzy Games

We will start with considering two-person games and specify what is meant by a classical two-person-nonzero-sum game. Let $s_{ik} \in S_k$, $k = 1,2$ be the ith pure strategy of player k. For any pair $\{s_{i1}, s_{j2}\}$ from $S_1 \otimes S_2$ there exists a unique real number $g_k(s_{i1}, s_{j2}) \in G_k$ which is called the gain of player k. A mixed strategy of player k is a (probability) vector $p^k = (p_1^k, \ldots, p_{n_k}^k)^T$ with $\sum_{i=1}^{n_k} p_i^k = 1$ and $p_i^k \geq 0$, which characterizes the probabilities with which player k plays his pure strategies s_{ik}. The set of T_k of all mixed strategies p^k of player k is the domain of the individual choices of player k in the game. If player 1 chooses his mixed strategy $p^1 \in T_1$ and player 2 chooses strategy $p^2 \in T_2$, player 1 receives as gain G_1 the expected value of possible gains:

$$G_1(p^1, p^2) = \sum_{i=1}^{n_1} \sum_{j=1}^{n_2} (p_i^1)^T g_1(s_{i1}, s_{j2}) p_j^2 \tag{3.1}$$

Butnariu [1978, p. 187] makes the criticism that one of the major assumptions of classical game theory is that all elements p^k are equally possible choices of player k. He argues that in real situations the max-min principle is not the only possible rule for selecting optimal strategies and that other considerations, such as moral, aesthetic, or philosophical motives may render some strategies more or less acceptable to a player. This is also true for the other player's choice of strategy. Butnariu therefore suggests considering only a fuzzy subset of T_k as the relevant set of strategies for player k. This fuzzy set may be unconditional or conditional on the strategy played by the adversary.

Several solution concepts to this problem are conceivable. One could consider the goals of the players as vector valued and apply procedures of multi-criteria analysis. (Such a suggestion will be presented further along.) For a special case—zero-sum matrix games with saddle points—one could reduce the problem to the symmetrical choice problem discussed in the first section of chapter 2. The "solution" for a player would then be a fuzzy set and the value of the game could be represented by a maximizing set (see definition 2.3).

Let us consider in more detail an approach suggested by Buckley [1984b]. He uses fuzzy set theory (a) to handle uncertainty in a more appropriate way than in classical game theoretic models, and (b) to combine multiple goals into one fuzzy program. Let

$$\Omega_p = \{p \mid p_i \geq 0, \sum_{i=1}^{m} p_i = 1\}$$

be the strategy space of player 1 and

$$\Omega_q = \{q \mid q_i \geq 0, \sum_{i=1}^{n} q_i = 1\}$$

be the strategy space of player 2. It is assumed that the game situation is symmetrical with respect to uncertainty about the other player's preferences for strategies. Therefore only player 1's view is considered. Player 2 could be considered analogously. Buckley assumes that each player has a number of goals, G_{ik}, characterized by functions that measure the attainment of the kth goal for the ith component, v_i, of the pay-off vector v for player 1, $1 \leq k \leq L_i$, $1 \leq i \leq r$. The goal function of player 2 is H_{jk}, $1 \leq k \leq M_j$, $1 \leq j \leq r$; and his pay-offs are w_j. Each goal function is assumed to be a function of both p and q, the strategy vectors of the players. The vectors v and w represent commodity bundles for players 1 and 2, respectively.

It is assumed that the components of v and w are real numbers. "For example, in labor negotiations the first component might be hourly wage, the second component medical benefits, the third component vacation time, etc." Labor and management would set separate goals for each component. Examples of possible goal statements are: (1) maximize the expected value of v_1 and minimize its variance; (2) the expected target value of v_2 should be approximately equal to some target value L_2 [Buckley 1984b, p. 109].

In alignment with Butnariu's suggestion, it is now assumed that player 1 constructs a conditional fuzzy set $\tilde{F}_{ik}$ in $p \in \Omega_p$ for each goal and conditioned for each value of $q \in \Omega_q$. This will allow player 1 to react to a change in his goal structure as well as to changes of q (i.e., his adversary's strategy). The membership function of $\tilde{F}_{ik}$ is suggested by Buckley to be

$$\mu_{\tilde{F}_{ik}} = \mu_{ik}(G_{ik}(p,q) \mid q) \tag{3.2}$$

A possible membership function for a player wishing to maximize $G_{ik}(p,q)$ is depicted in figure 3-1, where b_{ik} denotes the best possible value of G_{ik} and α_{ik} the worst possible value. The uncertainty of player 1 about the choice of strategy q of player 2 is also modelled as a fuzzy set $\tilde{F}$ in Ω_q with the membership function $\mu(q)$. Buckley assumes that player 1 uses past experience as well as knowledge of the raw score outcomes of the game to construct the fuzzy set $\tilde{F} = \{(q, \mu(q)) \mid q \in \Omega\}$.

To arrive at an optimal strategy, Buckley suggests the use of max- and min-operators such as described in example 2.1, even though other and probably more appropriate operators could be used as well. To arrive at unconditional fuzzy sets $\tilde{A}_{ik}$ representing the attainable goals, he suggests the membership function

$$\mu_{ik}(p) = \max_q \left(\min \{\mu_{ik}(G_{ik}(p,q) \mid q), \mu(q)\}\right) \tag{3.3}$$

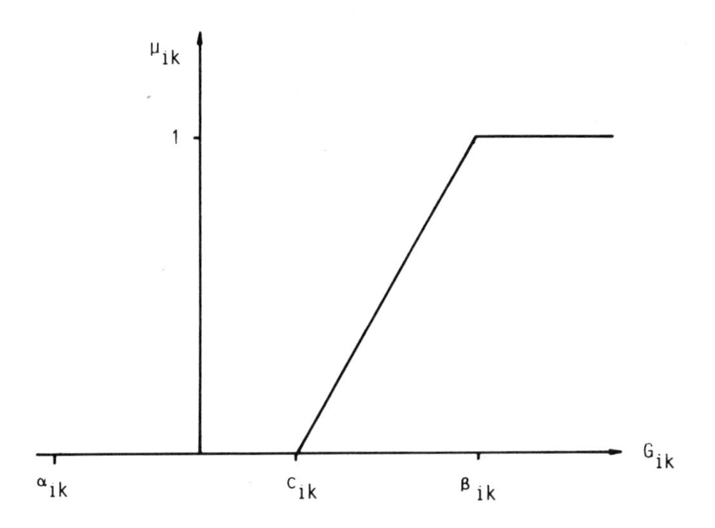

Figure 3-1: Conditional fuzzy set for maximizing G_{ik} for given value of q.

These fuzzy sets are aggregated in the sense of "and" by applying the min-operator to their membership functions

$$\mu(p) = \min_{i,k} (\mu_{ik}(p)) \tag{3.4}$$

The optimal strategy p^* is eventually determined as

$$\mu(p^*) = \max_{p} \mu(p) \tag{3.5}$$

Example 3.1 [Buckley 1984]

Let the pay-offs to player 1 be given in the following matrix:

$$\begin{array}{cc} & \text{Player 2} \\ \text{Player 1} & \begin{pmatrix} (2,1) & (-1,-1) \\ (-1,-1) & (1,2) \end{pmatrix} \end{array}$$

which corresponds to the structure of the well-known "battle of the sexes" [Luce, Raiffa 1957, p. 90]. The pay-off vector of player 1, $v = (v_1, v_2)$ has two components. Player 1 states his goals as (1) maximize the expected value of v_1 and minimize its variance; and (2) maximize the probability that v_2 exceeds zero. Hence player 1 has three goals, $\tilde{G}_{11}$: = maximize the expected value of

v_1; $\tilde{G}_{12}$: = minimize the variance of v_1; $\tilde{G}_{21}$: maximize $P(v_2 > 0)$.

Since $p = (p_1, 1 - p_1)$ and $q = (q_1, 1 - q_1)$ the membership functions are functions of p_1 and/or q_1 only. Let player 1 have the following triangular membership function $\mu(q_1)$ for $\tilde{F}$ in Ω_q:

$$\mu(q_1) = \begin{cases} 2q_1 & \text{if } 0 \leq q_1 \leq .5 \\ -2q_1 + 2 & \text{if } .5 \leq q_1 \leq 1 \end{cases} \tag{3.6}$$

Player 1 wants to maximize the expected value of v_1, hence

$$\begin{aligned} G_{11}(p_1,q_1) &= p_1, 2 \cdot q_1 + (1 - p_1)(-1)q_1 + p_1(-1)\cdot(1 - q_1) \\ &\quad + (1 - p_1)\cdot 1 \cdot (1 - q_1) \\ &= 1 + 5p_1q_1 - 2p_1 - 2q_1 \end{aligned}$$

The conditional membership function μ_{11} is defined to be

$$\mu_{11}(G_{11}(p_1,q_1) | q_1) = \begin{cases} 0 & \text{if } G_{11} \leq C_{11} \\ \dfrac{G_{11} - C_{11}}{2 - C_{11}} & \text{if } C_{11} \leq G_{11} \leq 2 \\ 1 & \text{if } G_{11} \geq 2 \end{cases} \tag{3.7}$$

where C_{11} is defined as

$$C_{11} = \begin{cases} -2q_1 + 1 & \text{if } 0 \leq q_1 \leq .5 \\ 2q_1 + 1 & \text{if } .5 \leq q_1 \leq 1 \end{cases} \tag{3.8}$$

Figure 3.2 depicts $\mu(q_1)$, as defined by equation (3.6), and $\mu_{11}(G_{11}|q_1)$.

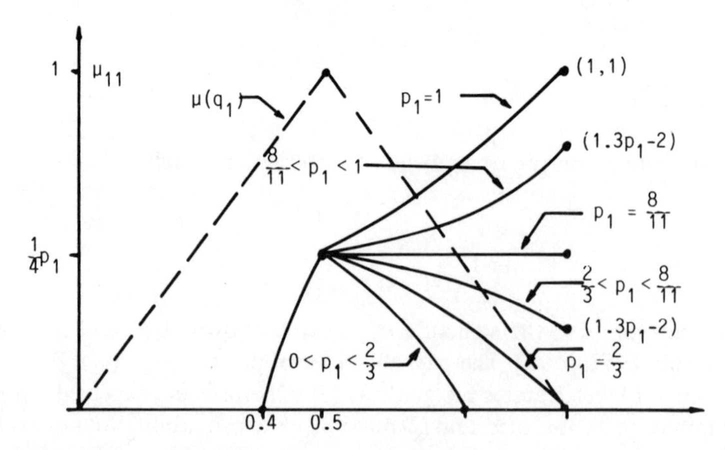

Figure 3-2: Membership functions $\mu(q_1)$ and $\mu_{11}(G_{11}|q_1)$.

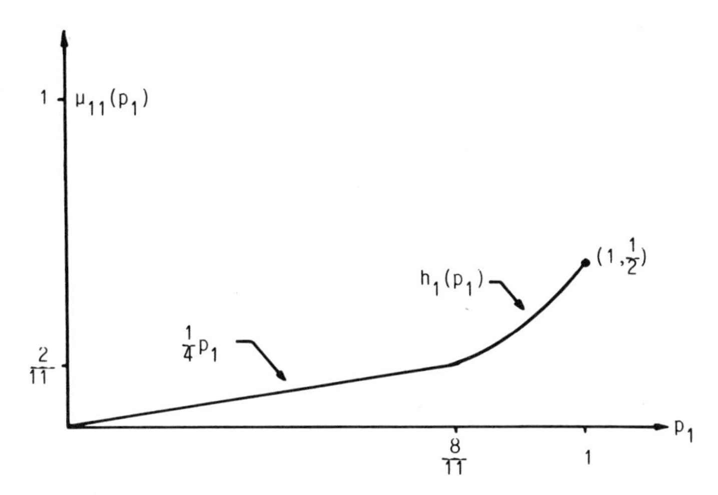

Figure 3-3: Fuzzy set representing the first goal.

Using equation (3.3), the membership function of $\tilde{A}_{11}$ can be determined as

$$\mu_{11}(p_1) = \begin{cases} .25p_1 & \text{if } 0 \le p_1 \le \frac{8}{11} \\ h_1(p_1) & \text{if } \frac{8}{11} \le p_1 \le 1 \end{cases} \tag{3.9}$$

with $h_1(p_1) = [2 - 5p_1(25(p_1)^2 + 28p_1 - 28)^{1/2}]/4$. This is shown in figure 3.3.

Analogously, the fuzzy sets representing the second goal (minimize the

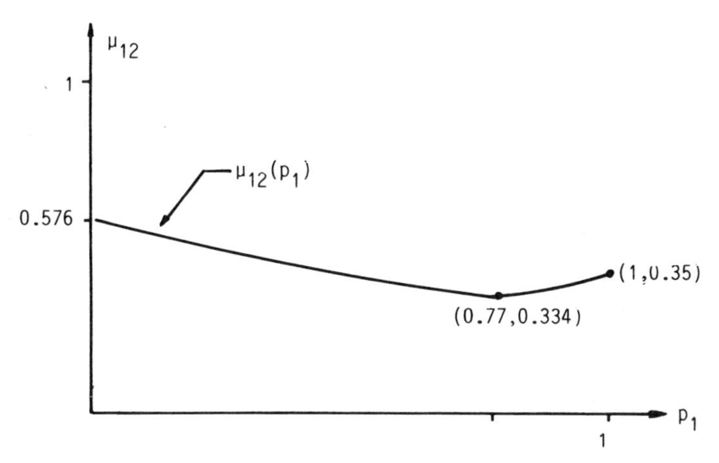

Figure 3-4: Fuzzy set representing the second goal.

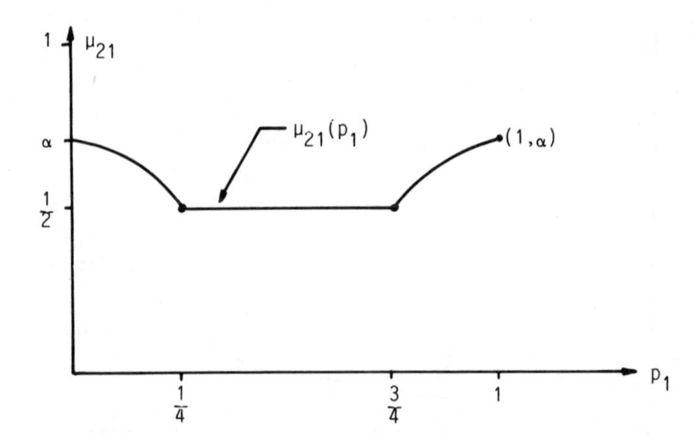

Figure 3-5: Fuzzy set representing the third goal.

variance of v_1) and the third goal (maximize Pr, $[v_2 > 0]$) can be determined. They are shown in figures 3-4 and 3-5 (for computational details see Buckley [1984b, pp. 117–120]). For this example p^* can be determined via equation (3.5) as $p_1 = 1, p_2 = 1 - p_1 = 0$. It is also possible to incorporate nonnumerical pay-offs. This is an attractive extension of Buckley's model which might render his approach even more user oriented.

Some very interesting contributions have been published concerning fuzzy n-person games [Aubin 1981, 1984; Butnariu 1978, 1979, 1980; Nurmi 1981a]. A detailed discussion of those highly mathematical papers would certainly exceed the scope of this book.

Let us, therefore, just indicate the direction of those publications. There are two major problem areas in the (classical) theory of n-person games: the bargaining problem and the formation of coalitions. The former is in character very similar to the problems and approaches in two-person games. Therefore the theory of fuzzy n-person games concentrates largely on the formation of coalitions and the stability of possible coalitions under different conditions. In this context a fuzzy coalition is defined as a symmetrical and transitive fuzzy relation between players such that $\tilde{R}(i,j) \geq \tilde{R}(i,k) \circ \tilde{R}(k,j)$ for all i, j, and k, where i, j, and k denote individual players of a game. Hence, by contrast to classical n-person game theory a player can belong to several coalitions to different degrees. The interested reader is referred to above-mentioned literature for further details.

Fuzzy Team Theory

Before discussing fuzzy team theory, we will specify in more detail the basic notions of team theory [Marshak, Radner 1972; MacCrimmon 1974; Ying 1969; Nojiri 1979].

Let a team consist of n members. The ith member can act individually and choose any of the actions a_i, $\{a_i\} = A_i$, available to him. The team as a whole can also act, and its feasible actions shall be denoted by

$$A = \{a\},\{a\} = \{(a_1,a_2,\ldots,a_n)\}$$

The set of possible states of nature shall be denoted by $S = \{s\}$. We shall assume that S is finite and does not contain any state that occurs with zero probability. By contrast to the theory of individual decision making it is not assumed that the decision makers have correct information about the states of the nature S. Let the information about the states of nature received by the team members be denoted by $y = (y_1,\ldots,y_n)$, where y_1, $i = 1(1)n$, is the information received by the ith member of the team; then s is related to y_i by a function $n_i(s)$.

A team member decides on action a_i on the basis of y_i. Hence $a_i = \alpha_i(y_i)$, where $\alpha = \{\alpha_1,\ldots,\alpha_n\}$ is called the decision function of a team. The decision function α_i is obviously a function from y_i to the set of feasible actions A_i. The n-tuple $n = (n_1,\ldots,n_n)$ is often called the information structure of the team. One generally assumes maximization of the expected utility to be the goal of the team. If $u(.,.)$—a mapping from $S \times A$ to the real line–denotes the utility function of the team, then the expected utility resulting from the information structure n and the team decision function α is

$$\begin{aligned} U(n,\alpha,u,p) &= \sum_s u(s,\alpha[n(s)])p(s) \\ &= \sum_s u(s,(\alpha_1[n_1(s)],\ldots,\alpha_n[n_n(s)]))p(s) \end{aligned} \tag{3.10}$$

where p denotes again the probability function over the various states of nature.

The aim of team theory is to find the optimal pair (n^*,α^*), that is, the information structure and the decision function which maximizes the expected utility for given sets of feasible actions and states of nature.

Nojiri [1979] supposes that the members of the team do not receive crisp information signals but, rather, fuzzy information about the states of nature. Let $\tilde{C}_i = \{(y_i,\mu_{\tilde{C}_i}(y_i)), y_i \in Y_i\}$, $i = 1,\ldots,n$, be the fuzzy set of information signals received by member i. If the information structure of the team is still a set of crisp functions $\{n_i\}$, $i = 1,\ldots,n$, then the inverse mapping of n_i, $n_i^{-1}(\tilde{C}_i)$ induces a fuzzy set $\tilde{B}_i = \{(s,\mu_{\tilde{B}_i}(s))\}$, $s \in S$ with $\mu_{\tilde{B}_i}(s) = \mu_{\tilde{C}_i}(y_i)$ in the space of states of nature. If $\tilde{B}$ is a fuzzy set in S the information function n_i induces a fuzzy set $\tilde{C}_i$ with the membership function [Nojiri 1979, p. 203]

$$\mu_{\tilde{C}_i}(y_i) = \begin{cases} \sup\limits_{s \in n_i^{-1}(y_i)} \{\mu_{\tilde{B}_i}(s)\} & \text{if } n_i^{-1}(y_i) \text{ is not empty} \\ 0 & \text{else} \end{cases} \tag{3.11}$$

Let $\tilde{B}$ denote the fuzzy set of states observed by the team as a whole. Assuming that this is the union of the fuzzy sets observed by the members of the team its membership function can be computed as

$$\mu_{\tilde{B}}(s) = \max(\mu_{\tilde{B}_1}(s),\ldots,\mu_{\tilde{B}_n}(s)) \tag{3.12}$$

Let $\tilde{C} = \tilde{C}_1 \times \cdots \times \tilde{C}_n$ be the fuzzy set of information signals to the team. The membership function of $\tilde{C}$ is then

$$\mu_{\tilde{C}}(y) = \min_i (\mu_{\tilde{C}_i}(y_i)) \qquad y_i \in Y_i \tag{3.13}$$

$\tilde{C}$ is an n-ary fuzzy relation in the product space $Y = Y_1 \times \cdots \times Y_n$.

Eventually the decision function of the team, $\alpha = (\alpha_1,\ldots,\alpha_n)$ induces a fuzzy-set decision, $\tilde{D} = (\tilde{D}_1 \times \cdots \times \tilde{D}_n)$, in the action spaces of the members. Hence

$$\tilde{D}_i = \{(a_i,\mu_{\tilde{D}_i}(a_i))\} \qquad a_i \in A_i \tag{3.14}$$

with

$$\mu_{\tilde{D}_i}(a_i) = \begin{cases} \sup\limits_{y_i \in \alpha_i^{-1}(a_i)} \{\mu_{\tilde{C}_i}(y_i)\} & \text{if } \alpha_i^{-1}(a_i) \text{ is not empty} \\ 0 & \text{else} \end{cases} \tag{3.15}$$

In analogy to equation (3.13) we obtain

$$\tilde{D} = \{(a,\mu_{\tilde{D}}(a))\} \qquad a \in A \tag{3.16}$$

with

$$\mu_{\tilde{D}}(a) = \min\{\mu_{\tilde{D}_1}(a_1),\ldots,\mu_{\tilde{D}_n}(a_n)\} \tag{3.17}$$

If $\tilde{B}$ is a fuzzy set of states observed and $\tilde{D}$ is the fuzzy set of relevant actions, then the maximal expected utility of the team, given its information structure n', is the expected utility maximized with respect to α. This can be computed as [Nojiri 1979, p. 205]

$$U(n',\alpha) = \sum_s u(s,\alpha[n'(s)]) \min\{\mu_{\tilde{B}}(s),\mu_{\tilde{D}}(\alpha[n'(s)])\} p(s) \tag{3.18}$$

where $U(n',\alpha)$ denotes the expected utility over the extension product of $\tilde{B}$ and

$\tilde{D}$. This approach is illustrated below by an abbreviated and slightly modified example from Nojiri [1979]:

Example 3.2

Let an urn be known to contain two balls, each of which may be either red or orange (fuzzy states). A single ball is drawn and its color observed. Of the 8 alternative states 2 are impossible (one could not draw a red ball if the urn only contains orange balls and vice versa!). Thus there are 6 possible states s_1 through s_6 shown in table 3–1.

The observing team may consist of 2 members. The states of the environment are $S = \{s_1, s_2, \ldots, s_6\}$; the possible informations about the states of nature are $\{y_1\} = \{y_{11}, y_{12}\}$ for the first member and $\{y_2\} = \{y_{21}, y_{22}\}$ for the second member, with $y_{11} = y_{22} =$ orange and $y_{12} = y_{21} =$ red. Hence,

$$y_{11} = n_1(s_1) = n_1(s_3) = n_1(s_3)$$

$$y_{12} = n_1(s_2) = n_1(s_4) = n_1(s_6)$$

$$y_{21} = n_2(s_2) = n_2(s_4) = n_2(s_6)$$

$$y_{22} = n_2(s_1) = n_2(s_3) = n_2(s_5)$$

Let members 1 and 2 receive, respectively, the fuzzy sets $\tilde{C}_1 = \{(y_{11}, .6), (y_{12}, .9)\}$ and $\tilde{C}_2 = \{(y_{21}, .8), (y_{22}, .7)\}$, where the degrees of membership indicate the degree to which a ball drawn is judged to be orange (y_{11}) or red (y_{12}). Therefore

$$\tilde{B}_1 = \{(s_1, .6), (s_2, .9), (s_3, .6), (s_4, .9), (s_5, .6), (s_6, .9)\}$$

$$\tilde{B}_2 = \{(s_1, .7), (s_2, .8), (s_3, .7), (s_4, .8), (s_5, .7), (s_6, .8)\}$$

Table 3-1

State	*Contents of urn* Ball 1	Ball 2	*Sample Ball Drawn*
s_1	O	O	O
s_2	R	O	R
s_3	R	O	O
s_4	O	R	R
s_5	O	R	O
s_6	R	R	R

and according to equation (3.12),

$$\tilde{B} = \{(s_1,.7),(s_2,.9),(s_3,.7),(s_4,.9),(s_5,.7),(s_6,.9)\}$$

There are four team information signals:

$$y^1 = (y_{11},y_{21}) \qquad y^2 = (y_{11},y_{22})$$
$$y^3 = (y_{12},y_{21}) \qquad y^4 = (y_{12},y_{22})$$

On the basis of these signals, $\tilde{C}$ can be determined according to equation (3.13):

$$\mu_{\tilde{C}}(y^1) = \mu_{\tilde{C}}(y_{11},y_{21}) = \min\{\mu_{\tilde{C}_1}(y_{11}),\mu_{\tilde{C}_2}(y_{21})\}$$
$$= \min\{.6,.8\} = .6$$

and so on. Thus

$$\tilde{C} = \{(y^1,.6),(y^2,.6),(y^3,.8),(y^4,.7)\}$$

Let us now turn to the decision function and assume that

$$a_{11} = \alpha_1(y_{11}) = \alpha_1(y_{12})$$
$$a_{21} = \alpha_2(y_{21})$$
$$a_{22} = \alpha_2(y_{22})$$

Hence there are two team actions:

$$a^1 = (a_{11},a_{21}) \quad \text{and} \quad a^2 = (a_{11},a_{22})$$
$$\tilde{D}_2 = \{(a_{21},\mu_{\tilde{D}_2}(a_{21})),(a_{22},\mu_{\tilde{D}_2}(a_{22}))\}$$

According to equation (3.15) we obtain

$$\tilde{D}_1 = \{(a_{11},.9)\}; \tilde{D}_2 = \{(a_{21},.8),(a_{22},.7)\},$$

and equation (3.17) yields

$$\tilde{D} = \{(a^1,.8),(a^2,.7)\} \quad \text{via}$$
$$\mu_{\tilde{D}}(a^1) = \mu_{\tilde{D}}(a_{11},a_{21}) = \min(.9,.8) = .8 \quad \text{and}$$
$$\mu_{\tilde{D}}(a^2) = \mu_{\tilde{D}}(a_{11},a_{22}) = .7$$

Let us now assume that the teams' utility matrix and the respective state probabilities are as shown in the pay-off matrix of table 3–2. The expected utilities are then

Table 3-2: Pay-off matrix

	State	s_1	s_2	s_3	s_4	s_5	s_6
	Probability p_i	.1	.3	.2	.1	.1	.2
Utility	Action a^1	1	0	0	0	1	0
	Action a^2	0	1	1	1	0	1

$$U(a^1) = \sum_{i=1}^{6} u(s_i,a^1)p(s_i) = .2$$

$$U(a^2) = .8$$

The best action is, therefore, $a^* = a^2$.

It has already been mentioned that the goal of team theory is to determine optimal decision functions, d^*, given a certain information structure n'. Equation (3.18) defined the utility function used for this purpose. Let us now assume that four decision rules, α^1 through α^4, are considered, and these lead to the following fuzzy decision sets:

$$\tilde{D}_1 = \{(a^1,.8),(a^2,.7)\}$$

$$\tilde{D}_2 = \{(a^1,.7),(a^2,.8)\}$$

$$\tilde{D}_3 = \{(a^1,.8),(a^2,.8)\}$$

$$\tilde{D}_4 = \{(a^1,0),(a^2,.8)\}$$

$\tilde{B}$ is as determined above. The expected utilities can then be computed via

$$U(n',\alpha^i) = \sum_{j=1}^{6} u(s_j,\alpha^i[n'(s_j)]) \min\{u_{\tilde{B}}(s_j),\mu_{\tilde{D}_i}(\alpha^i[n'(s_j)])\} p(s_j)$$

This yields

$$U(n',\alpha^1) = .12$$

$$U(n',\alpha^2) = .60$$

$$U(n',\alpha^3) = .12$$

$$U(n',\alpha^4) = .60$$

Hence, for the given $n' = (n'_1,n'_2)$, the best decision rules are α^2 and α^4.

Fuzzy Group Decision Making

Contributions of fuzzy set theory to group decision making have been made in several directions. Blin [1974] proposed to represent a relative group preference as a fuzzy preference matrix from individual preferences. Fung and Fu [1975] discussed the aggregation of individual preferences into a group preference from an axiomatic point of view. Orlovsky [1978] introduced two types of linearity of a fuzzy relation and studied the equivalence of crisp nondominated alternatives. He showed that crisp nondominated solutions to the decision-making problem exist if the original fuzzy relation satisfies some topological requirements. Kuz'min and Ovchinnikov [1980] introduced an appropriate distance in the space of fuzzy relation matrixes and studied group decision making on its basis. Nurmi [1981a,b, 1982] developed ways of determining the best alternatives on the basis of a fuzzy preference relation and of deriving a crisp group preference relation from fuzzy individual preference relations.

We shall consider in more detail two contributions which, from an application-oriented point of view, seem to be of particular appeal and which consider decision making as a process rather than basing it on the static choice model (see definition 1.1). First we will consider ways of aggregating individual preference functions in order to obtain group utility functions and then we shall discuss models that describe the degree of conformity or disagreement of the group for which the utility function has been determined. For this, we need some more basic definitions.

A fuzzy relation was defined in definition 2.6. For discrete supports, fuzzy relations can be defined by matrixes.

Example 3.3

Let $X = \{x_1, x_2, x_3\}$ and $Y = \{y_1, y_2, y_3, y_4\}$

$\tilde{R}$ = "x considerably larger than y"

	y_1	y_2	y_3	y_4
x_1	0	0	.1	.8
$= x_2$	0	.8	0	0
x_3	.1	.8	1	.8

and

$\tilde{Z}$ = "y much bigger than x"

	y_1	y_2	y_3	y_4
x_1	.4	.4	.2	.1
$= x_2$	.5	0	1	1
x_3	.5	.1	.2	.6

In what follows we will consider only fuzzy relations in $X \times X$. The reader should notice that the following definitions differ slightly from those used in chapter 2.

Definition 3.1

Let $0 \leq r_{ij} \leq 1$ express an individual's degree of preference for outcome x_i over outcome x_j. If r_{ij} and r_{ji} are reciprocal (i.e., $r_{ij} + r_{ji} = 1$), then the fuzzy relation $\tilde{R}(r_{ij})$ is called a fuzzy *preference relation* (reciprocal relation).

The interpretation of r_{ij} is obvious if $r_{ij} \in \{0,1\}$: if $r_{ij} = 1$, x_i is preferred to x_j; and if $r_{ij} = 0$, x_j is preferred to x_i. If, however, $0 < r_{ij} < 1$, the values of r_{ij} express either an uncertainty about the preference relationship between x_i and x_j or they express the intensity of preference. We shall adopt the latter view.

We want to discuss aggregated group utility functions and their properties. These properties will depend on the properties of the individual utility functions from which they have been derived. Therefore it is appropriate first to consider possible types and characters of individual preference relations:

Definition 3.2

A fuzzy preference relation that is also transitive is called a *fuzzy preference ordering.*

Usually transitivity is interpreted in fuzzy set theory as "max-min transitivity" (definition 2.9). For our purposes it is more appropriate to follow Tanino [1984] in defining the following types of transitivities, which do not coincide with definition 2.9.

Definition 3.3

Let $\tilde{R}$ be a fuzzy preference relation. This relation is called *max-min transitive* if

$$r_{ij} \geq \tfrac{1}{2}, r_{jk} \geq \tfrac{1}{2} \Rightarrow r_{ik} \geq \min\{r_{ij}, r_{jk}\} \qquad \forall\, i,j,k$$

This transitivity is also called moderate stochastic transitivity in the probabilistic choice theory [Luce, Suppes 1965].

Definition 3.4

A fuzzy preference relation is called *restricted max-max transitive* if

$$r_{ij} \geq \tfrac{1}{2}, r_{jk} \geq \tfrac{1}{2} \Rightarrow r_{ik} \geq \max\{r_{ij}, r_{jk}\} \qquad \forall\, i,j,k$$

This is called strong stochastic transitivity by Luce and Suppes, and it is obviously a stronger concept than definition 3.3.

If the intensities of preference are defined as $(r_{ij} - \tfrac{1}{2})$ [Tanino 1984] one can also define the following.

Definition 3.5

A fuzzy preference relation is called *additive transitive* if

$$r_{ij} \geq \tfrac{1}{2}, r_{jk} \geq \tfrac{1}{2} \Rightarrow (r_{ij} - \tfrac{1}{2}) + (r_{jk} - \tfrac{1}{2}) \leq r_{ik} - \tfrac{1}{2} \qquad \forall\, i,j,k$$

If a fuzzy preference relation is additive transitive it is also restricted max-max transitive.

Definition 3.6

When $r_{ij} > 0$ for all $i,j = 1,\ldots,n$, r_{ij}/r_{ji} shall indicate the ratio of the intensities of preferences, then a fuzzy preference relation is called *multiplicative transitive* if

$$\frac{r_{ji}}{r_{ij}} \cdot \frac{r_{kj}}{r_{jk}} \leq \frac{r_{ki}}{r_{ik}}$$

Multiplicative transitivity also implies restricted max-max transitivity.

The determination of group preference functions can be viewed as a three-stage process:

1. The determination of individual utilities.
2. The construction of individual preference relations.
3. The aggregation of individual preference relations to arrive at a group preference relation.

Let us first consider the transition from individual utilities to individual preference relations and then turn to the final aggregation of individual preference relations.

We will assume that there exists an individual utility function $u(x)$ on the set of events X. This utility function is supposed to be on a difference scale normalized in [0,1], that is

$$\max_i u(x_i) - \min_i u(x_i) \leq 1$$

then r_{ij} shall be defined as

$$r_{ij} = \tfrac{1}{2}(1 + u(x_i) - u(x_j)) \tag{3.19}$$

It can be shown [Tanino 1984] that if a set of utility values on a normalized scale level is given, the resulting preference relation according to equation (3.19) is a fuzzy preference order which satisfies additive transitivity.

Alternatively, one may assume that a utility function is given on a positive ratio scale and the preference intensity is defined as

$$r_{ij} = \frac{u(x_i)}{u(x_i) + u(x_j)} = \frac{1}{1 + \dfrac{u(x_j)}{u(x_i)}} \tag{3.20}$$

In this case the resulting fuzzy preference order relation is multiplicative transitive.

Given individual preference relations or fuzzy preference orderings, group preference relations can be determined in different ways. A simple aggregation rule is

$$r_{ij} = \frac{1}{m} \sum_{p=1}^{m} r_{ij}^{p} \tag{3.21}$$

where the superscript p denotes individual preferences of group member p.

If $\tilde{R}^p$, the individual preference orderings, satisfy additive transitvity then the resulting group preference relation $\tilde{R}$ is also additive transitive.

Example 3.4

The preference ordering of individual 1 is additive transitive:

$\tilde{R}^1 =$

	x_1	x_2	x_3
x_1	.5	.4	.7
x_2	.6	.5	.8
x_3	.3	.2	.5

The preference ordering of individual 2 is also additive transitive:

$\tilde{R}^2 =$

	x_1	x_2	x_3
x_1	.5	.7	1
x_2	.3	.5	.8
x_3	0	.2	.5

The resulting preference ordering of the group (according to equation (3.21)) $\tilde{R} = (r_{ij})$ is also additive transitive:

$\tilde{R} =$

	x_1	x_2	x_3
x_1	.5	.55	.85
x_2	.45	.5	.8
x_3	.15	.2	.5

Equation (3.21) is, of course, only the mean of the individual preference orders. It does not generate any new information nor does it give any indication of the diversity of individual preference orderings.

Tanino argues that for $r_{ij} \geq \frac{1}{2}$ for all $p = 1,\ldots,n$ and for $r_{ij} > \frac{1}{2}$ for some p, the group preference index should be 1 ($r_{ij} = 1$), indicating some type of Pareto-optimality. He, therefore, suggests the following aggregation rule.

$$r_{ij} = \begin{cases} \dfrac{\sum_{p=1}^{m} \max\left\{r_{ij}^{p} - \dfrac{1}{2}, 0\right\}}{\sum_{p=1}^{m} \left|r_{ij}^{p} - \dfrac{1}{2}\right|} + \dfrac{1}{2} & \text{for } i \neq j \\ \dfrac{1}{2} & \text{for } i = j \end{cases} \tag{3.22}$$

Tanino asserts that (3.22) is identical to (3.22a):

$$r'_{ij} = \begin{cases} \dfrac{\sum_{p=1}^{m}\left(r_{ij}^{p} - \frac{1}{2}\right)}{\sum_{p=1}^{m}\left|r_{ij}^{p} - \frac{1}{2}\right|} + \dfrac{1}{2} & \text{for } i \neq j \\ \dfrac{1}{2} & \text{for } i = j \end{cases} \tag{3.22a}$$

This, however, is not correct as shown by the following example. He proofs that if the individual preference orderings are additive transitive for all p then the fuzzy group preference ordering generated by (3.22) is also additive transitive. Moreover $r_{ij} = 1$ iff $r_{ij}^{p} \geq \frac{1}{2}$ for all p and $r_{ij}^{p} > \frac{1}{2}$ for some p.

Example 3.5 (continuation of example 3.4)

Fuzzy group preference ordering (3.22), $\tilde{R} = (r_{ij})$:

$\tilde{R} =$	x_1	x_2	x_3
x_1	.5	.67	1
x_2	.33	.5	1
x_3	0	0	.5

Relation $\tilde{R}' = (r'_{ij})$ according to (3.22a):

$\tilde{R}' =$	x_1	x_2	x_3
x_1	.5	.83	1
x_2	.17	.5	1
x_3	−.5	−1.5	.5

In general, (3.22a) does not lead to a preference ordering.

Tanino also suggests aggregation rules with analogous properties for individual preference orderings that are multiplicative transitive.

By contrast to equation (3.21) the group preference relation computed according to (3.22) conveys some additional information about the group consensus: $r_{ij} = 1$ does not indicate that *all* members of the group have an individual preference $r^p_{ij} = 1$ but that the group members predominantly have a positive attitude toward favoring x_i over x_j. Tanino also suggests a parametrized index that can be used to describe the degree of group consensus.

To describe the consensus of the group, or the different stages of a process aimed at achieving group concensus, we shall discuss in more detail an approach by Bezdek et al. [1978–1979] which seems very imaginative and applicable: These authors interpret r_{ij} as in definition 3.2. They are, however, not primarily concerned with determination of a specific $\tilde{R}$ of a group; they want to characterize the type of preference of consensus which has been reached by a certain $\tilde{R}$. Since we are only concerned about group consensus here we are interpreting all models and results with respect to group preferences only! To this end, Bezdek et al. define a number of scalar measures of consensus which characterize an arbitrary preference relation (of a group) with respect to either the location in the consensus space or with respect to specific kinds of consensus. We shall first consider the consensus space and specific kinds of consensus' contained in it and then discuss possible scalar measures of consensus.

Definition 3.7 [Bezdek et al. 1978]

Let V_n be the set of all real $n \times n$ matrixes and $\tilde{R}$ a fuzzy reciprocal-relation matrix representing a fuzzy preference relation such as defined in definition 3.1. Then the *consensus space*, M_n, is the set of all reciprocal relations, that is,

$$M_n = \{\tilde{R} \in V_n: 0 \leq r_{ij} \leq 1, \forall i,j;\ r_{ii} = 0 \,\forall i;\ r_{ij} + r_{ji} = 1 \,\forall i \neq j\}$$

The set of crisp reciprocal relations shall be called crisp consensus space, M_2,

$$M_2 = \{R \in M_n: r_{ij} \in \{0,1\} \,\forall i \quad \text{and} \quad j\}$$

Bezdek et al. suggest five specific kinds of consensus which can either be used as targets for consensus-reaching processes of a group or which can be used to better describe the consensus upon which a group has agreed.

Types of Consensus

Pairwise equal without choice:

$$M_1 = \{\tilde{R} \in M_n: r_{ij} = \tfrac{1}{2} \,\forall i \neq j\} = \{\tilde{R}_{1/2}\} \tag{3.23}$$

Pairwise definite without choice:

$$M_2 = \{\tilde{R} \in M_n: r_{ij} \in \{0,1\} \,\forall i \neq j\} \tag{3.24}$$

Pairwise equal with choice:

$$M_1^* = \{\tilde{R} \in M_n: \exists i \quad \text{with} \quad r_{ki} = 0 \,\forall\, k; r_{kj} = \tfrac{1}{2} \forall\, k \neq j \neq i\} \tag{3.25}$$

Pairwise definite with choice:

$$M_2^* = \{\tilde{R} \in M_2: \exists i \quad \text{with} \quad r_{ki} = 0 \,\forall\, k\} \tag{3.26}$$

Pairwise fuzzy with choice:

$$M_f^* = \{\tilde{R} \in M_n: \exists i \quad \text{with} \quad r_{ki} = 0 \,\forall\, k; 0 < r_{ki} < 1 \,\forall\, k \neq i \neq j\} \tag{3.27}$$

Of particular interest are

$\tilde{R}_1^* \in M_1^*$ which is called *Type 1* consensus

$\tilde{R}_2^* \in M_2^*$ which is called *Type 2* consensus

$\tilde{R}_f^* \in M_f^*$ which is called *Type f* consensus

Type 1 consensus means that the ith column of $\tilde{R}_1^*$ are zeros, that is, the ith alternative is unequivocally preferred. There is no other alternative that is preferred to another.

Type 2 consensus corresponds essentially to type 1 with the difference that the ratings of type 2 consensus refer to crisp rather than fuzzy preference relations.

Type f consensus is the third possible consensus in which one alternative is clearly preferred. By contrast to type 1 and type 2 consensus, the cardinalities of which are finite, this is not true for type f consensus. M_f^* is uncountable.

Scalar Measures of Consensus. Essentially two measures on M_n are suggested:

$$\text{average fuzziness } F(\tilde{R}) = \frac{2\,\text{tr}(\tilde{R}^2)}{n(n-1)} \tag{3.28}$$

$$\text{average certainty } C(\tilde{R}) = \frac{2\,\text{tr}(\tilde{R}\tilde{R}^T)}{n(n-1)} \tag{3.29}$$

Here, tr denotes the trace and $(\cdot)^T$ the transpose of $\tilde{R}$. F and C are not independent of each other. In fact Bezdek et al. prove the following properties:

For any $\tilde{R} \in M_n$ and $n > 1$,

$$F(\tilde{R}) + C(\tilde{R}) = 1 \tag{3.30}$$

$$F(\tilde{R}) = \tfrac{1}{2} \Leftrightarrow C(\tilde{R}) = \tfrac{1}{2} \Leftrightarrow \tilde{R} = \tilde{R}_{1/2} \tag{3.31}$$

$$F(\tilde{R}) = 0 \Leftrightarrow C(\tilde{R}) = 1 \Leftrightarrow R \in M_2 \quad \text{is crisp}$$

For $n > 1$,

$$\tilde{R}_1^* \in M_1^* \Rightarrow C(\tilde{R}_1^*) = \frac{n+2}{2n} = n^* < 1 \tag{3.32}$$

$$\tilde{R}_2^* \in M_2^* \Rightarrow C(\tilde{R}_2^*) = 1 \tag{3.33}$$

Even though $C(\tilde{R})$ seems to be a natural measure of the "degree of consensus" it may also prove useful for measuring the distance of an achieved $\tilde{R}$ to one of the specified distinct types of consensus—equations (3.23) through (3.27).

If, geometrically, we consider $\tilde{R}_{1/2}$ as a local "origin" and measure distances in M_n radially from $\tilde{R}_{1/2}$ we obtain [Bezdek et al. 1978, p. 264]

$$\tilde{R}_1^* \in M_1^* \Rightarrow \|\tilde{R}_1^* - \tilde{R}_{1/2}\| = \left(\frac{(n-1)}{2}\right)^{1/2} \tag{3.34}$$

$$\tilde{R}_2^* \in M_2^* \Rightarrow \|\tilde{R}_2^* - \tilde{R}_{1/2}\| = \left(\frac{n(n-1)}{4}\right)^{1/2} \tag{3.35}$$

$$\text{for } \|\tilde{R} - \tilde{R}_{1/2}\|^2 = \left(\frac{n(n-1)}{2}\right)\left(C(\tilde{R}) - \frac{1}{2}\right)$$

A normalized measure of radial distance inward from M_2 toward the centroid $\tilde{R}_{1/2}$ is

$$m_2(\tilde{R}) = 1 - \frac{\|\tilde{R} - \tilde{R}_{1/2}\|}{(n(n-1)/4)^{1/2}}$$

with the following properties:

$$0 \leq m_2(\tilde{R}) \leq 1 \; \forall \, \tilde{R} \in M_n \tag{3.36a}$$

$$m_2(\tilde{R}) = 1 \Leftrightarrow \tilde{R} = \tilde{R}_{1/2} \tag{3.36b}$$

$$m_2(\tilde{R}) = 0 \Leftrightarrow \tilde{R} \in M_2 \quad \text{is crisp} \tag{3.36c}$$

$$\tilde{R}_1^* \in M_1^* \Rightarrow m_2(\tilde{R}_1^*) = 1 - \left(\frac{2}{n}\right)^{1/2} \tag{3.36d}$$

$$\tilde{R}_2^* \in M_2^* \Rightarrow m_2(\tilde{R}_2^*) = 0 \tag{3.36e}$$

Figure 3-6 illustrates the relationship between consensus space M_n and the radial measure m_2 [Bezdek et al. 1978, p. 266].

Example 3.6 [Bezdek et al. 1979, p. 266]

Let the obtained group preference function be defined by the following fuzzy

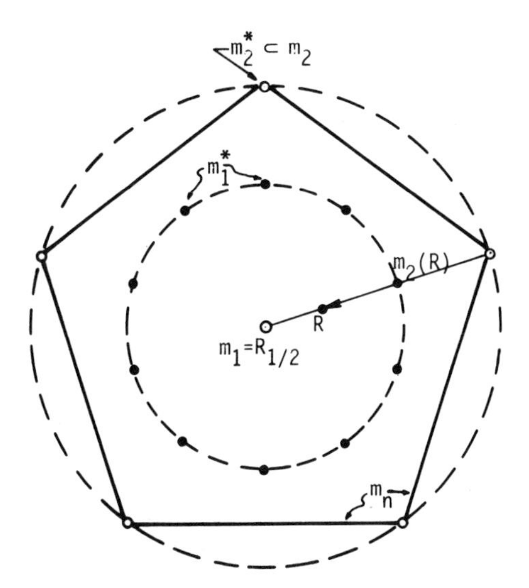

Figure 3-6: Consensus space and measure m_2.

reciprocal matrix $\tilde{R}$:

$$\tilde{R} = \begin{bmatrix} 0 & 1 & .5 & .2 \\ 0 & 0 & .3 & .9 \\ .5 & .7 & 0 & .6 \\ .8 & .1 & .4 & 0 \end{bmatrix}$$

For this fuzzy preference relation the following measures can be determined:

$$C(\tilde{R}) = .683$$

$$m_2(\tilde{R}) = .395$$

$$m_2(\tilde{R}_1^*) = .293$$

Graphically, this might be depicted as shown in figure 3-7. $m_2(R_1^*)$ is a measure of radial distance from M_2 to $R_{1/2}$. It also makes sense to measure the distance from an achieved consensus R to a type 1 consensus (3.25). As a measure one could also use

$$m_1(\tilde{R}) = \frac{|n^* - C(\tilde{R})|}{\max\{|n^* - \frac{1}{2}|, |n^* - 1|\}} \tag{3.37}$$

where, from (3.32)

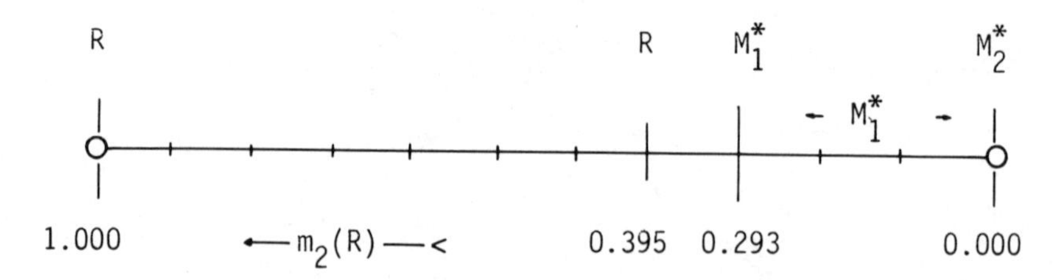

Figure 3-7: Graphical presentations of consensus measures.

$$n^* = C(\tilde{R}_1^*) = \frac{n+2}{2n}$$

Bezdek et al. [1979, p. 10] present an excellent example of the use of this measure. We shall, therefore, present an abbreviated version of their illustration.

Example 3.7

In an undergraduate speech communication class, four groups, G1–G4, were asked to develop a list of 10 topics one of which should be selected for research and presentation to the class. After a group had specified its alternative set, each group member was asked to provide the upper triangular portion of a 10×10 preference matrix. The first group of samples were averaged and then discussed. This process was repeated until the groups arrived at fixed individual preference relations, which in turn yielded a final group average that can be compared to type 1 consensus. For example, the final group average relation for G4 was

$$\tilde{R}_{4f} = \begin{pmatrix} 0 & 1 & 1 & 1 & 1 & 1 & 1 & 1 & 1 & 1 \\ & 0 & .5 & .5 & .5 & .5 & .46 & .5 & .5 & .5 \\ & & 0 & .56 & .5 & .58 & .46 & .56 & .54 & .5 \\ & & & 0 & .5 & .5 & .48 & .46 & .5 & .5 \\ & & & & 0 & .5 & .46 & .5 & .5 & .5 \\ & & & & & 0 & .46 & .44 & .5 & .5 \\ & & & & & & 0 & .56 & .5 & .5 \\ & & & & & & & 0 & .5 & .5 \\ & & & & & & & & 0 & .5 \\ & & & & & & & & & 0 \end{pmatrix}$$

indicating (true) consensus for alternative 1. This matrix is in M_f^*, and is quite close to M_1^*, as can be seen in the following table 3.3. All groups terminated fairly close to type 1 consensus. Figure 3-8 shows the evolution of group consensus for this experiment.

Table 3-3: Average normalized distances $m_1(\tilde{R}_t)$ to M_1^*.

Group	*Time*				
	0	1	2	3	4
G1	.164	.164	.219	—	—
G2	.004	.076	.023	.054	.188
G3	.018	.125	.018	—	—
G4	.021	.095	.048	.034	.003

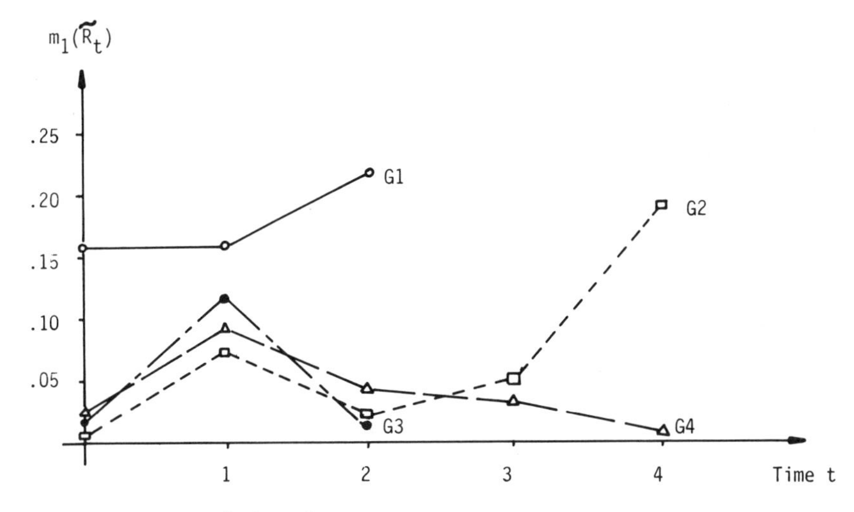

Figure 3-8: The evolution of group consensus.

4 FUZZY MATHEMATICAL PROGRAMMING

Mathematical programming is one of the areas to which fuzzy set theory has been applied extensively. The term *fuzzy programming* has been used in different ways in the past. Ostasiewicz [1982], Tanaka and Mizumoto [1975], as well as Chang [1975] define a fuzzy program essentially as an algorithm described by a flowchart in which each arc is associated with a fuzzy relation (called a fuzzy branching condition) and a fuzzy assignment. Input, output, and program variables represent fuzzy sets.

Here, the term *fuzzy mathematical programming* will be used as it is usually used in operations research—that is, to mean an algorithmic approach to solving models of the type

$$\begin{aligned} &\text{maximize} \quad f(x) \\ &\text{such that} \quad g_i(x) \leq 0 \qquad i = 1(1)m \end{aligned} \tag{4.1}$$

We shall primarily consider a special model of the problem "maximize an objective function subject to constraints," namely the *linear programming model*:

$$\begin{aligned} \text{maximize} \quad & z = c^T x \\ \text{such that} \quad & Ax \leq b \\ & x \geq 0 \end{aligned} \tag{4.2}$$

where c and x are n-vectors, b is an m vector, and A is an $m \times n$ matrix. (In chapter 5 we shall discuss this problem again but define c to be an $k \times n$ matrix!)

Equation (4.2) will be interpreted as a specific model of a decision in the sense of the choice model of definition 1.1. Here, A, b, and c describe the relevant state, x denotes the decision variable, z is the event resulting from combination of the state and the decision variable, and the utility function is expressed by the requirement to maximize z. For the time being the objective function $\max z = c^T x$ of (4.2) can be regarded as the utility function.

Obviously different parts of (4.2) can be considered fuzzy, and fuzziness can also be expressed in different ways: The elements of either A, b, or c can be fuzzy numbers rather than crisp numbers; the constraints can be represented by fuzzy sets rather than by crisp inequalities; and the objective function can be represented by either a fuzzy set or a fuzzy function.

Finally, the decision, or solution, can be either a fuzzy set or a crisp solution (maximizing solution). The discussion of the different cases will be structured according to the symmetry of the resulting fuzzy decision models. In doing so we shall assume that the min-operator is acceptable to model the intersection of fuzzy sets and that the membership functions are linear. Under the "Extensions" heading we will deal with nonlinear membership functions and with other ways of aggregating fuzzy constraints and objective functions.

Fuzzy Linear and Nonlinear Programming

Symmetrical Models

Our first assumption will be that we face a situation as described in definition 2.1 i.e., the goal of the decision maker can be expressed as a fuzzy set and the solution space is defined by constraints that can be modelled by fuzzy sets. In such a situation a better model than (4.2) would be:

Find x such that

$$\begin{aligned} c^T x &\gtrsim z \\ Ax &\lesssim b \\ x &\geq 0 \end{aligned} \tag{4.3}$$

Here, $\lesssim$ denotes the fuzzified version of $\leq$ and has the linguistic interpretation "essentially smaller than or equal." The objective function in (4.2) might have to be written as a minimizing goal in order to consider z as an upper bound.

We see that (4.3) is fully symmetric with respect to objective function and constraints and we want to make that even more obvious by substituting $\binom{c^T}{A} = B$ and $\binom{z}{b} = d$. Then (4.3) becomes:

Find x such that

$$\begin{aligned} Bx &\lesssim d \\ x &\geq 0 \end{aligned} \tag{4.3a}$$

Each of the $(m + 1)$ rows of (4.3a) shall now be represented by a fuzzy set, the membership functions of which are $\mu_i(x)$, $i = 1,\ldots,m + 1$. $\mu_i(x)$ can be interpreted as the degree to which x fulfills (satisfies) the fuzzy unequality $(Bx)_i \lesssim d_i$ (where $(Bx)_i$ denotes the ith row of B). Following definition 2.1 the membership function of the fuzzy set "decision" of model (4.3a) is

$$\mu_{\tilde{D}}(x) = \min_{i=1}^{m+1} \mu_i(x) \tag{4.4}$$

Assuming that the decision maker is interested not in a fuzzy set but in a crisp optimal solution x_0 we could suggest to him the "maximizing solution" to (4.4), which is the solution to the possibly nonlinear problem

$$\max_{x \geq 0} \min_{i=1}^{m+1} \mu_i(x) = \mu_M(x^0) \tag{4.5}$$

Now we have to specify the membership functions $\mu_i(x)$. $\mu_i(x)$ should be 0 if the constraints (including objective function) are strongly violated, 1 if they are very well satisfied (i.e., satisfied in the crisp sense), and should increase monotoneously from 0 to 1, that is,

$$\mu_i(x) = \begin{cases} 1 & \text{if } (Bx)_i \leq d_i \\ \in [0,1] & \text{if } d_i \leq (Bx)_i \leq d_i + p_i, \quad i = 1,\ldots,m + 1 \\ 0 & \text{if } (Bx)_i > d_i + p_i \end{cases} \tag{4.6}$$

Using the simplest type of membership function we assume them to be linearly increasing over the "tolerance interval" $[d_i, d_i + p_i]$:

$$\mu_i(x) = \begin{cases} 1 & \text{if } (Bx)_i \leq d_i \\ 1 - \dfrac{(Bx)_i - d_i}{p_i} & \text{if } d_i < (Bx)_i \leq d_i + p_i, \quad i = 1,\ldots,m + 1 \\ 0 & \text{if } (Bx)_i > d_i + p_i \end{cases} \tag{4.7}$$

The p_i are subjectively choosen constants of admissable violations of the constraints and the objective function. Substituting (4.7) into (4.5) yields, after some rearrangements [Zimmermann 1976],

$$\max_{x \geq 0} \min_{i=1}^{m+1} \left\{ 1 - \frac{(Bx)_i - d_i}{p_i} \right\} \tag{4.8}$$

Introducing one new variable λ, which corresponds essentially to (4.4), that is, to the membership function of the fuzzy set "decision," we arrive at

$$\begin{aligned} &\text{maximize} \quad \lambda \\ &\text{such that} \quad \lambda p_i + (Bx)_i \leq d_i + p_i, \quad i = 1,\ldots,m+1 \\ &\qquad 0 \leq \lambda \leq 1 \\ &\qquad x \geq 0 \end{aligned} \tag{4.9}$$

If the optimal solution to (4.9) is the vector (λ^0, x^0) then x^0 is the maximizing solution (4.5) of model (4.3), assuming membership functions as specified in (4.7). The reader should realize that this maximizing solution can be found by solving one standard (crisp) LP with only one more variable and one more constraint than model (4.2). This makes this approach computationally very efficient.

A slightly modified version of models (4.8) and (4.9) results if the membership functions are defined as follows: a variable t_i, $i = 1,\ldots,m+1$, $0 \leq t_i \leq p_i$, is defined which measures the degree of violation of the ith constraint. The membership function of the ith row is then

$$\mu_i = 1 - \frac{t_i}{p_i} \tag{4.10}$$

The crisp equivalent model is then

$$\begin{aligned} &\text{maximize} \quad \lambda \\ &\text{such that} \quad \lambda p_i + t_i \leq p_i, \qquad i = 1,\ldots,m+1 \\ &\qquad (Bx)_i - t_i \leq d_i \\ &\qquad t_i \leq p_i \\ &\qquad \lambda, x, t \geq 0 \end{aligned} \tag{4.11}$$

This model is larger than model (4.9). The set of constraints $t_i \leq p_i$ is actually redundant, it turns out to be useful, however, when interpreting dual prices. Model (4.11) has some advantages, in particular, when performing sensitivity analysis that will be discussed later. Its main advantage, compared to the unfuzzy problem formulation, is the fact that the decision maker is not forced into a crisp formulation for mathematical reasons even though he might only be able or willing to describe his problem in fuzzy terms. Linear membership functions are obviously only a very rough approximation. Membership functions that monotonically increase or decrease, respectively, in the interval of $[d_i, d_i + p_i]$ can also be handled quite easily, as will be shown later.

So far the objective function as well as all constraints have been considered fuzzy. If some of the constraints are crisp, $Dx \leq b$, then these constraints can easily be added to formulations (4.9) or (4.11), respectively. Thus (4.9) would, for instance, become

$$\begin{aligned} &\text{maximize} \quad \lambda \\ &\text{such that} \quad \lambda p_i + (Bx)_i \leq d_i + p_i, \qquad i = 1,\ldots,m+1 \\ &\qquad Dx \leq b \\ &\qquad \lambda \leq 1 \\ &\qquad x,\lambda \geq 0 \end{aligned} \tag{4.12}$$

A modification of model (4.3) would be to assume that the constraints can not be modelled directly as fuzzy sets, but that the decision maker is in a position to provide enough information to model the single elements of A or b as fuzzy numbers rather than as crisp real numbers. [Tanaka, Asai 1984] Whether this is the case will, of course, depend on the problem situation. The computational effort would certainly be larger. The reader can also imagine that an aggregation within each row could be performed resulting in a single fuzzy set per row as in model (4.3). So far we have not found in any real situation that a manager could provide that much information. We shall, therefore, not pursue this possible approach any further.

To this point, we have tried to determine a crisp solution to model (4.3). It might be desirable to determine not only the (crisp) maximizing decision but to provide more information about the fuzzy set "decision," that is, to compute explicitely (4.4).

In the case of linear membership functions and min-operator aggregation one can use parametric linear programming to compute $\mu_{\tilde{D}}(x)$ [Chanas 1983]. Let us consider the model

$$\begin{aligned} &\text{maximize} \quad z = c^T x \\ &\text{such that} \quad Ax \leq b + \theta p \\ &\qquad x \geq 0, \quad 0 \leq \theta \leq 1 \end{aligned} \tag{4.13}$$

where the vector p is defined as in (4.7). Then for any fixed parameter θ and a given solution x_K of (4.9)

$$\mu_i(x_K) \geq 1 - \theta \qquad i = 1,\ldots,m$$

Since the $\mu_{\tilde{D}}(x)$ is determined by applying the min-operator, there has to be at least one row, l, for which

$$\mu_l(x_K) = 1 - \theta$$

where $\mu_l(x_K) = \lambda$ is the degree to which solution x_K satisfies at least any of the fuzzy constraints and maximizes the fuzzy goal. Let $\mu_l(x_K)$ be this degree to which the constraints are satisfied. Hence

$$\mu_l(x_K) = 1 - \theta_l$$

We can now represent $z_{max}(x)$ of (4.9) as a function of θ. This function is continuous, piece-wise linear, and concave in θ. Via the relationship of θ and $z_{max}(x)$ the membership function of the goal, $\mu_0(x)$, can now be determined as a function of θ, where the fuzzy solution space is denoted by $\tilde{C}$.

$$\text{Since } \mu_{\tilde{D}}(x) = \min\{\mu_{\tilde{C}}(x), \mu_0(x)\} \text{ we obtain}$$

$$\mu_{\tilde{D}}(\theta) = \min\{\mu_{\tilde{C}}(\theta), \mu_0(\theta)\} \tag{4.14}$$

The maximizing decision x_M can now be determined via

$$\mu_M(\theta) = \max_{\theta} \mu_{\tilde{D}}(\theta) \tag{4.15}$$

and this has to be equal, of course, to $\mu_M(x)$ as determined in (4.5).

The approach described above is very similar to that described in definition 2.5, the main difference being that here a predefined aspiration level is assumed for the goal.

Example 4.1 [Chanas 1983]

The problem considered here is

$$\widetilde{\max}\, z = 3x_1 + 4x_2 + 4x_3$$

$$6x_1 + 3x_2 + 4x_3 \lesssim 1200$$

$$5x_1 + 4x_2 + 5x_3 \lesssim 1550$$

$$x_1, x_2, x_3 \geq 0$$

Let $b_0 = 1700$, $p_0 = 150$, $p_1 = 100$, $p_2 = 200$.

We study the following parametric programming problem:

$$\begin{aligned} \text{maximize } z &= 3x_1 + 4x_2 + 4x_3 \\ \text{such that} \quad & 6x_1 + 3x_2 + 4x_3 \leq 1200 + 100\theta \\ & 5x_1 + 4x_2 + 5x_3 \leq 1550 + 200\theta \\ & x_1, x_2, x_3 \geq 0 \end{aligned}$$

and obtain the following results:

$$x_\theta = \begin{cases} \left(0, \frac{775}{2} + 50 \cdot \theta\right) & \text{for } 0 \leq \theta \leq \frac{3}{8} \\ \left(0, \frac{1575}{4} + \frac{100}{3}\theta, 0\right) & \text{for } \frac{3}{8} \leq \theta \leq 1 \end{cases}$$

$$z(x_\theta) = \begin{cases} 1550 + 200\theta & \text{for } 0 \leq \theta \leq \frac{3}{8} \\ 1575 + \frac{400}{3}\theta & \text{for } \frac{3}{8} \leq \theta \leq 1 \end{cases}$$

$$\mu_0(x_\theta) = \begin{cases} \frac{4}{3}\theta & \text{for } 0 \leq \theta \leq \frac{3}{8} \\ \frac{1}{6} + \frac{8}{9}\theta & \text{for } \frac{3}{8} \leq \theta \leq \frac{15}{16} \\ 1 & \text{for } \theta \geq \frac{15}{16} \end{cases}$$

Figure 4-1 represents the graph of functions $\mu_{\tilde{C}}(x_\theta)$, $\mu_0(x_\theta)$, and $\mu_{\tilde{D}}(x_\theta)$. The maximal value of function $\mu_{\tilde{D}}$ equals $29/51 \approx .57$ and is attained for $\theta = 15/34$, which determines the maximizing solution

$$x_\theta = x_{15/34} \approx (0, 412.45, 0)$$

The reader should realize that parametric programming is used here to determine the fuzzy set "decision" and *not* to determine a parametric solution to model (4.3). This task will be discussed in the section on "Duality and Sensitivity Analysis."

It is obvious that the computational effort to determine the fuzzy set "decision" is larger than just to compute the (crisp) maximizing decision. This is not quite as serious in small problems as it might become in realistically large problems.

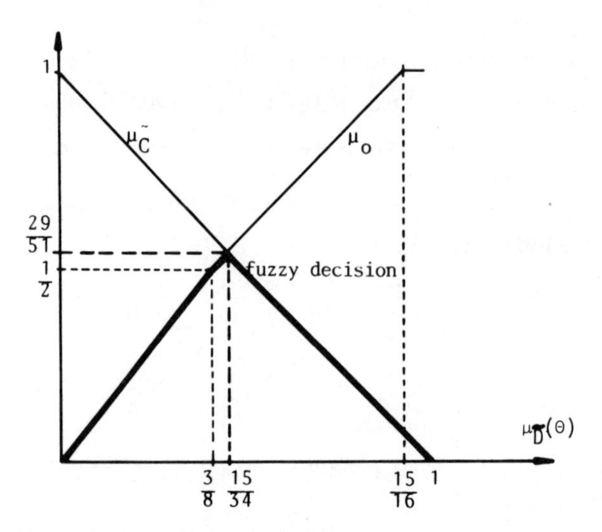

Figure 4.1: Fuzzy decision for example 4.1.

Nonsymmetrical Problems

The problem we are faced with is the determination of an extremum of a crisp function over a fuzzy domain, which we have already discussed in chapter 2. In definitions 2.3 and 2.4 we defined the notions of a maximizing set, which we will specify here and use as a vehicle to solve our LP problem. Two approaches are conceivable:

1. The determination of the fuzzy set "decision."
2. The determination of a crisp "maximizing decision" by aggregating the objective function after appropriate transformations with the constraints.

1: Determination of a Fuzzy Set "Decision." Orlovski [1977] and Tanaka et al. [1974] suggest computing for all α-level sets of the solution space the corresponding optimal values $r = f(x)$ of the objective function and considering as the fuzzy set "decision" the optimal values of the objective functions, r, with the degree of membership, $\mu_f(r)$, equal to the corresponding α-level of the solution space $\mu_{\tilde{C}}(x)$ with $x = f^{-1}(r)$.

For the case of fuzzy linear programming with linear membership functions and the min-operator, the $f(x) = r$'s and $\mu_f(r)$ can be obtained by parametric programming [Chanas 1983; Werners 1984]. For each α an LP of the following kind would have to be solved:

$$\begin{aligned} &\text{maximize} && f(x) \\ &\text{such that} && \alpha \leq \mu_i(x) \qquad i = 1,\ldots,m \\ & && x \in X \end{aligned} \tag{4.16}$$

The optimal solution (x^0,α^0) of each crisp LP determines $r_0 = f(x^0)$, $\mu_f(r^0) = \alpha^0$. The reader should realize, however, that the results yield fuzzy sets and that the decision maker would have to decide which pair $\{r_0,\mu_f(r_0)\}$ he considers optimal if he wants to arrive at a crisp optimal solution.

Example 4.2 [Werners 1984]

Consider the LP model

$$\begin{aligned} &\text{maximize} && r = 2x_1 + x_2 \\ &\text{such that} && x_1 \lessapprox 3 \\ & && x_1 + x_2 \lessapprox 4 \\ & && .5x_1 + x_2 \lessapprox 3 \\ & && x_1,x_2 \geq 0 \end{aligned}$$

The "tolerance intervals" of the constraints are $p_1 = 6$, $p_2 = 4$, $p_3 = 2$.

The parametric linear program for determining the relationships between $f(x) = r$ and degree of membership is then

$$\begin{aligned} &\text{maximize} && r = 2x_1 + x_2 \\ &\text{such that} && x_1 \leq 9 - 6\alpha \\ & && x_1 + x_2 \leq 8 - 4\alpha \\ & && .5x_1 + x_2 \leq 5 - 2\alpha \\ & && x_1,x_2 \geq 0 \end{aligned}$$

Figure 4-2 shows the feasible regions R_0 and R_1 for $\mu_{\tilde{R}}(x) = 0$ and $\mu_{\tilde{R}}(x) = 1$. Figure 4-3 shows the resulting membership function $\mu_f(r)$. Obviously the decision maker has to decide which combination $(r,\mu_f(r))$ he considers best.

In this respect, decision aids can either be derived from external sources or may depend on the problem itself. In the following we shall consider an approach that suggests a crisp solution which depends on the solution space.

Determination of a Crisp Maximizing Solution. We can now refer directly to definitions 2.4 and 2.5, and adapt them to the case of fuzzy linear program-

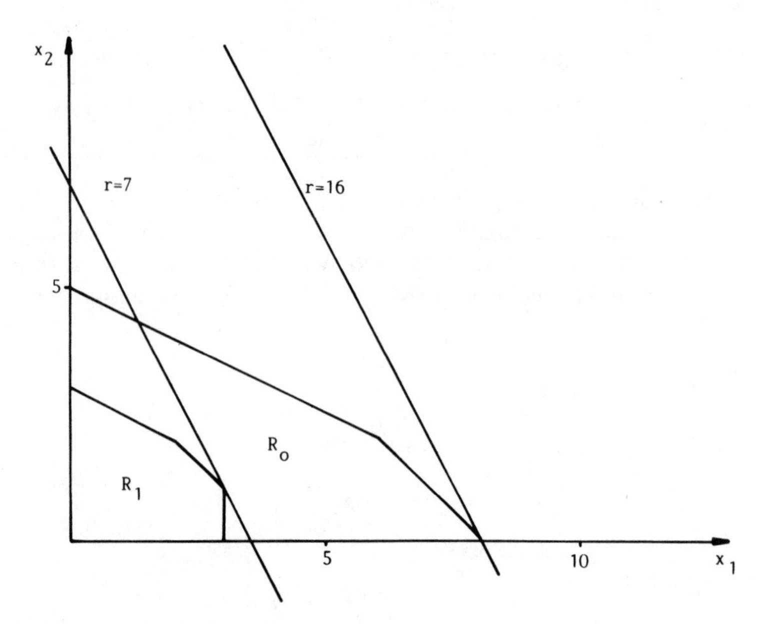

Figure 4-2: Feasible Regions.

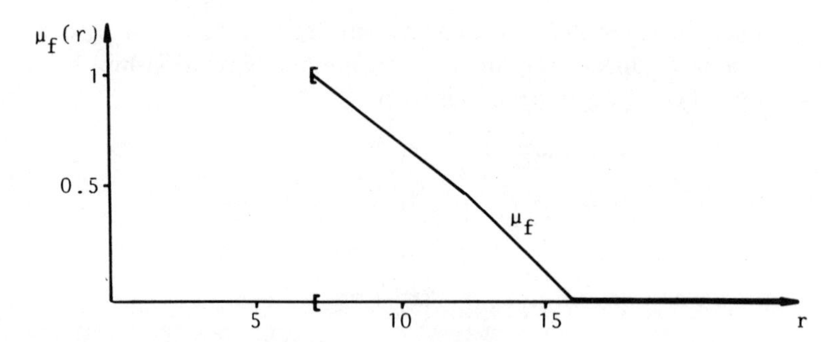

Figure 4-3: Membership function of "Decision".

ming. Werners [1984] argues that it does not seem reasonable for the decision maker to calibrate his judgment by looking at the smallest value of f over the feasible region. A better benchmark would be the smallest value for f that he can obtain at a degree of membership of 1 of the feasable region. This leads to the following definition.

Definition 4.1

Let $f: X \to \mathbb{R}^1$ (f be a mapping from X to $\mathbb{R}^1$), $\tilde{R}$ a fuzzy feasible region, $S(\tilde{R})$ the support of $\tilde{R}$, and R_1 the α-level-cut of $\tilde{R}$ for $\alpha = 1$. Then the *membership function of the goal given solution space* $\tilde{R}$ is defined as:

$$\mu_{\tilde{G}}(x) := \begin{cases} 0 & \text{if } f(x) \leq \sup_{R_1} f \\ \dfrac{f(x) - \sup_{R_1} f}{\sup_{S(\tilde{R})} f - \sup_{R_1} f} & \text{if } \sup_{R_1} f < f(x) < \sup_{S(\tilde{R})} f \\ 1 & \text{if } \sup_{S(\tilde{R})} f \leq f(x) \end{cases}$$

The corresponding membership function in functional space is then

$$\mu_{\tilde{G}}(r) := \begin{cases} \sup_{x \in f^{-1}(r)} \mu_{\tilde{G}}(x) & \text{if } r \in \mathbb{R} \wedge f^{-1}(r) \neq \emptyset \\ 0 & \text{else} \end{cases}$$

Example 4.3 [Werners 1984]

Consider the model of example 4.2. For this model, R_1 is the region defined by

$$\begin{aligned} x_1 \quad\quad &\leq 3 \\ x_1 + x_2 &\leq 4 \\ .5x_1 + x_2 &\leq 3 \\ x &\geq 0 \end{aligned}$$

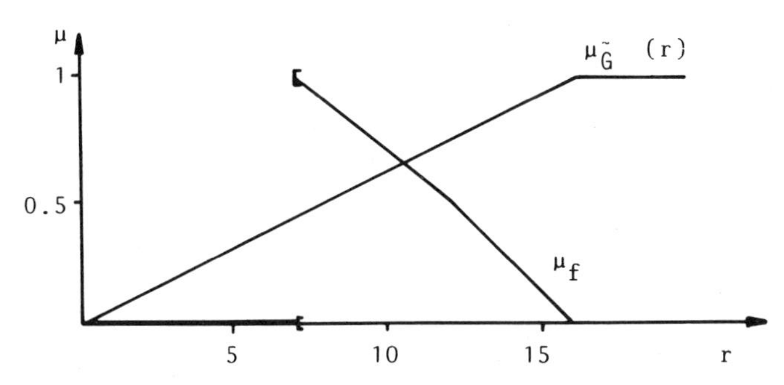

Figure 4-4: Fuzzy Decision.

The supremum of f over this region is

$$\sup_{R_1} (2x_1 + x_2) = 7$$

Figure 4-4 shows the membership functions $\mu_f(r)$ ad $\mu_{\tilde{G}}(r)$.

Using the max-min approach the resulting solution is $x_1^0 = 5.84$, $x_2^0 = .05$, $r_0 = 11.73$ and the attained degree of membership is $\mu_{\tilde{G}}(x_0) = .53$.

Let us now return to model (4.3) and modify it by considering the objective function to be crisp and by adding a set of crisp constraints $Dx \leq b'$:

$$\begin{array}{ll} \text{maximize} & f(x) = c^T x \\ \text{such that} & \left.\begin{array}{r} Ax \lessapprox b \\ Dx \leq b' \\ x \geq 0 \end{array}\right\} \quad \tilde{R} \end{array} \tag{4.17}$$

Let the membership functions of the fuzzy sets representing the fuzzy constraints be defined in analogy to (4.7) as

$$\mu_i(x) = \begin{cases} 1 & \text{if } (Ax)_i \leq b_i \\ \dfrac{b_i + p_i - (Ax)_i}{p_i} & \text{if } b_i < (Ax)_i \leq b_i + p_i \\ 0 & \text{if } (Ax)_i > b_i + p_i \end{cases} \tag{4.18}$$

The membership function of the objective function can be determined by solving the following two LP's:

$$\begin{array}{ll} \text{maximize} & f(x) = c^T x \\ \text{such that} & Ax \leq b \\ & Dx \leq b' \\ & x \geq 0 \end{array} \tag{4.19}$$

yielding $\sup_{R_1} f = (c^T x)_{\text{opt}} = f_1$, and

$$\begin{array}{ll} \text{maximize} & f(x) = c^T x \\ \text{such that} & Ax \leq b + p \\ & Dx \leq b' \\ & x \geq 0 \end{array} \tag{4.20}$$

yielding $\sup_{S(\tilde{R})} f = (c^T x)_{\text{opt}} = f_0$.

The membership function of the objective function is therefore

$$\mu_{\tilde{G}}(x) = \begin{cases} 1 & \text{if } f_0 \le c^T x \\ \dfrac{c^T x - f_1}{f_0 - f_1} & \text{if } f_1 < c^T x < f_0 \\ 0 & \text{if } c^T x \le f_1 \end{cases} \tag{4.21}$$

Now we have again achieved symmetry between constraints and the objective function and we can employ the approach used to derive model (4.9) as an equivalent formulation of (4.3): the equivalent model to (4.9) is

$$\begin{aligned} &\text{maximize} \quad \lambda \\ &\text{such that} \quad \lambda(f_0 - f_1) - c^T x \le -f_1 \\ &\qquad \lambda p + Ax \le b + p \\ &\qquad Dx \le b' \\ &\qquad \lambda \le 1 \\ &\qquad \lambda, x \ge 0 \end{aligned} \tag{4.22}$$

Example 4.4

We shall again consider the model in example 4.2. In example 4.3 we computed $f_1 = 7$. By solving (4.20) we obtain $f_0 = 16$. Therefore (4.22) is

$$\begin{aligned} &\text{maximize} \quad \lambda \\ &\text{such that} \quad 9\lambda - 2x_1 - x_2 \le -7 \\ &\qquad 6\lambda + x_1 \le 9 \\ &\qquad 4\lambda + x_1 + x_2 \le 8 \\ &\qquad 2\lambda + .5x_1 + x_2 \le 5 \\ &\qquad \lambda \le 1 \\ &\qquad \lambda, x_1, x_2 \ge 0 \end{aligned}$$

The solution is $(x_1, x_2) = (5.84, .05)$ with $\lambda^0 = .53$ and 11.73 value of the objective function.

Duality and Sensitivity Analysis

By contrast to classical (crisp) linear programming, the concept of duality for fuzzy linear programming is not uniquely defined. Verdegay [1984], for instance, considers the fuzzy mathematical programming problem as being adequately modelled by a (crisp) parametric programming model. The dual problem to this parametric (linear) programming model is then considered as "the dual" to the fuzzy mathematical programming problem. We shall consider two other approaches, one that bases on a weakened saddle-point definition [Rödder, Zimmermann 1980] and one that dualizes model (4.11) [Hamacher, Leberling, Zimmermann 1978]. To facilitate the interpretation of "fuzzy duality," we shall first consider the crisp linear programming model and its dual again.

Let us assume that model (4.2) describes the following situation [see Zangwill 1969, pp. 45ff.]: an industry (I) competes with the rest of the relevant market (M). (I) plans its production $(x_1,\ldots,x_n)^T = x$ on the basis of the following data:

A: technology matrix
b: I's available capacities
c: vector of prices that can be enforced in the market.

(I) can also purchase or sell resources (capacities) in the market at the prices $(u_1,\ldots,u_m) = u \geq 0$. Total profits (sales) that accrue to sector (I) will therefore be

$$L(x,u) = \underbrace{c^T x}_{\text{primary profit}} + \underbrace{u^T(b - Ax)}_{\text{secondary profit}} \tag{4.23}$$

per period, representing "primary profit" plus "secondary profit." Note that (4.23) is the Lagrangian function for (4.2).

It can be assumed that for the (primal) decision $x \geq 0$ (M) will set its prices at $u = u^0$ with

$$L(x,u^0) = \min_{u \geq 0} L(x,u) \tag{4.24}$$

(M) has to assume that (I) decides for a production vector $x = x^0$ for any given $u \geq 0$ such that

$$L(x^0,u) = \max_{x \geq 0} L(x,u) \tag{4.25}$$

Under appropriate regularity conditions, there exists a compromise solution $(x^0,u^0) \geq 0$ such that for $x = x^0$ in (4.24) $u = u^0$, and for $u = u^0$ in (4.25) $x = x^0$ is optimal, that is, that there exists an $(x^0,u^0) \geq 0$ such that

$$\begin{aligned} \forall (x,u) \geq 0\text{: } c^T x + u^{0^T}(b - Ax) &\leq c^T x^0 + u^{0^T}(b - Ax^0) \\ &\leq c^T x^0 + u^T(b - Ax^0) \end{aligned} \tag{4.26}$$

$(x^0,u^0) \geq 0$ is the saddlepoint of (4.23) in $(x,u) \geq 0$.

As it is well known, x^0 is the optimal solution of (4.2) and u^0 is the optimal solution of

$$\begin{aligned} \text{minimize} \quad & u^T b \\ \text{such that} \quad & u^T A \geq c^T \\ & u \geq 0 \end{aligned} \tag{4.27}$$

Because of the well-known properties just mentioned, (4.2) and (4.27) are called dual to each other.

Interpretation. If (I) chooses a production program that satisfies $Ax \leq b$ but does not maximize $c^T x$ in (4.2) (I) looses "primary profit." If (I) chooses $x \geq 0$, which violates $Ax \leq b$ (purchase of resources), it gives (M) a chance to increase prices $u \geq 0$ and so decrease (I)'s overall profit. Analogously for (M): if (M) chooses prices $u \geq 0$ satisfying $u^T A \geq c^T$ but not optimizing $u^T b$ in (4.27), it overrates the value of (I)'s excess resources. If (M) chooses prices $u \geq 0$ not satisfying $u^T A \leq c$ (i.e., for at least one product, costs are below price), (I) gets a chance to raise production (and profit) up to infinity.

We shall now "fuzzify" the objective function of (4.2) as follows.

Definition 4.2 [Rödder, Zimmermann 1977, p. 10]

Let $\{x,\mu(x) \mid x \in X\}$ be a fuzzy set on X and $\{(u,\sigma_x(u)) \mid u \in U\}$ be a family of fuzzy sets on U, conditioned by $x \in X$ which acts as a parameter for this family of sets.

Then the *mixture* of these fuzzy sets is defined by its membership function

$$\sigma_u(u) = \max_{x \geq 0} \min \{\mu(x), \sigma_x(u)\} \qquad u \in U$$

Example 4.5

Let us assume that a company sells different brands and types of cars and tries to optimize its marketing efforts. By extensive market research studies one knows which type of potential buyer (house wives, bachelors, civil servants, teenagers, etc.) really pretends to be buying rather than just gathering information. Let v: $X \rightarrow [0,1]$ express the "buy coefficient" for a member of class $x \in X$ of clients. Cars can be described by certain characteristics, so $y \in Y$ represents a specific brand and type of car. For those clients that definitely are willing to buy $\mu(\cdot \mid X)$: $Y \rightarrow [0,1]$ is the coefficient of affinity to a certain class of cars.

In other words: Once a housewife decides to buy, $\mu(y|x)$ is the coefficient that she buys a car of type y.

Now we can mix the two membership functions and calculate

$$\max_{x \in X} \min(v(x), \mu(y|x)) = (y)$$

where (y) is the market's coefficient of "sellability."

In contrast to the crisply defined situation we now assume that

- (I) not only considers the case in which (M) (strictly) minimizes but, for each $x \geq 0$, (I) has a membership function (evaluation, or utility function) on all possible decisions $u \geq 0$ of (M), which describes its own degree of satisfaction for (M)'s decisions u (and given x).
- (I) does not necessarily maximize but it has a membership function (evaluation or utility function) on $x \geq 0$, which describes its degree of satisfaction concerning primary profit (independent) of the adversary's action.

Thus, the strict imperative of maximizing the objective function as well as the imperative of strictly satisfying restrictions is relaxed as follows: (I) does not assume that (M) behaves in a strictly optimal way (i.e., minimizes), but rather suboptimizes probably because of other reasons. (In analogy to the concept of "bounded rationality" this could be called a "bounded optimality.") Therefore (I) has to consider all possible $u \geq 0$ (dependent on $x \geq 0$) and evaluates them by a membership function.

Similarly (I) is not a strict optimizer (maximizer) but rather considers all possible $x \geq 0$ and evaluates them with respect to their primary profits $c^T x$ by a membership function. The reason for this could be that (I) is a satisficer rather than a maximizer and has certain aspiration levels that can depend on a large number of different factors.

The following terms will be used:

$\mu^I(x)$ is the membership function of (I) on $\{x \mid x \geq 0\}$.
$\sigma_x^I(u)$ is the membership function of (I) on $\{u \mid u \geq 0\}$ for any given $x \geq 0$.
$\mu^M(u)$ is the membership function of (M) on $\{u \mid u \geq 0\}$.
$\sigma_u^M(x)$ is the membership function of (M) on $\{x \mid x \geq 0\}$ for any given $u \geq 0$.

The mixture of $\mu^I(x)$ and $\sigma_x^I(u)$,

$$\max_{x \geq 0} (\min\{\mu^I(x), \sigma_x^I(u)\}) \tag{4.28}$$

is the membership function of the fuzzy set of elements $x(u)$ for $u \geq 0$ which maximize $\mu^I(x)$ *and* $\sigma_x^I(u)$. For (M) the analogous fuzzy set is

$$\max_{u \geq 0} (\min(\mu^M(u), \sigma_u^M(x)) \tag{4.29}$$

A possible choice of nonnormalized membership functions could be

$$\mu^I(x) = \begin{cases} 1 & \text{if } c^T x^0 \leq c^T x \\ 1 - (c^T x^0 - c^T x) & \text{otherwise} \end{cases}$$

$$\sigma_x^I = \begin{cases} 1 & \text{if } u^T(b - Ax) \leq 0 \\ u^T(b - Ax) & \text{otherwise} \end{cases}$$

$$\mu^M(u) = \begin{cases} 1 & \text{if } u^T b \leq u^{0^T} b \\ 1 - (u^T b - u^{0^T} b) & \text{otherwise} \end{cases}$$

$$\sigma_u^M = \begin{cases} 0 & \text{if } (c^T - u^T A)x \geq 0 \\ -(c^T - u^T A)x & \text{otherwise} \end{cases}$$

where x^0 and u^0, respectively, denote the optimal solutions to models (4.2) and (4.27).

A possible interpretation for $\mu^I(x)$ and $\sigma_x^I(x)$ (the other two membership functions can be explained in analogy to the first two) is: $\mu^I(x)$ is the a priori evaluation of (I)'s own decisions x. For a solution the profit of which reaches the aspiration level $c^T x^0$, the membership function is 1, falling linearly in $c^T x$ with decreasing values of the objective function. $\sigma_x^I(u)$ is the evaluation function of the decisions u of his adversary (M) given a decision x. (I) is not satisfied (its utility is zero or smaller than zero) if $u^T(b - Ax) \geq 0$, and it increases linearly in $u^T(b - Ax)$.

Assuming the above-mentioned membership functions, an equivalent crisp formulation of model (4.28) is

$$\begin{aligned} &\text{maximize} && \lambda^1 \\ &\text{such that} && \lambda^1 \leq 1 - (c^T x^0 - c^T x) \qquad \text{for any given } u \\ & && \lambda^1 \leq u^T(b - Ax) \\ & && x \geq 0 \\ & && \lambda^1 \geq 0 \end{aligned} \tag{4.30}$$

and analogously (4.29) becomes the LP problem

$$\begin{aligned} &\text{minimize} && \lambda^2 \\ &\text{such that} && \lambda^2 \geq u^T b - u^{0^T} b - 1 \qquad \text{for any given } x \\ & && \lambda^2 \geq (c^T - u^T A)x \\ & && u \geq 0 \\ & && \lambda^2 \leq 0 \end{aligned} \tag{4.31}$$

Because (4.30) and (4.31) are interpretations of the fuzzy max-min and min-max problems, respectively, we call these problems a fuzzy dual pair.

Let us now consider the relationships between (4.30) and (4.31): It is obvious that (4.30) is unbounded if there exists an $x \geq 0$ with the following properties: $c^T x > 0, -u^T Ax > 0$. This is also a condition for $u \geq 0$! In this case (I) could increase the value of the objective function, λ^1, arbitrarily, which would certainly not be acceptable to (M). We, therefore, define (reasonable" decisions for both decision makers as follows.

Definition 4.3

Let x and u be solutions to (4.30) and (4.31), respectively. *reasonable decisions* are then defined as the following sets:

$$X^0 = \{x \geq 0 \mid \nexists u \geq 0\colon\ u^T b < 0, -u^T Ax < 0\}$$
$$U^0 = \{u \geq 0 \mid \nexists x \geq 0\colon\ c^T x > 0, -u^T Ax > 0\}$$

We shall analyze U^0 and X^0 more thoroughly and reduce them stepwise without losing any economically relevant solution:

U^0 can also be written as

$$\begin{aligned} U^0 &= \{u \geq 0 \mid \forall x \geq 0\colon\ c^T x \leq 0 \vee u^T Ax \geq 0\} \\ &= \{u \geq 0 \mid \forall x \geq 0\colon\ c^T x > 0 \Rightarrow u^T Ax \geq 0\} \end{aligned} \tag{4.32}$$

X^0 can be written as

$$\begin{aligned} X^0 &= \{x \geq 0 \mid \forall u \geq 0\colon\ u^T b \geq 0 \vee u^T Ax \leq 0\} \\ &= \{x \geq 0 \mid \forall u \geq 0\colon\ u^T b < 0 \Rightarrow u^T Ax \geq 0\} \end{aligned} \tag{4.33}$$

U^0 is the set of all price decisions of (M), for which the following is true: if (I) achieves positive profits ($c^T x > 0$) then the costs $u^T Ax$ are nonnegative. Prices u with negative $u^T Ax$ need not be considered any more.

We now make a further restriction concerning x and u, which is economically plausible: If

$$\begin{aligned} U^1 &= \{u \geq 0 \mid \forall x \geq 0\colon\ c^T x \geq 0 \Rightarrow u^T Ax \geq 0\} \\ X^1 &= \{x \geq 0 \mid \forall u \geq 0\colon\ u^T b \leq 0 \Rightarrow u^T Ax \leq 0\} \end{aligned} \tag{4.34}$$

the following relationships hold:

$$U^1 \subset U^0 \qquad \text{and} \qquad X^1 \subset X^0$$

If we restrict the possible decisions to U^1 and X^1, we do not lose economically relevant decisions. The reader can easily verify this statement. Now we can characterize U^1 and X^1 by using directly the Farkas-Lemma [Farkas 1902]

$$U^1 = \{u \geq 0 \mid \exists \alpha \in \mathbb{R}, \alpha \geq 0\colon \ \alpha \cdot c^T \leq u^T A\} \tag{4.35}$$

In analogy we can write:

$$X^1 = \{x \geq 0 \mid \exists \beta \in \mathbb{R}, \beta \geq 0\colon \ \beta b \geq Ax\} \tag{4.36}$$

Both competitors, however, are interested in considering only $x \geq 0$, $u \geq 0$ which are elements of U^1 and X^1, respectively. This leads to problems (4.37) and (4.38):

$$\begin{aligned} \text{maximize} \quad & \lambda^1 \\ \text{such that} \quad & \lambda^1 \leq 1 - (c^T x^0) - c^T x \\ & \lambda^1 \leq u^T(b - Ax) \\ & \alpha c^T \leq u^T A \qquad u \geq 0 \text{ fixed} \\ & \beta b \geq Ax \\ & x \geq 0, \alpha \geq 0, \beta \geq 0 \end{aligned} \tag{4.37}$$

and

$$\begin{aligned} \text{minimize} \quad & \lambda^2 \\ \text{such that} \quad & \lambda^2 \geq -u^{0^T} b + u^T b - 1 \\ & \lambda^2 \geq (c^T - u^T A)x \\ & \beta b \geq Ax \qquad x \geq 0 \text{ fixed} \\ & \alpha c^T \leq u^T A \\ & x \geq 0, \alpha \geq 0, \beta \geq 0 \end{aligned} \tag{4.38}$$

Obviously $\{x \mid Ax \geq b, x \geq 0\}$ and $\{u \mid u^T A \geq c^T, u \geq 0\}$ are subsets of the set of all feasible x vectors in (4.37) and all feasible u vectors in (4.38), respectively. This means that the "fuzzy" decision maker considers decisions that do not satisfy restrictions of the "classical" primal and dual LP problems.

Since we have

$$\forall (x,u) \in X^1 \times U^1 \ \exists \alpha, \beta \in \mathbb{R}^+\colon \ \alpha c^T x \leq u^T \beta b \tag{4.39}$$

the optimal solutions in (4.37) and (4.38) satisfy the following relationships:

$$\alpha \cdot c^T_{\text{opt}}(u) \leq u^T \beta(u) b \qquad \forall\, u \in U^1 \tag{4.40}$$

and

$$\alpha(x) c^T x \leq u^T_{\text{opt}}(x) \beta b \qquad \forall\, x \in X^1 \tag{4.41}$$

For the economically sensible case $\alpha \cdot \beta \neq 0$ we can derive

$$\frac{\alpha}{\beta(u)} \cdot c^T x_{\text{opt}}(u) \leq u^T b \tag{4.42}$$

and

$$c^T x \leq \frac{\beta}{\alpha(x)} u^T_{\text{opt}}(x) b \tag{4.43}$$

The reader should observe that (4.42) and (4.43) are generalizations of the classical relationship between the values of the primal and dual objectives.

Example 4.6

Let us consider a model of type (4.2) with

$$c = \begin{pmatrix} 1 \\ 1 \end{pmatrix} \qquad A = \begin{pmatrix} 1 & 2 \\ 2 & 1 \end{pmatrix} \qquad b = \begin{pmatrix} 2 \\ 2 \end{pmatrix}$$

We find:

$$x^{0^T} = \left(\frac{2}{3}, \frac{2}{3}\right) \qquad u^{0^T} = \left(\frac{1}{3}, \frac{1}{3}\right)$$

Model (4.37) has the following form:

$$\begin{aligned}
&\text{maximize} \quad \lambda^1 \\
&\text{such that} \quad \lambda^1 \leq 1 - \left(\frac{4}{3} - (x_1 - x_2)\right) \\
&\begin{pmatrix} \lambda^1 \\ \lambda^1 \end{pmatrix} \leq (u_1, u_2) \left[\begin{pmatrix} 2 \\ 2 \end{pmatrix} - \begin{pmatrix} 1 & 2 \\ 2 & 1 \end{pmatrix} \begin{pmatrix} x_1 \\ x_2 \end{pmatrix} \right] \qquad u_1, u_2 \text{ fixed} \\
&\alpha(1,1) \leq (u_1, u_2) \begin{pmatrix} 1 & 2 \\ 2 & 1 \end{pmatrix} \\
&\beta \begin{pmatrix} 2 \\ 2 \end{pmatrix} \geq \begin{pmatrix} 1 & 2 \\ 2 & 1 \end{pmatrix} \begin{pmatrix} x_1 \\ x_2 \end{pmatrix} \\
&x_1, x_2, \alpha, \beta \geq 0
\end{aligned}$$

Here U^1 is the nonnegative orthant, so is X^1. Thus the above mentioned problem reduces to

$$\begin{aligned}
&\text{maximize} \quad \lambda^1 \\
&\text{such that} \quad \lambda^1 \leq -\frac{1}{3} + x_1 + x_2 \\
&\qquad \lambda^1 \leq 2u_1 + 2u_2 + (-u_1 - 2u_2)x_1 + (-2u_1 - u_2)x_2 \\
&\qquad\qquad (u_1,u_2) \geq 0 \text{ fixed} \\
&\qquad x_1,x_2 \geq 0
\end{aligned}$$

This can be considered as a parametric problem in $(u_1,u_2) \geq 0$. For example, for $(u_1,u_2) = (\frac{1}{2},\frac{1}{2})$,

$$\lambda^1 = \frac{9}{15}, \quad x_1 = \frac{7}{15}, \quad x_2 = \frac{7}{15}$$

In analogy to above, for $x_1 = x_2 = \frac{2}{3}$,

$$\begin{aligned}
&\text{minimize} \quad \lambda^2 \\
&\text{such that} \quad \lambda^2 \geq -\frac{7}{3} + 2u_1 + 2u_2 \\
&\qquad \lambda^2 \geq \frac{4}{3} - 2u_1 - 2u_2 \\
&\qquad u_1,u_2 \geq 0
\end{aligned}$$

with optimal solution:

$$\lambda_2 = -\frac{1}{2}, \qquad u_1 = \frac{11}{48}, \qquad u_2 = \frac{11}{48}$$

Thus the result is

$$\lambda_1 = \frac{9}{15} \text{ is the degree of satisfaction of } (I) \text{ and}$$

$$\lambda_2 = -\frac{1}{2} \text{ is the degree of satisfaction of } (M)$$

Duality in the sense defined above and applied to the economic situation we used to interprete the relationships is a generalization of crisp duality theory. The following interpretation is possible.

Classical duality theory when applied to economic analysis suggests that market prices converge toward a fixed point, that is, the optimal solution of the Lagrangian function of the respective mathematical programming formulations. In this type of analysis rather unrealistic assumptions have to be made: for instance that of complete transparency of the market, that the competitors can always assume rational and "optimal" behavior of their counterparts, etc.

Fuzzy modelling assumes that the decision makers do not consider only the case in which their competitors minimize or maximize their "utility functions," but, rather, that they take into consideration all possible decisions of the competitors and have families of preference functions for their profits resulting from the competitor's decisions and their own. This could be considered as a special kind of "bounded rationality" of the decision makers when deciding about prices and quantities in competitive situations.

It has already been mentioned that duality in fuzzy mathematical programming can be defined in different ways. In the last section we started from the notion of a saddle point and derived dual pairs of models which generalized the classical duality theory in linear programming.

Another possible approach is to analyze the crisp duals of the (crisp) equivalent models to model (4.3). It is obvious that these crisp equivalents will differ from each other depending on the assumptions being made about connectives and kinds of membership functions when going from (4.3) to an equivalent crisp model. We shall illustrate this approach for the equivalent crisp model (4.11).

In order to keep the analyses as general as possible we shall first extend (4.11) by adding a set of crisp constraints. Hence we shall consider the primal problem [Hamacher, Leberling, Zimmermann 1978] to be

$$\begin{aligned} \text{maximize} \quad & \lambda \\ \text{such that} \quad & \lambda p + t + s_{\mathrm{I}} = p && \text{(I)} \\ & Ax - t + s_{\mathrm{II}} = b && \text{(II)} \\ & t + s_{\mathrm{III}} = p && \text{(III)} \\ & Dx + s_{\mathrm{IV}} = b' && \text{(IV)} \\ & \lambda \in \mathbb{R},\ x,t,s \geq 0 && \end{aligned} \tag{4.44}$$

s_{I} through s_{IV} are the vectors of slack variables corresponding to the respective blocks of restrictions. Let $y_{\mathrm{I}}, y_{\mathrm{II}}, y_{\mathrm{III}}, y_{\mathrm{IV}}$ denote the vectors of variables of the dual corresponding to (4.44). Then the dual is

$$\min y_{\mathrm{I}}^T p + y_{\mathrm{II}}^T b + y_{\mathrm{III}}^T p + y_{\mathrm{IV}}^T b'$$

$$
\begin{aligned}
&y_{\mathrm{I}}^T p && \geq 1 \\
&\qquad y_{\mathrm{II}}^T A \qquad + y_{\mathrm{IV}}^T D && \geq 0 \\
&y_{\mathrm{I}}^T E - y_{\mathrm{II}}^T E + y_{\mathrm{III}}^T E && \geq 0 \\
&\qquad\qquad y_{\mathrm{I}}, y_{\mathrm{II}}, y_{\mathrm{III}}, y_{\mathrm{IV}} && \geq 0
\end{aligned}
\tag{4.45}
$$

Here E is the $(m_1 + 1, m_1 + 1)$-identity matrix.

An equivalent LP to (4.45) is the following:

$$
\begin{aligned}
\min 1 \quad &+ y_{\mathrm{II}}^T b + y_{\mathrm{III}}^T p + y_{\mathrm{IV}}^T b' \\
&y_{\mathrm{I}}^T p && = 1 \\
&\qquad y_{\mathrm{II}}^T A \qquad + y_{\mathrm{IV}}^T D && \geq 0 \\
&y_{\mathrm{I}}^T E - y_{\mathrm{II}}^T E + y_{\mathrm{III}}^T E && \geq 0 \\
&\qquad\qquad y_{\mathrm{I}}, y_{\mathrm{II}}, y_{\mathrm{III}}, y_{\mathrm{IV}} && \geq 0
\end{aligned}
\tag{4.46}
$$

We shall first give an interpretation of the vectors y_{II} and y_{IV}. Separate treatment of the different blocks is necessary, because in blocks II and IV the dual variables in the optimum are the well known shadow prices; in blocks I and III we have to recognize that the activity matrix contains the right-hand-side vector p.

Problem (4.44) is a LP of special structure. So $y_{\mathrm{II}}^0, y_{\mathrm{IV}}^0$, the optimal dual variables, are, as usual, shadow prices. For example, $(y_{\mathrm{II}}^0)_i$ is the relative increase of the degree of satisfaction due to a marginal variation of b_i (fixed basis). Of course this statement remains true for the special case $\lambda_{\max} = 1$. Considering the dual (4.46) we recognize that $\lambda_{\max} = 1$ implies $t = 0$; thus there is no binding restriction in III ($p > 0$!) which in term implies $y_{\mathrm{III}}^0 = 0$. The objective function of (4.46) therefore necessarily contains the term $y_{\mathrm{II}}^{0^T} b + y_{\mathrm{IV}}^{0^T} b' = 0$. It is therefore appropriate to consider the following two cases:

(α) $(y_{\mathrm{II}}^0, y_{\mathrm{IV}}^0) = 0$
(β) $(y_{\mathrm{II}}^0, y_{\mathrm{IV}}^0) \neq 0$

For (α) we have a highly degenerate dual basis. If a component of y_{II}^0 or y_{IV}^0 is a positive number, this number nevertheless does not mean the relative increase of $\lambda_{\max}$ since a marginal variation of the right-hand side causes an immediate exchange of basis (otherwise $\lambda_{\max}$ could become greater than 1, contrary to the assumptions).

Case (α) economically implies the following: No tolerances are needed. There are even unused capacities. Overcapacities could be sold (optimality of basis will be guaranteed), the degrees of satisfaction remaining 1 for the optimal decision. An increase of capacities b, b' only enlarges the set of decisions with degree of satisfaction equal to 1.

For case (β), where $(y^0_{II}, y^0_{IV}) \neq 0$:

(β1) If a component of y^0_{II} is positive, we have the following statement: The optimal decision x_{opt} causes neither slack nor violation of the respective restriction. An increase of the capacity does not make sense, because the degree of satisfaction equals 1 anyway.

(β2) A discussion of the case in which a component of y^0_{IV} is positive is "classical" and can be omitted here.

Let us now consider the sensitivity of problem (4.44). That is, we will analyze the changes of λ_{max} as a function of the variations of the right-hand side of (4.44).

For the sensitivity analysis in blocks I and III we consider the following three cases:

(α) $\lambda_{max} = 1$
(β) $0 < \lambda_{max} < 1$
(γ) $\lambda_{max} = 0$

If, as in case (α), $\lambda_{max} = 1$, the optimal solution $(1, x_{opt}, 0)$ is invariant as to variations Δp of p for $p' = p + \Delta p > 0$, since $(1, x_{opt}, 0)$ still satisfies restrictions I and III after a variation. Restrictions II and IV are obviously not involved.

For case (β), $0 < \lambda_{max} < 1$, we reformulate (4.44) as follows:

$$\text{maximize} \quad \lambda$$

$$\text{such that} \quad A^* \begin{pmatrix} \lambda \\ x \\ t \end{pmatrix} \leq b^*$$

$$\lambda \in \mathbb{R},\ x \in \mathbb{R}^m_0,\ t \in \mathbb{R}^{m+1}_0, \text{ with } R^r_0 = \{y \in R^r \mid y \geq 0\},$$

$$b^* \in \mathbb{R}^{3(m_1+1)+m_2},\ A^*_{3(m_1+1)+m_2, n+1+m+1} \tag{4.47}$$

and

$$b^*: = \begin{pmatrix} p \\ b \\ p \\ b' \end{pmatrix} \qquad A^*: = \begin{pmatrix} p_{m_1+1,1} & \theta_{m_1+1,n} & E_{m_1+1,m_1+1} \\ \theta_{m_1+1,1} & A_{m_1+1,n} & -E_{m_1+1,m_1+1} \\ \theta_{m_1+1,1} & \theta_{m_1+1,n} & E_{m_1+1,m_1+1} \\ \theta_{m_2,1} & D_{m_2,n} & \theta_{m_2,m_1+1} \end{pmatrix}$$

Here θ and E are null and identity matrixes of adequate dimensions.

$$e_j^*: = (\overbrace{0,\ldots,\underset{\underset{j}{\uparrow}}{1},\ldots,0}^{m_1+2}, \overbrace{\theta}^{m_1+1}, \overbrace{0,\ldots,\underset{\underset{2(m_1+1)+j}{\uparrow}}{1},\ldots,0}^{m_1+n},\overbrace{0}^{m_2})^T$$

$$b: = b^* + \Delta p \cdot e_j^* \qquad \Delta p \in \mathbb{R}$$

$$\bar{A}: = A^* + \begin{pmatrix} \Delta p \cdot e_j & \\ \theta_{2(m_1+1)+m_2+1,1} & \theta_{3(m_1+1)+m_2,n+m_1+1} \end{pmatrix}$$

$$= \begin{pmatrix} \bar{p} & \theta & E \\ \theta & A & -E \\ \theta & \theta & E \\ \theta & D & \theta \end{pmatrix}$$

$\bar{b}$ and $\bar{A}$ are the right-hand-side vector b^* and activity matrix A^*, respectively, disturbed by variation p:

$$e_j: = (0,\ldots,0,\underset{\underset{j}{\uparrow}}{1},0,\ldots,0)^T$$

Assume the optimal solution of (4.47) to be $\lambda_{\max}$ and let $\lambda_{\max}(\Delta p)$ be the optimal solution of the following LP problem.

$$\text{maximize} \quad \lambda$$

$$\text{such that} \quad \bar{A}\begin{pmatrix} \lambda \\ x \\ t \end{pmatrix} \le \bar{b} \qquad \lambda \in \mathbb{R}, x,t \ge 0 \tag{4.48}$$

We want to determine the functional relationship $\lambda_{\max}(\Delta p)$. Note that this problem is a parametric LP problem with simultaneous parametrization in the right-hand-side b^* and the activity matrix A^*.

The following statements hold only for a transition from A to $\bar{A}$ and from b to $\bar{b}$, which does not influence the set of basic variables.

Since $0 < \lambda_{\max} < 1$, λ is a basic variable and thus the first column of A^*: $(p_0,\ldots,p_{m_1},\theta,\theta,\theta)^T$ is the column of basis B. Changing from B to $\bar{B}$ we obtain

$$\bar{B} = B + \Delta p \bar{E}_j \tag{4.49}$$

with

$$\bar{E}_j := \begin{bmatrix} 0 & \\ \vdots & \theta_{3(m_1+1)+m_2,\, 3(m_1+1)+m_2-1} \\ 0 & \\ 1 & \\ 0 & \\ \vdots & \\ 0 & \end{bmatrix} \leftarrow j$$

The optimal λ_{max} is, as usual,

$$\lambda_{max} = c_B^T B^{-1} b \qquad B^{-1} = \beta_{ij}$$

$$i,j = 1,\ldots,3(m_1 + 1) + m_2$$

c_B here is a unity vector, the position of the 1 is determined by B. In analogy to the above we obtain for the optimal $\lambda_{max}(\Delta p)$:

$$\lambda_{max}(\Delta p) = c_B^T \bar{B}^{-1} \bar{b} \tag{4.50}$$

We have $c_B = c_{\bar{B}}$ because no exchange of basis columns was performed. We now determine $\lambda_{max}(\Delta p)$ as a function of Δp: the relationship between $\bar{B}^{-1}$ and B^{-1} is [Gass 1964]

$$B^{-1} = (B + \Delta p \bar{E}_j)^{-1} = (E + B^{-1}\, \Delta p \bar{E}_j)^{-1} B^{-1} \tag{4.51}$$

Furthermore,

$$(E + B^{-1}\, \Delta p \bar{E})^{-1} = M + E$$

here M is the matrix

$$M = \begin{bmatrix} \dfrac{1}{\beta_{ij}\Delta p + 1} - 1 & \\ -\dfrac{\beta_{2j}\Delta p}{\beta_{ij}\Delta p + 1} & \theta_{3(m_1+1)+m_2,\, 3(m_1+1)+m_2-1} \\ \vdots & \\ -\dfrac{\beta_{3(m_1+1)+m_2 j} \cdot \Delta p}{\beta_{ij}\Delta p + 1} & \end{bmatrix}$$

Because of $\bar{B}^{-1} = (M + E)B^{-1}$ we obtain the following expression for $\lambda_{max}(\Delta p)$:

$$\begin{aligned} \lambda_{max}(\Delta p) &= c_B^T \bar{B}^{-1} \bar{b} \\ &= c_B^T \bar{B}^{-1} \bar{b} \end{aligned}$$

$$
\begin{aligned}
&= c_B^T(M + E)B^{-1}(b + \Delta p e_j^*) \\
&= c_B^T B^{-1} b + c_B^T [M B^{-1} b + (M + E) + B^{-1} \Delta p e_j^*] \\
&= \lambda_{\max} + c_B^T [M B^{-1} b + (M + E) B^{-1} \Delta p e_j^* \qquad (4.52)
\end{aligned}
$$

Obviously,

$$
\Delta\lambda(\Delta p){:} \quad = c_B^T [M B^{-1} b + (M + E) B^{-1} \Delta p e_j^*] \qquad (4.53)
$$

is the change of the optimal value of the objective function when the jth component of p changes from p_j to $(p_j + \Delta p)$.

Re. (γ), $\lambda_{\max} = 0$: there are two cases:

1. λ is basic variable.
2. λ is not basic variable.

The first case can be analyzed in analogy to (β), and one obtains $\lambda_{\max}(\Delta p) = \Delta\lambda(\Delta p)$. The second case has not yet been solved.

Example 4.7

We shall illustrate the above analyses by considering the following numerical example:

$$
\begin{aligned}
\text{maximize} \quad & x_1 + x_2 \\
\text{such that} \quad & -x_1 + 3x_2 \lesssim 21 \\
& x_1 + 3x_2 \lesssim 27 \\
& 4x_1 + 3x_2 \lesssim 45 \\
& 3x_1 + x_2 \leq 30 \\
& x_1 \geq 0, x_2 \geq 0
\end{aligned}
$$

with

$$
\begin{aligned}
b_0 &= 14{,}5; & p_0 &= 2 \\
b_1 &= 21; & p_1 &= 3 \\
b_2 &= 27; & p_2 &= 6 \\
b_3 &= 45; & p_3 &= 6
\end{aligned}
$$

This is a problem of type (4.31) extended by a set of crisp constraints. The equivalent crisp model (4.44) without the slack variables is therefore

$$
\begin{array}{llllllll}
\max \ \lambda & & & & & & & \\
2\lambda & & + t_0 & & & & \leq 2 & \\
3\lambda & & & + t_1 & & & \leq 3 & \text{I} \\
6\lambda & & & & + t_2 & & \leq 6 & \\
6\lambda & & & & & + t_3 & \leq 6 & \\
 & -x_1 - x_2 & - t_0 & & & & \leq -14{,}5 & \\
 & -x_1 + 3x_2 & & - t_1 & & & \leq 21 & \text{II} \\
 & x_1 + 3x_2 & & & - t_2 & & \leq 27 & \\
 & 4x_1 + 3x_2 & & & & - t_3 & \leq 45 & \\
 & & t_0 & & & & \leq 2 & \\
 & & & t_1 & & & \leq 3 & \text{III} \\
 & & & & t_2 & & \leq 6 & \\
 & & & & & t_3 & \leq 6 & \\
 & 3x_1 + x_2 & & & & & \leq 30 & \text{IV}
\end{array}
$$

$$\lambda \in R, \quad x_1 \geq 0, \quad x_2 \geq 0, \quad t_0 \geq 0, \quad t_1 \geq 0, \quad t_2 \geq 0, \quad t_3 \geq 0$$

Figure 4-5 illustrates this problem.

Solving the crisp equivalent we obtain

$$
\left.\begin{array}{ll}
\lambda_{max} = 0.625 & \text{(BV)} \\
x_1^0 = 6.0 & \text{(BV)} \\
x_2^0 = 7.75 & \text{(BV)}
\end{array}\right\} \quad \text{i.e., } x_0 = (6.0; 7.75)^T
$$

$$
\left.\begin{array}{ll}
t_0^0 = 0.75 & \text{(BV)} \\
t_1^0 = 0.0 & \text{(NBV)} \\
t_2^0 = 2.25 & \text{(BV)} \\
t_3^0 = 2.25 & \text{(BV)}
\end{array}\right\} \quad \text{i.e., } t_0 = (0.75; 0; 2.25; 2.25; 2.25)^T
$$

(Here BV denotes the basic variables.)

The corresponding optimal vectors of dual-variable or shadow-price are

$$y_{\text{I}}^0 = (.25; 0; .02778; .0556)^T$$

$$y_{\text{II}}^0 = (.25; 0; .02778; .0556)^T$$

$$y_{\text{III}}^0 = (0; 0; 0; 0)^T$$

$$y_{\text{IV}}^0 = (0)$$

Note that, for example, the first constraint of I is binding and the corre-

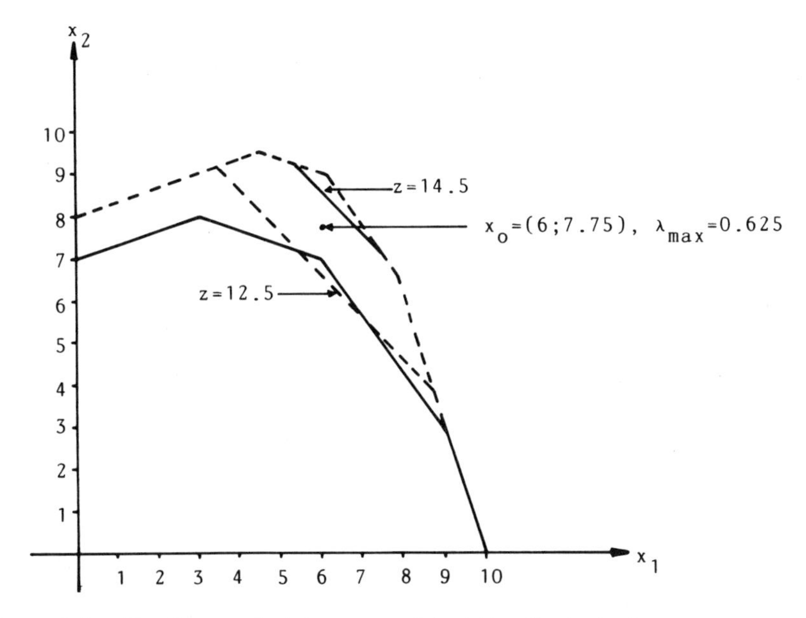

Figure 4-5: The Geometrical Structure of the Crisp Equivalent.

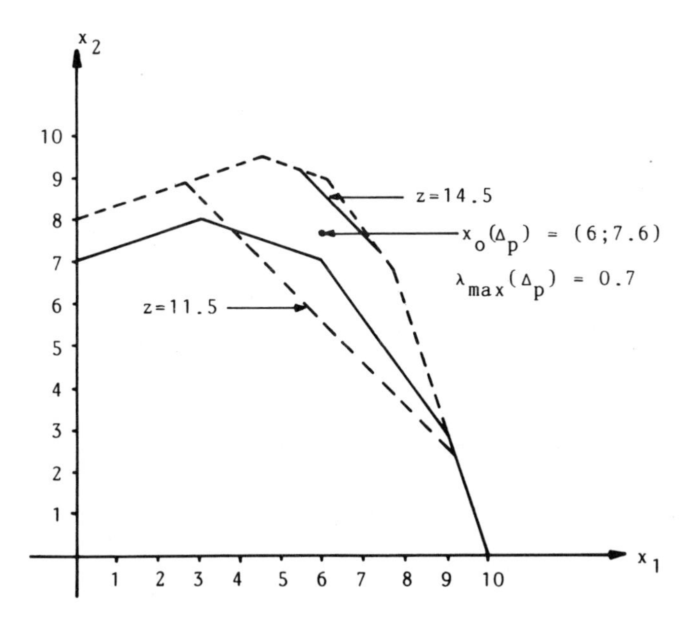

Figure 4-6: The Geometrical Structure of the Perturbed Problem.

sponding shadow price is .25.

For an admissible change of $\Delta p = 1$ we obtain the following LP problem (see figure 4-6):

$$
\begin{array}{lllllll}
\max \ \lambda & & & & & & \\
3\lambda & & + t_0 & & & & \leq 3 \\
3\lambda & & & + t_1 & & & \leq 3 \\
6\lambda & & & & + t_2 & & \leq 6 \\
6\lambda & & & & & + t_3 & \leq 6 \\
& -x_1 - \ x_2 & - t_0 & & & & \leq -14,5 \\
& -x_1 + 3x_2 & & - t_1 & & & \leq 21 \\
& x_1 + 3x_2 & & & - t_2 & & \leq 27 \\
& 4x_1 + 3x_2 & & & & - t_3 & \leq 45 \\
& & t_0 & & & & \leq 3 \\
& & & t_1 & & & \leq 3 \\
& & & & t_2 & & \leq 6 \\
& & & & & t_3 & \leq 6 \\
& 3x_1 + \ x_2 & & & & & \leq 30
\end{array}
$$

$$x_1 \geq 0, \quad x_2 \geq 0, \quad t_0 \geq 0, \quad t_1 \geq 0, \quad t_2 \geq 0, \quad t_3 \geq 0$$

By solving this LP we have the following results:

$$
\left.\begin{array}{ll}
\lambda_{\max}(\Delta p) = 0.7 & \text{(BV)} \\
x_1^0(\Delta p) = 6.0 & \text{(BV)} \\
x_2^0(\Delta p) = 7.6 & \text{(BV)}
\end{array}\right\} \quad \text{i.e., } x_0(\Delta p) = (6.0; 7.6)^T
$$

$$
\left.\begin{array}{ll}
t_0^0(\Delta p) = 0.9 & \text{(BV)} \\
t_1^0(\Delta p) = 0.0 & \text{(NBV)} \\
t_2^0(\Delta p) = 1.8 & \text{(BV)} \\
t_3^0(\Delta p) = 1.8 & \text{(BV)}
\end{array}\right\} \quad \text{i.e., } t_0(\Delta p) = (0.9; 0; 1.8; 1.8)^T
$$

Obviously the difference ($\lambda_{\max} - \lambda_{\max}(1)$) which is the difference of the optimal values of the objective functions of (4.2) and (4.3) is .075.

The same result is obtained when computing this difference by using (4.53).

$$\Delta\lambda_{\max}(\Delta p) = c_B^T[MB^{-1}b + (E + M)B^{-1}\,\Delta p e_j^*]$$

Extensions

Two of the major assumptions made in defining the crisp equivalent problem to (4.3) were:

1. Linear membership functions for all fuzzy sets involved.
2. Use of the min-operator for aggregating the fuzzy sets to arrive at the fuzzy set "decision."

It is quite obvious that linear membership functions will not always be adequate and it has been shown empirically (see also chapter 6) that the min-operator is often not an appropriate model for the "and" used in decision models. We shall first consider the problem of nonlinear membership functions—keeping the min-operator as aggregator—and then we shall investigate what happens if other aggregating procedures are used.

Nonlinear Membership Functions. The linear membership functions used so far could all be defined by fixing two points, the upper and lower aspiration levels or the two bounds of the tolerance interval. The most obvious way to handle nonlinear membership functions is probably to approximate them piece-wise by linear functions. Some authors [Hannan 1981; Nakamura 1985] have used this approach, and shown that the resulting equivalent crisp problem is still a standard linear programming problem.

This problem, however, can be considerably larger than model (4.44) because in general one constraint will have to be added for each "linear piece" of the approximation. Quite often S-shaped membership functions have been suggested, particularly if the membership function is interpreted as a kind of utility function (representing the degree of satisfaction, acceptance etc.). Leberling [1981], for instance, suggests such a function which is also uniquely determined by two parameters. He suggests

$$\mu_H(x) = \frac{1}{2}\,\frac{\exp\left[\left(x - \frac{a+b}{2}\right)\delta\right] - \exp\left[-\left(x - \frac{a+b}{2}\right)\delta\right]}{\exp\left[\left(x - \frac{a+b}{2}\right)\delta\right] + \exp\left[-\left(x - \frac{a+b}{2}\right)\delta\right]}$$

with $a,b,\delta \geq 0$. This hyperbolic function (see figure 4-7) has the following formal properties:

$\mu_H(x)$ is strictly monotonously increasing.

$$\mu_H(x) = \frac{1}{2} \text{ where } x = \frac{a+b}{2}.$$

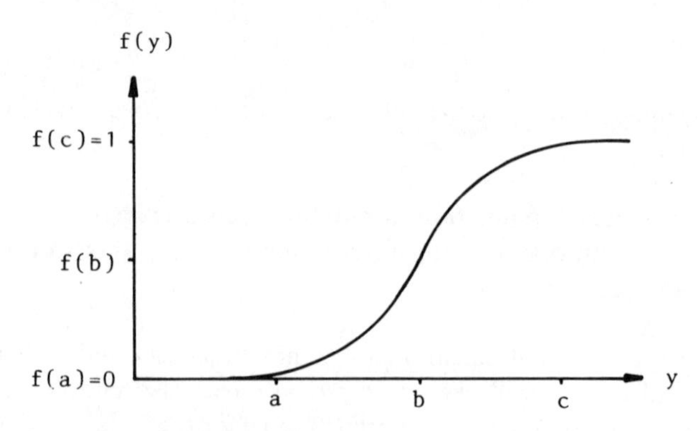

Figure 4-7: Hyperbolic Membership Function.

$\mu_H(x)$ is strictly convex on $[-\infty, (a+b)/2]$ and strictly concave on $[(a+b)/2, +\infty]$.

For all $x \in \mathbb{R}$: $0 < \mu_H(x) < 1$ and $\mu_H(x)$ approaches asymptotically $f(x) = 0$ and $f(x) = 1$, respectively.

Leberling shows that choosing as lower and upper aspiration levels for the fuzzy objective function $z = cx$ of an LP $a = \underline{c}$ (lower bound of z) and $b = \overline{c}$ (upper limit of the objective function), and representing this (fuzzy) goal by a hyperbolic function one arrives at the following crisp equivalent problem for one fuzzy goal and all crisp constraints:

$$\begin{aligned} &\text{maximize} \quad \lambda \\ &\text{such that} \quad \lambda - \frac{1}{2}\frac{e^{Z'(x)} - e^{-Z'(x)}}{e^{Z'(x)} + e^{-Z'(x)}} \leq \frac{1}{2} \\ &\qquad\qquad\qquad Dx \leq b' \\ &\qquad\qquad\qquad x, \lambda \geq 0 \end{aligned} \tag{4.55}$$

with $Z'(x) = (\Sigma_j c_j x_j - \frac{1}{2}(\overline{c} + \underline{c}))\delta$. For each additional fuzzy goal or constraint one of these exponential rows has, of course, to be added to (4.55).

For $x_{n+1} = \tanh^{-1}(2\lambda - 1)$, model (4.55) is equivalent to the following linear model:

$$\begin{aligned} &\text{maximize} \quad x_{n+1} \\ &\text{such that} \quad \delta \sum_j c_j x_j - x_{n+1} \geq \frac{1}{2}\delta(\overline{c} + \underline{c}) \end{aligned}$$

$$Dx \leq b'$$

$$x_{n+1}, x \geq 0 \tag{4.56}$$

This is again a standard linear programming model which can be solved, for instance, by any available simplex code.

The above equivalence between models with nonlinear membership functions is not accidental. It has been proven that the following relationship holds [Werners 1984, p. 143].

Theorem 4.1

Let $\{f_k\}$, $k = 1,\ldots,K$ be a finite family of functions $f_k: \mathbb{R}^n \to \mathbb{R}^1$, $x^0 \in X \subset \mathbb{R}^n$. $g: \mathbb{R}^1 \to \mathbb{R}^1$ strictly monotonously increasing and $\lambda, \lambda' \in \mathbb{R}$. Consider the two mathematical programming problems

$$\begin{aligned} \text{maximize} \quad & \lambda \\ \text{such that} \quad & \lambda \leq f_k(x) \qquad k = 1,\ldots,K \\ & x \in X \end{aligned} \tag{4.57}$$

$$\begin{aligned} \text{maximize} \quad & \lambda' \\ \text{such that} \quad & \lambda' \leq g(f_k(x)) \qquad k = 1,\ldots,K. \\ & x \in X \end{aligned} \tag{4.58}$$

If there exists a $\lambda^0 \in R'$ such that (λ^0, x^0) is the optimal solution of (4.57) then there exists a $\lambda'^0 \in R'$ such that (λ^0, x^0) is the optimal solution of (4.58).

Example 4.8 [Werners 1984]

Consider the linear programming model

$$\begin{aligned} \text{maximize} \quad & -x_1 + 2x_2 \\ \text{such that} \quad & 2x_1 + x_2 \gtrsim 21 \\ & -x_1 + 3x_2 \leq 21 \\ & x_1 + 3x_2 \leq 27 \\ & 4x_1 + 3x_2 \leq 45 \\ & 3x_1 + x_2 \leq 30 \\ & x_1, x_2 \geq 0 \end{aligned}$$

An absolute lower bound for the fuzzy restriction is 7.

With hyperbolic membership functions for the goals and the fuzzy constraint the following nonlinear crisp equivalent model results:

$$
\begin{aligned}
\text{maximize} \quad & \lambda \\
\text{such that} \quad & \lambda - \frac{1}{2}\frac{\exp a - \exp b}{\exp a + \exp b} \leq \frac{1}{2} \\
& \lambda - \frac{1}{2}\frac{\exp c - \exp d}{\exp c + \exp d} \leq \frac{1}{2} \\
& -x_1 + 3x_2 \leq 21 \\
& x_1 + 3x_2 \leq 27 \\
& 4x_1 + 3x_2 \leq 45 \\
& 3x_1 + x_2 \leq 30 \\
& x_1, x_2 \geq 0 \\
& \lambda \geq 0
\end{aligned}
$$

where

$$
\begin{aligned}
\exp a &= (-x_1 + 2x_2 - 5.5)\cdot(6/17) \\
\exp b &= -(-x_1 + 2x_2 - 5.5)\cdot(6/17) \\
\exp c &= (2x_1 + x_2 - 14)\cdot(6/14) \\
\exp d &= -(2x_1 + x_2 - 14)\cdot(6/14)
\end{aligned}
$$

With $g_H(x) = \frac{1}{6}\tanh^{-1}(2x - 1) + \frac{1}{2}$, the following linear equivalent model can be constructed and solved:

$$
\begin{aligned}
\text{maximize} \quad & x_3 \\
\text{such that} \quad & -6x_1 + 12x_2 - 17x_3 \geq 33 \\
& 12x_1 + 6x_2 - 14x_3 \geq 84 \\
& -x_1 + 3x_2 \leq 21 \\
& x_1 + 3x_2 \leq 27 \\
& 4x_1 + 3x_2 \leq 45 \\
& 3x_1 + x_2 \leq 30 \\
& x_1, x_2 \geq 0
\end{aligned}
$$

The optimal solution is $x^0 = (5.03, 7.32, 1.45)^t$ and the maximal degree of membership is

$$\lambda^{opt} = \tfrac{1}{2}\tanh(x_3^0) + \tfrac{1}{2}$$
$$= 0.95$$

Theorem 4.1 suggests that quite a number of nonlinear membership functions can be accomodated easily. Unluckily the same optimism is not justified concerning other aggregation operators.

Other Aggregation Operators. The computational efficiency of the approach mentioned so far has rested to a large extend on the use of the min-operator as a model for the logical "and" or the intersection of fuzzy sets, respectively. Axiomatic [Hamacher 1978] as well as empirical [Thole, Zimmermann, Zysno 1979, Zimmermann, Zysno 1980, 1983] investigations have shead some doubt on the general use of the min-operator in decision models. Quite a number of context free or context dependent operators have been suggested in the meantime [see, e.g., Zimmermann 1985b, ch. 3]. The disadvantage of these operators is, however, that the resulting crisp equivalent models are no longer linear [see, e.g., Zimmermann 1978, p. 45], which reduces the computational efficiency of these approaches considerably or even renders the equivalent models unsolvable within acceptable time limits. There are, however, some exceptions to this rule, and we will present two of them in more detail.

One of the objections against the min-operator (see, for instance, Zimmermann and Zysno [1980]) is the fact that neither the logical "and" nor the min-operator is compensatory in the sense that increases in the degree of membership in the fuzzy sets "intersected" might not influence at all membership in the resulting fuzzy set (aggregated fuzzy set or intersection). There are two quite natural ways to cure this weakness:

1. Combine the (limitational) min-operator as model for the logical "and" within the fully compensatory max-operator as a model for the inclusive "or." For the former, the product operator might be used alternatively and for the latter the algebraic sum might be used. This approach departs from distinguishing between "and" and "or" aggregation as being somewhere between the "and" and the "or." (Therefore it is often called *compensatory and.*)
2. Stick with the *distinction between "and" and "or"* aggregators and introduce a certain degree of compensation into these connectives.

Compensatory "and." For some apaplications it seems to be important that the aggregator used maps above the max-operator and below the min-operator. The γ-operator [Zimmermann, Zysno 1980] would be such a connective. For purposes of mathematical programming it has, however, the above-mentioned disadvantage of low computational efficiency. An acceptable compromise between empirical fit and computational efficiency seems to be the convex combination of the min-operator and the max-operator:

$$\mu_c(x) = \gamma \min_{i=1}^{m} \mu_i(x) + (1 - \gamma) \max_{i=1}^{m} \mu_i(x) \qquad \gamma \in [0,1] \tag{4.59}$$

For determining the maximizing decision the following problem has to be solved.

$$\max_{x \in X} \left(\gamma \min_{i=1}^{m} \{\mu_i(x)\} + (1 - \gamma) \max_{i=1}^{m} \{\mu_i(x)\} \right)$$

$$\begin{aligned} \text{maximize} \quad & \gamma \cdot \lambda_1 + (1 - \gamma)\lambda_2 \\ \text{such that} \quad & \lambda_1 \leq \mu_i(x) \qquad i = 1,\ldots,m \\ & \lambda_2 \leq \mu_i(x) \qquad \text{for at least one } i \in \{1,\ldots,m\} \\ & x \in X \end{aligned}$$

or

$$\begin{aligned} \text{maximize} \quad & \gamma\lambda_1 + (1 - \gamma)\lambda_2 \\ \text{such that} \quad & \lambda_1 \leq \mu_i(x) \qquad i = 1,\ldots,m \\ & \lambda_2 \leq \mu_i(x) + My_i \qquad i = 1,\ldots,m \\ & \sum_{i=1}^{m} y_i \leq m - 1 \\ & y \in \{0,1\}, \quad M \text{ is a very large real number} \\ & x \in X \end{aligned} \tag{4.59a}$$

For linear membership functions of the goals and the constraints (4.59a) is a mixed integer linear program that can be solved by the appropriate available codes.

Distinction Between Fuzzy "and" and Fuzzy "or." Now we shall distinguish between fuzzy "and," denoted by $\widetilde{\text{and}}$, and fuzzy "or," denoted by $\widetilde{\text{or}}$, and use models for these connectives which contain a certain degree of compensation:

Definition 4.4a [Werners 1984]

Let $\mu_i(x)$ be the membership functions of fuzzy sets which are to be aggregated in the sense of a *fuzzy and* ($\widetilde{\text{and}}$). The membership function of the resulting fuzzy set is defined to be

$$\mu_{\widetilde{\text{and}}}(x) = \gamma \cdot \min_{i=1}^{m} \mu_i(x) + (1-\gamma)\frac{1}{m}\sum_{i=1}^{m} \mu_i(x)$$

with $\gamma \in [0,1]$.

Definition 4.4b [Werners 1984]

Let $\mu_i(x)$ be membership functions of fuzzy sets to be aggregated in the sense of a *fuzzy or* ($\widetilde{\text{or}}$). The membership function of the resulting fuzzy set is then defined as

$$\mu_{\widetilde{\text{or}}}(x) = \gamma \max_{i=1}^{m} \mu_i(x) + (1-\gamma)\frac{1}{m}\sum_{i=1}^{m} \mu_i(x)$$

with $\gamma \in [0,1]$.

These two connectives are not inductive and associative, but they are commutative, idempotent, strictly monotonic increasing in each component, continuous, and compensatory [Werners 1984, p. 168]. These are certainly very useful and acceptable properties. Since we are used to conceiving the constraints and objective functions in mathematical programming in general to be valid simultaneously an $\widetilde{\text{and}}$ interpretation seems to be appropriate. We shall, therefore, show in some more detail the consequences of using $\widetilde{\text{and}}$ as an aggregator in model (4.3):

Consider again model (4.3a) extended by a block of crisp constraints, that is,

$$\begin{aligned} &\text{find} && x \\ &\text{such that} && Bx \lesssim b \\ & && Dx \leq d \\ & && x \geq 0 \end{aligned} \tag{4.60}$$

where B is an $m \times n$ matrix, D a $k \times n$ matrix, and all other components are assumed to be of appropriate dimensions.

By contrast to (4.4) the fuzzy set "decision" is now defined by the membership function

$$\mu_D(x) = \gamma \min_{i=1}^{m} \mu_i(x) + (1-\gamma)\frac{1}{m}\sum_{i=1}^{m} \mu_i(x)$$

$$x \in X, \quad \gamma \in [0,1] \qquad (4.61)$$

For (4.60), assuming (4.61), a crisp equivalent model can be determined [Werners 1984, p. 198] in analogy to (4.12):

$$\begin{aligned} \text{maximize} \quad & \lambda + (1-\gamma)\frac{1}{m}\sum_{i=1}^{m} \lambda_i \\ \text{such that} \quad & \lambda + \lambda_i \leq \mu_i(x) \qquad i = 1,\ldots,m \\ & Dx \leq d \\ & \lambda,\lambda_i,x \geq 0 \\ & 0 \leq \mu_i(x) \leq 1 \end{aligned} \qquad (4.62)$$

If $(\lambda^0,\lambda_i^0,x^0)$ is optimal solution of (4.62) then x^0 is a maximizing solution to (4.60). It is obvious that if $\mu_i(x)$ are linear (4.62) is again a standard linear programming problem.

Example 4.9

Model (4.62) for the linear programming model in example 4.8 with linear membership functions is

$$\text{maximize} \quad \lambda + \left(1 - \frac{1}{3}\right)\frac{1}{2}(\lambda_1 + \lambda_2) = \lambda + \frac{1}{3}\lambda_1 + \frac{1}{3}\lambda_2$$

such that

$$\begin{aligned} \lambda + \lambda_1 &\leq -.05882x_1 + .117x_2 + .1764 \\ \lambda + \lambda_2 &\leq +.1429x_1 + .0714x_2 - .5 \\ -x_1 + 3x_2 &\leq 21 \\ x_1 + 3x_2 &\leq 27 \\ 4x_1 + 3x_2 &\leq 45 \\ 3x_1 + x_2 &\leq 30 \end{aligned}$$

$$x_1,x_2 \geq 0$$

$$\lambda,\lambda_1,\lambda_2 \geq 0$$

Fuzzy Multi-Stage Programming

Introduction

The models and algorithms discussed in the last section considered the decision situation as a one-stage problem. In this mode, even a sequence of partial decisions, such as inventory decisions in a number of subsequent time periods, would be modelled in a one-stage linear programming model and the solution to all of them would be determined simultaneously. The computational effort for this type of model normally rises faster than the model size. In order to counteract the increase of computational effort and to decrease the required storage space when using computers, one tries to decompose large models into smaller ones, which are then solved sequentially. Thus multi-stage decision models can originate either from decomposing one-stage multi-variable decision problems or from modelling multi-stage (dynamic) decision problems. The latter is frequently found in control engineering [Kacprzyk 1983].

In operations research the best-known approaches to modelling and solving such multi-stage models are "Dynamic Programming" and "Branch-and-Bound" methods [Beckmann 1968; Bellman 1957; Gillett 1976; Nemhauser 1966; Norman 1975; White 1969]. We shall first sketch the basic crisp approach before we discuss fuzzy versions.

In traditional Dynamic Programming [Bellman 1957] models are generally formulated in terms of state variables x_i, decision variables d_i, stage rewards $r_i(x_i,d_i)$, a reward function $R_N = f(r_1,\ldots,r_N)$, and a transformation function $t_i(x_i,d_i)$. The basic structure of a decomposed mathematical programming model is depicted in figure 4-8. It consists of a set of stages, each corresponding to a one-decision variable problem, joined together in series such that the output of one stage (characterized by the state variables) becomes the input of the next stage. The backward numbering in figure 4-8 is used, because the first recursive sequential optimization generally starts at the last stage and then works backward to the first stage.

The decision variables, d_i, determine the transformations, t_i. It is assumed that x_i depends only on x_{i+1} and d_{i+1}, that is, $x_i = (x_{i+1},d_{i+1})$. Hence we can also write the stage return $r_i(x_i,d_i)$ as $r_i = (x_N,d_N,\ldots,d_i)$. The total reward R_N from stages N through i is a function of the individual stage returns of stages

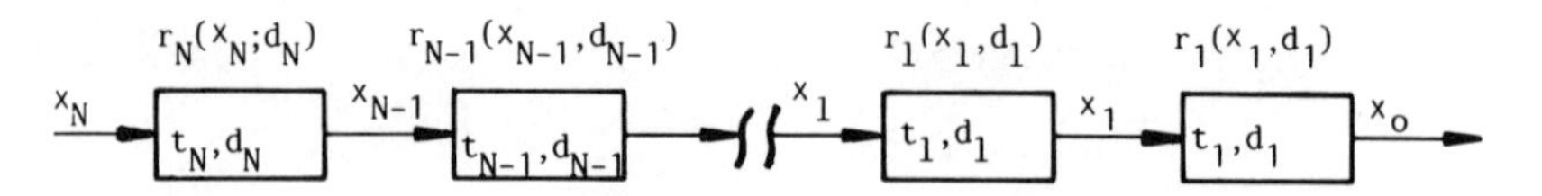

Figure 4-8: Serial multi-stage decision system.

N through 1, $R_N = f(r_N,\ldots,r_1) = f(x_N,d_N,\ldots,d_1)$. In most cases the total (cumulative) reward is taken to be the sum of the stage returns. In this case our general model is

$$\underset{d_1,\ldots,d_N}{\text{maximize}}\ R_N = \sum_{i=1}^{N} r_i(x_i,d_i)$$

$$\text{such that}\quad x_{i+1} = t_i(x_i,d_i)$$

This problem is now decomposed into N subproblems by using the following recursive equation:

$$\max_{d_i} R_i(x_i,d_i) = r_i(x_i,d_i) + R_{i-1}(t_i(x_i,d_i)) \qquad i = 2,\ldots,N$$

$$\max_{d_i} R_i(x_i,d_i) = r_i(x_i,d_i) \qquad i = 1 \tag{4.64}$$

Depending on the type of decision space, D, state space, X, reward function, R, transformation, t, and planning horizon, N, different numerical procedures have been suggested in the literature to solve (4.64). The reader is referred to the references given at the beginning of this section. For our purposes we shall, however, state briefly the assumptions underlying (crisp) dynamic programming as far as they are relevant for our further discussions and as they can be used to classify "fuzzy" approaches to multi-stage decision models.

1. *The decision space* is crisp. It can be discrete or continuous. On each stage this space is one dimensional—that is, only one decision variable is considered for optimization. The optimization is performed in such a way, however, that the global optimum of the total problem is obtained (recursively).
2. *The state space* is also crisp. The state variable can be crisp or continuous. Generally there exists only one state variable (for instance amount of inventory, available cash, speed of the system, etc.) which characterizes the states of the system. For more than one state variable, dynamic programming becomes very involved (see, for example, Nemhauser [1966, pp. 184–209]). The state spaces can be the same for all stages or they can vary.

3. *The transformation function* is crisp. It can be either deterministic or stochastic. In the latter case no uniquely optimal policy (solution) can be determined. The transformation function, which in the stochastic case is normally represented by a probability transition matrix, can vary from stage to stage.
4. *The reward function* (goal) is crisp. It has to be separable into stage rewards and monotonically nondecreasing in the stage rewards. Depending on the type of transformation function, it will be deterministic or stochastic. Generally it represents a one-criteria-type decision model. The introduction of multi-criteria decision considerations would cause considerable complications.
5. *The termination time* (planning horizon) is crisp. Usually is is finite (specified as the number of decision variables or stages N). There are, however, also models for infinite termination times [Nemhauser 1966; Howard 1960].

Discussing fuzzy versions of multi-stage decision models two more distinctive features of models become relevant:

6. *Operators* used to model "decisions." Even in crisp dynamic programming the question of operators plays a certain part: the stage rewards have to be aggregated to one cumulative reward function. Only those operators are permissable which maintain the separability and monotonicity of the reward function. This is generally the "addition." Other operators are, however, also possible (see, for example, Nemhauser [1966]). This also holds for the transformation function. In fuzzy models the additional question arises as to which operators model adequately the "confluence" of goals and constraints in decision models. (See discussion in chapters 2 and 6.)
7. *Algorithmic treatment* of crisp equivalent models. At the beginning of this chapter, the general procedure used to "solve" fuzzy decision problems was to design a fuzzy model of a fuzzy decision problem. Then a crisp model was developed which in certain aspects was equivalent to the fuzzy model. This crisp model was then solved by known and efficient crisp mathematical models. The methods used to solve the crisp equivalent do not have to be uniquely determined. The reader should realize that, even for "crisp" linear programming models, there exists a number of possible solution methods: for a nonlinear or integer crisp equivalent model of a fuzzy mathematical programming model even crisp dynamic programming might be an appropriate solution procedure.

   For multi-stage decision models the situation is similar: if crisp equivalent models for a fuzzy dynamic programming model are developed, then these models might best be solved by other algorithmic tools than (crisp) dynamic programming. One of those alternative approaches is, for instance, Branch-and-Bound.

The scope of fuzzy multi-stage decision models is obviously very wide, even if we exclude features 6 and 7. Each of the characteristics 1 through 5 and any combination of them can be modelled fuzzily. For all the resulting models one can develop a deterministic and a stochastic version. Not all of these models will be relevant for real applications. The reader who is particularly interested in this area is referred to Kacprzyk's book [Kacprzyk 1983]. We shall restrict our discussions to only two cases, which seem to be of particular interest at the present time: The classical deterministic model by Bellman and Zadeh [1970] with a crisp transformation function and crisp and finite termination time and a model by Kacprzyk with fuzzy transformations; crisp and finite termination time, the crisp equivalent of which will be solved by Branch-and-Bound. Whenever appropriate we shall indicate possible extensions and discuss their consequences and applicational relevance.

Fuzzy Dynamic Programming with Crisp Transformations

In their famous paper Bellman and Zadeh [1970] suggested for the first time a fuzzy approach to dynamic programming models. Conceivably they based their considerations on the symmetrical model of a decision as defined in definition 2.1. The following terms will be used to define the fuzzy dynamic programming model [Bellman, Zadeh 1970, p. B-151]:

$x_i \in X$, $i = 0,\dots,N$: (crisp) state variable where $X = \{\tau_1,\dots,\tau_N\}$ is the set of values permitted for the state variables.

$d_i \in D$, $i = 1,\dots,N$: (crisp) decision variable where $D = \{\alpha_1,\dots,\alpha_m\}$ is the set of possible decisions.

$x_{i+1} = t(x_i,d_i)$: (crisp) transformation function.

1. For each stage i, $i = 0,\dots,N-1$, we define: a fuzzy constraint $\tilde{C}_i$ limiting the decision space and characterized by its membership function

$$\mu_{\tilde{C}_i}(d_i)$$

2. A fuzzy goal $\tilde{G}_N$ characterized by the membership function

$$\mu_{\tilde{G}_N}(x_N)$$

3. The termination time is assumed to be deterministic and finite (N).
4. The state transformations, $x_{i+1} = t(x_i,d_i)$, are invariant and given as a matrix, T.

The reader should realize that decisions as well as state variables are crisp variables which are restricted by fuzzy constraints and that the goal—by contrast to traditional dynamic programming—refers to the state variables of stage N only and is formulated as a fuzzy set.

The aim is to determine the optimizing decision $\tilde{D}^0$ (see definition 2.2 or the maximizing decision (see (4.5))

$$D^0 = \{d_i^0\}, i = 0,\ldots,N, \text{ for a given } x_0$$

The Model. According to definition 2.1 the fuzzy set "decision" is the "confluence" of the constraints and the goal(s), that is,

$$\tilde{D} = \bigcap_{i=0}^{N-1} \tilde{C}_i \cap \tilde{G}_{\tilde{N}}$$

Using the min-operator for the aggregation of the fuzzy constraints and the goal, the membership function of the fuzzy set decision is

$$\mu_{\tilde{D}}(d_0,\ldots,d_{N-1}) = \min\{\mu_{\tilde{C}_0}(d_0),\ldots,\mu_{\tilde{C}_{N-1}}(d_{N-1}),\mu_{\tilde{G}_N}(x_N)\} \tag{4.65}$$

The membership function of the maximizing decision is then

$$\mu_{\tilde{D}^0}(d_0^0,\ldots,d_{N-1}^0) = \tag{4.66}$$

$$\max_{d_0,\ldots,d_{N-2}} \max_{d_{N-1}} [(\min \mu_{\tilde{C}_0}(d_0),\ldots,\mu_{\tilde{C}_{N-1}}(d_{N-1}),\mu_{\tilde{G}_N}(t_{N-1}(x_{N-1},d_{N-1}))]$$

where d_i^0 denotes the optimal decision on stage i.

If K is a constant and g is any function of d_{N-1}, we can write

$$\max_{d_{N-1}} (\min[g(d_{N-1}),K]) = \min[K, \max(g(d_{N-1}))]$$

and (4.66) can be expressed as

$$\mu_{\tilde{D}^0}(d_0^0,\ldots,d_{N-1}^0) = \max_{d_0,\ldots,d_{N-1}} (\min \mu_{\tilde{C}_0}(d_0),\ldots,\mu_{\tilde{C}_{N-2}}(d_{N-2}),\mu_{\tilde{G}_{N-1}}(x_{N-1})) \tag{4.67}$$

with

$$\mu_{\tilde{G}_{N-1}}(x_{N-1}) = \max_{d_{N-1}} (\min[\mu_{\tilde{C}_{N-1}}(d_{N-1}),\mu_{\tilde{G}_N}(t_{N-1}(x_{N-1},d_{N-1}))] \tag{4.68}$$

We can thus determine $\tilde{D}^0$ recursively.

Example 4.10 [Bellman, Zadeh 1970, p. B-153]

Let $\tilde{d}_1$, $\tilde{d}_2$ be the two decision variables, the possible values of which can be α_1,α_2; x_t, $t = 0,\ldots,2$, are the state variables with a finite range $X = \{\tau_1,\tau_2,\tau_3\}$. The fuzzy constraints for $t = 0$ and $t = 1$ are

$$\tilde{C}_0(\alpha_i) = \{(\alpha_1,.7),(\alpha_2,1)\}$$

$$\tilde{C}_1(\alpha_i) = \{(\alpha_1,1),(\alpha_2,.6)\}$$

The fuzzy goal is specified as

$$\tilde{G}(x_2) = \{(\tau_1,.3),(\tau_2,1),(\tau_3,.8)\}$$

and the crisp transformation function, $x_{i+1} = t(x_i,d_i)$, is defined by the following matrix:

	x_i		
d^0	τ_1	τ_2	τ_3
α_1	τ_1	τ_3	τ_1
α_2	τ_2	τ_1	τ_3

Solution: Using (4.68) we can compute the fuzzy goal induced at $i = 1$ as follows: start at stage $i = 2$. The state-decision combinations which yield τ_i on stage $i = 1$ are obtained from the above matrix. So we can compute:

$$\begin{aligned}
\mu_{G_1}(\tau_1) &= \max_{d_1} \{\min[\mu_{\tilde{C}_1}(d_1), \mu_{\tilde{G}_2}(t(\tau_1,\alpha_1))], \min[\mu_{\tilde{C}_1}(d_1), \mu_{\tilde{G}_2}(t(\tau_1,\alpha_2))]\}\\
&= \max\{\min[1,.3], \min[.6,1]\}\\
&= \max\{.3,.6\} = .6\\
&\to d_1^0 = \alpha_2
\end{aligned}$$

$$\begin{aligned}
\mu_{\tilde{G}_1}(\tau_2) &= \max\{\min[1,.8], \min[.6,.3]\}\\
&= \max\{.8,.3\} = .8\\
&\to d_1^0 = \alpha_1
\end{aligned}$$

$$\begin{aligned}
\mu_{\tilde{G}_1}(\tau_3) &= \max\{\min[1,.3], \min[.6,.8]\}\\
&= \max\{.3,.6\} = .6\\
&\to d_1^0 = \alpha_2
\end{aligned}$$

$$\mu_{\tilde{G}_0}(\tau_1) = \max\{\min[.7,.6], \min[1,.8]\} = .8$$

$$\rightarrow d_0^0 = \alpha_2$$

$$\mu_{\tilde{G}_0}(\tau_2) = \max\{\min[.7,.6], \min[1,.6]\} = .6$$

$$\rightarrow d_0^0 = \alpha_1 \quad \text{or} \quad \alpha_2$$

$$\mu_{\tilde{G}_0}(\tau_3) = \max\{\min[.7,.6], \min[1,.6]\} = .6$$

$$\rightarrow d_0^0 = \alpha_1 \quad \text{or} \quad \alpha_2$$

Thus, for

$$x_0 = \tau_1\colon \quad d_0^0 = \alpha_2, d_1^0 = \alpha_1 \qquad \text{with } \mu_{\tilde{G}_2}^0 = .8$$

$$x_0 = \tau_2\colon \quad d_0^0 = \alpha_1, d_1^0 = \alpha_2, \text{ or}$$

$$d_0^0 = \alpha_2, d_1^0 = \alpha_2 \qquad \text{with } \mu_{\tilde{G}_2}^0 = .6$$

$$x_0 = \tau_3\colon \quad d_0^0 = \alpha_1, d_1^0 = \alpha_2, \text{ or}$$

$$d_0^0 = \alpha_2, d_1^0 = \alpha_2 \qquad \text{with } \mu_{\tilde{G}_2}^0 = .6$$

Fuzzy Dynamic Programming with Fuzzy State Transformations

In the foregoing discussion, the state transformations were assumed to be crisp and deterministic. Baldwin and Pilsworth argue that for

> political decision making, economic planning, ... domestic and other human problem solving, the state mappings from stage to stage [i.e., the state transformations] will only be known in an imprecise manner. We all feel that we are able to choose the best car route when going on holiday and this is arrived at using a very fuzzy decision analysis. Nevertheless human intelligence is limited to relatively simple chains of argument and often the analysis of complex multi-stage decision problems is over simplified. This motivates the need for a dynamic programming method for systems with fuzzy state mappings, fuzzy constraints and fuzzy goals. [Baldwin, Pilsworth 1982]

Consequently, they suggest a model with fuzzy state transformations, fuzzy constraints on state and decision variables, and a fuzzy goal. Optimization is performed in the framework of dynamic programming via a specially defined truth functional which expresses the degree of truth of the statement "the decisions match constraints and goal well." This is certainly a very interesting approach and the reader is referred to Baldwin and Pilsworth [1982], Kacprzyk [1983, pp. 47–52], and Zimmermann [1985b] for further details. We shall not pursue this approach here, primarily for two reasons:

1. This type of model leads to almost prohibitively high computational effort for a realistic number of stages. The authors realize this and suggest "fuzzy interpolation" as a remedy. It appears, however, that more research in this direction is needed before this approach can be considered ready for a textbook or for real application.
2. We find it difficult to envisage fuzzy stage decisions in reality. In most real application of fuzzy models, such as linear programming or fuzzy control (see, for instance, Zimmermann [1985, ch. 13]), fuzzy decisions are transformed into crisp decisions before they are implemented.

We shall, therefore, describe another model [Kacprzyk 1979] which is somewhat older than that of Baldwin and Pilsworth but has the advantage of crisp stage decisions, is easier to understand, needs less computations, and gives us the opportunity to illustrate the use of Branch-and-Bound in multi-stage decision analysis. The model is characterized by the following features:

1. There is a crisp and fixed termination time N.
2. The states of the system, $\tilde{x}_i$, are represented by fuzzy sets with discrete supports $\{\sigma_1,\ldots,\sigma_n\}$.
3. The stage decisions, d_i, are crisp with possible values $\{\alpha_1,\ldots,\alpha_m\}$.
4. The stage decisions are constrained by fuzzy sets $\tilde{C}_i(d_i)$.
5. The goal is defined as a fuzzy set $\tilde{G}_N(\tilde{x}_N)$ with reference to state N of the system. Alternatively, subgoals for the different stages can be defined as fuzzy sets $\tilde{G}_i(\tilde{X}_i)$.
6. The transformation from one stage to the next is defined by a function $\tilde{F}$ which maps from the product space $D \times X$ to the space of fuzzy sets in X; that is,

$$\tilde{X}_{i+1} = \tilde{F}(\tilde{X}_i,d_i)$$

Using the notion of a conditioned fuzzy set (see definition 4.2) one can write the membership function of the fuzzy set $\tilde{X}_{i+1}$ as

$$\mu_{\tilde{X}_{i+1}}(x_{i+1}) = \min_{x_i}(\mu_{\tilde{x}_i}(x_i), \mu_{\tilde{x}_{i+1}}(\tilde{x}_{i+1} \mid x_i,d_i)) \tag{4.69}$$

Here $\mu_{\tilde{x}_{i+1}}(\tilde{x}_{i+1} \mid \tilde{x}_i,d_i)$ is the membership function of a fuzzy set conditioned on $\tilde{x}_i$ and d_i. The notation was slightly changed from that of definition 4.2 because otherwise the subscripts would have become too numerous. (In definition 4.2 no other subscript than that of the conditioning parameter was needed.) For the subsequent examples with discrete state and decision spaces the transformation equations can be expressed in a more convenient way.

The Model. The goal is to find the maximizing decision the membership function of which is in analogy to (4.66):

$$\mu_{\tilde{D}^0}(d_0^0,\ldots,d_{N-1}^0) = \max_{d_0,\ldots,d_{N-1}} \min(\mu_{\tilde{C}_0}(d_0),\ldots,\mu_{\tilde{C}_{N-1}}(d_{N-1}),\mu_{\tilde{G}_N}(x)) \quad (4.70)$$

Kacprzyk now suggests formulating (4.69) for the discrete case by using a transformation matrix $\tilde{T}(d_i)$, the (i,j)th element of which is given by

$$T_{ij}(d_i) = \mu_{\tilde{x}_i}(\tilde{x}_i \mid \tilde{x}_j,d_i) \quad (4.71)$$

$\tilde{x}_{i+1}$ and $\tilde{x}_i$ are represented by the column vectors whose ith elements are $\mu_{\tilde{x}_{i+1}}(\tilde{x}_{i+1})$ and $\mu_{\tilde{x}_i}$, respectively. Equation (4.69) can then be written as

$$\tilde{x}_{i+1} = \tilde{T}(d_i)\tilde{x}_i \quad (4.72)$$

which is the max-min matrix product of $\tilde{T}(d_i)$ and $\tilde{x}_i$. Accordingly

$$\tilde{x}_{i+k} = \tilde{T}(d_{i+k-1})\tilde{T}(d_{i+k-2})\ldots\tilde{T}(d_i)\tilde{x}_i \quad (4.73)$$

Since the states of the system are fuzzy Kacprzk also reinterpretes the fuzzy goal $\tilde{G}_N$. He requests the state of the system on stage N to be "as close as possible" to $\tilde{G}_N$; that is, he wants the fuzzy set $\tilde{X}_N$ to be as similar as possible to $\tilde{G}_N$. This similarity is operationalized by the minimization of measures of relative distance, for which he suggests linear or quadratic expressions. We shall here use his linear distance

$$l(\tilde{x}_N,\tilde{G}_N) = \frac{1}{n}\sum_{i=1}^{n} \mid \mu_{\tilde{x}_N}(x_i) - \mu_{\tilde{G}_N}(x_i) \mid \quad (4.74)$$

The degree of membership of $\tilde{G}_N$ might then be considered to be

$$\mu_{\tilde{G}_N}(\tilde{x}_N) = 1 - l(\tilde{x}_N,\tilde{G}_N) \quad (4.74a)$$

Similar constraints can be added for intermediate stages.

Algorithmic Approach. To determine the maximizing decision, Kacprzyk suggests a crisp Branch-and-Bound procedure: since the number of possible decisions at each stage is finite he branches with respect to the $\alpha_j, j = 1,\ldots,m$, mentioned in point 3 of the "features of the model." The bounding and the selection of the node from which to branch next is performed as follows.

Let $D_k = \{d_0,d_1,\ldots,d_k\}$ be called a partial decision. The degree of membership of this partial decision in the fuzzy set decision $\tilde{D}$ is

$$\mu_{\tilde{D}}(d_0,\ldots,d_k) = \min(\mu_{\tilde{C}_0}(d_0),\ldots,\mu_{\tilde{C}_k}(d_k),\ldots,\mu_{\tilde{G}_1},\mu_{\tilde{G}_2},\ldots\mu_{\tilde{G}_k}) \quad (4.75)$$

where the $\mu_{\tilde{G}_j}$ are the membership functions of the goals imposed on intermediary stages.

Let

$$v_k = v_k(D_k) = \mu_{\tilde{D}} \tag{4.76}$$

be called the value of the partial decision D_k and let

$$v'_k = v'_k(D_k) = \min(\mu_{\tilde{C}_0}(d_0), \ldots, \mu_{\tilde{G}_{k-1}}) \tag{4.77}$$

that is, (4.75) without considering the degree of membership of the goal on stage k.

The values of v_k and v'_k are monotonously nonincreasing with increasing k. No partial decision, v_l, containing the partial decision at a node k can therefore attain a value for which $v_l > v_k$. Since we want to maximize $\mu_{\tilde{D}_N}(d_0,\ldots,d_N)$ in (4.73), v can conveniently be used as a bound. Hence branching is always done from the unterminated node with the highest v_k or v'_k and the process terminates when we obtain a complete decision with the value greater than that of all others considered so far.

We shall now present two numerical examples from Kacprzyk [1979], one which only one goal imposed and one with intermediary goals.

Example 4.11

Let $x = \{\sigma_1,\ldots,\sigma_5\}$ and $D = \{\alpha_1,\alpha_2,\alpha_3\}$ be the state and decision spaces, respectively. The (conditional) transformation matrixes (time invariant) T are assumed to be

$$d = \alpha_1$$

x_1 \ x_{t+1}	σ_1	σ_2	σ_3	σ_4	σ_5
σ_1	1	.1	.9	.1	.2
σ_2	.8	.5	.7	.3	.5
σ_3	.7	.9	.5	.5	.7
σ_4	.5	.7	.7	.3	.4
σ_5	.2	.3	.9	.7	.3

$$d = \alpha_2$$

$x_t \backslash x_{t+1}$	σ_1	σ_2	σ_3	σ_4	σ_5
σ_1	.3	.9	1	.4	.6
σ_2	.5	.7	.5	.2	.3
σ_3	.8	.5	.3	.5	.2
σ_4	.9	.7	.7	.9	.5
σ_5	.7	.9	.7	1	.7

$$d = \alpha_3$$

$x_1 \backslash x_{t+1}$	σ_1	σ_2	σ_3	σ_4	σ_5
σ_1	.5	.7	.7	1	.7
σ_2	.7	.8	.1	.5	.9
σ_3	.8	.1	.2	.3	1
σ_4	.9	.2	.3	.5	.8
σ_5	1	.5	.4	.7	.4

The (crisp) termination time is $N = 3$. The fuzzy constraints imposed on state x_0, the decisions of stages 0 through 2, and the fuzzy (terminal) goals are given as follows:

$$\tilde{X}_0 = \{(\sigma_1,.1),(\sigma_2,.2),(\sigma_3,.3),(\sigma_4,.7),(\sigma_5,1)\}$$

$$\tilde{C}_0 = \{(\alpha_1,.3),(\alpha_2,.7),(\alpha_3,1)\}$$

$$\tilde{C}_1 = \{(\alpha_1,.5),(\alpha_2,1),(\alpha_3,.7)\}$$

$$\tilde{C}_2 = \{(\alpha_1,1),(\alpha_2,.8),(\alpha_3,.6)\}$$

$$\tilde{G}_3 = \{(\sigma_1,.4),(\sigma_2,.7),(\sigma_3,1),(\sigma_4,.7),(\sigma_5,.4)\}$$

Solution: Figure 4-9 depicts the Branch-and-Bound tree. We shall describe the computations in more detail.

In node 0 the first decision, d_0, which determines the transformation from stage 0 to stage 1 has to be analyzed. It is constrained by $\tilde{C}_0$ and we compute $v_k(\alpha_j)$ for $k = 0$ and $j = 1,2,3$. We obtain directly from $\tilde{C}_0$

$$v_1(\alpha_1) = .3$$

$$v_1(\alpha_2) = .7$$

$$v_1(\alpha_3) = 1 \leftarrow \max$$

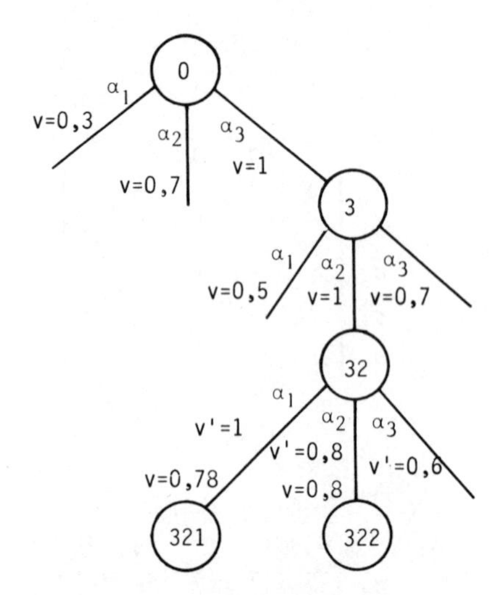

Figure 4-9: Branch-and-Bound tree for Example 4-11.

Since the maximal $v_1(\alpha_j)$ is attained for $j = 3$ we branch to node 3 (the numbers in the nodes indicate the indexes of the partial decision that lead to the node!). Node 3 is on the next level of the tree hierarchy. Hence the decision process proceeds by applying the stage decision α_3 (crisp) to state $\tilde{x}_0 = \{(\sigma_1,.1),(\sigma_2,.2),(\sigma_3,.3),(\sigma_4,.7),(\sigma_5,1)\}$.

Using (4.72) we compute the min-max product of $T(\alpha_3)$ with $\tilde{x}_0$. That is, we first determine componentwise the minimum of $\mu_{\tilde{x}_0}$ and the columns of $T(\alpha_3)$. The degrees of membership of the σ_j for stage 1 are then the maxima of those minima:

For σ_1: $\max(\min\{(.1,.5),(.2,.7),(.3,.8),(.7,.9),(1,1)\})$

$$\mu_{\sigma_1} = \max(.1,.2,.3,.7,1) = 1$$

After the same computations for σ_2 through σ_5 we arrive at

$$\tilde{x}_1(\tilde{x}_0,\sigma_3) = \{(\sigma_1,1),(\sigma_2,.5),(\sigma_3,.4),(\sigma_4,.7),(\sigma_5,.7)\}$$

To determine the next branch from node 3 we have to determine the $v_2(d_1)$ using (4.75):

$$\min(\mu_{d_0}(\alpha_3),\mu_{d_1}(\alpha_1))$$

$$\min(\mu_{d_0}(\alpha_3),\mu_{d_1}(\alpha_2))$$

$$\min(\mu_{d_0}(\alpha_3),\mu_{d_1}(\alpha_3))$$

$$\left.\begin{aligned} v_2(\alpha_3,\alpha_1) &= \min(1,.5) = .5 \\ v_2(\alpha_3,\alpha_2) &= \min(1,1) = 1 \\ v_2(\alpha_3,\alpha_3) &= \min(1,.7) = .7 \end{aligned}\right\} \rightarrow v_2 \max$$

Hence we apply stage decision $d_1 = \alpha_2$ and using (4.73) we arrive at

$$\tilde{x}_2(\tilde{x}_0,\alpha_3,\alpha_2) = \{(\sigma_1,.7),(\sigma_2,.9),(\sigma_3,1),(\sigma_4,.7),(\sigma_5,.7)\}$$

For the next branching we use (4.77) to compute the respective v_3':

$$\begin{aligned} v_3'(\alpha_3,\alpha_2,\alpha_j) &= \min(v_2,\mu_{\tilde{C}_2}(\alpha_j)) \\ v_3'(\alpha_3,\alpha_2,\alpha_1) &= \min(1,1) = 1 \quad \rightarrow v_3' \max \\ v_3'(\alpha_3,\alpha_2,\alpha_2) &= \min(1,.8) = .8 \\ v_3'(\alpha_3,\alpha_2,\alpha_3) &= \min(1,.6) = .6 \end{aligned}$$

Hence we first branch along α_1 and obtain $\tilde{x}_3(\tilde{x}_0,\alpha_3,\alpha_2,\alpha_1)$ by using again (4.73):

$$\tilde{x}_3(\tilde{x}_0,\alpha_3,\alpha_2,\alpha_1) = \{(\sigma_1,.8),(\sigma_2,.9),(\sigma_3,.7),(\sigma_4,.7),(\sigma_5,.7)\}$$

We have not yet taken into consideration the fuzzy goal $\tilde{G}_3$! Hence we determine the distance of $\tilde{G}_3$ as given and $\tilde{x}_3$ as computed by using (4.74) and obtain

$$l(\tilde{x}_3(\cdot),\tilde{G}_3) = \tfrac{1}{5}(.4 + .2 + .3 + .3) = .24$$

According to (4.74a) $\mu_{\tilde{G}_3}(\tilde{x}_3,\tilde{G}_3) = .76$. Now we can determine $v_3(\alpha_3,\alpha_2,\alpha_1)$ as

$$v_3(\alpha_3,\alpha_2,\alpha_1) = \min(v_3',\mu_{\tilde{G}_3}) = \min(1,.76) = .76$$

Before we terminate we have to check whether the partial decision $D_3(\alpha_3,\alpha_2,\alpha_2)$ considering $\tilde{G}_3$ leads to a better value than $D_3(\alpha_3,\alpha_2,\alpha_1)$. Hence we determine $\tilde{x}_3(\alpha_3,\alpha_2,\alpha_2)$ by using (4.73) together with $T(\alpha_2)$ and obtain

$$\begin{aligned} \tilde{x}_3(\tilde{x}_0,\alpha_3,\alpha_2,\alpha_2) &= \{(\sigma_1,.8),(\sigma_2,.7),(\sigma_3,.7),(\sigma_4,.7),(\sigma_5,.7)\} \\ l(\tilde{x}_3,\tilde{G}_3) &= \tfrac{1}{5}(.4 + .3 + .3) = .2 \\ \mu_{\tilde{G}_3}(\tilde{x}_3,\tilde{G}_3) &= 1 - .2 = .8 \end{aligned}$$

and eventually

$$v_3(\alpha_3,\alpha_2,\alpha_2) = \min(v_3,\mu_{\tilde{G}_3}) = \min(.8,.8) = .8$$

In fact the decision $D_3(\alpha_3,\alpha_2,\alpha_2)$ is better than $D_3(\alpha_3,\alpha_2,\alpha_1)$! $D_3(\alpha_3,\alpha_2,\alpha_3)$ can not be better because $v_3'(\alpha_3,\alpha_2,\alpha_3) = .6$! Therefore we can terminate the evaluation process and $D^0 = (\alpha_3,\alpha_2,\alpha_2)$ is the maximizing decision.

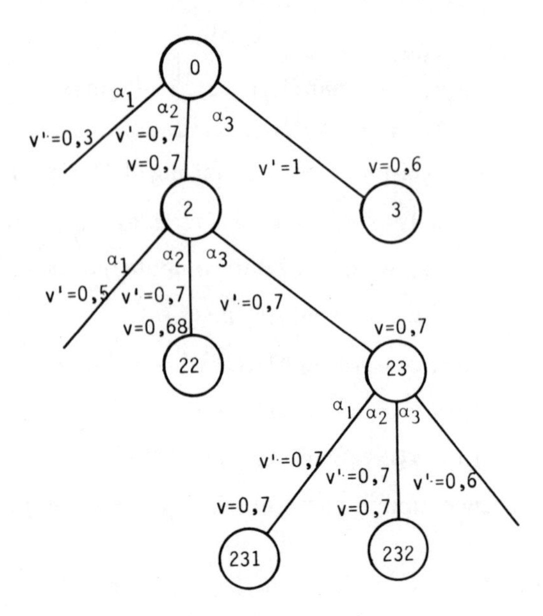

Figure 4-10: Branch-and-Bound tree for example 4.12.

Example 4.12 [Kacprzyk 1979]

Let us modify example 4.11 by adding the two intermediate goals:

$$\tilde{G}_1 = \{(\sigma_1,.7),(\sigma_2,1),(\sigma_3,.7),(\sigma_4,.4),(\sigma_5,.1)\}$$

$$\tilde{G}_2 = \{(\sigma_1,.2),(\sigma_2,.5),(\sigma_3,.7),(\sigma_4,.8),(\sigma_5,1)\}$$

Since we have described the computations in detail for example 4.11 we shall now concentrate on the difference between these two examples. Figure 4-10 shows the Branch-and-Bound tree for this example.

Essentially we just have to insert the evaluations of the intermediate goals at appropriate places into the computations of example 4.11. The v_1 of example 4.11 become the v_1' of example 4.12 because no goal had been excluded in computing the v_2 in example 4.11. Since $\max v_1'(.) = v_1'(\alpha_3) = 1$ we first determine via (4.74) the membership grade of $\tilde{G}_1$ given $x_1(x_0,\alpha_3)$ as computed in example 4.11.

$$\mu_{\tilde{G}_1}(x_1,\tilde{G}_1) = 1 - \tfrac{1}{5}(.3 + .5 + .3 + .6) = .6$$

Hence $v_1(\alpha_3) = \min(1,.6) = .6$.

Since $v_1'(\alpha_2) \Rightarrow .7 > .6$, we also have to evaluate the branch for $d_0 = \alpha_2$! By using (4.73) for α_2 we obtain

$$x_1(x_0,\alpha_2) = \{(\sigma_1,.7),(\sigma_2,.9),(\sigma_3,.7),(\sigma_4,1),(\sigma_5,.7)\}$$

Evaluating with respect to $\tilde{G}_1$:

$$\mu_{\tilde{G}_1}(x_1,\tilde{G}_1) = 1 - \tfrac{1}{5}(.1 + .6 + .6) = .74$$

$$v_1(\alpha_2) = \min(v_1'(\alpha_2),\mu_{\tilde{G}_1})$$

$$= \min(.7,.74) = .7$$

Hence $v_1(\alpha_2) > v_1(\alpha_1)$ and α_2 is preferable.

To branch from node 2 we compute

$$v_2'(\alpha_2,\alpha_1) = \min(.7,.5) = .5$$

$$v_2'(\alpha_2,\alpha_2) = \min(.7,1) = .7$$

$$v_2'(\alpha_2,\alpha_3) = \min(.7,.7) = .7$$

Accordingly we determine $\tilde{x}_1(\tilde{x}_1,\alpha_2)$ and $\tilde{x}_2(\tilde{x}_1,\alpha_3)$ using (4.73):

$$\tilde{x}_2(\alpha_2) = \{(\sigma_1,.9),(\alpha_2,.7),(\sigma_3,1),(\sigma_4,.9),(\sigma_5,.7)\}$$

$$\tilde{x}_2(.,\alpha_3) = \{(\sigma_1,.9),(\sigma_2,.8),(\sigma_3,.7),(\sigma_4,.7),(\sigma_5,.9)\}$$

With respect to these two states we compute $\tilde{G}_2$:

$$\mu_{\tilde{G}_2}(\tilde{x}_1(\alpha_2)) = 1 - \tfrac{1}{5}(.7 + .2 + .3 + .1 + .3) = .68$$

$$\mu_{\tilde{G}_2}(\tilde{x}_1(\alpha_3)) = 1 - \tfrac{1}{5}(.7 + .3 + .1 + .1) = .76$$

Hence,

$$v_2(\alpha_2,\alpha_2) = \min(.7,.68) = .68$$

$$v_2(\alpha_2,\alpha_3) = \min(.7,.76) = .7$$

and α_3 is better than α_2 on stage 2.

On stage 3 we first compute

$$v_3'(\alpha_2,\alpha_3,\alpha_1) = \min(.7,1) = .7$$

$$v_3'(\alpha_2,\alpha_3,\alpha_2) = \min(.7,.8) = .7$$

$$v_3'(\alpha_2,\alpha_3,\alpha_3) = \min(.7,.6) = .6$$

Thus using (4.73), we determine states

$$\tilde{x}_3(\tilde{x}_2,\alpha_1) = \{(\sigma_1,.9),(\sigma_2,.7),(\sigma_3,.9),(\sigma_4,.7),(\sigma_5,.7)\}$$

$$\tilde{x}_3(\tilde{x}_2,\alpha_2) = \{(\sigma_1,.7),(\sigma_2,.9),(\sigma_3,.9),(\sigma_4,.9),(\sigma_5,.7)\}$$

The evaluation of $\tilde{G}_3$ with respect to these two states yields:

$$\mu_{\tilde{G}_3}(x_2,\alpha_1) = 1 - \tfrac{1}{5}(.5 + .1 + .3) = .82$$

$$\mu_{\tilde{G}_3}(x_2,\alpha_2) = 1 - \tfrac{1}{5}(.3 + .1 + .1) = .78$$

and

$$v_3(\alpha_2,\alpha_3,\alpha_1) = \min(.7,.82) = .7$$

$$v_3(\alpha_2,\alpha_3,\alpha_2) = \min(.7,.78) = .7$$

There are two other partial decisions which could possibly lead to a value $v_3 > .7$. Hence we can terminate and the maximizing decisions are

$$D^0 = \{\alpha_2,\alpha_3,\alpha_1\} \qquad \text{and} \qquad D^0 = \{\alpha_2,\alpha_3,\alpha_2\}$$

These two examples have demonstrated that the approach suggested by Kacprzyk seems to be interesting and computationally feasable. The reader should realize, however, that only min-max compositions and a linear distance measure was used. For other operators and more complicated measures of distance the computational effort will certainly increase.

Whether the operators and measures of distance are appropriate and whether the fuzzy constraints, transformation functions, and goals can be interpreted meaningfully depends certainly on the real problem situation that has to be solved—as for any formal model used in practice.

5 MULTI-CRITERIA DECISION MAKING IN ILL-STRUCTURED SITUATIONS

In the recent past it has become more and more obvious that comparing different ways of action as to their desirability, judging the suitability of products, and determining "optimal" solutions in decision problems can in many cases not be done by using a single criterion or a single objective function. This has led to the area of Multi-Criteria Decision Making—in the framework of which numerous evaluation schemes (for instance in the areas of cost benefit analysis or marketing) have been suggested—and to the formulation of the vector-maximum problems in mathematical programming.

Two major areas have evolved both of which concentrate on decision making with several criteria: Multi-Objective Decision Making (MODM) and Multi-Attribute Decision Making (MADM). The main difference between these two directions is that the former concentrates on continuous decision spaces, primarily on mathematical programming with several objective functions, the latter focuses on problems with discrete decision spaces. There are some exceptions to this rule (for instance integer programming with multiple objectives), but for our purposes this distinction seems to be appropriate and sufficient.

The literature on multi-criteria decision making has grown tremendously in the recent past. We shall only mention one survey reference for each of the two areas: Hwang and Yoon [1981] for MADM and Hwang and Masud [1979] for MODM. The interested reader is also referred to Roy and Vincke [1981], to Steuer [1986], and to issues 25(2) and 26(1) of the *European Journal of Operational Research*, which concentrate on problems and models of Multi-Criteria Decision Making.

From another point of view—and referring to the *Optimization*, ... section of chapter 1—one can classify decision models with respect to the type of decision—e.g., is an optimal decision required, is the determination of non-dominated solutions desired, is a certain type of ranking sufficient, is the main problem to evaluate just one alternative with respect to several criteria?

Fuzzy set theory has been applied to most of these types of models. The first section of this chapter considers continuous decision spaces combined with optimization approaches in the framework of (fuzzy) mathematical programming. Models that assume discrete decision spaces will be discussed in the next section, and approaches that apply fuzzy set theory to ranking and outranking models will be discussed in the final part of the chapter. The entire chapter 5 is devoted to global models. The local or interactive approaches in multi-criteria analyses that use fuzzy sets will be discussed in chapter 7.

Fuzzy Multi-Criteria Programming

Multi-Objective Decision Making

In mathematical programming the MODM problem is often called the "vector-maximum" problem, which was first mentioned by Kuhn and Tucker [Kuhn, Tucker 1951].

Definition 5.1

The *vector-maximum problem* is defined as

$$\text{“maximize”}\ \{Z(x) \mid x \in X\}$$

where $Z(x) = (z_1(x), \ldots, z_K(x))$ is a vector-valued function of $x \in \mathbb{R}^n$ into $\mathbb{R}^K$ and X is the *solution space*.

Two stages can generally be distinguished at least categorically, in vector-maximum optimization:

1. The determination of efficient solutions
2. The determination of an optimal compromise solution

Definition 5.2

Let "max" $\{Z(x) | x \in X\}$ be a vector-maximum problem such as defined in definition 5.1. Then x is an *efficient solution* if there is no $x' \in X$ such that

$$z_i'(x') \geq z_i(x) \qquad i = 1,\ldots,K$$

and

$$z_{i_0}(x') > z_{i_0}(x) \qquad \text{for at least on } i_0 \in \{1,\ldots,K\}$$

The set of all efficient solutions is generally called the *complete solution.*

Definition 5.3

An *optimal compromise solution* of a vector-maximum problem is a solution $x \in X$ which is preferred by the decision maker to all other solutions, taking into consideration all criteria contained in the vector-valued objective function.

It is generally accepted, that an optimal compromise solution has to be an efficient solution according to definition 5.2. In the following we shall restrict our considerations to the determination of optimal compromise solutions in mathematical programming problems with vector-valued objective functions.

Three major approaches are known to single out, from the set of efficient solutions, one specific solution which qualifies as an optimal compromise solution:

1. The utility approach [e.g., Keeney, Raiffa 1976]
2. Goal programming [e.g., Charnes, Cooper 1961]
3. Interactive approaches [e.g., Dyer 1972/1973].

The first two of these approaches assume that the decision maker can specify his "preference function" with respect to the combination of the individual objective functions in advance. This can either take the form of a weighted aggregation of the individual objective functions or it can be a distance function referring, for instance, to the ideal solution. Generally they assume that the combination of the individual objective functions that yields the compromise solution with the highest overall utility is achieved by linear combinations (i.e., by adding the weighted individual objective functions). The third approach uses only local information in order to arrive at an acceptable compromise solution, and will be discussed in chapter 7.

We shall first discuss the case with several crisp objective functions and crisp constraints—the classical vector-maximum problem.

For the case of linear programming, the vector-maximum problem is

$$\text{“maximize”} \quad z = \begin{Bmatrix} f_1(x) \\ \vdots \\ f_K(x) \end{Bmatrix} \mathrel{\widehat{=}} \begin{Bmatrix} c_1^T x \\ \vdots \\ c_K^T x \end{Bmatrix} \tag{5.1}$$

$$\text{such that} \quad Ax \le b$$

$$x \ge 0$$

where z is a k-vector and all other components are defined as usual. Let us transform this problem by assuming that the decision maker does not exhibit maximizing behavior, but rather acts as a satisfier: this assumption is usually made in “goal programming,” one of the usual ways to solve the vector-maximum problem. The objective functions are thus calibrated by aspiration levels z_i and (5.1) becomes

$$\text{find } x$$

$$\text{such that} \quad c_i^T x \ge z_i \qquad i = 1,\ldots,K \tag{5.2}$$

$$Ax \le b$$

$$x \ge 0$$

To illustrate a fuzzy-set approach to this problem we shall use the following example [Zimmermann 1983b].

Example 5.1

A company manufactures two products, 1 and 2, on given capacities. Product 1 yields a profit of $2 per piece and product 2 of $1 per piece. While product 2 can be exported, yielding a revenue of $2 per piece in foreign countries, product 1 needs imported raw materials at $1 per piece. Two goals are established: (a) profit maximization and (b) maximum improvement of the balance of trade (that is, maximum difference of exports minus imports). This problem can be modelled as follows:

$$\text{“maximize”} \quad Z(x) = \begin{pmatrix} -1 & 2 \\ 2 & 1 \end{pmatrix} \begin{pmatrix} x_1 \\ x_2 \end{pmatrix} \quad \begin{matrix} \text{(effect on balance of trade)} \\ \text{(profit)} \end{matrix}$$

$$\text{such that} \quad -x_1 + 3x_2 \le 21$$

$$x_1 + 3x_2 \le 27$$

$$4x_1 + 3x_2 \le 45$$

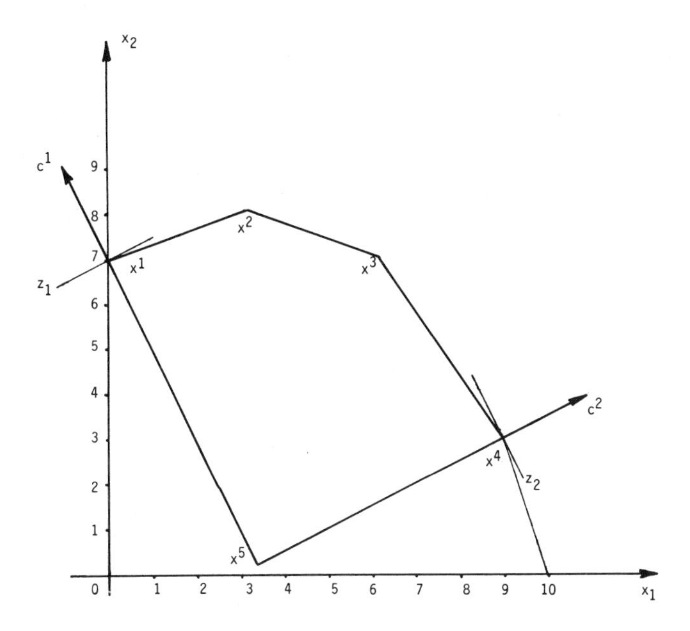

Figure 5-1: The Vector-maximum Problem.

$$3x_1 + \quad x_2 \leq 30$$

$$x_1, x_2 \geq 0$$

Figure 5-1 shows the solution space of this problem. The "complete solution" is the edge $x^1 - x^2 - x^3 - x^4$. x^1 is optimal with respect to objective function $z_1(x) = -x_1 + 2x_2$ (i.e., best improvement of balance of trade). x^4 is optimal with respect to objective function $z_2(x) = 2x_1 + x_2$ (profit). The "optimal" values are $z_1(x^1) = 14$ (maximum net export) and $z_2(x^4) = 21$ (maximum profit), respectively. For $x^1 = (0,7)^T$, total profit is $z_2(x^1) = 7$ and $x^4 = (9,3)^T$ yields $z_1(x^4) = -3$ (a net import of 3).

Solution $x^5 = (3.4;0.2)^T$ is the solution that yields $z_1(x^5) = -3$, $z_2(x^5) = 7$, which is the lowest "justifiable" value of the objective functions in the sense that a further decrease of the value of one objective function can not be balanced or even counteracted by an increase of the value of the other objective function.

It seems reasonable that the satisfaction of the decision maker increases or decreases monotonously as he approaches the aspiration levels (depending on whether they represent upper or lower bounds of acceptability).

Assuming that the decision maker has upper and lower bounds $\overline{c}_i$ and $\underline{c}_i$

for his aspirations, such that he does not accept solutions for which $c_i^T x$ is smaller than $\underline{c}_i$, and assuming that he is fully satisfied whenever $c_i^T x$ is equal or larger than $\bar{c}_i$, we can express his objectives by fuzzy sets whose membership functions increase monotonously from 0 at $\underline{c}_i$ to 1 at $\bar{c}_i$. Denoting these fuzzy sets as fuzzy constraints, $\tilde{C}(x)$, (5.2) can be written as

$$\begin{aligned} &\text{find } x \\ &\text{such that} \quad Cx \gtrsim \underline{c} \\ &\qquad\qquad\quad Ax \leq b \\ &\qquad\qquad\quad\ \ x \geq 0 \end{aligned} \tag{5.3}$$

Now we can directly apply model (4.12). The only problem that remains is how to establish the $\underline{c}_i$ and $\bar{c}_i$, respectively. We can either assume that the decision maker establishes aspiration levels for himself, or we can compute those levels as a function of the solution space. For the latter approach it was suggested [Zimmermann 1978] we use the individual optima as upper bounds and "least justifiable" solutions as lower bounds.

Example 5.1 (continued)

We first assume that the decision maker can not specify aspiration levels for the objective functions. We, therefore, define properties of the solution space for "calibration" of the objective functions. Let us consider the objective functions as fuzzy sets of the type "solutions acceptable with respect to objective function 1, or 2, respectively." In this example we would have to construct two fuzzy sets: "solutions acceptable with respect to objective function 1" and "solutions acceptable with respect to objective function 2." As calibration points we shall use the respective "individual optima" and the "least justifyable solution."

The membership functions $\mu_1(x)$ and $\mu_2(x)$ of the fuzzy sets characterizing the objective functions rise linearly from 0 to 1 at the highest achievable values of $z_1(x) = 14$ and $z_2(x) = 21$, respectively. This means that we assume that the level of satisfaction with respect to the improvement of the balance of trade rises from 0 for imports of 3 units or more to 1 for exports of 14 and more and that the satisfaction level with respect to profit rises from 0 if the profit is 7 or less to 1 if total profit is 21 or more.

$$\mu_1(x) = \begin{cases} 0 & \text{for } z_1(x) \leq -3 \\ \dfrac{z_1(x) + 3}{17} & \text{for } -3 < z_1(x) \leq 14 \\ 1 & \text{for } 14 < z_1(x) \end{cases}$$

$$\mu_2(x) = \begin{cases} 0 & \text{for } z_2(x) \leq 7 \\ \dfrac{z_2(x) - 7}{14} & \text{for } 7 < z_2(x) \leq 21 \\ 1 & \text{for } 21 < z_2(x) \end{cases}$$

We are now faced with a problem of type 4.3a in which crisp constraints have been added (i.e., the problem consists of 2 rows representing our fuzzified objectives and 4 crisp constraints). We can now employ (4.12).

In analogy to formulation (4.12) and including the crisp constraints we arrive at the following problem formulation:

$$\begin{aligned} \text{maximize} \quad & \lambda \\ \text{such that} \quad & \lambda \leq .05882x_1 + .117x_2 + .1764 \\ & \lambda \leq .1429x_1 + .714x_2 - .5 \\ & 21 \geq -x_1 + 3x_2 \\ & 27 \geq x_1 + 3x_2 \\ & 45 \geq 4x_1 + 3x_2 \\ & 30 \geq 3x_1 + x_2 \\ & x \geq 0, \end{aligned} \tag{5.4}$$

depicted in figure 5-2.

The maximum degree of overall satisfaction ($\lambda = .74$) is achieved for the solution $x^0 = (5.03;7.32)^T$. This is the "maximizing solution" which yields in our example a profit of \$17.38 and an export contribution of \$4.58. The basic solutions x^1 and x^4 yield $\lambda = 0$.

If the optimal solution to (5.4) is a singleton then this is also the desired optimal solution. Werners [1984, p. 73] has pointed to the fact, however, that the final simplex tableau of (5.1) might indicate multiple optimal solutions (dual degeneracy). In this case not all of the optimal solutions might be efficient solutions to the vector-maximum problem—that is, it might be possible to improve these nonefficient solutions by increasing λ_0 further by using the slack of the constraints that are not binding with respect to the first optimal solution.

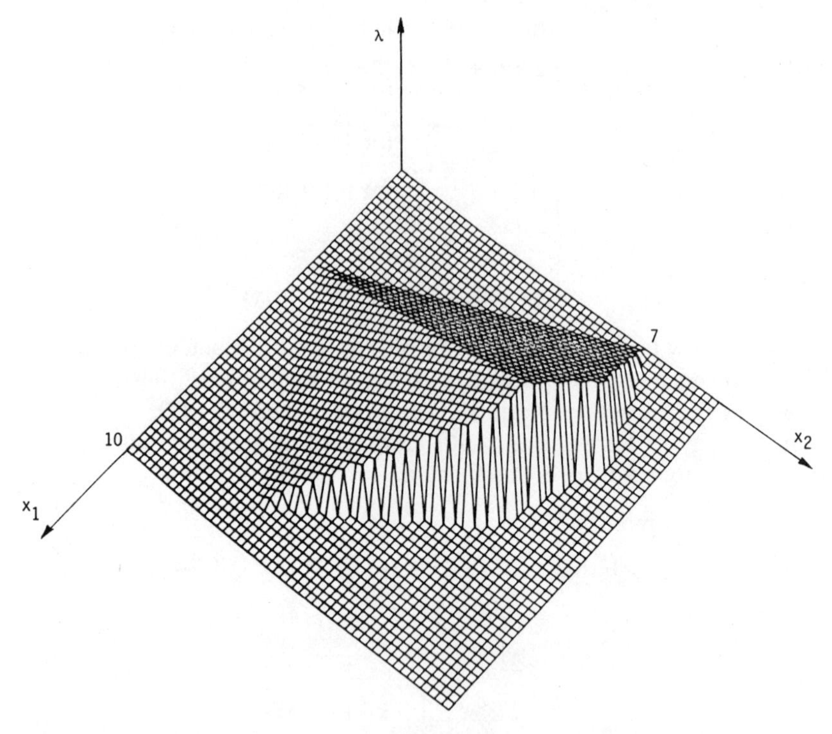

Figure 5-2: Maximizing Decision for Vector-Maximum Problem.

When we consider the case in which fuzzy constraints have to be taken into consideration, the problem is of the type:

$$\begin{aligned} \text{“maximize”} \quad & z = Cx \\ \text{such that} \quad & Ax \lessapprox b \\ & Dx \leq b' \\ & x \geq 0 \end{aligned} \tag{5.5}$$

where C is a $k \times n$ matrix, z is a vector with k components, and all the other elements are of the usual dimension.

Essentially, for this case, we could use the approach described above. However, two additional complications arise.

The first complication is that, in classical (crisp) vector-maximum theory, "efficiency of solutions" has been defined under the assumption that solutions can only be split into feasable and nonfeasable solutions and that only the former are considered as applicants for efficient solutions. But in (5.2), solutions do only not differ with respect to the associated values of the objective functions, they also differ with respect to their degree of feasibility. Definition 5.2, therefore, has to be extended. Werners [1984, p. 79] notion of fuzzy-efficiency gives us the following definition.

Definition 5.4

Let f_l: $X \to \mathbb{R}^1$, $l = 1,\ldots,K$, be objective functions of problem (5.2) and μ_i: $X \to [0,1]$, $i = 1,\ldots,m$, the membership functions representing the fuzzy constraints of (5.5). A solution $x \in X$ is called *fuzzy efficient* if there is no $x' \in X$ such that

$$f_l(x') \geq f_l(x) \qquad \text{for all } l = 1,\ldots,K$$

and

$$\mu_i(x') \geq \mu_i(x) \qquad \text{for all } i = 1,\ldots,m$$

and

$$(f_{l_0}(x') > f_{l_0}(x) \qquad \text{for at least one } l_0 \in \{1,\ldots,K\}$$

or

$$\mu_{i_0}(x') > \mu_{i_0}(x) \qquad \text{for at least one } i_0 \in \{1,\ldots,m\})$$

The second complication is that in problems there may not exist uniquely defined individual optima that can be used as upper bounds to calibrate the fuzzy sets representing the objective functions. The "least justifiable" solution used above may not be available either. However, we can then, employ the approach used to derive model (4.22). The extension to multiple objectives is straightforward.

Some modifications have to be made concerning the lower bound when calibrating the fuzzy goal sets: We still consider as a lower bound of aspiration, for which the degree of membership is equal to 0, the least functional value a decision maker can obtain if the individual optimal solutions, x_l^0, x_l^1, of the other objective functions are choosen. Since, however, these optima are no longer uniquely defined the respective degrees of belonging to the solution space also have to be taken into account. $\mu_l(x)$, $l = 1,\ldots,k$, is therefore considered to be zero if either

$$f_l(x) \leq \min_{l'=1}^{k} f_l(x_{l'}^1) = f_l' \tag{5.6}$$

or

$$f_l(x) \leq \min_{l'=1}^{k} f_l(x_{l'}^0) = f_{l'}'$$

Then $\quad f_{02} = \min \{f_{l}', f_{l'}'\}$.

The crisp equivalent model to (5.5) is then

$$\begin{aligned} &\text{maximize} \quad \lambda \\ &\text{such that} \quad \lambda(F_1 - F_0) - Cx \leq -F_0 \\ &\qquad\qquad \lambda p \qquad + Ax \leq b + p \\ &\qquad\qquad\qquad\qquad Dx \leq b' \\ &\qquad\qquad\qquad\qquad \lambda, x \geq 0 \end{aligned} \tag{5.7}$$

Here $F_0 = (f_{01}, \ldots, f_{0K})^T$, $F_1 = (f_{11}, \ldots, f_{1K})^T$, with f_{1l}, $l = 1, \ldots, K$, fuzzy individual optimal values; C is the $k \times n$ matrix defined in (5.5); and all the other coefficients are defined as before.

If there exists a unique optimal solution to (5.6) then this solution is also fuzzy efficient [Werners 1984, p. 88]. If this is not the case a solution that is fuzzy efficient can be determined by using the lexmaxmin algorithm [see Werners 1984; Behringer 1977, 1981].

The use of model (5.6) shall now be illustrated by using an example by Leberling [see Leberling 1983; Werners 1984]:

Example 5.2

Let us consider the following model:

$$\begin{aligned} &\text{“maximize”} \quad F = \begin{cases} 100x_1 + 150x_2 \\ .1x_1 + .05x_2 \end{cases} \\ &\text{such that} \quad x_1 + x_2 \lessapprox 1000 \\ &\qquad\qquad 3x_1 + 2x_2 \lessapprox 2400 \\ &\qquad\qquad x_1 \lessapprox 600 \\ &\qquad\qquad x_2 \lessapprox 800 \\ &\qquad\qquad x_1, x_2 \geq 0 \end{aligned} \tag{5.8}$$

The tolerance intervales of the constraints are assumed to be $p_1 = 100$, $p_2 = 200$, $p_3 = 200$, and $p_4 = 100$.

The f_{1l} and f_{0l} can be determined to be: the individual optima for $\mu_i = 0$ are $x_1^0 = (200{,}900)$ and $x_2^0 = (800{,}100)$ for $\mu_i = 1$, $x_1^1 = (200{,}800)$, $x_2^1 = (600{,}300)$. Hence,

$$f_1(x_1^0) = 155{,}000 \qquad f_2(x_1^0) = 65$$
$$f_1(x_2^0) = 95{,}000 \qquad f_2(x_2^1) = 85$$

According to (5.6) the lower bounds of the acceptable functional values are therefore

$$f_{01} = 95{,}000 \qquad f_{02} = 60$$

and the upper bounds above which $\mu_l(x) = 1$ are

$$f_{11} = 155{,}000 \qquad f_{12} = 85$$

The crisp equivalent model to (5.8) is now

$$\begin{aligned}
&\text{maximize} \quad \lambda \\
&\text{such that} \quad \lambda(155{,}000 - 95{,}000) - 100x_1 - 150x_2 \leq -95{,}000 \\
&\qquad \lambda(85 - 60) - .1x_1 - .05x_2 \leq -60 \\
&\qquad \lambda 100 + x_1 + x_2 \leq 1100 \\
&\qquad \lambda 200 + 3x_1 + 2x_2 \leq 2600 \\
&\qquad \lambda 200 + x_1 \leq 800 \\
&\qquad \lambda 100 + x_2 \leq 900 \\
&\qquad \lambda, x_1, x_2 \geq 0
\end{aligned} \tag{5.9}$$

The optimal solution to (5.9) is $\lambda_0 = .56$, $x^0 = (466.7, 544.4)$. Even though this solution is not the only optimal one further investigation shows, that it is fuzzy efficient.

Multi-Attribute Decision Making (MADM)

By contrast to the multi-objective decision-making problem, an example of which is the vector-maximum problem as defined in definition 5.1, the basic model of multi-attribute decision making can be described as follows:

Let $X = \{x_i\}$, $i = 1,\ldots,n$, be a (finite) set of decision alternatives and $G = \{g_j\}, j = 1,\ldots,m$, a (finite) set of goals, attributes or criteria according to which the desirability of an alternative is to be judged. The aim of MADM is to determine the optimal alternative x^0 with the highest degree of desirability with respect to all relevant goals g_j.

Basically MADM consists of two phases:

I. The aggregation of the judgments with respect to all goals and per decision alternatives.
II. The rank ordering of the decision alternatives according to the aggregated judgments.

In crisp MADM models it is usually assumed that the final judgments of the alternatives are expressed as real numbers. In this case the second phase does not pose any particular problems and, therefore, suggested algorithms concentrate on phase I. Fuzzy models are sometimes justified by the argument, that the goals g_j or their attainment by the alternatives x_i, cannot be defined or judged crisply but only as fuzzy sets. In this case the final judgments are also represented by fuzzy sets, which have to be ordered to determine the optimal alternative. Then the second phase is, of course, by far not trivial.

The approaches that have been suggested to solve the MADM problem with fuzzy components differ from each other in a number of points:

- They either consider phase I, phase II, or both phases of MADM.
- They determine crisp or fuzzy solutions to the problem, or they offer vectors of measures of dominance and leave the final evaluation to the decision maker.
- They use different methods for the aggregation of phase I and for ranking of phase II and hence are computationally more or less efficient.
- They differ in their assumptions.
- They are more or less discriminatory—that is, they differ with respect to the degree to which they distinguish between different alternatives and their characteristics. Some authors strive after very sensitive methods and others stress the stability of their resulting ratings.

Among the numerous models and methods available we shall present representatives of the different kinds, trying to cover the entire scope as well as possible. None of these methods can be considered best. Which of them is most appropriate will depend on the problem and the attitude of the decision maker. After presentation of the methods we will compare some of their results and the reader should be able to judge by himself whether the additional effort and sophistication of some models is justified by their results.

One approach which has been successfully applied to MADM and which has some relationships to the fuzzy-set approach is Saaty's *Analytic Hierarchy Process* [Saaty 1978, 1980; Saaty, Vargas 1982]. It will not be described here in detail because the literature on it is voluminous and well accessable to everybody and because it is not characteristic for the fuzzy-set models considered in this section. It rather competes and supplements the type of analysis that will be described in this section and to the evaluational model in chapter 2. We will, however, use Saaty's approach as part of other models.

The fuzzy MADM model that is closest to the Bellman-Zadeh model of definition 2.1 and resembles the approaches adopted in fuzzy linear programming is Yager's [1978] model, which will be described first:

Fuzzy MADM on the Basis of Saaty's Priorities

Using Crisp Weights [Yager 1978]. Essentially, Yager assumes a finite set of alternative actions $X = \{x_i\}, i = 1,\ldots,n$, and a finite set of goals (attributes) $G = \{\tilde{g}_j\}, j = 1,\ldots,m$. The $\tilde{g}_j$, $\tilde{g}_j = \{x_i, \mu_{\tilde{g}_j}(x_i)\}$, are fuzzy sets the degrees of membership of which represent the normalized degrees of attainment of the jth goal by alternative x_i. The fuzzy set decision, $\tilde{D}$, is then the intersection of all fuzzy goals, that is,

$$\mu_{\tilde{D}}(x_i) = \min_{j=1}^{m} \mu_{\tilde{g}_j}(x_i), \qquad i = 1,\ldots,n,$$

and the maximizing decision is defined to be the x_i' for which

$$\mu_{\tilde{D}}(x_i') = \max_{x_i} \min_{j} \mu_{\tilde{g}_j}(x_i) \tag{5.10}$$

Yager now allows for different importance of the goals and expresses this by exponentially weighting of the membership functions of the goals. If w_j are the weights of the goals the weighted membership functions, $\mu'_{\tilde{g}_j}$, are

$$\mu'_{\tilde{g}_j}(x_i) = (\mu_{\tilde{g}_j}(x_i))^{w_j} \tag{5.11}$$

For determination of the w_j Yager suggests the use of Saaty's method—viz the determination of the reciprocal matrix [Saaty 1978] by pairwise comparison of the goals with respect to their relative importance. The components of the eigenvector of this $m \times m$ matrix corresponding to the maximal eigenvalue are then used as weights.

The rational behind using the weights as exponents to express the importance of a goal can be found in the definition of the modifier *very* [Zimmermann 1985b, p. 128]. There the modifier *very* was defined as the squaring operation. Thus the higher the importance of a goal the larger should be the exponent of its representing fuzzy set, at least for normalized fuzzy sets and when using the min-operator for the intersection of the fuzzy goals.

Example 5.3 [Yager 1978]

Let $X = \{x_i\}$, $i = 1,\ldots,3$, be the set of alternatives and $G = \{\tilde{g}_j\}$, $j = 1,\ldots,4$, the goals.

$$\tilde{g}_1 = \{(x_1,.7),(x_2,.5),(x_3,.4)\}$$

$$\tilde{g}_2 = \{(x_1,.3),(x_2,.8),(x_3,.6)\}$$

$$\tilde{g}_3 = \{(x_1,.2),(x_2,.3),(x_3,.8)\}$$

$$\tilde{g}_4 = \{(x_1,.5),(x_2,.1),(x_3,.2)\}$$

By pairwise comparison the following reciprocal matrix has been determined, expressing the relative importance of the goals with respect to each other:

$$W = \begin{array}{c} \\ g_1 \\ g_2 \\ g_3 \\ g_4 \end{array} \begin{array}{c} \begin{array}{cccc} g_1 & g_2 & g_3 & g_4 \end{array} \\ \begin{pmatrix} 1 & 3 & 7 & 9 \\ \frac{1}{3} & 1 & 6 & 7 \\ \frac{1}{7} & \frac{1}{6} & 1 & 3 \\ \frac{1}{9} & \frac{1}{7} & \frac{1}{3} & 1 \end{pmatrix} \end{array}$$

The eigenvector $w = (w_j)$, $j = 1,\ldots,4$, for which $\Sigma_{i=1}^{4} w_i = 4$, is

$$w = (2.32, 1.2, .32, .16)$$

Weighting the g_j appropriately yields

$$\tilde{g}'_1 = \{(x_1,.44),(x_2,.2),(x_3,.12)\}$$

$$\tilde{g}'_2 = \{(x_1,.24),(x_2,.76),(x_3,.54)\}$$

$$\tilde{g}'_3 = \{(x_1,.2),(x_2,.68),(x_3,.93)\}$$

$$\tilde{g}'_4 = \{(x_1,.9),(x_2,.69),(x_3,.77)\}$$

Hence,

$$D_{\max} = \max_{x_i} \min_{\mu_j} (\mu'_{\tilde{g}_j}(x_i)) = (x_1,.24)$$

The reader is encouraged to reflect upon the effect that the suggested weighting procedure has on the membership functions of the goals and what $D_{\max} = (x_1,.24)$ means.

The measure of ranking the decision alternatives is obviously the $\mu_{\tilde{D}}(x_i)$. For the ranking of fuzzy sets in the unit interval Yager [1981] suggests another criterion, which bases on properties of the supports of the fuzzy sets rather than on the degree of membership. This is particularly applicable when ranking different (fuzzy) degrees of truth and similar linguistic variables and will be described further down.

Using Fuzzy Numbers as Weights [Laarhoven, Pedrycz 1983]. The authors concentrate on the first phase of MADM—that is, on the determination of fuzzy ratings for the decision alternatives, which can then be used for the ranking in phase II. Laarhoven and Pedrycz's approach is characterized by three features:

- They can use fuzzy numbers with triangular membership functions to simplify the calculations.
- It is possible to handle decision situations in which there is either no information or multiple information available with respect to the preferability of alternatives,
- Using the principle of hierarchic composition, the authors apply priority theory on two levels: in assigning weights to the criteria and for weighting the alternatives with respect to each of their criteria separately!

The method follows closely the classical weighting procedure:

1. It first rates the importance of the criteria (goals) with respect to each other. This results in criteria weights.
2. It rates all alternatives x_i by pairwise comparison with respect to each single criterion. This results in relative ratings per alternative and criteria.
3. It computes a final rating per alternative by adding for each alternative x_i relative ratings with respect to all criteria, multiplied by their criteria weights.

The main difference from the classical approach is, of course, that the weights are all considered to be fuzzy numbers and that the eigenvector of Saaty's reciprocal matrix also consists of fuzzy numbers. This makes the computations much more involved than when dealing with ordinary matrixes.

To understand the fuzzy mathematics involved we have to introduce some definitions [see also Zimmermann 1985b, ch. 5].

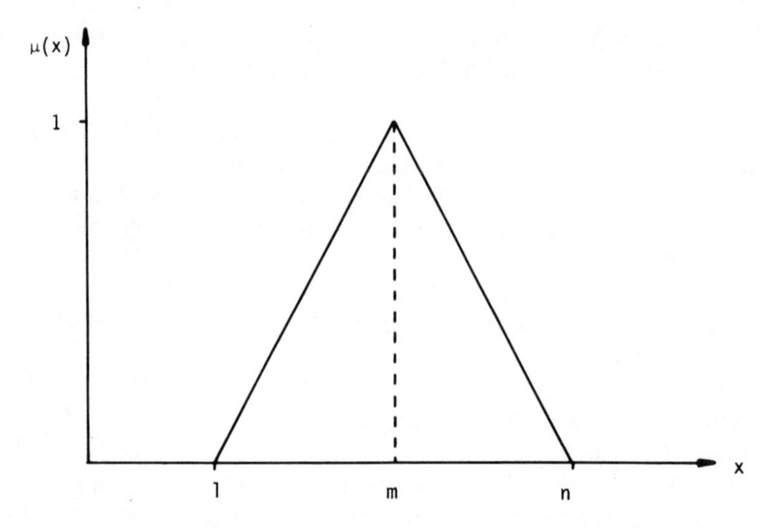

Figure 5-3: Triangular Fuzzy Number.

Definition 5.5

A *triangular fuzzy number* on $\mathbb{R}$ (figure 5-3) is characterized by its membership function $\mu_{\tilde{N}}(x)$: $\mathbb{R} \to [0,1]$ with

$$\mu_{\tilde{N}}(x) = \begin{cases} \dfrac{1}{m-1}x - \dfrac{1}{m-1} & \text{for } x \in [l,m] \\ \dfrac{1}{m-n}x - \dfrac{n}{m-n} & \text{for } x \in [m,n] \\ 0 & \text{otherwise} \end{cases}$$

Definition 5.6

On the basis of the extension principle, addition and multiplication of two fuzzy numbers $\tilde{N}_1$ and $\tilde{N}_2$ are defined via their membership functions as follows.

Addition:

$$\mu_{\tilde{N}_1 \oplus \tilde{N}_2}(z) = \sup_{\substack{(x,y) \in \mathbb{R}^2 \\ z=x+y}} (\min(\mu_{\tilde{N}_1}(x), \mu_{\tilde{N}_2}(y)))$$

$$= \sup_{x \in \mathbb{R}} (\min(\mu_{\tilde{N}_1}(x), \mu_{\tilde{N}_2}(z-x)))$$

Multiplication:

$$\mu_{\tilde{N}_1 \odot \tilde{N}_2}(z) = \sup_{\substack{(x,y) \in \mathbb{R}^2 \\ z = x \cdot y}} (\min(\mu_{\tilde{N}_1}(x), \mu_{\tilde{N}_2}(y)))$$

$$= \sup_{x \in \mathbb{R}} (\min(\mu_{\tilde{N}_1}(x), \mu_{\tilde{N}_2}(z/x)))$$

For triangular fuzzy numbers, the computations involved in definition 5.6 are rather laborious. Laarhoven and Pedrycz, therefore, use the approximation formulas given by Dubois and Prade [1980]. These are

$$\tilde{N}_1(l_1, m_1, n_1) \oplus \tilde{N}_2(l_2, m_2, n_2) = \tilde{N}_3(l_1 + l_2, m_1 + m_2, n_1 + n_2)$$

$$\tilde{N}_1(l_1, m_1, n_1) \odot \tilde{N}_2(l_2, m_2, n_2) \simeq \tilde{N}_3(l_1 \cdot l_2, m_1 \cdot m_2, n_1 \cdot n_2) \tag{5.12}$$

The weights in the first and the second step are now determined by extending Saaty's operations to fuzzy-extended operations—that is, by considering the ratios w_i/w_j as fuzzy numbers. For the details of the computations see the original paper by Laarhoven and Pedrycz [1983]. We shall illustrate the procedure by the authors' example.

Example 5.4

Suppose that at a university the post of professor in Operations Research is vacant. After a first selection, three serious candidates remain, we shall call them A, B, and C. A committee has been installed to give advice as to which applicant is the best qualified for the job. The committee has three members and they have identified the following decision criteria:

C_1: mathematical creativity
C_2: creativity in implementations
C_3: administrative capabilities
C_4: human maturity

The members of the committee estimate the relative importance of the 4 criteria (goals) by providing fuzzy numbers as shown in table 5-1. This table indicates that not all committee members have provided estimates for each pairwise comparison. The authors provide rules to normalize the lack and abundance of judgments to come up with appropriate numbers for each element of Saaty's reciprocal matrix.

The relative importances of the criteria are derived from table 5-1 and shown in table 5-2. The three numbers in each row of table 5-2 denote again the l, m, and n of the fuzzy numbers representing the weights $\tilde{w}_i$. Independent of the ranking of the criteria the experts now estimate pairwise the alternatives as to their merit for each single criteria. The results may be as shown in tables 5-3a through 5-3d. The resulting ratings, λ_{i_j}, and the final scores of the alternatives are shown in table 5-4. These ratings are multiplied—using

Table 5-1: Pairwise comparisons of the criteria

	C_1	C_2	C_3	C_4
C_1	(1,1,1)	$(\frac{2}{3},1,\frac{3}{2})$ $(\frac{2}{5},\frac{1}{2},\frac{2}{3})$ $(\frac{3}{2},2,\frac{5}{2})$	$(\frac{2}{3},1,\frac{3}{2})$	$(\frac{2}{7},\frac{1}{3},\frac{2}{5})$ $(\frac{2}{7},\frac{1}{3},\frac{2}{5})$ $(\frac{2}{5},\frac{1}{2},\frac{2}{3})$
C_2	$(\frac{2}{3},1,\frac{3}{2})$ $(\frac{3}{2},2,\frac{5}{2})$ $(\frac{2}{5},\frac{1}{2},\frac{2}{3})$	(1,1,1)	$(\frac{5}{2},3,\frac{7}{2})$ $(\frac{5}{2},3,\frac{7}{2})$	$(\frac{2}{3},1,\frac{3}{2})$ $(\frac{2}{3},1,\frac{3}{2})$ $(\frac{3}{2},2,\frac{5}{2})$
C_3	$(\frac{2}{3},1,\frac{3}{2})$	$(\frac{2}{7},\frac{1}{3},\frac{2}{5})$ $(\frac{2}{7},\frac{1}{3},\frac{2}{5})$	(1,1,1)	$(\frac{2}{5},\frac{1}{2},\frac{2}{3})$
C_4	$(\frac{5}{2},3,\frac{7}{2})$ $(\frac{5}{2},3,\frac{7}{2})$ $(\frac{3}{2},2,\frac{5}{2})$	$(\frac{2}{3},1,\frac{3}{2})$ $(\frac{2}{3},1,\frac{3}{2})$ $(\frac{2}{5},\frac{1}{2},\frac{2}{3})$	$(\frac{3}{2},2,\frac{5}{2})$	(1,1,1)

Table 5-2: Relative importance of criteria

Criterion	*Estimated weight* ($\tilde{w}_i$)
C_1	(0.149,0.194,0.256)
C_2	(0.235,0.319,0.431)
C_3	(0.112,0.140,0.180)
C_4	(0.263,0.347,0.451)

extended multiplication—by the fuzzy weights $\tilde{w}_i$ and added per alternative x_j. The resulting ratings, $\tilde{r}_j$, are the fuzzy triangular numbers shown in figure 5-4. They can now be used in phase II to rank the alternatives.

Table 5-3a: $\tilde{R}_1$ pairwise comparison of alternatives under criterion 1

	x_1	x_2	x_3
x_1	(1,1,1)	$(\frac{2}{3},1,\frac{3}{2})$ $(\frac{2}{3},1,\frac{3}{2})$	$(\frac{2}{3},1,\frac{3}{2})$ $(\frac{2}{5},\frac{1}{2},\frac{2}{3})$
x_2	$(\frac{2}{3},1,\frac{3}{2})$ $(\frac{2}{3},1,\frac{3}{2})$	(1,1,1)	$(\frac{2}{5},\frac{1}{2},\frac{2}{3})$
x_3	$(\frac{2}{3},1,\frac{3}{2})$ $(\frac{3}{2},2,\frac{5}{2})$	$(\frac{3}{2},2,\frac{5}{2})$	(1,1,1)

Table 5-3b: The matrix $\tilde{R}_2$: pairwise comparison of alternatives under criterion 2

	x_1	x_2	x_3
x_1	$(1,1,1)$	$(\frac{5}{2},3,\frac{7}{2})$	$(\frac{3}{2},2,\frac{5}{2})$
x_2	$(\frac{2}{7},\frac{1}{3},\frac{2}{5})$	$(1,1,1)$	—
x_3	$(\frac{2}{5},\frac{1}{2},\frac{2}{3})$	—	$(1,1,1)$

Table 5-3c: $\tilde{R}_3$: Pairwise comparison of alternatives under criterion 3

	x_1	x_2	x_3
x_1	$(1,1,1)$	$(\frac{5}{2},3,\frac{7}{2})$ $(\frac{5}{2},3,\frac{7}{2})$ $(\frac{3}{2},2,\frac{5}{2})$	$(\frac{5}{2},3,\frac{7}{2})$
x_2	$(\frac{2}{7},\frac{1}{3},\frac{2}{5})$ $(\frac{2}{7},\frac{1}{3},\frac{2}{5})$ $(\frac{2}{5},\frac{1}{2},\frac{2}{3})$	$(1,1,1)$	$(\frac{2}{3},1,\frac{3}{2})$
x_3	$(\frac{2}{7},\frac{1}{3},\frac{2}{5})$	$(\frac{2}{3},1,\frac{3}{2})$	$(1,1,1)$

Table 5-3d: The matrix $\tilde{R}_4$: pairwise comparison of alternatives under criterion 4

	x_1	x_2	x_3
x_1	$(1,1,1)$	—	$(\frac{3}{2},2,\frac{5}{2})$ $(\frac{2}{5},\frac{1}{2},\frac{2}{3})$
x_2	—	$(1,1,1)$	$(\frac{3}{2},2,\frac{5}{2})$
x_3	$(\frac{2}{5},\frac{1}{2},\frac{2}{3})$ $(\frac{3}{2},2,\frac{5}{2})$	$(\frac{2}{5},\frac{1}{2},\frac{2}{3})$	$(1,1,1)$

Table 5-4: Fuzzy ratings for alternatives

Criterion	x_1	x_2	x_3
C_1	(0.196,0.289,0.431)	(0.195,0.265,0.368)	(0.344,0.449,0.561)
C_2	(0.405,0.546,0.714)	(0.162,0.182,0.204)	(0.277,0.273,0.340)
C_3	(0.540,0.579,0.603)	(0.163,0.217,0.292)	(0.158,0.205,0.267)
C_4	(0.162,0.250,0.394)	(0.313,0.500,0.763)	(0.209,0.250,0.305)
	x_1	x_2	x_3
Final score	(0.227,0.398,0.705)	(0.168,0.313,0.579)	(0.188,0.289,0.504)

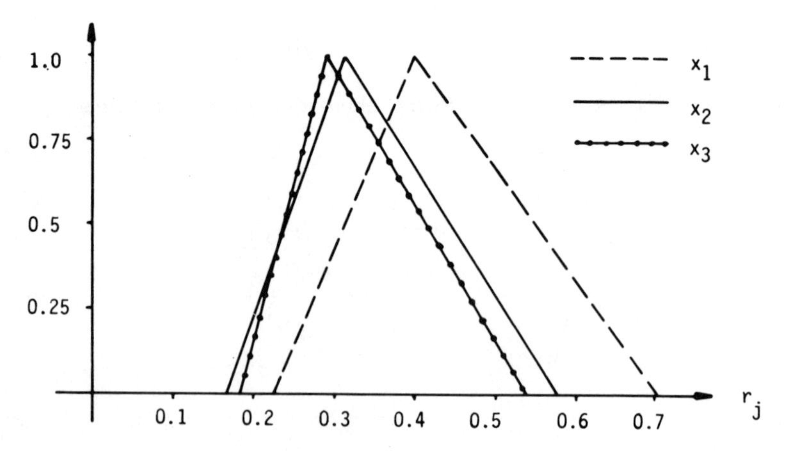

Figure 5-4: Final ratings of alternatives.

Ranking Fuzzy Sets in the Unit Interval [Yager 1981]

Since normalized fuzzy ratings will be used in some of the following approaches we shall briefly sketch Yager's proposal for ranking fuzzy sets in the unit interval. He first defines the mean value, $M(V)$ for (crisp) sets V as follows:

If $V = \{x_1, \ldots, x_n\}$ then $M(V) = \frac{1}{n} \sum_{i=1}^{n} x_i$

If $V = \{a \leq x \leq b\}$ then $M(V) = \dfrac{a+b}{2}$

If $0 \leq a_1 \leq b_1 \leq a_2 \leq b_2 \leq \cdots \leq a_n \leq b_n \leq 1$ then $M(V) =$

$$= \frac{\sum_{i=1}^{n} \left(\frac{a_i + b_i}{2}\right)(b_i - a_i)}{\sum_{i=1}^{n} (b_i - a_i)}$$

and $V = \bigcup \{a_i \leq x \leq b_i\}$ (5.13)

His "ordering function," $F: I^I \rightarrow I$, where I^I is the set of all fuzzy sets in the unit interval, is then

$$F(\tilde{A}) = \int_0^{\alpha_{max}} M(V)\, d\alpha \tag{5.14}$$

with α_{max} being the highest degree of membership of the fuzzy set A in the unit

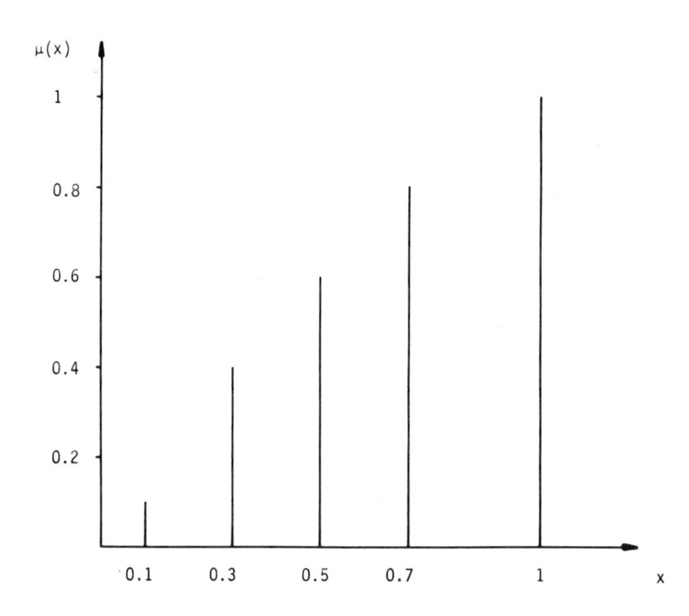

Figure 5-5: Fuzzy Set $\tilde{A}$.

interval.

For a crisp set $A = \{a\}$ this yields $\alpha_{max} = 1$ and

$$F(A) = \int_0^1 a\, d\alpha = a$$

***Example** 5.5* [Yager 1981, p. 147]

Let $\tilde{A}$ be the fuzzy set shown in figure 5-5. X could, for instance, represent a normalized rating. The α-level sets are then

α	A_α
.1	{.1,.3,.5,.7,1}
.4	{.3,.5,.7,1}
.6	{.5,.7,1}
.8	{.7,1}
1	{1}

Now M can be computed for the different A_α using (5.13):

$M(A_\alpha)$	α
.52	.1
.625	.4
.733	.6
.85	.8
1	1

According to (5.14) we obtain

$$\begin{aligned} F(\tilde{A}) &= \int_0^1 M(A_\alpha)\, d\alpha \\ &= \int_0^{.1} .52\, d\alpha + \int_{.1}^{.4} .625\, d\alpha \\ &\quad + \int_{.4}^{.6} .733\, d\alpha + \int_{.6}^{.8} .85\, d\alpha + \int_{.8}^{1} 1\, d\alpha \\ &= (.52)(.1) + (.625)(.3) + (.733)(.2) \\ &\quad + (.85)(.2) + (1)(.2) \\ &= .7561 \end{aligned}$$

Yager considers as one of the most important advantages of his method "its ability to compare crisp numbers, discrete fuzzy sets and continuous fuzzy sets of the unit interval. It does not require convexity, nor does it require normality of the sets compared. It is easy to implement and intuitively appealing [Yager 1981, p. 143]."

Rating and Ranking Multiple-Aspect Alternatives Using Fuzzy Sets [Baas, Kwakernaak 1977]

The approach suggested by Baas and Kwakernaak has become almost classic in this area. It is often used as a benchmark for other models and one finds many references to this approach in the literature [see, e.g., Baldwin and Guild 1979; Chen 1985; Tong and Bonissone 1979; Jain 1979]. We shall, therefore, describe it in more detail even though the proofs will be omitted because they are of more mathematical interest.

Baas and Kwakernaak's publication was a reaction to a probabilistic suggestion by Kahne [1975]. To facilitate the understanding of the former let us briefly sketch Kahne's model:

He considers the alternatives a_i, $i = 1,\ldots,n$, and the criteria $c_j, j = 1,\ldots,m$. r_{ij} denotes the rating of alternative i with respect to criteria j. The weight of criteria j, its relative importance, is called w_j. The ranking of the alternatives is performed according to their rank.

$$R_i = \frac{\sum_{j=1}^{m} w_j r_{ij}}{\sum_{j} w_j} \tag{5.15}$$

The optimal alternative is that for which R_i is maximal.

In Kahne's model the w_j and hence the R_i are assumed to be stochastic variables and the optimal alternative is determined by using Monte Carlo simulation.

Baas and Kwakernaak [1977] suggest the following fuzzy version of above model:

Let again $X = \{x_i\}$, $i = 1,\ldots,n$, be the set of alternatives and $G = \{\tilde{g}_j\}$, $j = 1,\ldots,m$, be the set of goals. $\tilde{R}_{ij}$ is the fuzzy rating of alternative i with respect to goal j and $\tilde{W}_j \in \mathbb{R}$ is the weight (importance) of goal j. It is assumed that the rating of alternative i with respect to goal j is fuzzy and is represented by the membership function $\mu_{\tilde{R}_{ij}}(r_{ij})$. Similarly, the weight (relative importance) of goal j is represented by a fuzzy set $\tilde{W}_j$ with membership function $\mu_{\tilde{W}_j}(w_j)$. All fuzzy sets are assumed to be normalized (i.e., have finite supports and take on the value 1 at least once!).

Phase I (Determination of ratings for alternatives). The evaluation of an alternative x_i is assumed to be a fuzzy set which is computed on the basis of the $\tilde{R}_{ij}$ and $\tilde{W}_j$ as follows.

Consider a function $g(z)$: $\mathbb{R}^{2n} \to \mathbb{R}$ defined by

$$g(z) = \frac{\sum_{j=1}^{n} w_j r_{ij}}{\sum_{j=1}^{n} wj} \tag{5.16}$$

with $z \doteq (w_1,\ldots,w_n,r_{i1},\ldots,r_{in})$.

On the product space $\mathbb{R}^{2n}$ a membership function $\mu_{\tilde{Z}_i}$ is defined as

$$\mu_{\tilde{Z}_i}(z) = \min\left\{\min_{j=1}^{n} (\mu_{\tilde{W}_j}(w_j)), \min_{k=1}^{n} (\mu_{\tilde{R}_{ik}}(r_{ik}))\right\} \tag{5.17}$$

Through the function g the fuzzy set $\tilde{Z}_i = \{(z,\mu_{\tilde{Z}_i})\}$ induces a fuzzy set

$$\tilde{R}_i = \{(r,\mu_{\tilde{R}_i})\} \text{ with the membership function}$$

$$\mu_{\tilde{R}_i}(r) = \sup_{z:g(z)=r} \mu_{\tilde{Z}_i}(z) \qquad r \in \mathbb{R} \tag{5.18}$$

$\mu_{\tilde{R}_i}(r)$ is the final rating of alternative x_i on the basis of which the rank ordering is performed in phase II.

Phase II (Ranking). For the final ranking of the x_i Baas and Kwakernaak start from the observation that, if the x_i had received crisp rating $r_i = \tilde{R}_i$ then a reasonable procedure would be to select the x_i that have received the highest rating—that is, to determine the set of preferred alternatives as

$$\{x_i \in X \mid r_i \geq r_j, \forall j \in I\}, I = \{1,\ldots,m\}.$$

Since here the final ratings are fuzzy the problem is somewhat more complicated. The authors suggest in their model two different fuzzy sets in addition to $\tilde{R}_i$ which supply different kinds of information about the preferability of an alternative.

1. They first determine the conditional set $\{I \mid \tilde{R}\}$ with the characteristic function

$$\mu_{(I|\tilde{R})}(x_i \mid r_1,\ldots,r_m) = \begin{cases} 1 & \text{if } r_i \geq r_j, \forall j \in I \\ 0 & \text{else} \end{cases} \tag{5.19}$$

This "membership function" indicates that a given alternative x_i belongs to the preferred set if and only if

$$r_i \geq r_j \qquad \forall j \in I$$

The final fuzzy ratings $\tilde{R}$ define on $\mathbb{R}^m$ a fuzzy set

$$\tilde{R} = \{(r_1,\ldots,r_m),\mu_{\tilde{R}}(r_1,\ldots,r_m)\}$$

with the membership function

$$\mu_{\tilde{R}}(r_1,\ldots,r_m) = \min_{i=1,\ldots,m} \mu_{\tilde{R}_i}(r_i) \tag{5.20}$$

This fuzzy set together with the conditional fuzzy set (5.19) induces a fuzzy set $\tilde{I} = \{(x_i,\mu_{\tilde{I}}(x_i))\}$ with the membership function

$$\mu_{\tilde{I}}(x_i) = \sup_{r_1,\ldots,r_m} (\min\{\mu_{\tilde{R}}(x_i),\mu_{(\tilde{I}|\tilde{R})}(x_i)\}) \tag{5.21}$$

which can be interpreted as the degree to which alternative x_i is the best alternative. If there is a unique i for which the supremum of (5.21) is attained, $\mu_{\tilde{I}}(x_i) = 1$, then alternative x_i dominates crisply all other alternatives.

2. $\tilde{I}$ is, of course, not all the information that can be provided. x_i might not be the unique best alternative, but there might be some x_i attaining their maximum degree of membership at r^*. They might, however, be represented by different fuzzy sets $\tilde{R}_i$. Baas and Kwakernaak therefore try to establish other criteria which might be able to distinguish such "preferable" alternatives from each other and rank them:

If the final ratings are crisp, $r_1,\ldots,r_m$, then

$$p_i = r_i - \frac{1}{m-1}\sum_{i=1}^{m} r_i \qquad \text{for fixed } i$$

can be used as a measure of preferability of alternative x_i over all others.

If the ratings $\tilde{R}_i$ are fuzzy, then the mapping h_i: $\mathbb{R}^m \to \mathbb{R}$ induces a fuzzy set $\tilde{P}_i = \{(p,\mu_{\tilde{P}_i}(p)\}$ with the membership function

$$\mu_{\tilde{P}_i}(p) = \sup_{\substack{r_1,\ldots,r_m \\ h_i(r_i)=p}} \mu_{\tilde{R}}(\bar{r}_1,\ldots,\bar{r}_m) \qquad p\in\mathbb{R} \tag{5.22}$$

in which $\mu_{\tilde{R}}$ is defined by (5.20).

This fuzzy set can be used to judge the degree of preferability x_i over all other alternatives.

In summary, we have

$\mu_{\tilde{R}_i}(r)$ as the fuzzy rating of x_i,

$\mu_{\tilde{I}}(x_i)$ as the degree to which x_i is best alternative, and

$\mu_{\tilde{P}_i}(p)$ as the degree of preferability of x_i over all other alternatives.

To determine explicitely the membership functions defined is still a problem which might not be solvable at all in general. Baas and Kwakernaak proof three theorems, ommitted here, which for certain cases guarantee that the required membership functions and their maxima exist. They assume throughout their article that the membership functions are piecewise continuous, differentiable, bounded, and nonnegative and that there exists a finite support. Baas and Kwakernaak suggest that sometimes trial-and-error methods may be the only way to find membership functions of $\tilde{R}_i$ that satisfy all the assumptions.

We shall now present two examples from Baas and Kwakernaak [1977], the first of which leads to satisfactory results and the second of which shows a result that will give rise to approaches described thereafter.

Example 5.6

Let x_1 and x_2 be two alternatives which shall be ranked according to two criteria g_1 and g_2. The rating is expressed by linguistic variables (see chapter 7). Table 5-5 shows the ratings and weights of the criteria. The fuzzy sets representing the linguistic variables (terms) are shown in figure 5-6: The membership functions of the final ratings $\mu_{\tilde{R}_i}$ are shown in figure 5-7.

The fuzzy set $\tilde{I} = \{(1,1),(2,.7)\}$ indicates the degree to which x_i is the best alternative. Finally, the degree of preferability of x_1 over x_2 (x_1 over all other alternatives), that is, $(\mu_{\tilde{R}_1} - \mu_{\tilde{R}_2})$, is shown in figure 5-8.

Given the ratings of the alternatives and the weights of the criteria, these results look quite plausible and appealing.

Example 5.7

Let us now slightly modify example 5.6. Rather than rating alternative 1 with respect to criterion 2 "fair" we shall rate it "not clear." The final ratings that result are shown in figure 5-9. The fuzzy set $\tilde{I}$ becomes $\tilde{I} = \{(1,1),(2,1)\}$; and $\mu_{\tilde{P}_i}(p)$ is shown in figure 5-10.

Table 5-5: Ratings of 2 alternatives

	Weight	r_{1j}	r_{2j}
goal 1	very important	good	fair
goal 2	rather unimportant	fair	good

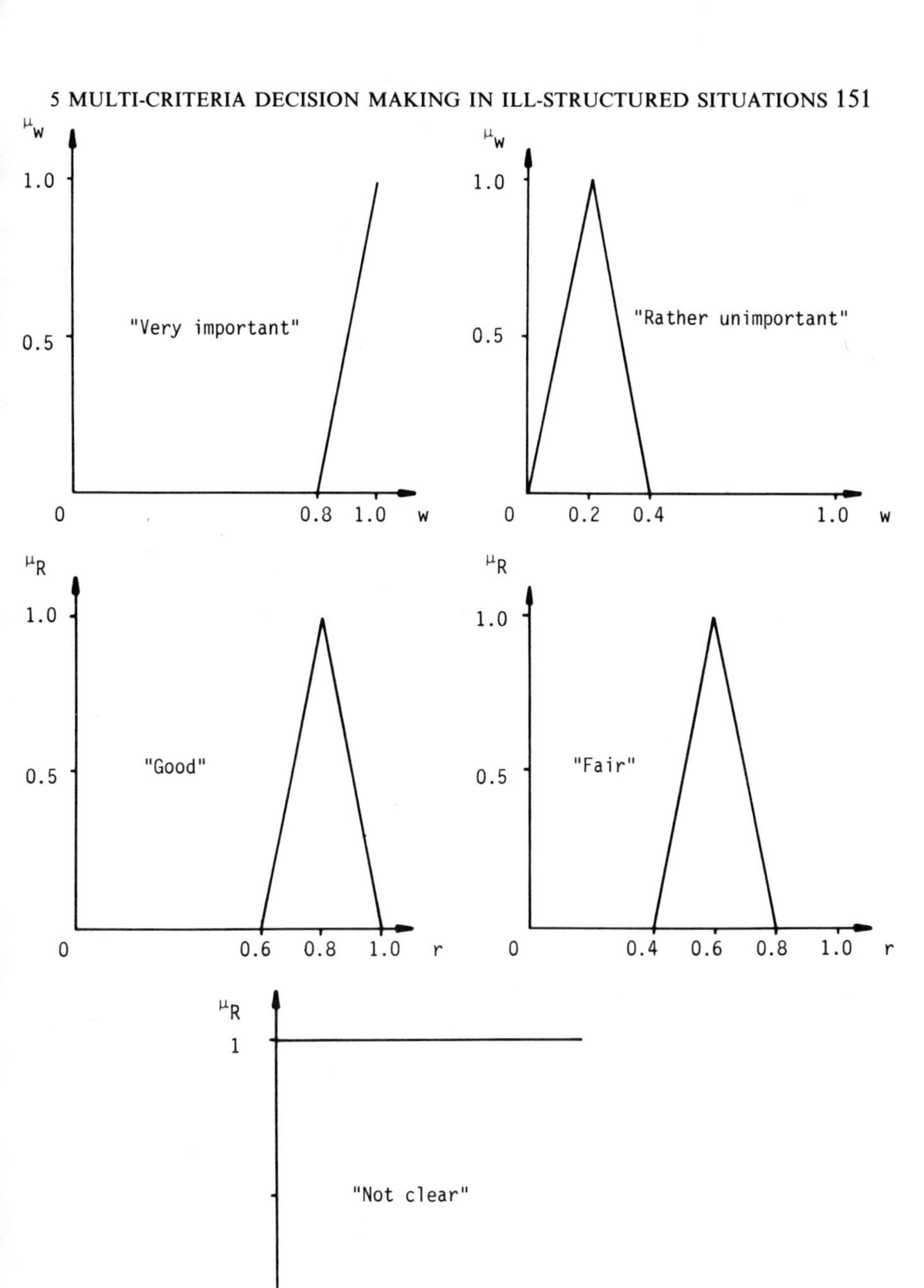

Figure 5-6: Linguistic Variables.

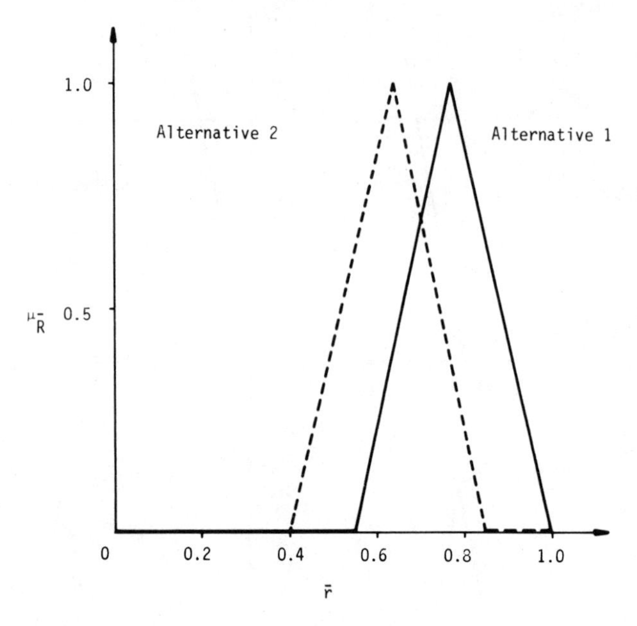

Figure 5-7: Membership Functions of Final Ratings.

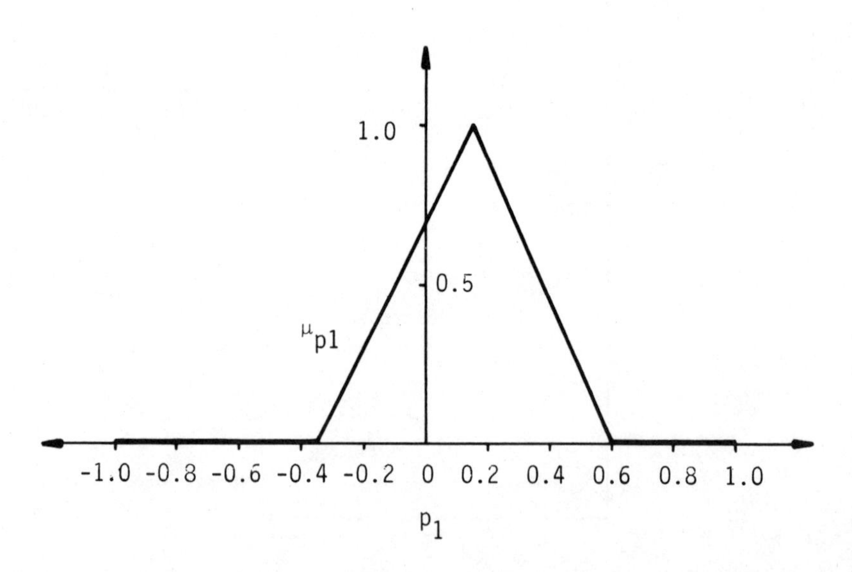

Figure 5-8: Membership Function of Preferability of Alternative 1 or Alternative 2.

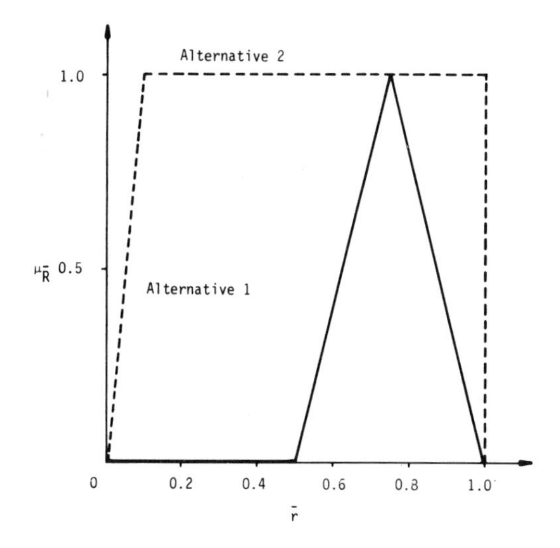

Figure 5-9: Membership Functions of Final Ratings of Alternatives 1 and 2.

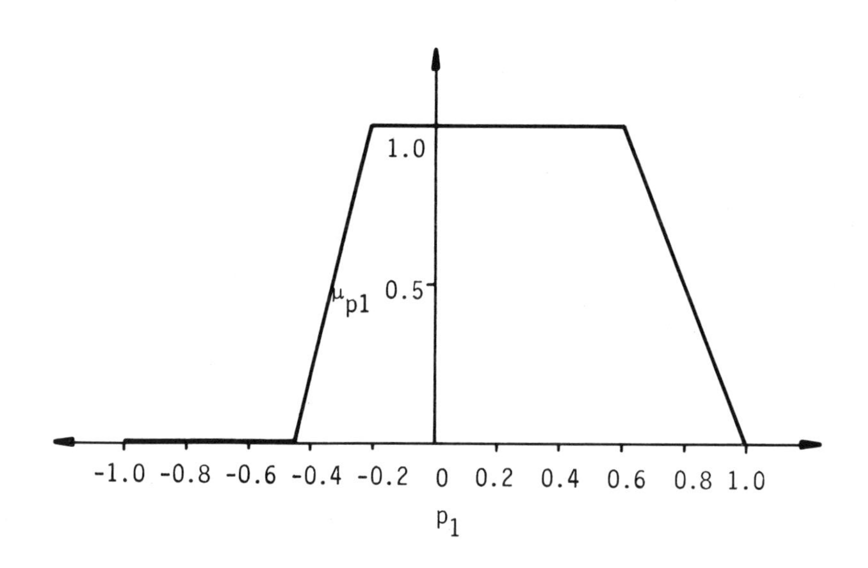

Figure 5-10: Preferability of Alternative over 2.

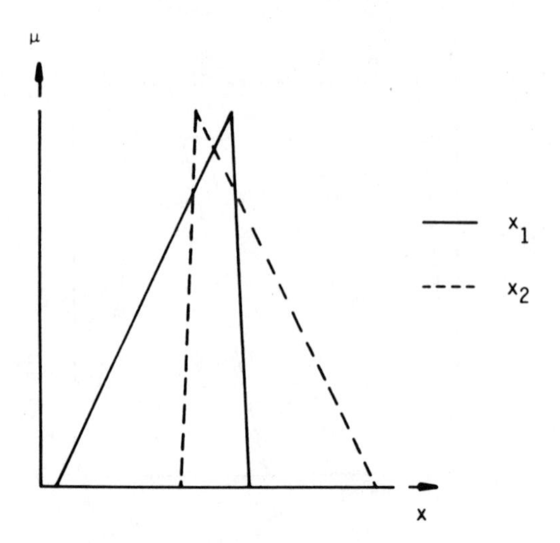

Figure 5-11: Ratings of two alternatives.

The result of example 5.7 is not quite satisfactory because it does not distinguish (enough) between alternatives 1 and 2, even though they differ from each other. Baas and Kwakernaak recognize this feature of their method themselves.

Sometimes this method also leads to results that are against our intuition. Baldwin and Guild [1979], for example, present the following example in which the model of Baas and Kwakernaak would indicate x_1 as the optimal alternative, whereas intuition might regard alternative x_2 as preferable to x_1. (See figure 5-11.)

A modification of the ranking approach described above is offered by Jain, who argues: "The balances approach for the ranking of the alternatives should consider both, the maximum rating associated with various alternatives, and the grade of membership of the ratings" [Jain 1977, p. 4]. For this he uses a special concept of the "maximizing set": namely, if

$$S = \bigcup_{i=1}^{n} S(\tilde{R}_i)$$

that is, if S is the union of all supports of the fuzzy ratings $\tilde{R}_i = \{(r, \mu_{\tilde{R}_i}(r))\}$, and

$$\mu_{\tilde{M}}(r) = \left[\frac{r}{r_{\max}}\right]^n \qquad \text{with } r_{\max} = \sup_{r \in S} r$$

then the maximizing set is

$$\tilde{M}(S) = \{(r, \mu_{\tilde{M}}(r))\} \tag{5.23}$$

n is supposed to be an integer, which should be choosen context dependently. For each alternative a fuzzy set $\tilde{R}_i^0(r_{ij}) = \{(r_{ij}, \mu_{\tilde{R}_i^0}(r_{ij}))\}$ is formed for which

$$\mu_{\tilde{R}_i^0}(r_{ij}) = \min(\mu_{\tilde{M}}(r_{ij}), \mu_{\tilde{R}_i}(r_{ij})) \tag{5.24}$$

The fuzzy set $\tilde{R}_i^0$ is considered to represent the different ratings for alternative x_i. The "fuzzy optimal alternative" is represented by the fuzzy set

$$\tilde{O} = \{(x_i, \mu_{\tilde{O}}(x_i))\} \tag{5.25}$$

with

$$\mu_{\tilde{O}}(x_i) = \max_k \mu_{\tilde{R}_i^0}(r_{ik})$$

To some authors, neither Baas and Kwakernaak's approach nor Jain's model seem to be discriminative enough. Baldwin and Guild present an example which illustrates this weakness of Jain's proposal. Figure 5-12 presents the fuzzy ratings of two projects as they would be ordered properly by Jain's method.

$\mu_{\tilde{M}}$ indicates the membership function of Jain's maximizing set for $n = 1$ and $\mu_{\tilde{O}}(x_1)$ and $\mu_{\tilde{O}}(x_2)$, respectively, the degrees of membership of these alternatives in the set $\tilde{O}$. Obviously the choice of n in (5.23) influences the shape of $\mu_{\tilde{M}}(x)$ (for $n < 1$ it is a concave, for $n > M$ it is a convex curve). In any case only the "right side" (decreasing parts) of the fuzzy ratings are taken into

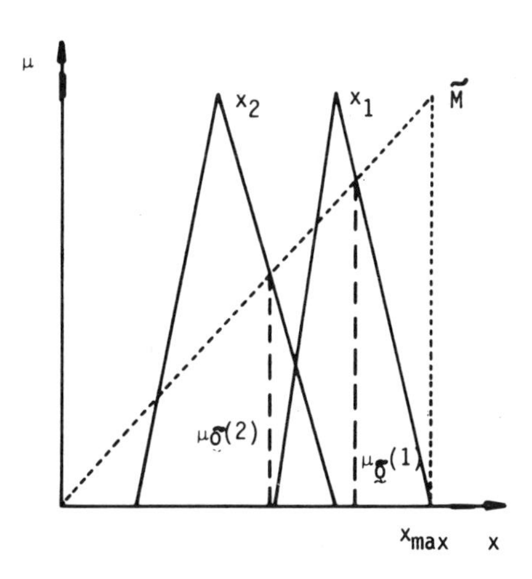

Figure 5-12: Ratings of two alternatives.

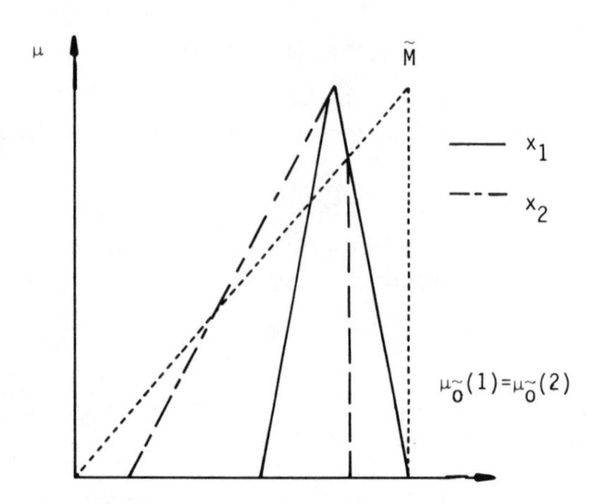

Figure 5-13: Ratings of three alternatives.

consideration when determining (5.25). Differences of those ratings in their left increasing part are, therefore, neglected. This is shown in figure 5-13.

A procedure suggested by Baldwin and Guild [1979] for ranking fuzzy sets differs essentially from that of Baas and Kwakernaak in the definition of the set of preferred alternatives—in (5.18) and (5.20), respectively,

Ranking Fuzzy Sets Using "Cardinal Utilities"
[Baldwin, Guild 1979]

Rather than using (5.18), Baldwin and Guild define the two-dimensional relation

$$\tilde{P}_{ij} = \{[(r_i,r_j), \mu_{\tilde{P}_{ij}}(r_i,r_j)]\} \qquad i,j \in \mathbb{N}, i \neq j \tag{5.26}$$

where

$$\mu_{\tilde{P}_{ij}}(r_i,r_j) = f(r_i,r_j)$$

expresses the "difference" between the ratings of x_i and x_j (the difference of utilities!). For linear utilities:

$$\mu_{\tilde{P}_{ij}}(r_i,r_j) = r_i - r_j \qquad i,j \in \mathbb{N}, i \neq j$$

The set $\tilde{O}$ is then defined similar to (5.20) as

$$\tilde{O}(x_i) = \{(x_i, \mu_{\tilde{O}}(x_i)) \qquad i \in \mathbb{N}\} \tag{5.27}$$

with

$$\mu_{\tilde{O}}(x_i) = \sup_{r_i, r_j} \min \{\mu_{\tilde{R}_i}(r_i), \mu_{\tilde{R}_j}(r_j), \mu_{\tilde{P}_{ij}}(r_i, r_j)\} \tag{5.28}$$

Equation (5.28) expresses the degree to which alternative x_i is preferable to its best rival. $\tilde{O}(x_i)$ corresponds to the max-min-composition of $\tilde{R}_i$, $\tilde{R}_j$, and $\tilde{P}_{ij}$. The determination of $\mu_{\tilde{O}}(x_i)$, if the $\tilde{R}_i$ are discrete fuzzy sets, can be performed directly. For continuous membership functions Baldwin and Guild suggest and prove the applicability of procedures for fuzzy relations $\tilde{P}_{ij}$ whose membership functions are one sided and either strictly increasing or decreasing in each argument; for fuzzy ratings with unimodal membership functions the sides of which are strictly increasing or decreasing; and for membership functions that range over the whole interval [0,1]. The computations are particularly easy if the ratings are restricted to the shapes shown in figure 5-14.

In this case the following $(n - 1)$ sets of equations have to be solved:

$$\hat{\mu}_j = \frac{\delta - r_i}{\delta - \gamma} (= \mu_{\tilde{R}_i}(r_i))$$

$$\hat{\mu}_j = \frac{r_j - \alpha}{\beta - \alpha} (= \mu_{\tilde{R}_j}(r_j))$$

$$\hat{\mu}_j = r_i - r_j (= \mu_{\tilde{P}_{ij}}(r_i, r_j))$$

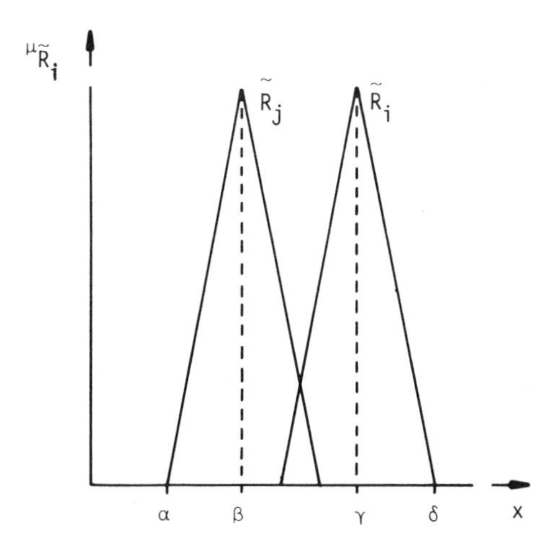

Figure 5-14: Membership Functions of Ratings $\tilde{R}_i$, $\tilde{R}_j$.

which have the solution

$$\hat{\mu}_j = \frac{\delta - \alpha}{1 + (\delta - \gamma) + (\beta - \alpha)} \quad \text{and} \quad \mu_{\tilde{O}}(x_i) = \min_j (\hat{\mu}_j) \tag{5.29}$$

Example 5.8

Consider the two fuzzy sets $\tilde{R}_1$ and $\tilde{R}_2$ in figure 5-14a. Then the results according to (5.29) can easily be determined

$$\text{for } x_1: \quad \hat{\mu}_2 = \frac{3 - 1}{1 + (3 - 2.5) + (1.5 - 1)} = 1 \qquad \mu_{\tilde{O}}(x_1) = 1$$

$$\text{for } x_2: \quad \hat{\mu}_1 = \frac{3 - 1}{1 + (3 - 1.5) + (2.5 - 1)} = .5 \qquad \mu_{\tilde{O}}(x_2) = .5$$

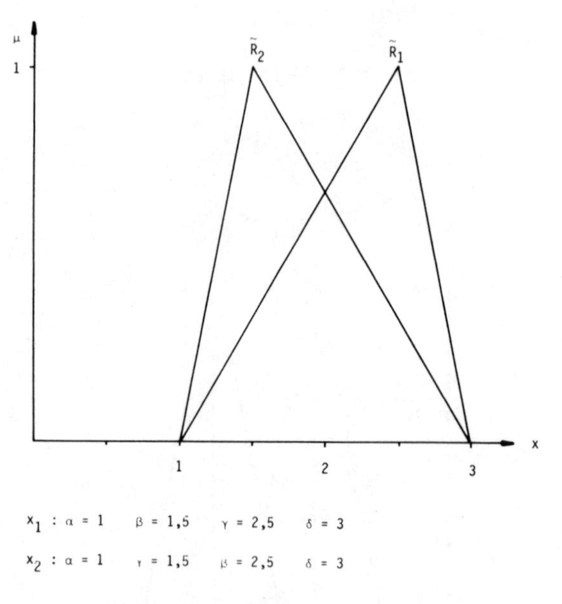

Figure 5-14a: Ratings of Projects 1 and 2.

Ranking Fuzzy Sets by Maximizing and Minimizing Sets [Chen 1985]

Chen suggests modifications to Jain's procedure which allow a better discrimination and also the treatment of negative and of subnormal ratings. He modifies Jain's "maximizing set" (5.22) by defining the membership function of it as

$$\mu_{\tilde{M}}(r) = \begin{cases} \left[\dfrac{r - r_{\min}}{r_{\max} - r_{\min}}\right]^n & \text{for } r \in [r_{\min}, r_{\max}] \\ 0 & \text{otherwise} \end{cases} \tag{5.30}$$

where $[r_{\min}, r_{\max}]$ is a real interval. $R(x_i)$ is then defined using Jain's approach by

$$R(x_i) = \sup_r \min \{\mu_{\tilde{R}_i}(r), \mu_{\tilde{M}}(r)\} \tag{5.31}$$

By introducing in addition to this maximizing set a "minimizing set" Chen increases the discriminating quality of the procedure because he can now also use the increasing left sides of the fuzzy ratings for distinguishing and ranking nonidentical fuzzy ratings.

The minimizing set, $\tilde{N}$, is defined by the membership function

$$\mu_{\tilde{N}}(r) = \begin{cases} \left[\dfrac{r - r_{\max}}{r_{\min} - r_{\max}}\right]^n & \text{for } r \in [r_{\min}, r_{\max}] \\ 0 & \text{otherwise} \end{cases} \tag{5.32}$$

In analogy to (5.31) Chen defines $L(x_i)$ as follows:

$$L(x_i) = \sup_r \min \{(\mu_{\tilde{R}_i}(r), \mu_{\tilde{N}}(r)\} \tag{5.33}$$

The ranking is then performed via

$$O(x_i) = \frac{R(x_i) + 1 - L(x_i)}{2} \tag{5.34}$$

Example 5.9

Let us consider two alternatives the ratings of which, $\tilde{R}_1$ and $\tilde{R}_2$, are shown in figure 5-15. The membership functions of the ratings are suggested to be

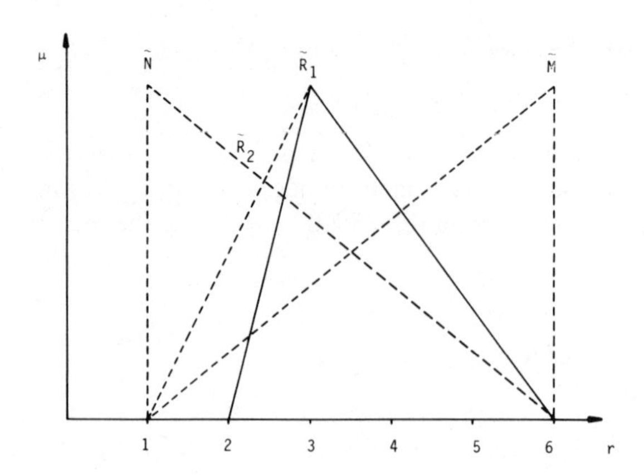

Figure 5-15: Ratings of alternatives.

$$\mu_{\tilde{R}_1}(r) = \begin{cases} \dfrac{r-2}{1} & 2 \le r \le 3 \\ \dfrac{6-r}{3} & 3 < r \le 6 \\ 0 & \text{otherwise} \end{cases}$$

$$\mu_{\tilde{R}_2}(r) = \begin{cases} \dfrac{r-1}{2} & 1 \le r \le 3 \\ \dfrac{6-r}{3} & 3 < r \le 6 \\ 0 & \text{otherwise} \end{cases}$$

Maximizing and minimizing sets can now be calculated for $n = 1$ as

$$\mu_{\tilde{M}}(r) = \begin{cases} \dfrac{r-1}{5} & 1 \le r \le 6 \\ 0 & \text{otherwise} \end{cases}$$

$$\mu_{\tilde{N}}(r) = \begin{cases} \dfrac{6-r}{5} & 1 \le r \le 6 \\ 0 & \text{otherwise} \end{cases}$$

For alternative 1 we can compute its ranking value $O(x_1)$ as follows:

$$R(x_1) = \sup_r \min \left\{ \frac{6-r}{3}, \frac{r-1}{5} \right\} = \frac{5}{8} = .625$$

$$L(x_1) = \sup_r \min \left\{ \frac{r-2}{1}, \frac{6-r}{5} \right\} = \frac{2}{3} = .67$$

$$O(x_1) = \frac{.625 + 1 - .67}{2} = .48$$

For alternative 2 we obtain

$$R(x_2) = \sup_r \min \left\{ \frac{6-r}{3}, \frac{r-1}{5} \right\} = \frac{5}{8} = .625$$

$$L(x_2) = \sup_r \min \left\{ \frac{r-1}{2}, \frac{6-r}{5} \right\} = \frac{5}{7} = .71$$

$$O(x_2) = \frac{.625 + 1 - .71}{2} = .46$$

Hence alternative x_1 is slightly preferred to x_2.

Let us now compare the behavior of the approaches described so far by considering some situations used frequently in the literature [see in particular, Baldwin, Guild 1979; Bortolan, Degani 1985; and Chen 1985].

In most of the easy structures, that is, if preference relationships are clear cut, the order of the alternatives according to their preferability are identically determined by all methods, even though the intensities (i.e., the numerical values) of preferences differ considerably.

For situations in which the order of the alternatives are not as intuitively obvious, the methods differ with respect to discrimination as well as order. We shall consider the six situations shown in figure 5-16 and compare the *order* of preferability according to Yager (unit interval), Baas and Kwakernaak, Jain, and Baldwin and Guild (linear). The differences among the *intensities* are, of course, much larger.

In table 5-6, where $1 \succ 2$ indicates that alternative 1 is preferred to alter-

Table 5-6

Situation	*Yager*	*Baas & Kwakernaak*	*Jain*	*Baldwin & Guild*
1	$1 \succ 2 \succ 3$	$1 \succ 2 \succ 3$	$1 \succ 2 \succ 3$	$1 \succ 2 \succ 3$
2	$1 \approx 2$	$1 \approx 2$	$1 \succ 2$	$1 \approx 2$
3	$1 \succ 2 \succ 3$	$1 \approx 2 \approx 3$	$1 \approx 2 \approx 3$	$1 \succ 2 \approx 3$
4	$1 \succ 2 \succ 3$	$1 \approx 2 \approx 3$	$1 \succ 2 \succ 3$	$1 \succ 2 \succ 3$
5	$2 \succ 1$	$1 \succ 2$	$1 \succ 2$	$2 \succ 1$
6	$3 \succ 2 \succ 1$	$1 \approx 3 \succ 2$	$3 \succ 2 \succ 1$	$2 \approx 3 \succ 1$

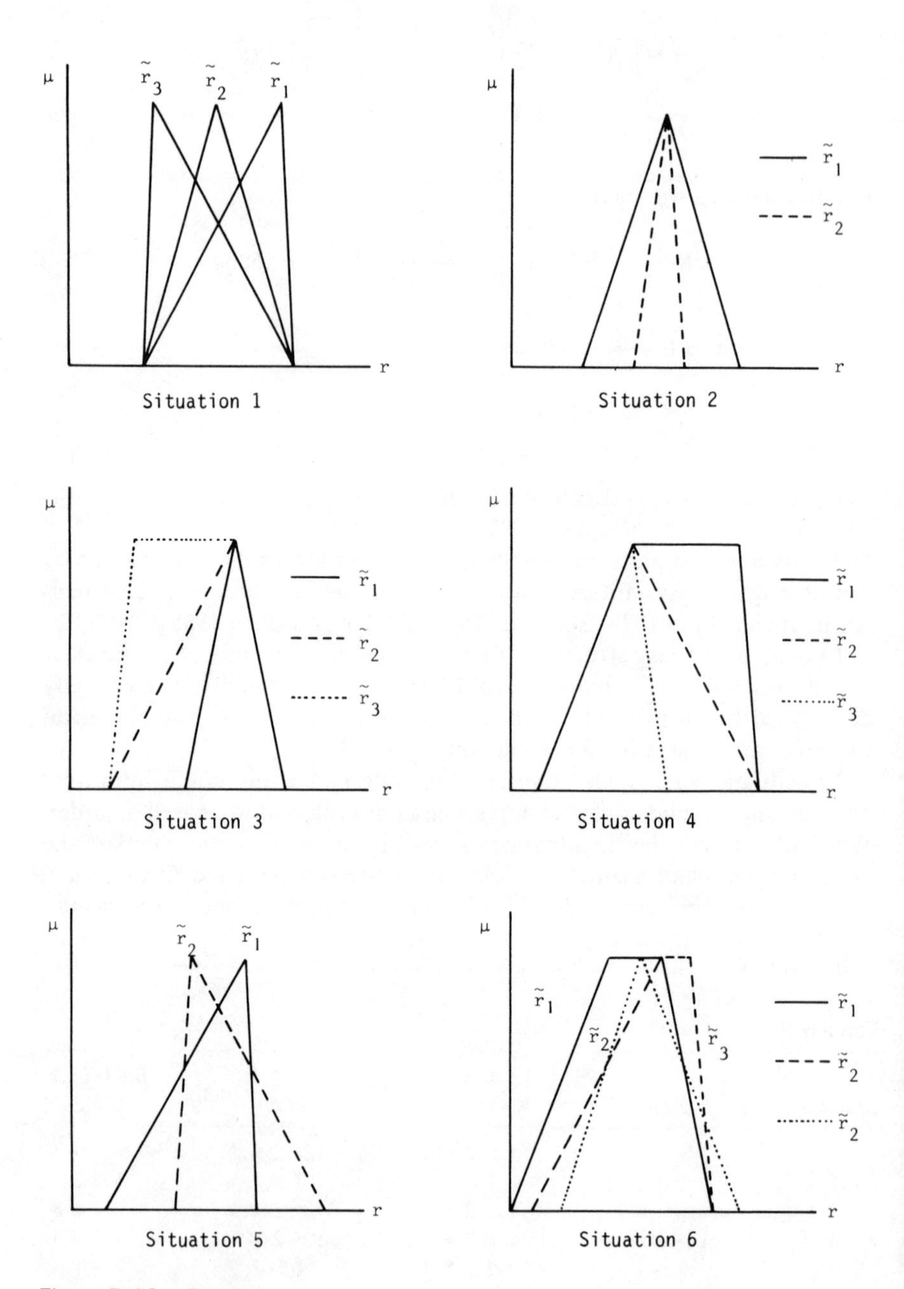

Figure 5-16: Ratings.

native 2 and $\approx$ indicates indifference. Only in situation 1 are all the results identical. In situations 2, 3, and 4 they differ from each other, but they do not contradict each other. In situations 5 and 6 the rankings not only differ, they even contradict each other. Obviously Baas and Kwakernaak differentiate least often. Whether this has to be judged negative or positive is a matter of personal preference. The authors mentioned above all strive after a high degree of discrimination. From this point of view a low degree of discrimination would certainly be considered negative. We will see, however, that the opposite view has also been taken.

Linguistic Solutions to Multi-Attribute Decision Problems [Tong, Bonissone 1984]

Tong and Bonissone are not interested in refining even further the discrimination capabilities of fuzzy MADM approaches. They argue, on the contrary, that

> "Previous attempts to solve fuzzy decision problems have produced numerical rankings of the alternatives. We believe that this is misguided since in situations where fuzzy sets are a suitable way of representing uncertainty the final choice must itself be fuzzy. It is certainly not appropriate to give the decision some artificial precision—solutions should be linguistic rather than numerical." [Tong, Bonissone 1984, p. 334]

The authors are concerned only with phase II of MADM—with the ranking of (normal convex) fuzzy sets, $\tilde{R}_i$, which represent ratings of decision alternatives, x_i, and which may already include the aggregation of the merits of alternatives with respect to different criteria (goals).

Ranking of the final ratings, $\tilde{R}_i$, $i = 1,\ldots,n$, of the alternatives, x_i, $i = 1,\ldots,n$, is achieved in two steps. First a fuzzy preference set is determined which corresponds essentially to Baas and Kwakernaak's $\tilde{P}_i$ (see (5.22)). In the second step a linguistic approximation and truth qualification of the final decision proposal is generated. We shall consider these steps in turn.

Step 1 (determination of fuzzy decision sets). Dominance sets, $\tilde{D}_i$, are defined by the following membership functions:

$$\mu_{\tilde{D}_i}(r_1, r_j) = \max_{\substack{j=1,\ldots,n \\ i \neq j}} (\min\{\mu_{\leq r_i}(r_i), \mu(r_j)\}) \qquad i = 1,\ldots,n \quad (5.35)$$

with

$$\mu_{\leq r_i}(r_i) = \begin{cases} 1 & \text{for } r_i < r_i^* \\ \mu_i(r_i) & \text{for } r_i \geq r_i^* \end{cases} \quad (5.36)$$

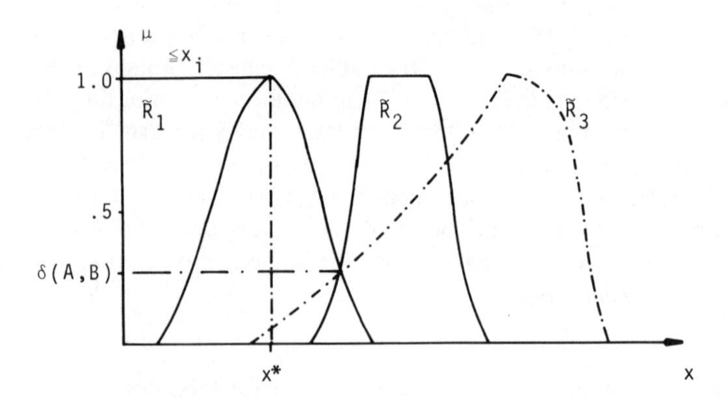

Figure 5-17: Dominance of Fuzzy Sets.

where r_i^* is the leftmost (lowest) value of r_i for which $\mu_i(r_i) = 1$.

The rationale behind (5.35) and (5.36) is to get a clear indication on which alternatives are nondominated or preferred. Equation (5.35) does not consider the shapes of the $\tilde{R}_i$ but only the location of the peaks of the ratings. In figure 5-17, for instance, $\tilde{R}_3$ and $\tilde{R}_2$ would dominate $\tilde{R}_1$ to the same degree, $\mu_{\tilde{D}_2}(r_2,r_1) = .25$.

On the basis of the $\tilde{D}_i$ a dominance relation, $\tilde{R}_D(r_i,r_j)$, can be constructed, indicating the dominance of all x_i over x_j. This relation is reflexive but neither symmetrical nor min-max transitive and is therefore not a partial ordering of the x_i! Nor does it take into consideration the shapes of the membership functions $\mu_{\tilde{R}_i}(r)$, but it already offers very useful information.

Example 5.10 [Tong, Bonissone 1984]

Consider the four ratings $\tilde{R}_1$ through $\tilde{R}_4$ shown in figure 5-18. The dominance sets are then as follows (the first elements in the brackets of (5.35) have been dropped):

$$\tilde{D}_1 = \{(r_1,1),(r_2,.5),(r_3,0),(r_4,0)\}$$

$$\tilde{D}_2 = \{(r_1,1),(r_2,1),(r_3,.8),(r_4,.5)\}$$

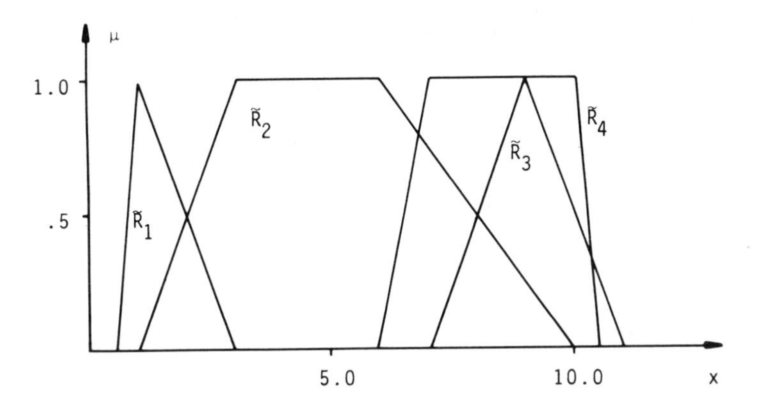

Figure 5-18: Fuzzy ratings of alternatives.

$$\tilde{D}_3 = \{(r_1,1),(r_2,1),(r_3,1),(r_4,1)\}$$
$$\tilde{D}_4 = \{(r_1,1),(r_2,1),(r_3,1),(r_4,1)\}$$

and the dominance relation is, accordingly,

$$\tilde{R}_D = \begin{Bmatrix} 1 & .5 & 0 & 0 \\ 1 & 1 & .8 & .5 \\ 1 & 1 & 1 & 1 \\ 1 & 1 & 1 & 1 \end{Bmatrix}$$

Obviously $\tilde{R}_3$ and $\tilde{R}_4$ are nondominated alternatives according to (5.35) because the 3rd and 4th row of $\tilde{R}_D$ contains only 1's.

To differentiate further between nondominated alternatives, Tong and Bonissone define a vector $v(x_i) = \min_j \tilde{R}_D(x_i,x_j)$, the components of which indicate the degree to which an alternative dominates all others (on the basis of (5.25)!). To include also the shapes of the membership functions of $\tilde{R}_i$ they define the following difference function:

$$g_k(r_1,\ldots,r_n) = r_k - \frac{\sum_{\substack{i=1 \\ i\neq k}}^{n} v(x_i)\cdot r_i}{\sum_{\substack{i=1 \\ i\neq k}}^{n} v(x_i)} \tag{5.37}$$

The index k in (5.37) corresponds to a position in $v(x_i)$ for which $v(x_k) = 1$. If, in (5.37), r_i is replaced by $\tilde{R}_i$, the result is a fuzzy set which the authors call

$\tilde{Z}_k(\tilde{R}_i)$. The membership function of this fuzzy set can be determined via the extension principle as

$$\mu_{\tilde{Z}_k}(u) = \max_{r_1,\ldots,r_n} \min_{i=1}^{n} \mu_{\tilde{R}_i}(r_i) \tag{5.38}$$

$$\text{such that } g_k(\cdot) = u$$

These fuzzy sets (one for each nondominated alternative) are now offered as a decision aid, expressing for the nondominated alternatives the degree of preference over other alternatives.

Example 5.10 (continued)

Calculating vector $v(x_i)$ from $\tilde{R}_D$ yields

$$v = \{0,.5,1,1\}$$

Since this vector has two components equal to one, two fuzzy sets $\tilde{Z}_k$ have to be determined via (5.38). They are shown in figure 5-19 [Tong, Bonissone 1984, p. 326]. The membership functions of these two fuzzy sets are very similar, indicating that the attractiveness of alternative x_3 is not much different from that of x_4. x_4 seems to be slightly superior to x_3. The doubt about the relative desirability of x_3 and x_4 gives rise to the second step of Tong and Bonissone's procedure.

Step 2 (truth qualification and linguistic approximation). The rationale behind this second step is the belief that human decision makers understand better a linguistic statement characterizing the decision set than a (numerical) membership function. The form of the linguistic expressions searched for by the authors is: "It is very true that x_k is marginally preferred to all other alternatives." This statement obviously contains three important pieces of information:

- the crisp decision x_k
- the intensity of preference (marginally)
- the degree of truth of the statement (truth qualification)

Formally the statement has the structure:

"x_k is $\tilde{P}$ over all other alternatives is τ."

To translate the decision set $\tilde{Z}_k$ meaningfully in the above-mentioned way, the authors interpret $\tilde{P}$ as a fuzzy set on the same universe of discourse as $\tilde{Z}_k$

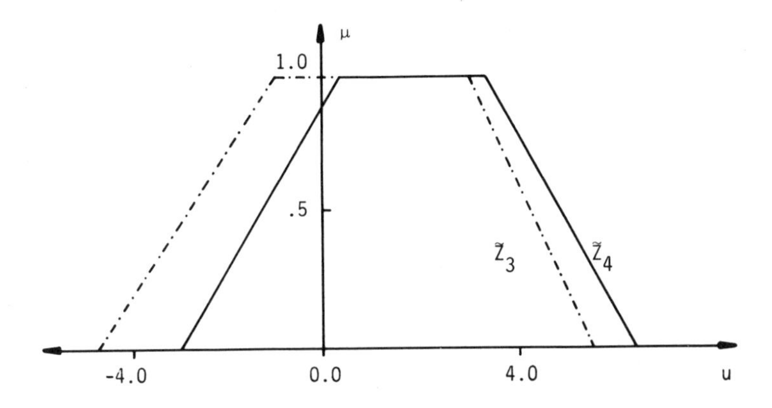

Figure 5-19: Decision sets for nondominated alternatives.

and τ as a term of the linguistic variable "truth" [see Zimmermann 1985, ch. 9]. They then try to find terms in the term sets of the linguistic variables "Preference" ($\tilde{P}$) and "Truth" which approximate the unlabelled $\tilde{Z}_k$ as well as possible and then use the linguistic label of these approximating terms to express $\tilde{Z}_k$ in natural language. As a tool for the linguistic approximation they suggest pattern recognition techniques [Bonissone 1979a] and a context-free grammar such as suggested by Zadeh [1973]. We shall illustrate *step 2* by using the following example from Tong and Bonissone [1984, p. 328]. (For linguistic approximation see also Wenstop [1980, 1981].)

Example 5.11

A person wants to invest and considers the following alternatives:

x_1 = investment in the commodity market

x_2 = investment in the stock market

x_3 = purchase of gold and/or diamonds

x_4 = investment in real estate

x_5 = investment in long term bonds

Table 5-7: Ratings of alternatives and criteria

Criteria	c_1	c_2	c_3	c_4
Importance / *Alter-natives*	*Moderately important*	*More or less important*	*Very important*	*More or less unimportant*
x_1	High	More or less high	Very high	Fair
x_2	Fair	Fair	Fair	More or less good
x_3	Low	From fair to more or less low	Fair	Good
x_4	Low	Very low	More or less high	Bad
x_5	Very low	High	More or less low	Very good

The criteria considered relevant by the investor are:

c_1 = the risk of losing the capital

c_2 = the risk of losing by inflation

c_3 = the amount of interest received

c_4 = the cash realizability of the investment

On the basis of the data in table 5-7, which shows the investor's ratings, the ratings shown in figure 5-20 can be determined. Using (5.35) and (5.36) the following dominance sets and dominance relation, respectively, can be derived:

$$\tilde{R}_D = \begin{bmatrix} 1 & 1 & .91 & .58 & 1 \\ 1 & 1 & .99 & .72 & 1 \\ 1 & 1 & 1 & 1 & 1 \\ 1 & 1 & 1 & 1 & 1 \\ 1 & .96 & .81 & .51 & 1 \end{bmatrix}$$

The vector $v(x_i) = (.58,.72,1,1,.51)$ indicates that alternatives x_3 and x_4 are nondominated. Therefore for these alternatives $\tilde{Z}_3$ and $\tilde{Z}_4$ are derived via (5.37). They are shown in figure 5-21.

It can be seen from figure 5-21 that $\tilde{Z}_3$ and $\tilde{Z}_4$ are very similar, indicating

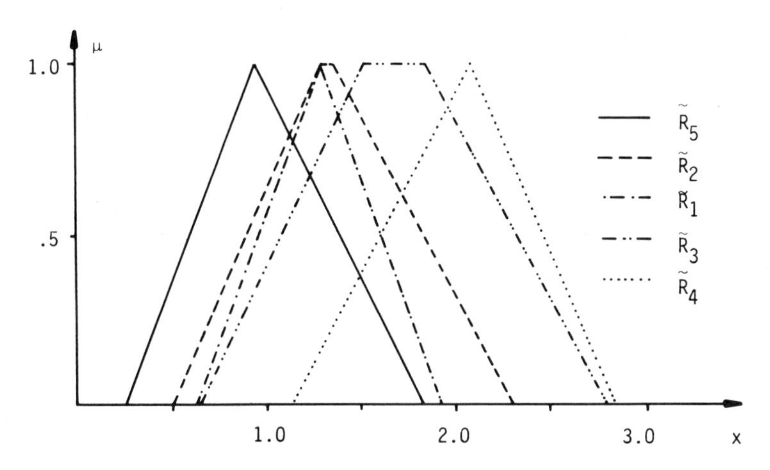

Figure 5-20: Ratings of alternatives.

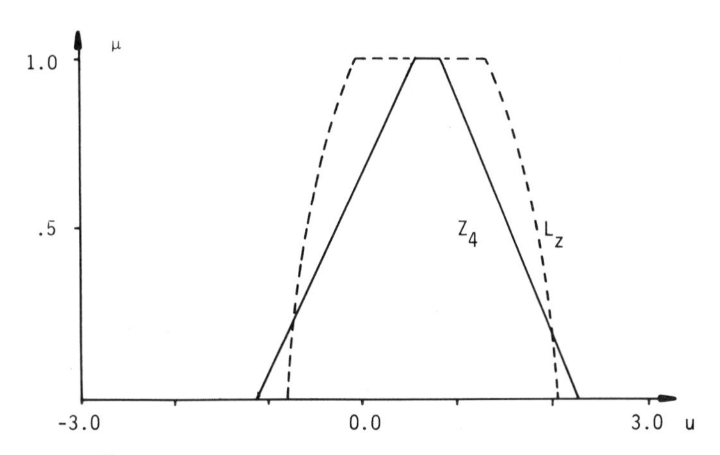

Figure 5-21: $\tilde{Z}_k$ for nondominated alternatives.

that the investor hardly distinguishes between an investment in real estate or one in gold (diamonds). It is therefore not surprising that Tong and Bonissone suggest, on the basis of step 2, one common linguistic term ($\tilde{L}_Z$) as a linguistic approximation for $\tilde{Z}_3$ and $\tilde{Z}_4$, with the interpretation

x_k = real estate and/or gold and diamonds

$\tilde{P}$ = from indifferent to marginally better than (other alternatives!)

τ = more or less true

If the investor still wants a discrimination between x_3 and x_4 he could, for instance, consider only these two (rather than all) alternatives and supply more information on his preferences, which might lead to a modification of $\tilde{R}_3$ and of $\tilde{R}_4$ and hence to different $\tilde{Z}_3$ and $\tilde{Z}_4$, respectively.

The distinguishing feature of Tong and Bonissone's procedure is that it offers a (fuzzy) linguistic solution to a (possibly) fuzzy problem rather than the pretense of a preciseness not inherent in the problem. The final approach to multi-attribute decision making to be presented here goes even one step further and offers the decision maker a vector of four "measures" characterizing decision alternatives. It is then left to the decision maker to derive a final judgment.

Possibilistic Multi-Indexes ranking [Dubois, Prade 1983]

Dubois and Prade also concentrate on the second phase of the MADM problem, on ranking of fuzzy sets representing, for instance, the desirability of decision alternatives. They suggest four indexes for ranking two fuzzy numbers $\tilde{R}_i$ and $\tilde{R}_j$:

1. Possibility of dominance:

$$PD(\tilde{R}) = \text{Poss}(\tilde{R}_i \geq \tilde{R}_j) = \sup_{\substack{r_i, r_j \\ r_i \geq r_j}} \min [\mu_{\tilde{R}_i}(r_i), \mu_{\tilde{R}_j}(r_j)] \tag{5.39}$$

2. Possibility of strict dominance:

$$PSD(\tilde{R}_i) = \text{Poss}(\tilde{R}_i > \tilde{R}_j) = \sup_{r_i} \inf_{\substack{r_j \\ r_j \geq r_i}} \min [\mu_{\tilde{R}_i}(r_i), 1 - \mu_{\tilde{R}_j}(r_j)] \tag{5.40}$$

3. Necessity of dominance:

$$ND(\tilde{R}_i) = \text{Nec}(\tilde{R}_i \geq \tilde{R}_j) = \inf_{r_i} \sup_{\substack{r_j \\ r_j \geq r_i}} \max [1 - \mu_{\tilde{R}_i}(r_i), \mu_{\tilde{R}_j}(r_j)] \tag{5.41}$$

4. Necessity of strict dominance:

$$NDS(\tilde{R}_i) = \text{Nec}(\tilde{R}_i > \tilde{R}_j) = 1 - \sup_{r_i \le r_j} \min [\mu_{\tilde{R}_i}(r_i), \mu_{\tilde{R}_j}(r_j)] \tag{5.42}$$

In order to extend these indexes to the ranking of n fuzzy ratings they define the dominance of $\tilde{R}_i$ over all other $\tilde{R}_j$, $i \neq j$, as the grades of dominance of $\tilde{R}_i$ over $\max_{j \neq i} r_j$. Hence,

1. Possibility of dominance:

$$PD(\tilde{R}_i) = \text{Poss}\left(\tilde{R}_i \geq \widetilde{\max_{j \neq i}} \tilde{R}_j\right) = \min_{j \neq i} \text{Poss}(\tilde{R}_i \geq \tilde{R}_j) \tag{5.39a}$$

2. Possibility of strict dominance:

$$PSD(\tilde{R}_i) = \text{Poss}\left(\tilde{R}_i > \widetilde{\max_{j \neq i}} \tilde{R}_j\right) \tag{5.40a}$$

3. Necessity of dominance:

$$ND(\tilde{R}_i) = 1 - \text{Poss}\left(\tilde{R}_i < \widetilde{\max_{j \neq i}} \tilde{R}_j\right) \tag{5.41a}$$

4. Necessity of strict dominance:

$$NSD(\tilde{R}_i) = 1 - \text{Poss}\left(\tilde{R}_i \leq \widetilde{\max_{j \neq i}} \tilde{R}_j\right) \tag{5.42a}$$

The reader can find a more detailed interpretation of these indexes in the later part of chapter 7.

The ratings $\tilde{R}_i$ can then be ranked in descending order in terms of decreasing values of each index. If these orders are identical there is no problem in ranking the $\tilde{R}_i$. If this is not the case a more detailed interpretation can be given than if only one index would exist. We will illustrate this in the following example.

Example 5.12

Let us consider the situations shown in figure 5-22, for which table 5-8 shows the results of applying Dubois and Prade's method as shown in Bortolan and Degani 1985.

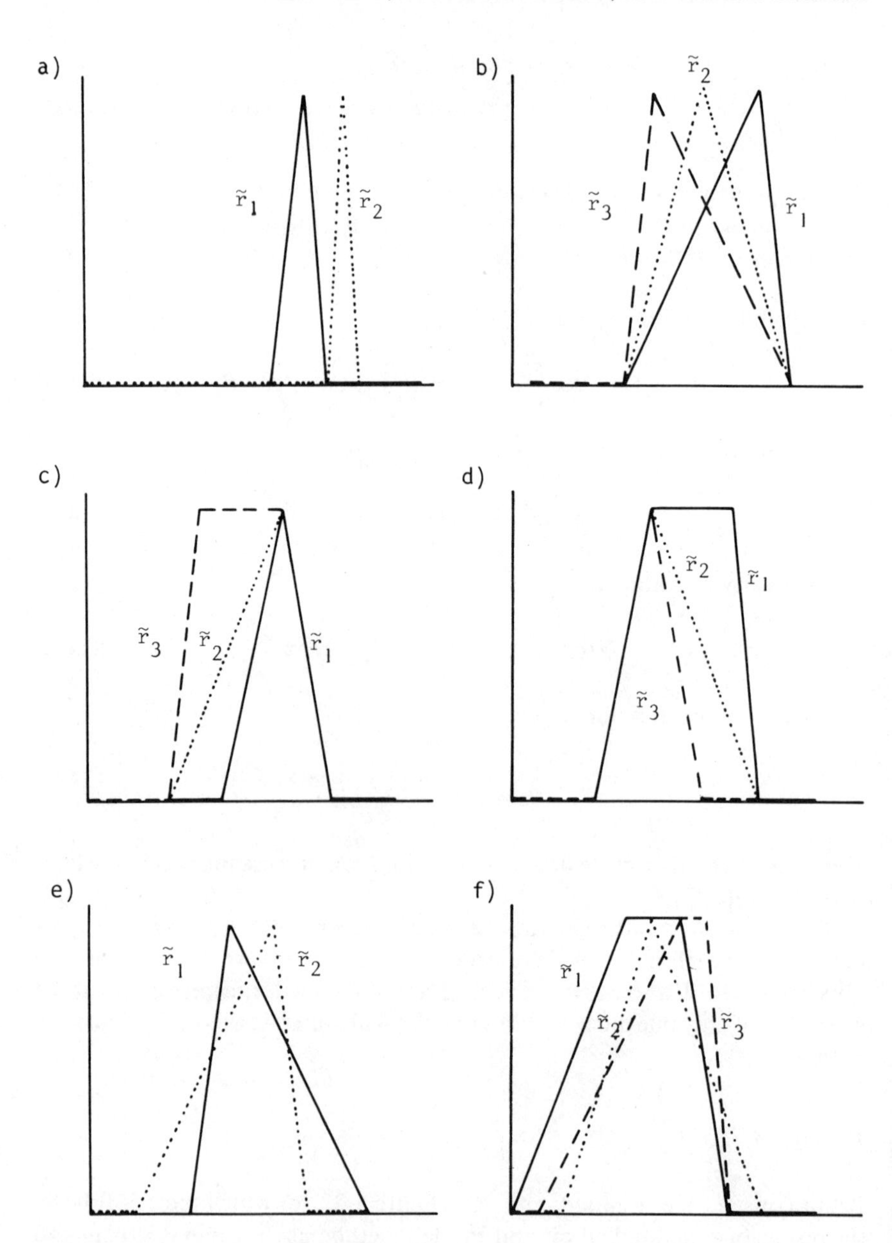

Figure 5-22: Ranking with Multiple Indices.

Table 5-8

Case	5-22*a*		5-22*b*			5-22*c*			5-22*d*			5-22*e*		5-22*f*		
	$\tilde{r}_1$	$\tilde{r}_2$	$\tilde{r}_1$	$\tilde{r}_2$	$\tilde{r}_3$	$\tilde{r}_1$	$\tilde{r}_2$	$\tilde{r}_3$	$\tilde{r}_1$	$\tilde{r}_2$	$\tilde{r}_3$	$\tilde{r}_1$	$\tilde{r}_2$	$\tilde{r}_1$	$\tilde{r}_2$	$\tilde{r}_3$
PD	0	1	1	.74	.60	1	1	1	1	1	1	.84	1	1	.88	1
PSD	0	1	.74	.23	.16	.5	.5	.5	.8	.2	0	.54	.46	.3	.4	.6
ND	0	1	.63	.38	.18	.67	.35	0	.5	.5	.5	.54	.46	.3	.5	.5
NSD	0	1	.26	0	0	0	0	0	0	0	0	0	.16	0	0	0

Case 5-22a is clearcut: $\tilde{r}_2$ obviously dominates $\tilde{r}_1$. Case 5-22b is still without problems and both results coincide with the results shown in table 5-6. Case 5-22c shows a slight dominance of $\tilde{r}_1$ over $\tilde{r}_2$, which would still not contradict the results in table 5-6. The same holds for case 5-22d. For case 5-22e, the results are rather confusing: $\tilde{r}_2$ shows a slight superiority of possibility of dominance but not of strict dominance and vice versa for the necessity of dominance. This is also the case in which the methods compared in table 5.6 lead to contradicting results.

The most difficult case seems to be case 5-22f. A possible, though probably not very helpful for the DM, interpretation could be: none of the alternatives dominates strictly because all three supports overlap. $\tilde{r}_2$ and $\tilde{r}_3$ dominate $\tilde{r}_1$ on the left (ND) while $\tilde{r}_3$ is better than $\tilde{r}_1$ and $\tilde{r}_2$ on the right (PSD). $\tilde{r}_1$ and $\tilde{r}_3$ can both be better than $\tilde{r}_2$ on the right (PD).

It is of interest to compare the ratings of the other metholds for this case: Yager: $\tilde{r}_1 \succ \tilde{r}_3 \succ \tilde{r}_2$; Jain: $\tilde{r}_3 \succ \tilde{r}_1 \succ \tilde{r}_2$; Baas and Kwakernaak: $\tilde{r}_1 \approx \tilde{r}_3 \succ \tilde{r}_2$; and Baldwin and Guild: $\tilde{r}_2 \approx \tilde{r}_3 \succ \tilde{r}_1$. Obviously none of the orderings coincide with any other!

Summarizing, it can be stated, that the methods shown lead to almost the same results if all the problems have clearcut solutions. If this is not the case the results contradict each other to different degrees. Dubois and Prade's method seems to allow the most detailed interpretations. Before turning to a quite different, order-focussed approach, we should ask the question, "Which is the best MADM method so far?" This question can not be answered with certainty because the answer will depend largely on the situation for which the method is to be used, on subjective evaluations, and on other factors. Some help in selecting a suitable method might, however, be provided by a classification of the methods according to a number of criteria.

A first classification could be done by looking at the three aspects—scope, process, and focus—as shown in table 5-9. This classification is rather mechanistic. It considers the method from a technical point of view. More appropriate would probably be a multidimensional classification taking into consideration more aspects of the different approaches. The following possible dimensions are sketched in figure 5-23:

Generality refers to the degree of general applicability of the method: are special types of fuzzy sets assumed or can the ratings have arbitrary forms; is the method restricted to special operators or can they be adopted to the context; etc.

Discrimination refers to the capability of a method to differentiate between alternatives the ratings of which differ only slightly from each other. As mentioned above authors have different views on whether a method should be very discriminatory or rather "stable."

Table 5-9: Classification of Methods by Criteria

Criterion			
Scope	Step 1	Step 2	Steps 1 and 2
Process	Simultaneous	Hierarchical	Interactive
Focus	Aggregation	Distance	Order-relation

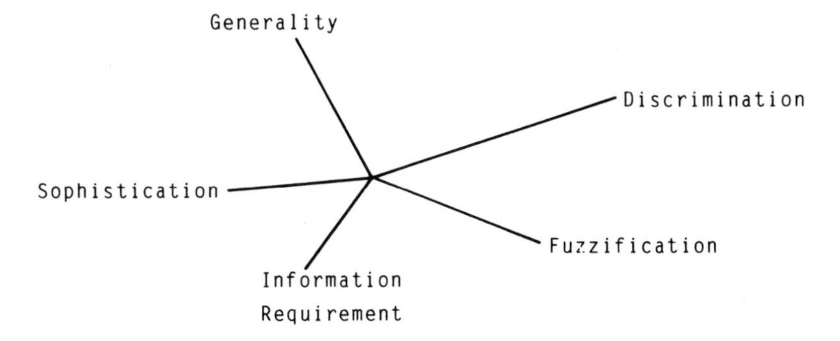

Figure 5-23: Classification of methods.

Fuzzification: Obviously different components of the MADM-problem can be represented by fuzzy sets. One extreme would be to consider only the relative weights of the criteria as fuzzy sets. Another extreme could be to consider the ratings, the weights and the alternatives as fuzzy.

Information requirements: The more standardized the input data the less information has to be processed but the rougher might be the model of the real problem! If, for instance, only triangular fuzzy numbers are allowed each of them can be characterized by three real numbers. If arbitrary fuzzy sets are used much more information has to be provided and processed. The amount of information to be processed would increase even further if type-2 fuzzy sets are used.

Sophistication refers to the mathematical tools used in phases I and/or II.

An evaluation of the methods according to the above criteria would obviously be rather subjective. Table 5-10, therefore, describes rather than evaluates the methods we have discussed in this section.

Table 5-10: Comparison of Approaches to solve Multi-Attribute Decision Problems

	Phase	*Weights*	*Criteria*	*Aggreg. Phase I*	*Crit. f. ranking*	*Solution*
Yager [1981]	I + II	fuzzy	fuzzy sets (norm)	weighted sum	max + min (Phase II)	crisp
Baas & Kwakernaak [1977]	I + II	fuzzy	fuzzy sets	max − min	preference sets	crisp
Laarhoven & Pedrycz [1983]	I	fuzzy triangular numbers	crisp	hierarchical aggregation	—	fuzzy ratings
Jain [1977]	II	—	fuzzy	—	maximizing set	crisp
Baldwin & Guild [1979]	II	—	fuzzy (special)	—	relative preference	fuzzy
Chen [1985]	II	—	fuzzy	—	maximizing and minimizing set	crisp
Tong & Bonissone [1984]	II	ling. variables	crisp	—	fuzzy truth qualification of dominance	fuzzy
Dubois & Prade [1984]	II	—	fuzzy	—	multiple	vectorial

Fuzzy Outranking

In the preceeding chapters and sections it was generally assumed that the decision-making body, individual or group, wanted to maximize utility and that a rather well-specified preference function was known or could be determined. Preferences were normally expressed as either preference relations (see definitions 2.15 through 2.17) or as ratings of actions or alternatives with respect to criteria or goals, or expressed the preference of the decision maker with respect to one alternative compared to another. The general framework of argumentation was that of a formal theory: that is, "given that the individual preference orderings satisfy additive transitivity, so does the resulting group preference relation" (see chapter 3, *Fuzzy Group...*).

Since the end of the sixties there has appeared an increasing concern about the usefulness of the usual notion of a utility function for real decision making. Together with the growth of multi-criteria analysis there has been an increase in attempts to enrich decision models beyond the strictly optimizing choice model and to render the assumptions about the (mathematical) properties of utility or preference functions more realistic. One of the most prominent representatives of this direction is Bernhard Roy who proposed to substitute for the classical choice model–striving for a complete order of the actions or alternatives–the classification of types of decisions, as mentioned in chapter 1, optimization, ...

Classical assumptions for preference relations are *transitivity*, *reflexivity*, and *antisymmetry* (see definition 2.14). It is generally assumed that a decision maker can make either of two judgments about two alternatives x_i and x_j: the decision maker either prefers (strictly or fuzzily) one or the other or is indifferent with respect to the alternatives under consideration. The case of *incomparability* is normally excluded. Roy [1976, p. 182] gives three good reasons for not excluding incomparability and for distinguishing it from indifference:

1. One cannot compare alternatives due to the lack of information or because the available information is too uncertain.
2. One does not want to compare alternatives, because at a certain stage it might not seem appropriate to adopt value systems that would allow a comparison.
3. One does not know how to compare alternatives due to either a multi-criteria problem, a lack of knowledge about existing preferences, or the high imprecision of the knowledge about preferences.

Under these circumstances, it makes sense to renounce what Roy [1976, p. 6] calls the "axiom of complete transitive comparability," that is, the assumption that preferences can be modelled by means of the two binary relations "preference" (irreflexive, antisymmetric, and transitive) and "indifference" (reflexive, symmetric, and transitive). This assumption would be well replaced by answers to the question:

> How can alternatives be ranked if $c_j(x_i) \neq c_j(x_j), j \in J \subset F$; and $|J| > 1$, where c_j are multiple vector-valued criteria, J is the index set of the criteria, and F is a so-called consistent family of criteria? [Roy 1976, pp. 5, 24]

In search of such answers, Roy [1976] suggests considering, in addition to "indifference"(I) and "strict preference" (P), two binary relations "large preference" (Q) and "incomparability" (Y) which he defines as follows:

Definition 5.7

Large preference, $x_i Q x_j$ or $x_j Q x_i$, prevails if one of the alternatives is not strictly preferred to the other and if it is impossible to decide whether the other is strictly preferred or indifferent to the first. This insufficient "decidability" may be due to a lack of information or to the small degree of difference between the alternatives.

Example 5.13

The relation "large preference" may exist, if for two alternatives $x_i, x_j \in A \subseteq X$ and several criteria $c_i(x_i)$, $i = 1,\ldots,m$, the following is true:

$$c_i(x_i) = c_i(x_j) \qquad \forall\, i \neq k$$

and

$$c_k(x_i) - c_k(x_j) \leq s_k$$

where s_k is a threshold below which a unique statement about a preference relationship cannot be made.

Definition 5.8

Incomparability between x_i and x_j prevails, $x_i Y x_j$, if for x_i and x_j none of the relations $x_i P x_j$, $x_i I x_j$, $x_i Q x_j$ (and vice versa) exist.

Example 5.14

The relationship $x_i \, Y \, x_j$ may, for instance, exist if for $x_i, x_j \in A \subset X$ the following holds:

$$c_j(x_i) > c_j(x_j) \qquad \text{for } j = 1,\ldots,k < m$$

$$c_j(x_i) < c_j(x_j) \qquad \text{for } j = k + 1,\ldots,m$$

For the foregoing four preference relationships the following properties are assumed to exist:

I (indifference): reflexive and symmetric

P (strict preference): irreflexive and antisymmetric

Q (large preference): irreflexive and antisymmetric

Y (incomparability): irreflexive and symmetric.

To establish preference relationships for these four kinds of possible situations the (fuzzy) indifference and preference relations as defined in definitions 2.16 and 2.17 are obviously no longer sufficient. To cope with this extended view of decision models Roy suggested the use of so called outranking relations, $x_i \, R_A^d \, x_j$, which are defined via the degree of outranking d, as follows [Roy 1973, p. 183; 1976, p. 26]:

Definition 5.9

"x_i *outranks* x_j" if the scientist has enough reasons (in particular with respect to what $c(x_i)$ and $c(x_j)$ really mean) to admit that in the eyes of the decision maker x_i is at least as good as x_j (hence x_i is indifferent from or preferred to x_j).

"x_i does not outrank x_j" signifies that the arguments in favor of the proposition "x_i is at least as good as x_j" are judged insufficient, and that there exist arguments in favor of the proposition "x_j is at least as good as x_i." Hence x_i is preferred or incomparable to x_j.

Fuzzy outranking relations $\tilde{R}_A^d$, also, are defined via the degree of outranking, d [Roy 1973, p. 183; 1976, p. 27]:

Definition 5.10

The *degree of outranking* of x_i over x_j, $d(x_i,x_j)$, $x_i,x_j \in X$, is a function of the evaluations of x_i and x_j, that is,

$$d(x_i,x_j) = d(c(x_i),c(x_j)) \qquad \forall\, i,j \in J,\ x \in A \subseteq X$$

$d(x_i,x_j)$ is a nondecreasing function of $c(x_i)\,\forall\, i$ and a nonincreasing function of $c(x_j)\,\forall\, j$.

$d(x_i,x_j) = 1$ implies a certain outranking of x_i over x_j.

$d(x_i,x_j) = 0$ implies either a certain nonoutranking of x_j by x_i or the total absence of arguments in favor of such an outranking. Hence,

$$0 \le d(x_i,x_j) \le 1$$

Note that $d(x_i,x_j)$ does not necessarily represent an intensity of preference of x_i over x_j. It is rather the credibility of a preference existing of x_i over x_j!

In analogy to the α-level cuts of fuzzy set theory we can also define a crisp outranking relation R_A^α:

Definition 5.11

Using the terminology of the definitions above a (*crisp*) *outranking relation* is defined by

$$x_i\, R_A^\alpha\, x_j \Leftrightarrow d(x_i,x_j) \ge \alpha$$

The four possible relationships between decision alternatives x_i and x_j can be represented by outranking relationships as follows (s_k indicates the "outranking threshold" concerning the kth criterion):

1. Indifference

   Criteria:

$$c_l(x_i) = c_l(x_j) \qquad \forall\, l \ne k$$

$$c_k(x_i) - c_k(x_j) < s_k(C_k)$$

   Outranking:

$$\tilde{R}^d(x_i,x_j) = \tilde{R}^d(x_j,x_i) \qquad 0 \le d(x_i,x_j) \le 1$$

   Example:

$$x_i \underset{d\,=\,.6}{\overset{d\,=\,.6}{\rightleftarrows}} x_j$$

2. Incomparability

a.
$$c_l(x_i) = c_l(x_j) \qquad \forall\, l \neq k,h$$
$$0 < c_k(x_i) - c_k(x_j) < s_k$$
$$0 < c_h(x_j) - c_h(x_i) < s_h$$

b.
$$c_l(x_i) = c_l(x_j) \qquad \forall\, l \neq h,k$$
$$0 < c_k(x_i) - c_k(x_j) > s_k$$
$$0 < c_h(x_j) - c_h(x_i) > s_h$$

Outranking:

$$\tilde{R}^d(x_i,x_j) = \tilde{R}^d(x_j,x_i) \qquad 0 < d < s$$

Example:

$d = .1$

$x_i \rightleftarrows x_j$

$d = .1$

3. Large Preference

$$c_l(x_i) = c_l(x_j) \qquad \forall\, l \neq k,h$$
$$0 < c_h(x_i) - c_h(x_j) > s_h$$
$$0 < c_k(x_j) - c_k(x_i) < s_k$$

Outranking:

$$\tilde{R}^d(x_i,x_j) > \tilde{R}^d(x_j,x_i) > S$$

Example:

$d = .3$

$x_i \rightleftarrows x_j$

$d = .8$

4. Strict Preference

a.
$$c_l(x_i) > c_l(x_j) \qquad \forall\, l$$

b.
$$c_l(x_i) > c_l(x_j) \qquad \forall\, l \neq k$$
$$0 \leq c_k(x_j) - c_k(x_i) < s$$

Outranking:

$$\tilde{R}^d(x_i,x_j) > 1 - s \qquad \tilde{R}^d(x_j,x_i) = 0$$

Example:

$$x_j \xrightarrow{d = .9} x_j$$

The Construction of Fuzzy Outranking Relations

Several ways have been suggested for construction of fuzzy outranking relations [see, for example, Roy 1976, p. 31; Martel et al. 1986]. We shall focus our attention on one that seems particularly interesting—the use of degree of concordance and discordance—using the following terminology:

$x_i \in X, \quad i = 1,\ldots,m$	are the decision alternatives.
$C_l, \quad l = 1,\ldots,n$	are the criteria according to which the alternatives are evaluated (rated).
$c_l(x_i), \quad i = 1,\ldots,m$; $l = 1,\ldots,n$	is the rating of alternative x_i with respect to *criterion l.*
$w_l \geq 0, \quad \sum_{l=1}^{n} w_l = 1$	are the weights (relative importance) of the criterion C_l.

We shall also use the following thresholds:

s^i indifference threshold
s^p preference threshold
s^v veto threshold

The interpretation is for $c_l(x_i) \in \mathbb{R}^+$ where

$$c_l(x_i) \geq c_l(x_j) + s^i(C_l)$$

indicates x_i is at least as good as x_j,

$$c_l(x_i) \geq c_l(x_j) + s^p(C_l)$$

indicates x_i is strictly preferred to x_j, and

$$c_l(x_i) \geq c_l(x_l) + s^v(C_l)$$

indicates x_i is considerably better than x_j. Obviously, $0 \leq s^i < s^p \leq s^v$ for any criterion C_l!

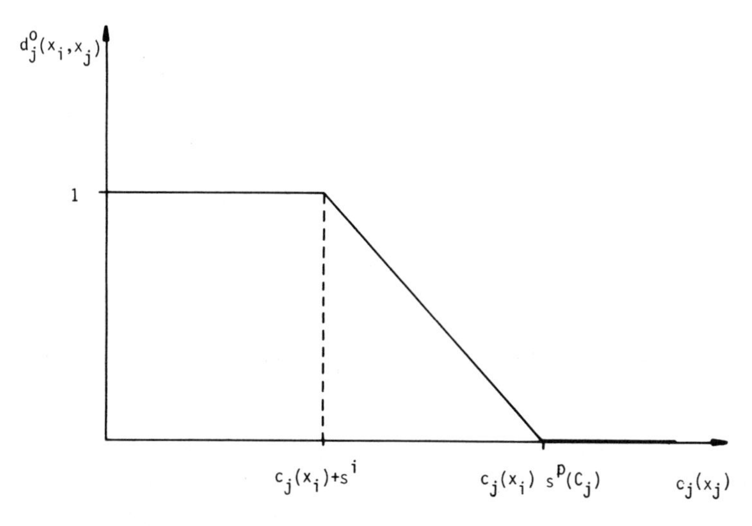

Figure 5-24: Fuzzy concordance.

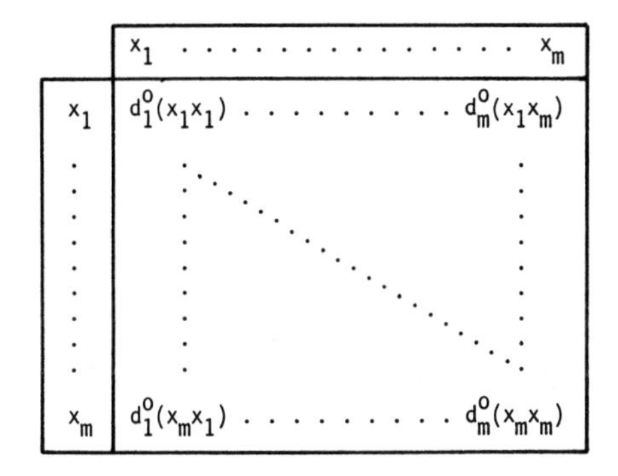

Figure 5-25: Fuzzy concordance matrix.

We now define a degree of concordance, d^0, which expresses the credibility of the hypothesis that x_i is at least as good as x_j with respect to criterion C_l. A simple way to do this is [Roy 1980, p. 475] to define:

$$d_l^0(x_i,x_j) = \begin{cases} 0 & \text{for } c_l(x_j) \geq c_l(x_i) + s^p(C_l) \\ \dfrac{c_l(x_j) - (c_l(x_i) + s^p(C_l))}{s^i(C_l) - s^p(C_l)} & \text{for } c_l(x_i) + s^i \\ & \quad \leq c_l(x_j) \leq c_l(x_i) + s^p(C_l) \\ 1 & \text{for } c_l(x_i) + s^i(C_l) \geq c_l(x_j) \end{cases} \tag{5.43}$$

Figure 5-24 depicts this kind of fuzzy concordance relation. For the set of feasible alternatives, the fuzzy concordance relation $\tilde{D}_1^0$ can be written as the matrix shown in figure 5-25.

The concordance relation for criterion C_l is now supplemented by a *discordance* relation which expresses the credibility of the hypothesis that alternative x_i is not at least as good as alternative x_j. In analogy to (5.43), fuzzy discordance is defined as

$$d_l^i(x_i,x_j) = \begin{cases} 0 & \text{for } c_l(x_i) + s^p(C_l) \geq c_l(x_j) \\ \dfrac{c_l(x_j) - (c_l(x_i) + s^p(C_l))}{s^v(C_l) - s^p(C_l)} & \text{for } c_l(x_i) + s^p(C_l) \\ & \quad \leq c_l(x_j) \leq c_l(x_i) + s^v(C_l) \\ 1 & \text{for } c_l(x_i) \geq c_l(x_j) + s^v(C_l) \end{cases} \tag{5.44}$$

Figure 5-26 depicts this relation. For all pairs of alternatives, this can be written as the fuzzy discordance matrix

$$\tilde{D}_l^i = (d_l^i(x_i,x_j))$$

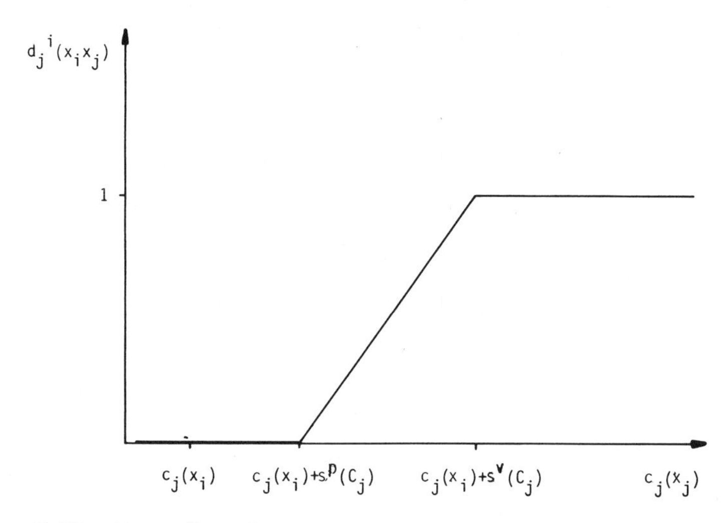

Figure 5-26: Fuzzy discordance.

Concordance and discordance have so far been defined for each pair of alternatives and with respect to single criteria C_l. Since we are concerned with multicriteria problems the concordance and discordance relations have to be aggregated for all criteria. Roy's suggestion is to compute the weighted sum of the concordance relations in order to arrive at the total concordance. As weights, the relative criteria weights w_l are used. Hence,

$$d^0(x_i,x_j) = \sum_{l=1}^{n} w_l d_l^0(x_i,x_j) \qquad x_i,x_j \in X \tag{5.45}$$

and

$$\tilde{D}^0 = w_1 \tilde{D}_1^0 + \cdots + w_n \tilde{D}_n^0 \tag{5.46}$$

Eventually concordance and discordance have to be aggregated to arrive at the outranking relation. To this end a discordance multiplier is defined in order to reduce the concordance by the discordance. Roy defines the discordance multiplier $d^i(x_i,x_j)$ by

$$d^i(x_i,x_j) = \frac{1}{n} \sum_{l=1}^{n} fak(d_l^i(x_i,x_j) \qquad d^0(x_i,x_j)) \tag{5.47}$$

where the operation $fak(d_l^0(.), d_l^i(.)$ is defined as

$$fak(d_l^i(.),d^0(.)) = \begin{cases} 1 & \text{for } d_l^i(.) \leq d^0(.) \\ \dfrac{1 - d_l^i(.)}{1 - d^0(.)} & \text{for } d_l^i(.) > d^0(.), d^0(.) \neq 1 \end{cases} \tag{5.48}$$

Table 5-11: Ratings

	c_1	c_2	c_3
x_1	0.72	0.73	0.60
x_2	0.50	0.50	0.60
x_3	0.72	0.73	0.30
x_4	0.60	0.60	0.30
x_5	0.60	0.60	0.60

The degree of outranking is then computed as

$$d_{ij} = d^{o}(x_i,x_j) \cdot d^{i}(x_i,x_j) \tag{5.49}$$

resulting in the fuzzy outranking relation

$$\tilde{R}_A^d = ((d_{ij})) \, \forall \, i,j \tag{5.50}$$

Example 5.15

Let us consider an example with three criteria, c_1, c_2, and c_3, and five alternatives, x_1 through x_5. The ratings, $c_l(x_i)$, of the alternatives are given in table 5-11.

We shall choose the following numerical values for the parameters of the outranking procedure:

$$\begin{aligned} w_l &= \tfrac{1}{3} && l = 1,2,3 \text{ (equal weights)} \\ s_l^i &= .05 && l = 1,2,3 \\ s_l^p &= .15 && l = 1,2,3 \\ s_l^v &= .25 && l = 1,23 \end{aligned}$$

The concordance matrixes according to (5.43) are then as shown in tables 5-12 through 5-14. Now, using (5.44); we can determine the discordance matrixes depicted in tables 5-15, 5-16, and 5-17. The total concordance matrix using equal weights is shown in table 5-18.

If we use (5.47) through (5.50) to reduce the concordance by the discordance we arrive eventually at the fuzzy outranking relation shown in table 5-19. Then, for different values of d_{ij} (corresponding to α-level cuts) we can give the

Table 5-12: Concordance matrix $\tilde{D}_1^0$

$\tilde{D}_1^0$	x_1	x_2	x_3	x_4	x_5
x_1	1	1	1	1	1
x_2	0	1	0	0.5	0.5
x_3	1	1	1	1	1
x_4	0.3	1	0.3	1	1
x_5	0.3	1	0.3	1	1

Table 5-13: Concordance matrix $\tilde{D}_2^0$

$\tilde{D}_2^0$	x_1	x_2	x_3	x_4	x_5
x_1	1	1	1	1	1
x_2	0	1	0	0.5	0.5
x_3	1	1	1	1	1
x_4	0.2	1	0.2	1	1
x_5	0.2	1	0.2	1	1

Table 5-14: Concordance matrix $\tilde{D}_3^0$

$\tilde{D}_1^0$	x_1	x_2	x_3	x_4	x_5
x_1	1	1	1	1	1
x_2	1	1	1	1	1
x_3	0	0	1	1	0
x_4	0	0	1	1	0
x_5	1	1	1	1	1

respective dominance relations or graphs. These are shown for $d_{ij} = 1$ and for $1 \geq d_{ij} \geq .45$ in figures 5-27 and 5-28.

Given the fuzzy outranking relation $\tilde{R}_A^d$ we can now alternatively consider

Table 5-15: Discordance matrix $\tilde{D}_1^i$

$\tilde{D}_1^i$	x_1	x_2	x_3	x_4	x_5
x_1	0	0	0	0	0
x_2	0.7	0	0.7	0	0
x_3	0	0	0	0	0
x_4	0	0	0	0	0
x_5	0	0	0	0	0

Table 5-16: Discordance matrix $\tilde{D}_2^i$

$\tilde{D}_2^i$	x_1	x_2	x_3	x_4	x_5
x_1	0	0	0	0	0
x_2	0.8	0	0.8	0	0
x_3	0	0	0	0	0
x_4	0	0	0	0	0
x_5	0	0	0	0	0

Table 5-17: Discordance matrix $\tilde{D}_3^i$

$\tilde{D}_3^i$	x_1	x_2	x_3	x_4	x_5
x_1	0	0	0	0	0
x_2	0	0	0	0	0
x_3	1	1	0	0	1
x_4	1	1	0	0	1
x_5	0	0	0	0	0

any of the decision situations α, β, or γ, described at the beginning of this book. We shall discuss them in turn.

Table 5-18: Total concordance matrix

D^0	x_1	x_2	x_3	x_4	x_5
x_1	1	1	1	1	1
x_2	0.33	1	0.33	0.67	0.67
x_3	0.67	0.67	1	1	0.67
x_4	0.17	0.67	0.5	1	0.67
x_5	0.5	1	0.5	1	1

Table 5-19: Fuzzy outranking relation

$\tilde{R}^d_A =$

d_{ii}	x_1	x_2	x_3	x_4	x_5
x_1	1	1	1	1	1
x_2	0.19	1	0.19	0.67	0.67
x_3	0.45	0.45	1	1	0.45
x_4	0.113	0.45	0.5	1	0.45
x_5	0.5	1	0.5	1	1

α. Selecting Best Alternatives (Dichotomy Method) [Roy 1976, p. 37; 1980, p. 483]. First of all we can derive from $\tilde{R}^d_X$ a crisp outranking relation R^α_X as defined in definition 5.11. If for $\alpha = 1$ there exists an alternative x_k for which $x_k R^1 x_j \forall j \neq k$ this alternative(s) is certainly a candidate for the best choice.

In general the chances of such an x_k existing are not too good. Then the decision analyst will have to determine R^α_k for $\alpha \neq 1$ such that α is considered high enough to assert "dominance" of alternative x_k over the others. If this is not possible one can still try to determine the minimal outranking set.

Definition 5.12 [Roy 1976, p. 38]

Let X be the set of feasible alternatives. $N \subset X$ is called the *minimal outranking set* with regard to R^α_X if each action in X but not in N is outranked by at least one action in N and if the reduction of N by one action causes N to be no longer an outranking set.

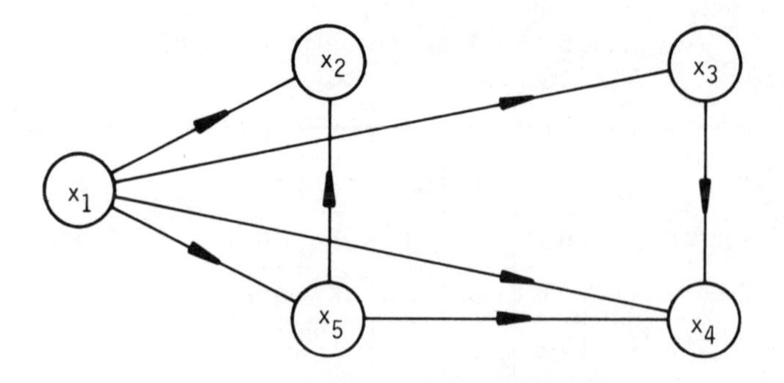

Figure 5-27: Outranking graph for $d_{ij} = 1$.

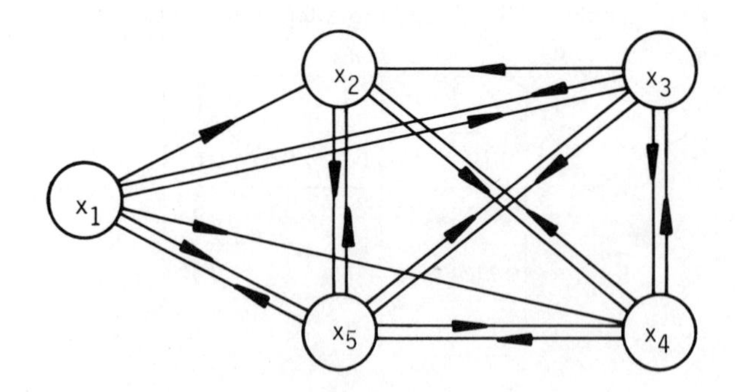

Figure 5-28: Outranking graph for $1 \geq d_{ij} \geq .45$.

Example 5.16

Let us consider figure 5-29, the (crisp) outranking graph, R_x^α, of the alternatives x_1 through x_6. $N = \{x_1, x_5\}$, then, is a minimal outranking set with regard to R_x^α. If we now consider the (fuzzy) outranking graph of figure 5-30, we can determine the following minimal outranking sets, for instance, for $\alpha = .95$ and for $\alpha = .7$:

$$N \text{ for } R_x^{.95} = \{x_1, x_2, x_6, x_7\}$$

$$N \text{ for } R_x^{.7} = \{x_1, x_6\}$$

β. Determining the Set of All Good Alternatives (Trichotomy method). The goal of this type of decision model is to sort or classify feasible alterna-

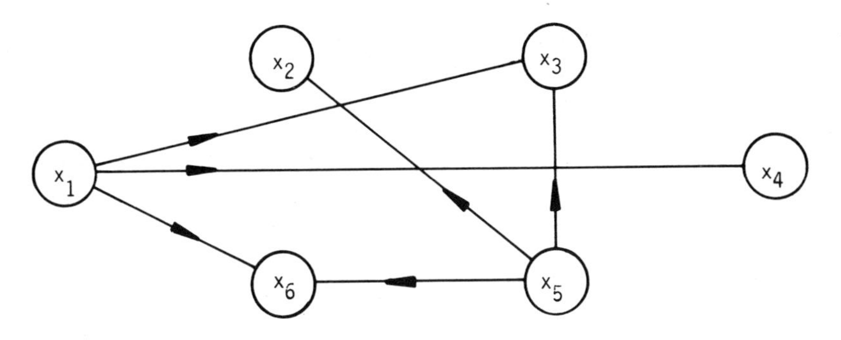

Figure 5-29: Outranking Graph.

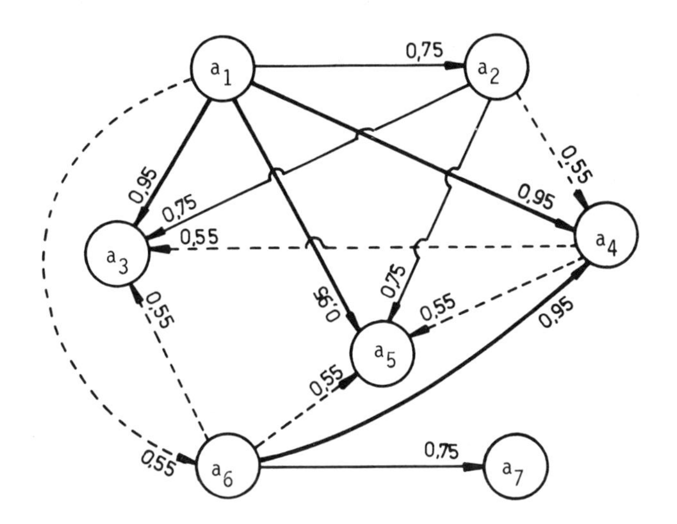

Figure 5-30: Fuzzy Outranking Graph.

tives into a number of classes such as "acceptable," "nonacceptable," "non-decidable" alternatives.

Let us assume that we want to classify all elements $x_i \in X$ into three subsets X_1, X_2, X_3 where

$x_i \in X_1$	means accept alternative
$x_i \in X_2$	means reject alternative
$x_i \in X_3$	means additional examinations by communicating with the decision maker

Again, we start from a fuzzy outranking relation $\tilde{R}_X^d$. We could, for example, determine an overall acceptance threshold $0 \leq \lambda^1 \leq 1$, above which acceptance is indicated and a rejection level $0 \leq \lambda^2 \leq 1$, below which definite rejection is advised. If we define $d_i^1 = \min_j d_{ij}$ and $d_i^2 = \max_j d_{ij}$, figure 5-31 sketches the way a sorting algorithm could look. The rejection and acceptance indicators might not be defined with reference to the aggregated outranking relation, but with respect to different subsets of criteria.

γ. Rank-Ordering the Decision Alternatives. Here the decision maker might want to rank all alternatives or the alternatives in the subset of "acceptable" alternatives. This approach or task is obviously most similar to the types of models discussed in the first two sections of this chapter. In other words, the decision maker tries to establish a preorder or a total order of a set of alternatives.

This is not a difficult task if a scalar-valued value—or utility function with appropriate properties—exists. As we have seen, however, it involves a number of problems for multi-criteria situations (vector-valued objective functions). Algorithms for outranking relations and fuzzy outranking relations have been designed and used in the framework of ELECTRE II and ELECTRE III. The interested reader is referred for more detailed descriptions of those approaches to Roy [Roy 1976, p. 491; Moscarola, Roy 1977, p. 145–173].

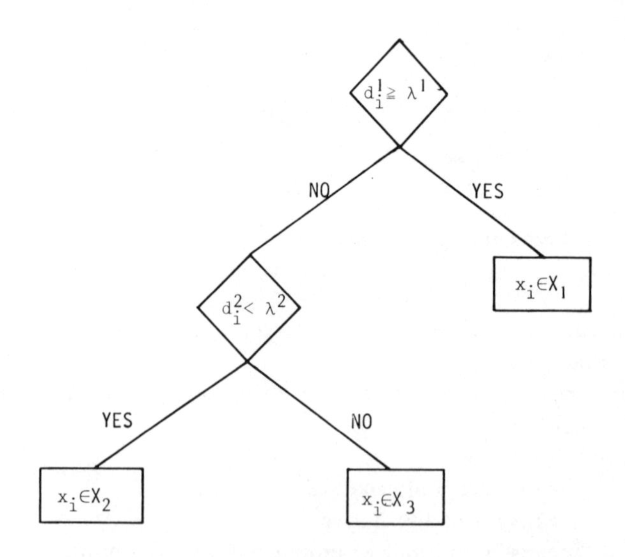

Figure 5-31: Algorithm for Trichotomy model.

6 OPERATORS AND MEMBERSHIP FUNCTIONS IN DECISION MODELS

Axiomatic, Pragmatic, and Empirical Justification

Many papers in the area of fuzzy sets start with statements such as "Given membership function $\mu_A(x)$ and assuming that the minimum operator is an appropriate model for the intersection of fuzzy sets...." If fuzzy set theory is considered to be a purely formal theory, such statements are certainly acceptable, even though some kind of formal justification of these assumptions would be desirable. If, however, fuzzy set theory is used to model real phenomena and we assert these models to be true models of reality then some kind of empirical justification is absolutely necessary.

In the first section of chapter 1 we made some remarks concerning the relationship between formal theories, factual theories, and technologies [see also Zimmermann 1980]. So far hardly any formal axiomatic justification for specific kinds of membership functions has been offered. Authors normally argue pragmatically by assuming some kind of membership function and then going on to see "whether it works." Some formal arguments can be found in fuzzy logic when membership functions for the linguistic variable "truth" are defined. The results of empirically testing models for membership functions will be described shortly. The situation is slightly better for operators. In

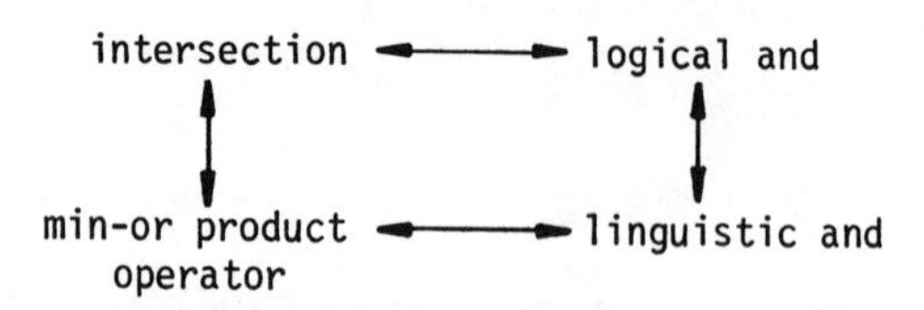

Figure 6-1: Relationships of "and-aggregation".

most of the models of chapters 2 through 5 we have assumed the following relationships.

The *linguistic and*, that is, the "and" we use in our daily language and in statements such as "the objective function *and* the constraints have to be satisfied," corresponds to the *logical and*. This in turn corresponds to the set theoretic intersection. As a mathematical model for this intersection, either the minimum operator or the product operator have been used, following the custom in dual logic or in Boolean algebra. Figure 6-1 depicts these relationships. The relationship between the "linguistic and" and its mathematical model is a factual statement, the truth of which, obviously can only be tested empirically. The other relationships are of a more formal character and can, therefore, be justified axiomatically.

Two of the best-known *formal justifications*, which lead to different results, are sketched in the following.

Bellman and Giertz [1973, p. 151] argued from a logical point of view, interpreting the intersection as "logical and," the union as "logical or," and the fuzzy set $\tilde{A}$ as the statement "The element x belongs to set $\tilde{A}$," which can be accepted as more or less true. It is very instructive to follow their line of argument, which is an excellent example for an axiomatic justification of specific mathematical models. We shall therefore sketch their reasoning: consider two statements, S and T, for which the truth values are μ_S and μ_T, respectively, $\mu_S, \mu_T \in [0,1]$. The truth value of the "and" and "or" combination of these statements, $\mu(S \text{ and } T)$ and $\mu(S \text{ or } T)$, both from the interval $[0,1]$, are interpreted as the values of the membership functions of the intersection and union, respectively, of S and T. We are now looking for two realvalued functions f and g such that

$$\mu_{S \text{ and } T} = \mu_{S \cap T} = f(\mu_S, \mu_T)$$

and

$$\mu_{S \text{ or } T} = \mu_{S \cup T} = g(\mu_S, \mu_T)$$

Bellman and Giertz feel that the following restrictions are reasonably imposed on f and g:

1. f and g are nondecreasing and continuous in μ_S and μ_T.
2. f and g are symmetrical, that is,

$$f(\mu_S,\mu_T) = f(\mu_T,\mu_S) \quad \text{and} \quad g(\mu_S,\mu_T) = g(\mu_T,\mu_S)$$

3. $f(\mu_S,\mu_S)$ and $g(\mu_S,\mu_S)$ are strictly increasing in μ_S.
4. $f(\mu_S,\mu_T) \leq \min(\mu_S,\mu_T)$ and $g(\mu_S,\mu_T) \geq \max(\mu_S,\mu_T)$.
   This implies that accepting the truth of the statements "S and T" requires more, and accepting the truth of the statement "S or T" requires less than accepting S or T alone as true.
5. $f(1,1) = 1$ and $g(0,0) = 0$.
6. Logically equivalent statements must have equal truth values and fuzzy sets with the same contents must have the same membership functions; that is,

$$S_1 \quad \text{and} \quad (S_2 \text{ or } S_3)$$

   is equivalent to

$$(S_1 \text{ and } S_2) \quad \text{or} \quad (S_1 \text{ and } S_3)$$

   and therefore must be equally true.

Bellman and Giertz [1973, p. 154] then prove mathematically that

$$f(\mu_S,\mu_T) = \min(\mu_S,\mu_T) \quad \text{and} \quad g(\mu_S,\mu_T) = \max(\mu_S,\mu_T)$$

This is the justification for using the minimum operator to model the "logical and," and the maximum operator to model the "inclusive or."

Hamacher [1978] justifies another mathematical model for the "logical and," $\wedge$, by starting from the following reduced set of axioms:

A1. The operator $\wedge$ is associative, that is,

$$\tilde{A} \wedge (\tilde{B} \wedge \tilde{C}) = (\tilde{A} \wedge \tilde{B}) \wedge \tilde{C}$$

A2. The operator $\wedge$ is continuous.

A3. The operator $\wedge$ is injective in each argument, that is,

$$(\tilde{A} \wedge \tilde{B}) = (\tilde{A} \wedge \tilde{C}) \Rightarrow \tilde{B} = \tilde{C}$$

and

$$(\tilde{A} \wedge \tilde{B}) = (\tilde{C} \wedge \tilde{B}) \Rightarrow \tilde{A} = \tilde{C}$$

(This is the essential difference from the Bellman-Giertz axioms).

A4. $\mu_{\tilde{A}}(x) = 1 \Rightarrow \mu_{\tilde{A} \wedge \tilde{A}}(x) = 1$.

Hamacher then proves that a function $f: \mathbb{R} \rightarrow [0,1]$ exists with

$$\mu_{\tilde{A} \wedge \tilde{B}}(x) = f(f^{-1}(\mu_{\tilde{A}}(x)) + f^{-1}(\mu_{\tilde{B}}(x)))$$

If f is a rational function in $\mu_{\tilde{A}}(x)$ and $\mu_{\tilde{B}}(x)$, then the only possible mathematical model for the "and" operator is (6.1). It is obvious that this operator—in contrast to the Bellman-Giertz arguments—reduces to the product operator for $\gamma = 1$.

$$\mu_{\tilde{A} \cap \tilde{B}}(x) = \frac{\mu_{\tilde{A}}(x)\mu_{\tilde{B}}(x)}{\gamma + (1 - \gamma)(\mu_{\tilde{A}}(x) + \mu_{\tilde{B}}(x) - \mu_{\tilde{A}}(x)\mu_{\tilde{B}}(x))} \quad \gamma \geq 0 \tag{6.1}$$

Analogous considerations were made by Hamacher for the "or" operator. In the meantime other authors have generalized this approach by considering so-called t-norms and t-conorms as models for these connectives [Alsina 1985; Yu 1985].

By *pragmatic justification* of an operator we mean some heuristic arguments that support the use of a specific operator either in general or in a specific context. Before we discuss in more detail the empirical verification of operators, we consider the following rules for selecting appropriate operators which, with the exception of the first two, are of more pragmatic character.

1. Axiomatic strength. We have listed the axioms that Bellman-Giertz and Hamacher wanted their operators to satisfy. Obviously, everything else being equal, an operator is the better the less limiting are the axioms it satisfies.

2. Empirical fit. If fuzzy set theory is used as a modelling language for real situations or systems, it is not only important that the operators satisfy certain axioms or have certain formal qualities (such as associativity, commutativity), which are certainly of importance from a mathematical point of view. The operators must in this case also be appropriate models of real system behavior, which can normally only be proven by empirical testing.

3. Adaptability. It is rather unlikely that the type of aggregation is independent of context and semantic interpretation. That is, the type of aggregation used is more likely to be dependent than independent of whether the aggregated fuzzy sets model a human decision, a fuzzy controller, a medical diagnostic system, or a specific inference rule in fuzzy logic. If one wants to use a very small number of operators to model many situations, then these operators have to be adaptable to the specific context. This can be achieved, for example, by parametrization. Thus min- and max-operators cannot be adapted at all. They are acceptable in situations in which they fit and under no other circumstances. (Of course, they have other advantages such as numerical efficiency.) By contrast, Yager's operators [1980] or the γ-operator (to be considered later in the chapter) can be adapted to certain contexts by setting the p's or γ's appropriately.

4. *Numerical efficiency.* Comparing the min-operator with, for instance, Yager's intersection-operator or the γ-operator it becomes quite obvious, that the latter two require considerably more computational effort than the former. In practice, this might be quite important, in particular, when large problems have to be solved.

5. *Compensation.* The "logical and" does not allow for compensation at all, that is, an element of the intersection of two sets cannot compensate a low degree of belonging to one of the intersected sets by a higher degree of belonging to another of them; in (dual) logic, one cannot compensate by higher truth of one statement for lower truth of another statement when combining them by "and." *Compensation* in the context of aggregation operators for fuzzy sets has the following meaning: assuming that $\mu_{\tilde{C}} = \mu_{\tilde{A}} * \mu_{\tilde{B}}$, the operator $*$ is compensatory if a change in $\mu_{\tilde{C}}$ due to a change in $\mu_{\tilde{A}}$ can be counteracted (compensated) by a change in $\mu_{\tilde{B}}$. Thus, the min-operator is not compensatory, while the product operator, the γ-operator, and so forth are.

6. *Range of resulting membership.* If one used a convex combination of min- and max-operators, the resulting degree of membership would obviously lie between min and max. The product operator can result in degrees of the entire open interval (0,1). In general, the larger the range the better the operator.

7. *Aggregating behavior.* Considering normal or subnormal (see definition 1.2) fuzzy sets, the degree of membership in the aggregated set depends very frequently on the number of sets combined. When combining fuzzy sets by the product operator, for instance, each additional fuzzy set "added" will normally decrease the resulting aggregate degrees of membership. Although this might be a desirable feature, it also might not be adequate. Goguen [1967], for instance, argues that for formal reasons the resulting degree of membership should be nonincreasing.

8. *Required scale level of membership functions.* The scale level (nominal, interval, ratio, or absolute) on which membership information can be obtained depends on a number of factors. Different operators may require different scale levels of membership information to be admissible. (For example, the min-operator is still admissable for ordinal information while the product operator, strictly speaking, is not!) In general, again everything else being equal, the operator that requires the lowest scale level is the most preferable from the point of view of information gathering.

The Measurement of Membership Functions

Aside from statements suggesting that one or the other shape makes sense for membership functions, few justifications have been offered for models of membership functions. The concept of probabilistic sets has been offered by Hirota [Hirota 1981], primarily for the area of control engineering. Norwich and Turksen [1981] present their suggestions within measurement theory. For decision making, Schwab [1983] axiomatically justified membership functions on the basis of spline functions. The empirical validity of his 11 axioms remains to be shown.

In the following, we shall present two models for determining the membership function empirically. They differ with respect to their mapping properties. Basically, measurement means assigning numbers to objects such that certain relations between numbers reflect analogous relations between objects. Put differently, measurement is the mapping of object relations into numerical relations of the same type. Let us consider the following two examples.

Example 6.1

Let X be the set of clients x_i of a certain bank:

$$X = \{x_1, x_2, x_3, x_4, x_5, x_6, x_7, x_8\}$$

Then the fuzzy set "creditworthy clients" might be

$$\tilde{F} = \{(x_1, 1), (x_2, .4), (x_3, 1), (x_4, .6), (x_5, .5), (x_6, .7), (x_7, .1), (x_8, 0)\}$$

Example 6.2

Let X be the set of noise levels, measured in Phon, that occur in streets. Then the fuzzy set "acceptable noise levels in streets" for a residential area might be given by the membership function presented in figure 6.2.

Examples 6.1 and 6.2 show two ways of representing a fuzzy set. Often the latter version is preferred because it visualizes the relationships better. It presupposes, however, that the set of objects can be mapped not only into the space M of membership grades, but also into a scaled variable we call the base variable. In the above example this is represented by the Phon scale.

In the case of type A membership functions (which will be discussed shortly; also, see example 6.1), μ maps an empirical relational structure "$X, S_1, \ldots, S_n$" with a set X of elements and n-tuple of empirical relations S_1 to S_n defined on X into a numerical relational structure "$[0,1]$, $U_1, \ldots, U_n$" of the same type: μ: "$X, S_1, \ldots, S_n$" $\rightarrow$ "$[0,1]$, $U_1, \ldots, U_n$." In example 6.2, two numerical structures "$R, T_1, \ldots, T_n$" (Phon scale) and "$[0,1]$, $U_1, \ldots, U_n$" (interval of membership

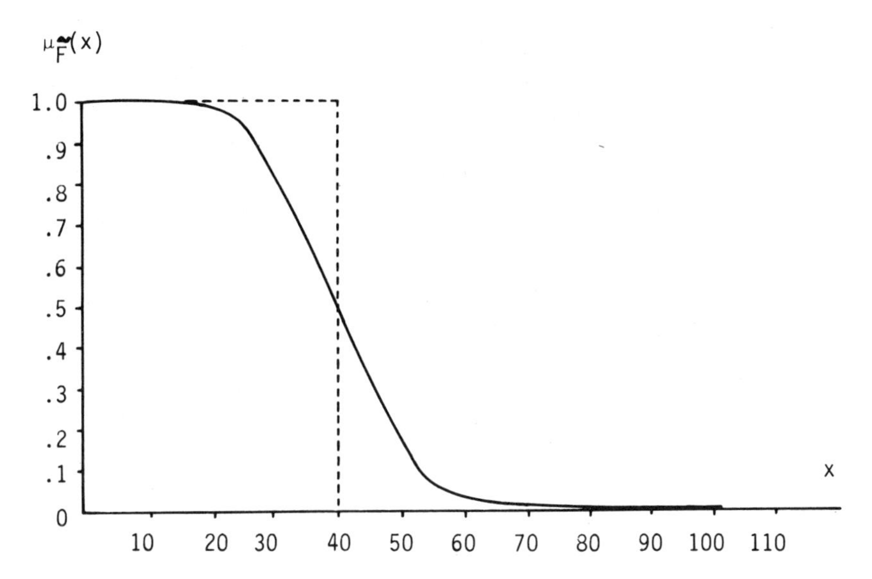

Figure 6-2: Membership function of the fuzzy set "acceptable noise levels in streests for a residential area".

grades) are given. In this case the membership function abandons fundamental measurement. It is basically a transformation, since it maps one numerical structure into another numerical structure of the same type of relations: μ': "$R, T_1, \ldots, T_n$" and "$[0,1], U_1, \ldots, U_n$." The respective model to be developed will be called type B model.

At the very beginning of measurement there should be a semantic definition of the central concepts, which would considerably facilitate the consistent use of the relevant principles. This has not yet been possible for the concept of membership, which has a clear-cut formal but not an explicit empirical definition. Apart from first steps by Norwich and Turksen [1981] genuine measurement structures have not yet been developed.

Under these circumstances one could wait until a satisfactory definition is available. However, one should remember that up to the beginning of the twentieth century even in the "hard sciences" measures were used without the support of adequate measurement theories. Usually measurement tools were used, and these were based on not much more than plausible reasoning. Nevertheless, the success of the natural sciences is undoubted. Hence, for the purpose of empirical research it may be tolerable to use plausible techniques.

Firstly, such a scale can serve as an operational definition of membership. Secondly a specified concept can be criticized and consequently may lead to useful improvements. Of primary importance is the determination of the lowest necessary scale level of membership for a specific application. The requested scale level should be as low as possible in order to facilitate data acquisition, which usually involves the participation of human beings. On the other hand a suitable numerical handling is desirable in order to insure mathematically appropriate operation. Regarding the five classical scale levels—nominal, ordinal, interval, ratio, and absolute—the interval scale seems to be most adequate. In this respect we can not follow Sticha, Weiss, and Donnell [1979] who assert that membership has to be measured on an ordinal scale. Usually the intended mathematical operations require at least interval scale quality.

Type A Model

The easiest way to obtain data is to ask some subjects directly for membership values. However, it is well known that scales developed by using the so-called direct methods may be distorted by a number of response biases [Cronbach 1950; Sixtl 1967]. On the other hand, indirect methods work on the basis of much weaker assumptions using ordinal judgments only. Their advantages are simplicity and robustness with respect to response biases. Their disadvantage is that many judgments are needed since the ordinal judgment provides relatively little information. However, if there is no instrument available for controlling such effects, this increased experimental effort should be accepted in order to avoid distortions of the data. The first scaling method to be described yields an interval scale on the basis of ordinal ratings.

Experimental Procedure. After a set of suitable objects has been established subjects are asked for the grades of membership on a percentage scale. People are accustomed to this type of judgment and a division by 100 provides the normalized 0–1-values. The obtained data are interpreted as ranks. The subsequent scaling procedure refers mainly to a method suggested by Diederich, Messick, and Tucker [1957] and based on Thurstone's "law of categorical judgment" [Thurstone 1927].

Model. Let S be a set of stimuli with elements s, and T be a set of category boundaries (on a percentage scale) with elements t. The subjective reactions s and t are assumed to be normally distributed:

$$s = N(\mu_s, \sigma_s^2) \tag{6.2}$$

$$t = N(\mu_t, \sigma_t^2) \tag{6.3}$$

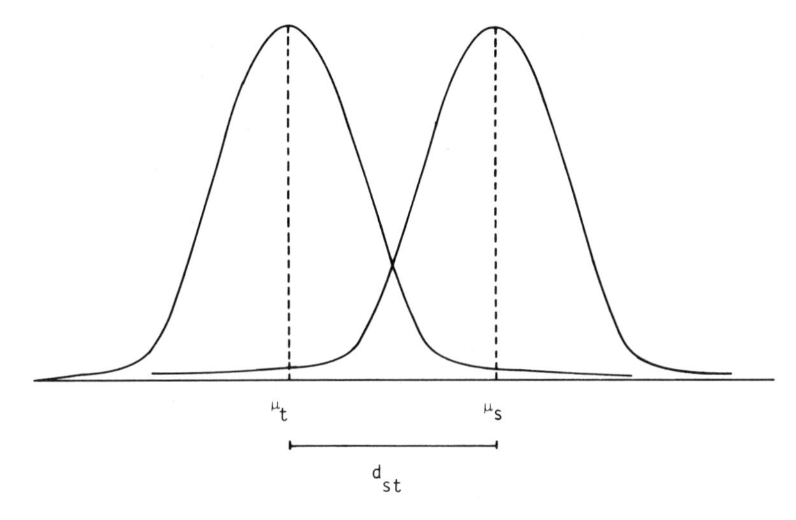

Figure 6-3: Distinction of the positions of stimulus *s* and category boundary *t* perceived by a subject.

The location of the stimulus μ_s and the category boundary μ_t can be estimated by the modal values, $\bar{s}$, $\bar{t}$, of their reaction distributions (figure 6-3):

$$\mu_s = \bar{s} \tag{6.4}$$

$$\mu_t = \bar{t} \tag{6.5}$$

Of course, as there is some fluctuation with respect to the subjects' perception of the position of stimuli and category boundaries, the perception of the difference d_{st} between s and t is also stochastic:

$$d_{st} = N(\mu_{d_{st}}, \sigma^2_{d_{st}}) \tag{6.6}$$

Its variance can be determined via the variances of the individual judgments and the correlation r_{st}:

$$\sigma^2_{d_{st}} = \sigma^2_s + \sigma^2_t + 2r_{st}\sigma_s\sigma_t \tag{6.7}$$

The value of the modal distance d_{st} can be estimated by the distance of the modal values of the stimuli from the category boundaries:

$$\bar{d}_{st} = \bar{s} - \bar{t} \tag{6.8}$$

Now the interaction of reactive behavior and the kind of stimulus has to be specified. The categorical judgment of a subject implies that a dominance relationship is perceived between a certain stimulus and a certain categorical boundary. It is assumed that the probability $p_{s>t}$ is a function of the distance between s and t:

$$p_{s>t} = F(d_{st}) \tag{6.9}$$

The discriminative process concerning d_{st} is assumed to be normally distributed. Unfortunately, its parameter values are unknown. However, as the difference d_{st} is related to the associated standard deviation σ_{st}, z-values of the standard normal distribution can be used:

$$p'_{s>t} = F(d_{st}(\sigma_{st})) = F(z_{st}) \tag{6.10}$$

where the σ_{st} are the standard deviations of the individual perceptions. The probabilities are estimated by the respective cumulative frequencies for each stimulus along the category boundaries. Then the z-values are given by the inverse function

$$F^{-1}(p'_{s>t}) = z_{st} \tag{6.11}$$

As

$$z_{st} = \frac{\bar{d}_{st}}{\sigma_{st}} = \frac{\bar{s} - \bar{t}}{\sigma_{st}} \tag{6.12}$$

the modal distance between stimulus and category boundary equals the product of the z-value and standard deviation:

$$\bar{s} - \bar{t} = z_{st}\sqrt{\sigma_s^2 + \sigma_t^2 + 2r_{st}\sigma_s\sigma_t} \tag{6.13}$$

Formula (6.13) represents Thurstone's "law of categorical judgment" [Thurstone 1927]. It is not directly solvable since there are more unknowns than equations. With n stimuli sorted into $m + 1$ categories there are $2n$ unknown parameter values of the stimuli, $2m$ parameter values of the category boundaries, and $m \cdot n$ correlation terms. Two parameters (e.g., the origin and the unit) can be specified arbitrarily; still, $2(n + m - 1) + mm$ unknowns are left. Hence simplifying conditions have to be introduced. For our purposes it seems reasonable to assume that

- there is no correlation within the fluctuation of stimuli and category boundaries ($r_{st} = 0$), and
- the variances of the category boundaries are constant ($\sigma_t^2 = c$).

Then (6.13) reduces to

$$\bar{s} - \bar{t} = z_{st}\sigma_s^* \tag{6.14}$$

with $\sigma_s^* = \sqrt{\sigma_s^2 + c}$; as interval scales are invariant with respect to linear transformations the additive constant c can be neglected. The remaining system with $2n + m - 2$ unknowns is solvable.

An efficient iterative algorithm minimizing the experimental error was offered by Diederich, Messick, and Tucker [1957]. The method developed by these authors has been implemented on a Cyber 175 computer and used to generate degrees of membership for a finite number of elements on at least interval-scale level for observed date [Thole, Zimmermann, Zysno 1979].

These degrees of membership can be used for different purposes. In the section on *Selecting Appropriate Operators* we will show how degrees of membership are employed in order to test certain models of operators empirically. It should, however, be obvious that these degrees of membership pertain only to the set of objects for which they have been obtained. In other words, they are not "generalizable" to other fuzzy sets and one can generally not interpolate degrees of membership for elements or quantities not included in the original set. When determining membership functions that are to represent the fuzzy constraints of mathematical programming models, for instance, the type A model for degrees of membership is not suitable because degrees of membership have to be defined for all solutions of the solution space, (i.e., infinitely many). Then one can use pragmatic models of membership, as we did in chapter 4 or one can resort to the type B model of membership described in the following.

Type B Model of Membership

Often a certain concept can be considered as a context-specific version of a more general feature. For instance, the set of "young men" is a subset of all objects with the feature "age." We call this general feature the "base variable." By contrast to the context-specific version the base variable is already scaled and the scale is commonly accepted. If both features are scaled, a mapping from one numerical relational structure into the other would be possible and reflects the difference of the basic empirical relational structure with respect to the same set of elements. If on the other hand the scale of the base variable and the mapping function were known, then the scale of the special feature could be determined. Concerning the required scale level of the membership function, essentially the same holds as for the type A model.

However, for the type B model we used direct scaling methods. This involves less experimental effort and is justified by the existence of the base variable which provides some control with respect to judgmental errors of the subjects. To express this lower aspiration concerning the validity of the scale, we call this scale an "evaluative" scale.

Model. The judgment (valuation) of membership can be regarded as the comparison of object x with a standard (ideal) that results in a perceived distance $d(x)$ which is not necessarily a distance in the mathematical sense. If the object has all the features of the standard, the distance shall be zero, if no similarity between standard and object exists, the distance shall be ∞. If the evaluation concept is represented formally by a fuzzy set $\tilde{F} \subset X$, then a certain degree of membership $\mu_{\tilde{F}}(x)$ is assigned to each element x. In the following we will denote the degree of membership, $\mu_{\tilde{F}}(x)$, simply by $\mu(x)$.

$$\mu(x) = \frac{1}{1 + d(x)} \tag{6.15}$$

Membership is defined as a function of the perceived distance $d(x)$ between a given object x and a standard (ideal). Hence, $d(x) = 0 \rightarrow \mu(x) = 1$;

$$d(x) = \infty \rightarrow \mu(x) = 0.$$

Equation (6.15) is only a transformation rule from one numerical structure into another: Real numbers $r = d(x)$ are mapped into the interval $[0, 1]$.

The distance function now has to be specified. Experience shows that ideals are very rarely fully realized. As an aid to determine the relative position very often a context-dependent standard b is created. It facilitates a fast and rough preevaluation such as "rather positive," "rather negative," etc. As another context-dependent parameter we can use the evaluation unit a, similar to a unit of length such as feet, meters, yards, etc. If one realizes, furthermore, that the relationship between physical units and perceptions is generally exponential [Helson 1964], the following distance function seems appropriate:

$$d(x) = e^{-a(x-b)}. \tag{6.16}$$

Substituting (6.16) into (6.15) yields the logistic function

$$\mu(x) = \frac{1}{1 + e^{-a(x-b)}} \tag{6.17}$$

It is S-shaped, as demanded by several authors [Goguen 1969; Zadeh 1971].

From the point of view of linear programming (6.17) has the additional advantage that it can easily be linearized by the following transformation:

$$-\ln \frac{1-\mu}{\mu} = \ln \frac{\mu}{1-\mu} = a(x-b) \tag{6.18}$$

The parameters a and b will have to be interpreted differently depending on the situation that is modelled. From a linguistic point of view a and b can be considered as semantic parameters.

Since concepts or categories, which are formally represented by sets, are

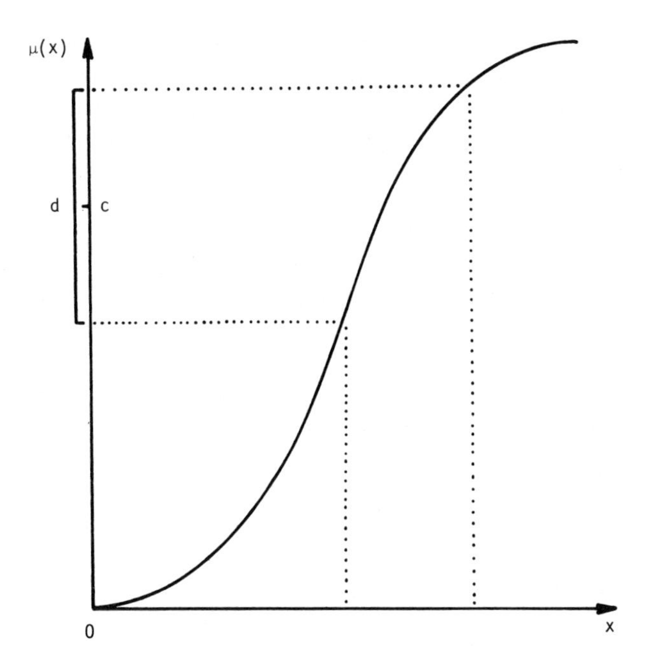

Figure 6-4: Calibration of the interval for measurement.

normally linguistically described, the membership function is the formal representation of meaning. The vagueness of the concept is operationalized by the slope a and the identification threshold by b. For managerial terms such as "appropriate dividend" or "good utilization of capacities" the parameter a models the slope of the membership function in the tolerance interval and b represents the point at which the tendency of the subject's attitude changes from rather positive into rather negative.

Model (6.17), however, is still too general to fit subjective models of different persons. Frequently only a certain part of the logistic function is needed to represent a perceived situation. This is also true for measuring devices such as scales, thermometers, etc., designed for specific measuring areas only. In order to allow for calibration it is assumed that only a certain interval of the physical scale is mapped into the open interval $(0,1)$ (see figure 6-4). Whenever stimuli are smaller or equal to the lower bound or larger or equal to the upper bound, the grade of membership of 0 or 1, respectively, is assigned to them. This is achieved by changing the range by means of legitimate scale transformations so that the desired interval is mapped into $[0,1]$.

Since we requested an interval scale the interval of the degrees of membership may be transformed linearly. On this scale level the ratios of two distances are invariant. Let $\bar{\mu}$ be the upper and $\underline{\mu}$ the lower bound of the normalized membership scale and μ_i be a degree of membership between these bounds, $\underline{\mu} < \mu_i < \bar{\mu}$; and let $\underline{\mu}' < \mu_i' < \bar{\mu}'$ be the corresponding values on the transformed scale. Then

$$\frac{\mu_i - \underline{\mu}}{\bar{\mu} - \underline{\mu}} = \frac{\mu_i' - \underline{\mu}'}{\bar{\mu}' - \underline{\mu}'} \tag{6.19}$$

For the normalized membership function we have $\underline{\mu} = 0$ and $\bar{\mu} = 1$. Hence,

$$\mu_i' = \mu_i(\bar{\mu}' - \underline{\mu}') + \underline{\mu}' \tag{6.20}$$

Generally it is preferable to define the range of validity by specifying the interval d with the center c (figure 6-4) as follows:

$$\bar{\mu}' - \underline{\mu}' = d \tag{6.21a}$$

so

$$\bar{\mu}' = d + \underline{\mu}' \tag{6.21b}$$

and

$$(\bar{\mu}' + \underline{\mu}')/2 = c \tag{6.22a}$$

so

$$\bar{\mu}' = 2c - \underline{\mu}' \tag{6.22b}$$

Inserting (6.21b) into (6.22b) yields

$$\underline{\mu}' = 2c - d - \underline{\mu}' \tag{6.22c}$$

solving (6.22c) for $\underline{\mu}'$ gives

$$\underline{\mu}' = c - d/2 \tag{6.22d}$$

and inserting (6.22d) and (6.21a) into (6.20) yields

$$\mu_i' = d(\mu_i - 1/2) + c \tag{6.23}$$

The general model of membership (6.17) is specified by two parameters of calibration, if μ_i is replaced by μ_i'. Solving this equality for μ_i leads to the complete model of membership:

$$\mu_i = {}^{0}\!\left[\left(\frac{1}{1 + e^{-a(x-b)}} - c\right)\frac{1}{d} + \frac{1}{2}\right]^{1} \tag{6.24}$$

where ${}^{0}[\ ]^{1}$ indicates that values outside of the interval [0,1] have no real meaning. The measurement instrument does not differentiate in these areas. Hence,

$$x < \underline{x} \Rightarrow \mu(x) = 0 \tag{6.25a}$$

$$x > \bar{x} \Rightarrow \mu(x) = 1 \tag{6.25b}$$

Determination of the parameters from an empirical data base does not pose any difficulties in the general model. On the basis of (6.18) the original membership values μ_i are transformed into y values:

$$y_i = \ln \frac{\mu}{1 - \mu_i} \tag{6.26}$$

Between x and y there exists a linear relationship. The straight line of the model is then defined by the least squares of deviations.

Estimation of parameters c and d in the extended model still poses some problems. We cannot yet provide a direct way for a numerically optimal estimation. However, an iterative procedure is suggested. We assume now that a set of stimuli, x_i, which is equally spread over the physical continuum, was chosen such that the distance, s, between any two of the neighboring stimuli is constant:

$$x_{i+1} - x_i = s \tag{6.27}$$

This condition serves as a criterion for precision. If c and d are correctly estimated, then those scale values x_i' are reproducable that are invariant with respect to x_i, with the exception of the additive and multiplicative constant. This becomes obvious when rewriting (6.24) as follows:

$$\ln \frac{d(\mu_i - \frac{1}{2}) + c}{1 - (d(\mu_i - \frac{1}{2}) + c} = x_i' = a(x_i - b) \tag{6.28}$$

Let s' be the distance between the pairs x_i' and x_{i+1}' and M' their mean value. If the estimated values $\hat{d}$ and $\hat{c}$ are equal to their true values then the estimated distance $\hat{s}'$ and the mean $\hat{M}'$ are equal to their respective true values and vice versa:

$$(\hat{d} = d) \wedge (\hat{c} = c) \Leftrightarrow (\underline{s}' = s) \wedge (\hat{M}' = M) \tag{6.29}$$

Our aim is therefore to reach the equivalence of $\hat{s}'$ and s as well as $\hat{M}'$ and M.

Using appropriate starting values c_1 and d_1 one can now determine the x_i' that correspond to the empirically determined μ_i:

$$\hat{M}' = \frac{1}{n} \Sigma x_i \tag{6.30}$$

$$\hat{s}' = \frac{1}{n-1} \sum_{i=1}^{n-1} (x'_{i+1} - x'_i) = \frac{x_n - x_1}{n-1} \tag{6.31}$$

If the absolute difference between two estimates does not exceed a certain ε, then the last estimate is accepted as sufficiently exact:

$$|\hat{M}'' - \hat{M}'| \leq \varepsilon_M \tag{6.32}$$

$$|\hat{s}'' - \hat{s}'| \leq \varepsilon_s \tag{6.33}$$

If this is not the case, we estimate the interval of the base variable that corresponds to the (0, 1) interval of the membership values. To this end, an upper bound $\bar{x}'$ and a lower bound $\underline{x}'$ is determined:

$$\bar{x}' = \hat{M}' + \frac{n}{2}\hat{s}' \tag{6.34}$$

$$\underline{x}' = \hat{M}' - \frac{n}{2}\hat{s}' \tag{6.35}$$

Now the corresponding $\bar{\mu}'$ and $\underline{\mu}'$, respectively, are computed; and via (6.21a) and (6.22a) new parameters $\hat{c}$ and $\hat{d}$ are estimated. Experience has shown that it usually takes less than 10 iterations to reproduce the values of the base variable up to an accuracy of three digits behind the decimal point. As starting points we used

$$c_1 = \frac{1}{n}\Sigma\mu_i \tag{6.36}$$

$$d_1 = \min\left(1 - \frac{1}{k}, 2(1-c), 2c\right) \tag{6.37}$$

where n is the number of stimuli and k is the number of different degrees of membership. If only the values 0 and 1 occur, $d_1 = \frac{1}{2}$. Only the "linear" interval in the middle of the logistic function is used. With increasing k, d converges to 1; that is, $\lim_{k\to\infty} d = 1$, the entire range of the function is used. In any case, d must not exceed the minor part of $2c$ or $2(1-c)$. Finally it should be mentioned that unimodal functions can be described by an increasing (S_I) and a decreasing (S_D) part of two monotonic functions represented as the minimum

$$\mu_{S_I S_D}(x) = \min {}^0\lceil \mu_{S_I}(x), \mu_{S_D}(x) \rceil^1 \tag{6.38}$$

(6.39)

Empirical evidence. Sixty-four subjects (16 for each set) from 21 to 25 years of age individually rated 52 different statements of age concerning one of the

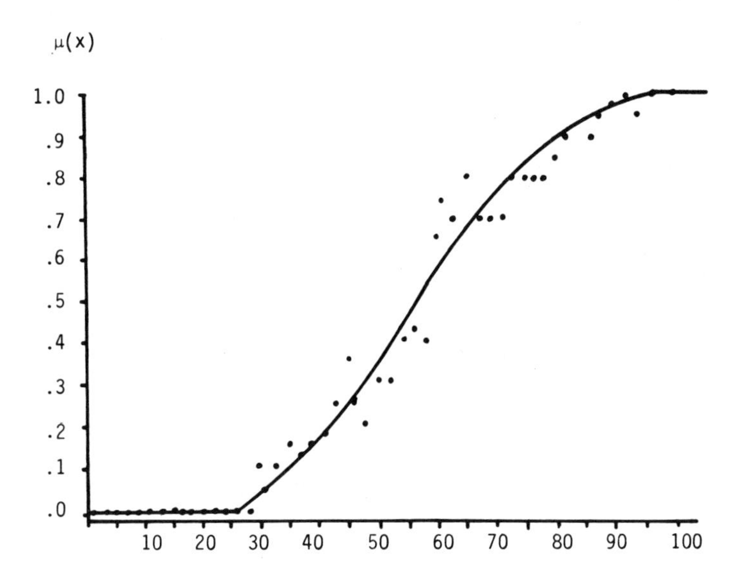

Figure 6-5: Subject 34, "old man" (om).

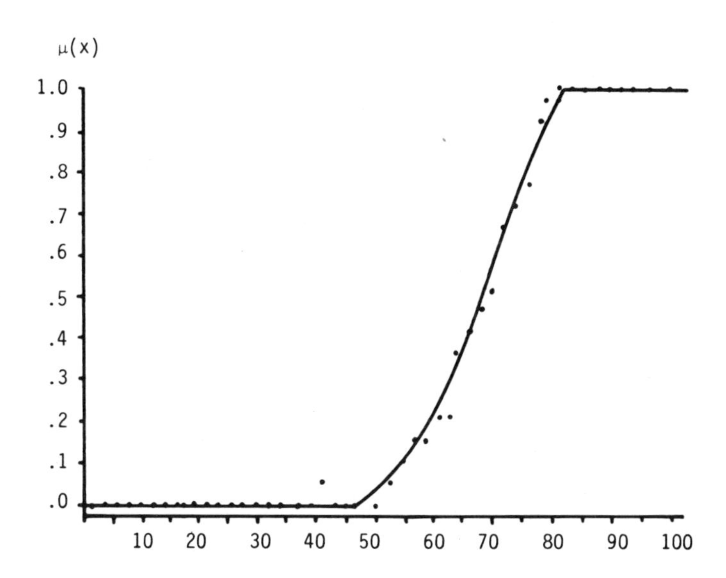

Figure 6-6: Subject 58, "very old man" (vom).

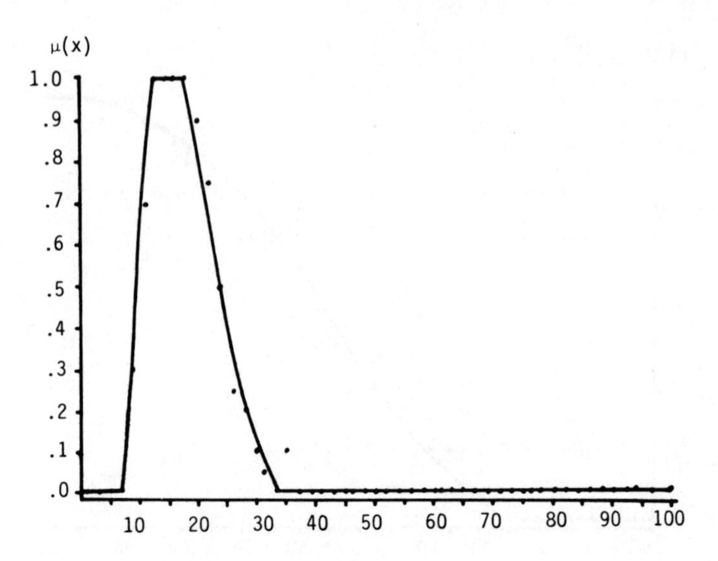

Figure 6-7: Subject 5, "very young man" (vym).

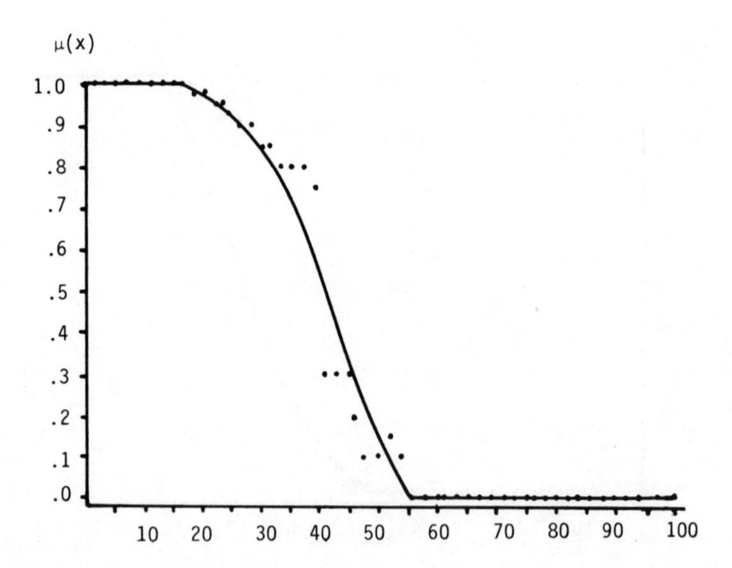

Figure 6-8: Subject 15, "very young man" (vym).

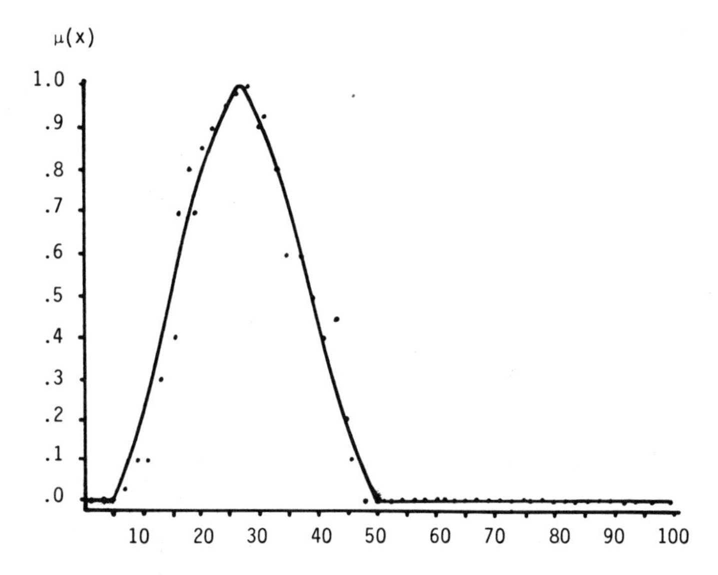

Figure 6-9: Subject 17, "young man" (ym).

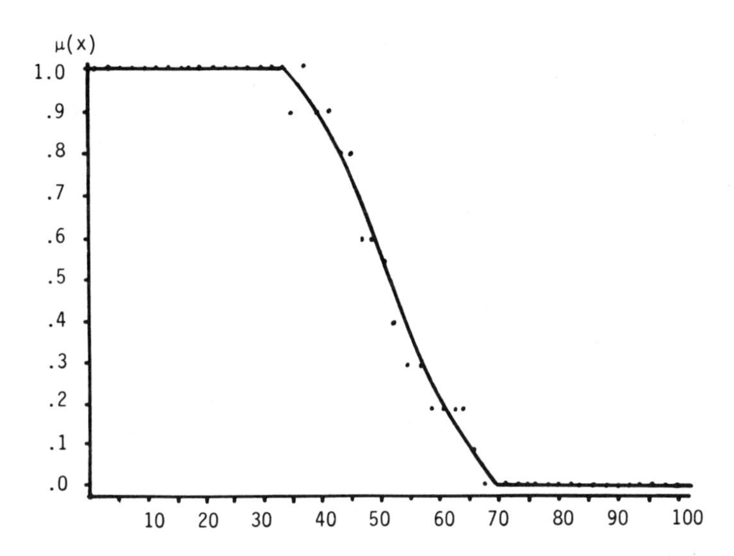

Figure 6-10: Subject 32, "young man" (ym).

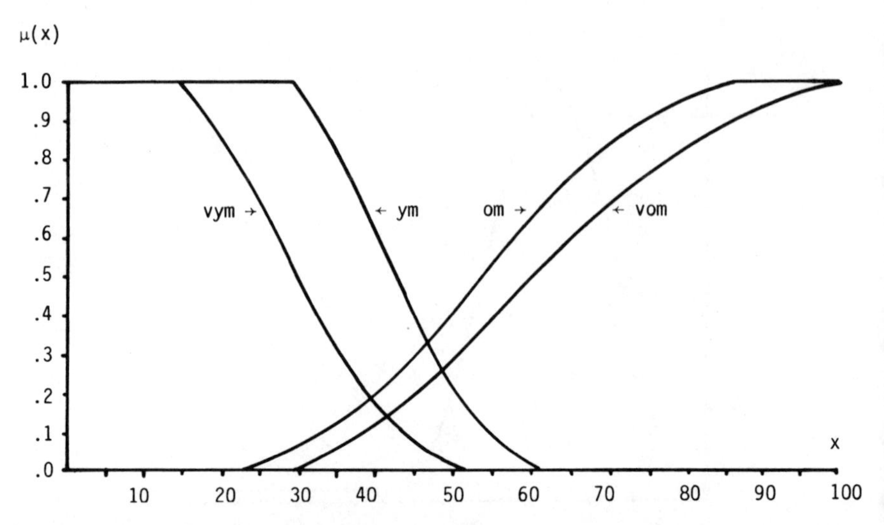

Figure 6-11: Generalized membership function (monotonic type) "very young man" (vym), "young man" (ym), "old man" (om), "very old man" (vom).

four fuzzy sets "very young man" (vym), "young man" (ym), "old man" (om), and "very old man" (vom). Evaluation of the data shows a good fit of the model. Figures 6-5 to 6-10 show the membership functions given by six different persons. As can be seen, the concepts "vym" and "ym" are realized in the monotonic type as well as in the unimodal. The detailed data and results can be found in a major report by the authors [Zimmermann, Zysno 1982].

One may ask whether a general membership function for each of the four sets can be established. Even though the variety of conceptual comprehension is rather remarkable, there should be an overall membership function at least in order to have a standard of comparison for the individuals. This is achieved by determining the common parameter values, a, b, c, and d for each set. Obviously the general membership functions of "old man" and "very old man" (figure 6-11) are rather similar. Practically, they differ only with respect to their inflection points, indicating a difference of about five years between "old man" and "very old man." The same holds for the monotonic type (figure 6-11) of "very young man" and "young man"; their inflection points differ by nearly 15 years. It is interesting to note that the modifier "very" has a greater effect on "young" than on "old," but in both cases it can be formally represented by a constant. Several subjects provided the unimodal type in connection with "very young" and "young." Again the functions show a striking congruency (figure 6-12).

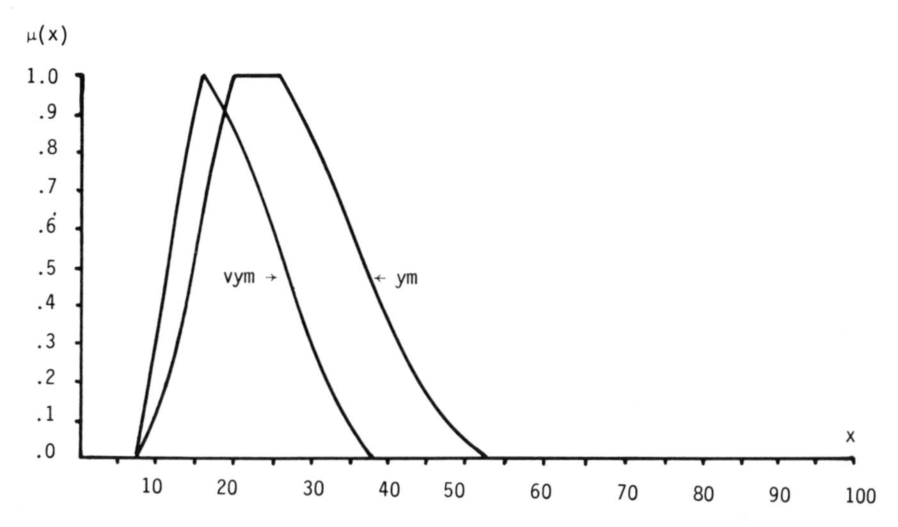

Figure 6-12: Generalized membership function (unimodal type) for "very young man" (vym) and "young man" (ym).

Selecting Appropriate Operators in Decision Models

We have already described approaches for formally justifying operators and have also suggested some criteria that can be helpful when pragmatically deciding about the operator to be used. We shall now concentrate on one of these criteria—the empirical fit. In terms of figure 6-1, we now investigate the relationships between the "linguistic and" and its mathematical models on one hand and between the "logical and" and the "linguistic and" on the other hand.

In formal justifications one starts from certain assumptions and then "derives" an operator with the desired properties.

In empirically testing operators we used an approach similar to that described for model B membership functions. First we decided on the model that had to be tested. For this purpose the minimum and the product operator were chosen first. The appropriate experimental design was then chosen according to the goals of the test: we wanted to test whether the minimum or the product modelled the "logical and" well enough. The reader should visualize the intersection in the sense of the "logical and," and see that it has, among others, two properties:

1. Elements of the sets $\tilde{A}$ and $\tilde{B}$ to be intersected are considered to be of

equal weight.

2. Members of the sets $\tilde{A}$ and $\tilde{B}$ are independent. That is, the degree to which an element belongs to $\tilde{A}$ is not affected by the degree to which it belongs to $\tilde{B}$, and the degree to which it belongs to the intersection cannot be higher than the minimum of the degrees to which it belongs to $\tilde{A}$ or $\tilde{B}$. Roughly speaking, we can say that there is no positive compensation between the degrees of membership.

These properties of the base material had to be checked carefully. For more details see [Thole, Zimmermann, Zysno 1979].

With respect to the rather simple structure of the two candidate models, it seemed reasonable to demand that the following conditions concerning the judgmental "material" are satisfied:

1. The attributes characterizing the members of the sets $\tilde{A}$ and $\tilde{B}$ are independent, that is, some magnitude of $\mu_{\tilde{A}}$ is not affected by some magnitude of $\mu_{\tilde{B}}$ and vice versa. As an operational criterion for this kind of independence a correlation of zero is demanded:

$$r_{\mu_{\tilde{A}}\mu_{\tilde{B}}} = 0$$

2. If $\mu_{\tilde{A}\cap\tilde{B}}$ represents the aggretation of $\mu_{\tilde{A}}$ and $\mu_{\tilde{B}}$, modelling the intersection, and if $W_{\tilde{A}}$ and $W_{\tilde{B}}$ are weights, then $\mu_{\tilde{A}\cap\tilde{B}}$ can be described by

$$\mu_{\tilde{A}\cap\tilde{B}} = (W_{\tilde{A}}\mu_{\tilde{A}}) \cdot (W_{\tilde{B}}\mu_{\tilde{B}})$$

where $\cdot$ stands for some algebraic operation. But as the models proposed do not take into account different importance of the sets with respect to their intersection, equal weights are demanded:

$$W_{\tilde{A}} = W_{\tilde{B}}$$

As operational criterion for equal correlations are demanded we have

$$r_{\mu_A \mu_{A\cap B}} = r_{\mu_B \mu_{A\cap B}}.$$

With regard to these conditions, three fuzzy sets were chosen: "metallic object" (Metallgegenstand), "container" (Behälter), and "metallic container" (Metallbehälter). It has to be proved that these sets satisfy the conditions mentioned above.

This investigation has been carried out in Western Germany. In brackets you find the corresponding German words. It should be realized that the German language allows the forming of compound words. Hence the intersection is labeled by one word.

The following hypothesis may now be formulated: Let $\mu_{\tilde{M}}(x)$ be the grade of membership of some object x in the set "metallic object" and $\mu_{\tilde{C}}(x)$ be the grade of membership of x in the set "container," then the grade of membership of x in the intersecting set "metallic container" can be predicted by

$$H_1: \mu_{\tilde{M} \cap \tilde{C}}(x) = \min[\mu_{\tilde{M}}(x), \mu_{\tilde{C}}(x)]$$

$$H_2: \mu_{\tilde{M} \cap \tilde{C}}(x) = \mu_{\tilde{M}}(x) \cdot \mu_{\tilde{C}}(x)$$

The pretest showed that the requested properties existed [see Thole, Zimmerman, Zysnö 1979]. The main test resulted in the three sets of observed degrees of membership shown in table 6-1. The results of comparing the observed degrees of membership of the objects in the intersection with the degrees computed by using the min-operator and the product-operator, respectively, are shown in table 6-2. The relationship between empirical and theoretical grades of membership is shown graphically in figures 6-13 and 6-14. The straight line indicates locations of perfect prediction (i.e., if the operator makes perfect predictions and the data are free of error, then all points lie on the straight line). The question arises, whether the observed deviations are small enough to be tolerable. To answer this question we chose two criteria: if (a) the mean difference between observed and predicted values is not different from zero ($\alpha = .25$, two-tailed) and (b) the correlation between observed and predicted values is higher than .95, the connective operator in question should be accepted.

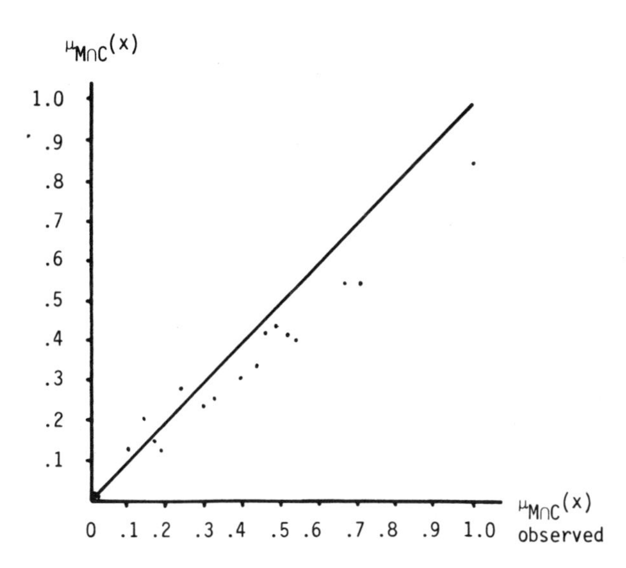

Figure 6-13: Min-operator: Observed versus expected grades of membership.

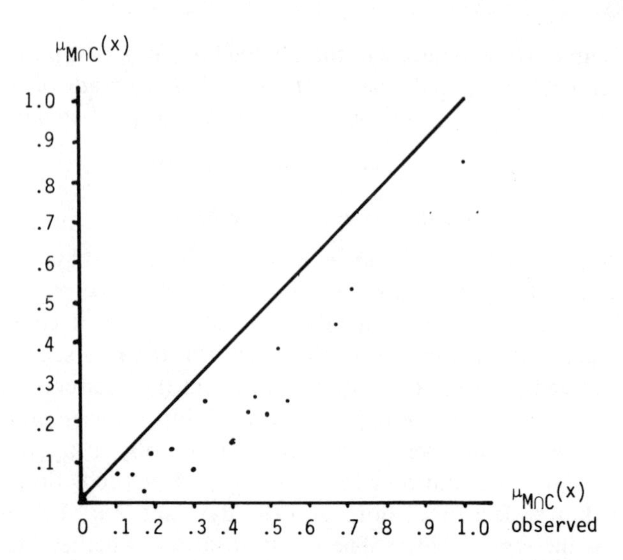

Figure 6-14: Product-operator: Observed versus expected grades of membership.

Table 6-1: Empirically determined grades of membership

Stimulus x	$\mu_{\tilde{M}}(x)$	$\mu_{\tilde{C}}(x)$	$\mu_{\tilde{M}\cap\tilde{C}}(x)$
1. bag	0.000	0.985	0.007
2. baking-tin	0.908	0.419	0.517
3. ball-point-pen	0.215	0.149	0.170
4. bathing-tub	0.552	0.804	0.674
5. book wrapper	0.023	0.454	0.007
6. car	0.501	0.437	0.493
7. cash register	0.629	0.400	0.537
8. container	0.847	1.000	1.000
9. fridge	0.424	0.623	0.460
10. hollywood-swing	0.318	0.212	0.142
11. kerosene lamp	0.481	0.310	0.401
12. nail	1.000	0.000	0.000
13. parkometer	0.663	0.335	0.437
14. pram	0.283	0.448	0.239
15. press	0.130	0.512	0.101
16. shovel	0.325	0.239	0.301
17. silver-spoon	0.969	0.256	0.330
18. sledge-hammer	0.480	0.012	0.023
19. water-bottle	0.546	0.961	0.714
20. wine-barrel	0.127	0.980	0.185

Table 6-2: Empirical versus predicted grades of membership

Stimulus x	$\mu_{\tilde{M}\cap\tilde{C}}(x)$	$\mu_{\tilde{M}\cap\tilde{C}}(x)\mid$Min	$\mu_{\tilde{M}\cap\tilde{C}}(x)\mid$Prod.
1. bag	0.007	0.000	0.000
2. baking-tin	0.517	0.419	0.380
3. ball-point-pen	0.170	0.149	0.032
4. bathing tub	0.674	0.552	0.444
5. book wrapper	0.007	0.023	0.010
6. car	0.493	0.437	0.219
7. cash register	0.537	0.400	0.252
8. container	1.000	0.847	0.847
9. fridge	0.460	0.424	0.264
10. hollywood-swing	0.124	0.212	0.067
11. kerosene lamp	0.401	0.310	0.149
12. nail	0.000	0.000	0.000
13. parkometer	0.437	0.335	0.222
14. pram	0.239	0.283	0.127
15. press	0.101	0.130	0.067
16. shovel	0.301	0.239	0.078
17. silver-spoon	0.330	0.256	0.248
18. sledge-hammer	0.023	0.012	0.006
19. water-bottle	0.714	0.546	0.525
20. wine-barrel	0.185	0.127	0.124

Since the observed differences are normally distributed we used the student t as test statistic. It is entered by the mean of the population (in this case: 0), the mean of the sample (.052 for min-operator, .134 for product operator), the observed standard deviation (.067 for minimum, .096 for product), and the sample size. For the min-rule, the result is $t = 3.471$, which is significant (df $= 19$; p, the probability of transition, is less than .01). For the product rule, the result is $t = 6.242$, which is also significant (df $= 19$; p is less than .001). Thus, both hypotheses H_1 and H_2 have to be rejected.

Despite the fact that none of the connective operators tested seems to be a really suitable model for the intersection of subjective categories, there is a slight superiority of the min-rule, as can be seen from the figures. If one was forced to use one of these aggregation rules, the minimum certainly would be the better choice.

A more severe weakness of the results and of the experimental design becomes obvious when considering the semantic meaning of the "and" used in decisions and comparing it with the properties of the "logical and" tested here: as we have already mentioned, the "logical and" does not allow for any

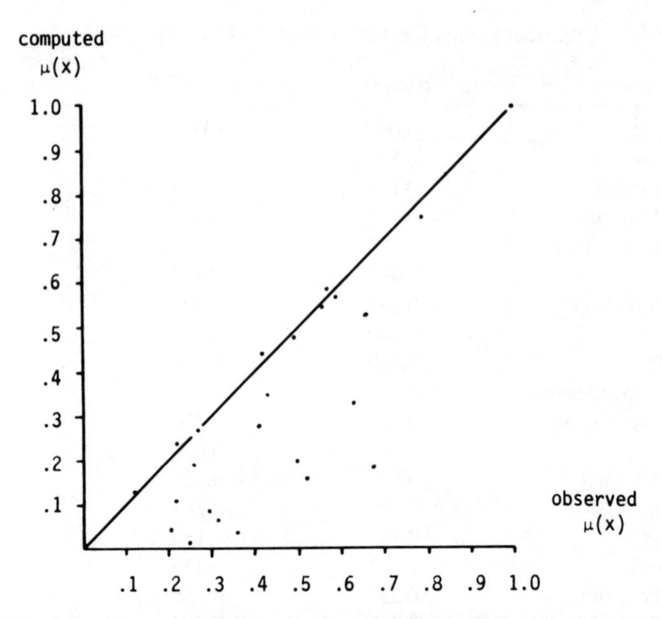

Figure 6-15: Min-Operator; observed versus computed degrees of membership.

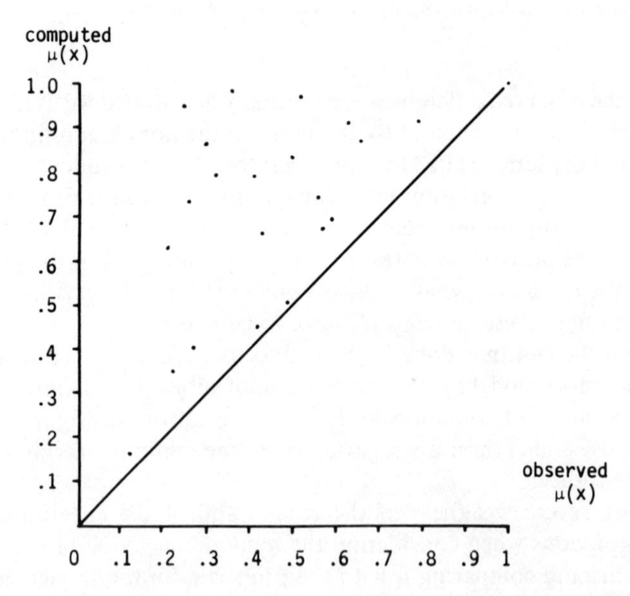

Figure 6-16: Max-Operator, observed versus computed degrees of membership.

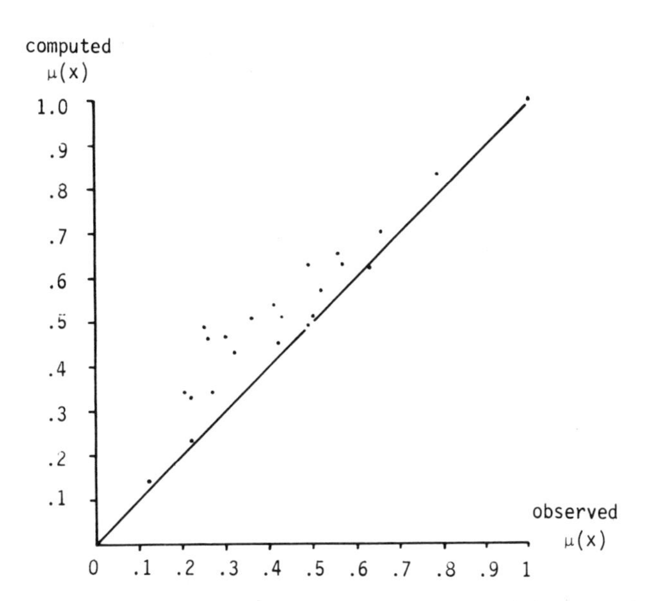

Figure 6-17: Arithmetic Mean; observed versus computed degrees of membership.

compensation; that is, the degree of membership of an element to the intersection cannot be increased by increasing the nonminimum degree of membership to the respective set. This property was ensured for the experiment in the pretest.

In decision making, the "and" connecting, for instance, two goals or criteria most often allows for such a compensation. Let us assume that we are looking for an "attractive car," where "attractive" means "comfortable *and* fast." Then the same degree of attractiveness can be reached by having a less comfortable but faster car and vice versa. That is, the higher degree of "comfort" compensates for the lower degree of membership in the set of "fast cars."

First of all, this kind of (linguistic) "and" has never been formally or mathematically defined. There is not even a special name for it—just "and." For the sake of distinguishability this "and" will be called "compensatory and" by contrast to the (noncompensatory) "logical and." Possible mathematical models for such a "compensatory and" are, for instance, the arithmetic or the geometric mean, which showed quite good results when tested in appropriate experiments. It seemed as if different operators performed best in different situations and contexts.

Figures 6-15 through 6-17 show the results of using three different mathematical models for the "compensatory and." They were obtained in an ex-

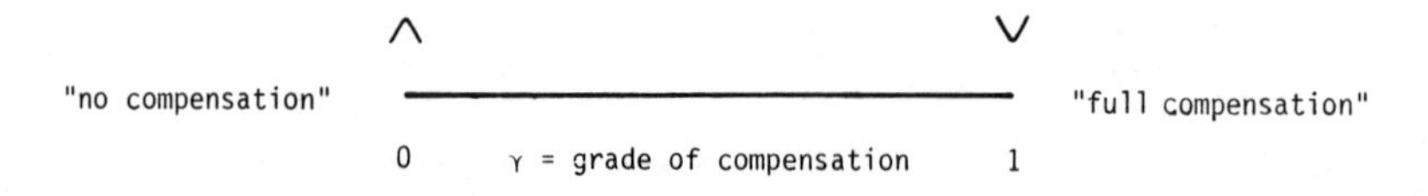

Figure 6-18: Generalized concept of connectives.

periment especially designed to test models for the "compensatory and" [Zimmermann, Zysno 1980].

If several operators are necessary in order to describe a variety of phenomena, the question arises, how many operators are needed—in practice, each important situation would then call for an adequate model. Moreover, one would be forced to assume that man has a decision rule enabling him to chose the right connective for each situation. The pursuit of this train of thought and especially its application implies a lot of difficulties. We feel that one way to by-pass these difficulties is to generalize the classical concept of connectives by introducing a parameter γ which may be interpreted as "grade of compensation." If one realizes that the "logical and" does not allow any compensation, and the 'logical' "inclusive or" provides full compensation, then γ can be regarded as a parameter indicating the position of the "compensatory and" between the two extremes (see figure 6-18). Each point on the continuum between "and" and "or" represents a different operator.

One way to formalize this idea is to find an algebraic representation for a weighted combination of the noncompensatory "and" and the fully compensatory "or." The more there is a tendency for compensation the more the "or" becomes effective and vice versa. As "extremal" operators we prefer the product and the algebraic sum [Oden 1977; Zaden 1976]. Of course, other "extremes" are conceivable, for instance minimum and maximum. But in our opinion these models are handicapped because they do not reflect the interaction of membership values. Thus we define

$$\mu_{\tilde{A}\theta\tilde{B}} = \mu_{\tilde{A}\cap\tilde{B}}^{1-\gamma} \cdot \mu_{\tilde{A}\cup\tilde{B}}^{\gamma} \tag{6.40}$$

The membership of an object in the set $\tilde{A}\,\theta\,\tilde{B}$ equals the product of the weighted membership values for the intersection and the union. If the intersection and the union are algebraically represented by the product and the algebraic sum, respectively, then (6.40) becomes for several sets

$$\mu_\theta = \left(\prod_{i=1}^{m} \mu_i\right)^{1-\gamma} \left(1 - \prod_{i=1}^{m} (1 - \mu_i)\right)^{\gamma} \qquad \begin{matrix} 0 \le \mu_i \le 1 \\ 0 \le \gamma \le 1 \end{matrix} \tag{6.41}$$

where $i = 1,2,\ldots,m$, m = number of sets to be connected. Then, if $\gamma = 0$,

$$\mu_\cap = \prod_{l=1}^{m} \mu_i \tag{6.42}$$

This is the product and provides the truth values for the connective "and." If $\gamma = 1$, then

$$\mu_\cup = 1 - \prod_{i=1}^{m} (1 - \mu_i) \tag{6.42}$$

This formula equals the generalized algebraic sum and provides the truth values for the connective "or."

If it is desired to introduce different weights for the sets in question, μ_i and $1 - \mu_i$, for example, could be replaced by

$$\mu_i = v_i^{\delta_i} \quad \text{and} \quad 1 - \mu_i = (1 - v_i)^{\delta^i} \tag{6.44}$$

where v_i are the (raw) membership values and δ_i their corresponding weights. In order to preserve the structure of our model, the sum of weights δ_i should be equal to the number of sets connected:

$$\sum_i \delta_i = m \tag{6.45}$$

In our opinion, the consideration of different weights plays an important role if real-world situations are modelled by fuzzy sets.

In order to use this class of operators in a meaningful manner an operational definition should, of course, be available for the empirical determination of γ. At present, such a definition is still missing. However, we can try to find out if there is any value of γ that enables us to predict our experimental data. If such a value does not exist, the adequacy of the operator suggested must be doubted. On the other hand, if the operator works on the basis of some γ, it seems reasonable to search for an operational definition.

If (6.41) is solved for γ the result is

$$\gamma = \frac{\log \mu_\theta - \log \prod_{i=1}^{m} \mu_i}{\log\left(1 - \prod_{i=1}^{m} (1 - \mu_i)\right) - \log \prod_{i=1}^{m} \mu_i} \tag{6.46}$$

where $i = 1,2,\ldots,m$, m = number of sets to be connected. Naturally, γ will show some fluctuations because of experimental error. We therefore used $\hat{\gamma}$ to find the results in figure 6-19:

$$\hat{\gamma} = \frac{1}{n} \prod_{j=1}^{n} \gamma_j \tag{6.47}$$

where n is the number of experimental objects in each of the sets selected ($\tilde{A}$, $\tilde{B}$, $\tilde{A}\,\theta\,\tilde{B}$).

Other operators are, of course, conceivable. For instance, the aggregation of two sets may be defined by

$$\begin{aligned}\mu_{\tilde{A}\theta\tilde{B}} &= (1-\gamma)\mu_{\tilde{A}\cap\tilde{B}} + \gamma\mu_{\tilde{A}\cup\tilde{B}} \\ &= \mu_{\tilde{A}\cap\tilde{B}} + \gamma(\mu_{\tilde{A}\cup\tilde{B}} - \mu_{\tilde{A}\cap\tilde{A}})\end{aligned} \tag{6.48}$$

If the intersection and the union are represented by the product and the algebraic sum, respectively, (6.48) becomes

$$\mu_\theta = (1-\gamma)\prod_{i=1}^{m}\mu_i + \gamma\left(1 - \prod_{i=1}^{m}(1-\mu_i)\right) \tag{6.49}$$

Again, μ_i may be replaced by weighted membership values:

$$\mu_\theta = (1-\gamma)\prod_{i=1}^{m}v_i^{\delta_i} + \gamma\left(1 - \prod_{i=1}^{m}(1-v_i)^{\delta_i}\right) \tag{6.50}$$

$$0 \le v_i \le 1, \quad 0 \le \gamma \le 1, \quad \Sigma\delta_i = m$$

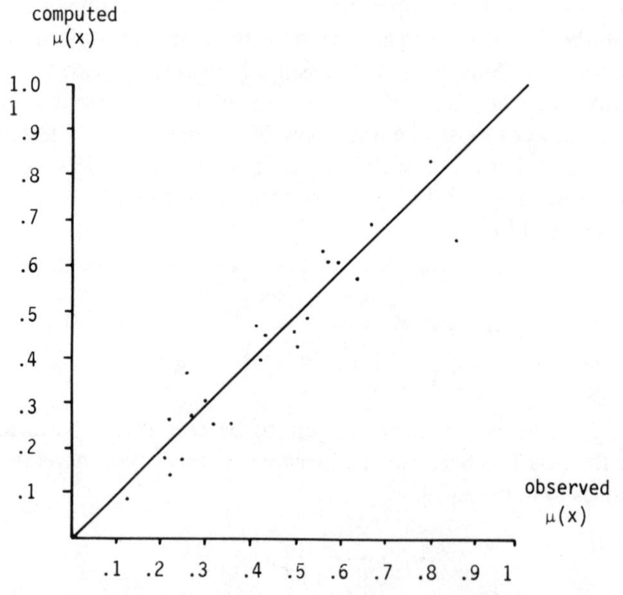

Figure 6-19: γ-operator; observed versus computed degrees of membership.

If $\gamma = 0$ and $\delta_i = 1$, then (6.50) becomes

$$\mu_\cap = \prod_i \mu_i \tag{6.51}$$

If $\gamma = 1$ and $\delta_i = 1$, then (6.50) becomes

$$\mu_\cup = 1 - \prod_i (1 - \mu_i) \tag{6.52}$$

This class of operators is again in accordance with the truth tables of dual logic and allows the use of different weights. Its performance, however, did not match that of (6.41).

Of interest is the performance of the operator in complex situations. In particular, our interest concerns its capacity in real decision situations with—as usual—multi-level hierarchies of evaluation criteria. To characterize the aggregation system we first need a descriptive model (a paradigm), which explains and describes the central aspects and their relations in a manner easily understandable. The essential features of the paradigm will be represented formally. In order to test the model, an empirical study has been carried out, in which the adequacy of the model with respect to a typical decision situation was examined.

Our paradigm assumes that people either learn or generate "evaluative concepts" or "subjective categories." These terms refer to two sides of one coin: the first refers to the intensional aspects of a set, which can be described by a list of attributes; the second stresses the accumulation of objects (extensional aspects of a set). We assume that human beings have such concepts or categories at their disposition and that they can relate them to each other.

Attributes constituting a concept may be interpreted other than psychologically. They can be replaced by any mental information unit—for instance, the status of neural elements or the adjectives of a language. The relationships may actually be modelled by operators, connectives, rules, or other means. For our purposes we will limit our considerations to a specific type of amalgamation. We assume a hierarchy of concepts in which there are several levels of complexity (see figure 6-20). The bottom level contains basic concepts which can stepwise be aggregated until the top concept of the hierarchy is attained. For reasons of practical relevance of the model we shall allow that (a) the subcategories are of unequal importance for the respective super category, and (b) the description of categories of each level may partly contain the same attributes.

Decision Situation. In searching for an appropriate decision situation our choice fell on the rating of creditworthiness for the following reasons:

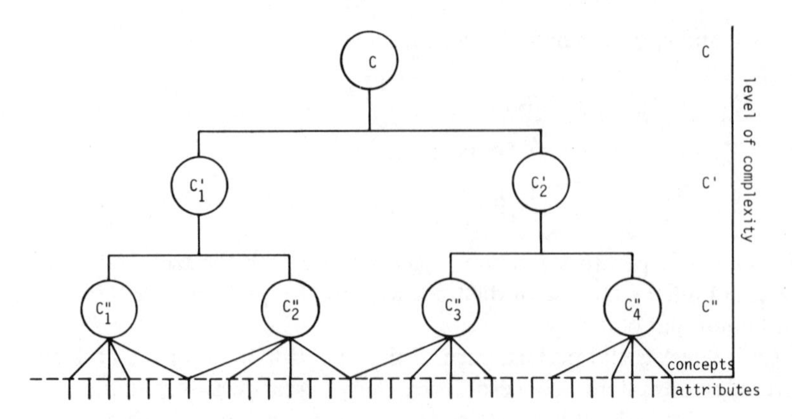

Figure 6-20: Hierarchy of concepts/categories.

a. This is a decision problem which is complex enough, though it is still relatively transparent and definable. In addition, this situation is highly standardized. Even though test subjects come from different organizations similar evaluation schemes can be assessed.
b. A sufficiently large number of decision makers is available, with about the same training background and similar levels of competence.
c. The decision problems to be solved can be formulated and presented in a realistic manner with respect to contents and appearance.

Before beginning an empirical investigation it was necessary to explore whether a conceptual system on creditworthiness could be established. Three groups of six credit clerks each were asked to design a hierarchical system of aspects for the evaluation of borrowers. Three sessions were arranged, each of which lasted five hours and was divided into three sections.

Section I. After an introducing discourse exposing the principal questions and intentions of the study the participants' task was explained. Then four completed credit applications of fictitious borrowers had to be rated by "thinking aloud." Finally, each expert was asked to develop a concept hierarchy of creditworthiness on a piece of paper. On this basis the group tried to find a first common criteria system, beginning from the top and going down successively to the lower levels.

Section II. The system arrived at so far was extended, refined, and modified by means of four more credit applications.

Section III. Clarification and agreement—superfluous aspects were eliminated, conceptual extensions were accepted only by majority consent of the group.

The final concept hierarchy has a symmetrical structure (figure 2-4). Credit experts distinguish between the financial basis and the personality of an applicant. The financial basis comprises all realities, movables, assets, liquid funds, and others. Evaluation of the economic situation depends on the actual securites (i.e., the difference between property and debts), and on the liquidity (i.e., the continuous difference between income and expenses). Personality, on the other hand, denotes the collection of traits by which a potent and serious person may be distinguished. A persons achievement potential is based on mental and physical capacity as well as on the individual's motivation. Business conduct includes economic standards. While the former means setting of realistic goals, reasonable planning, and economic success, the latter is directed toward the applicant's disposition to obey business laws and mutual agreements. Hence, a creditworthy person lives in secure circumstances and guarantees successful profit-oriented cooperation. The interested reader will find details of the experimental procedure in Zimmermann and Zysno [1983].

The predictive quality of each model can be evaluated by comparing observed μ-grades with theoretical μ-grades. The latter can be computed for higher-level concepts by aggregation of the lower-level concepts using the candidate formula.

The membership values for higher-level concepts should be predicted sufficiently well by any lower level of the corresponding branch. The quality of a model can be illustrated by a two-dimensional system, the axes of which

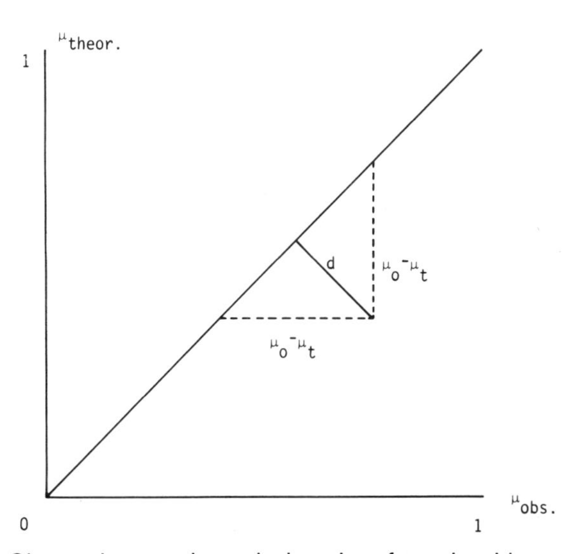

Figure 6-21: Observed versus theoretical grades of membership.

represent the observed versus theoretical μ-values (see figure 6-21). Each applicant is represented by a point. In the case of exact prognoses, all points must be located on a straight diagonal line. Since data are collected empirically, there will be deviations from this ideal.

In order to evaluate the goodness of fit, the "prognostic error" was computed. This is defined as the distance between the empirical value and its theoretically expected counterpart [Zysno 1982]. From the underlying geometric explanation given by figure 6-21 we see that the squared error is determined by

$$d^2 = \tfrac{1}{2}(\mu_o - \mu_t)^2 \tag{6.53}$$

where μ_0 = observed μ-values and μ_t = theoretically expected μ-values.

The "average prognostic error" s_p^2 can be defined by

$$s_p^2 = \frac{\Sigma \frac{1}{2}(\mu_o + \mu_t)^2}{n-1} = \frac{\Sigma(\mu_o - \mu_t)^2}{2(n-1)}. \tag{6.54}$$

In table 6-3 the abbreviations refer to the concept hierarchy: the first two letters indicate the respective fuzzy set (e.g., CW = creditworthiness, BB = business behavior), and the roman number refers to the level in which the term stands in the hierarchy. The descriptive measure s_p can be used to compare the different models and to find the one with the best fit.

Tentatively, a level for rejection is introduced—the "intolerable error," which is fixed at $s_e^2 = .005$. At present such a standard is somewhat arbitrary. Principally, it should be fixed on the basis of general consent, external requirements, or experimental experience. Practically, it serves as a criterion of acceptance or rejection: if $s_p^2 < s_e^2$, the model will be accepted. Therefore, if the ratio of variance $F_{\text{comp}} = s_e^2/s_p^2$ is greater than $F_{\text{crit}}(\text{df}_1 = \text{df}_2 = n - 1)$ from the F-distribution, then the average prognostic error is regarded as "significantly less" than the intolerable error. Accordingly, the values of table 6-3 are marked by two stars ($F_{\text{crit}} = 1.95, \alpha = .01$) or one star ($F_{\text{crit}} = 1.67, \alpha = .05$).

It is obvious that the minimum and the maximum can not be accepted as suitable operators. However, as soon as compensatory models come into consideration, the goodness of fit increases immediately. Figure 6-22 to 6-29 give a visual orientation for the prediction of creditworthiness (CW) by level III and of security (SE) by the corresponding low concepts.

Unfortunately, the weighted geometric mean fails drastically in predicting security by unmortgaged real estate and other net properties (figure 6-28). In our view, this is due to the fact that the model does not regard different grades of compensation. The inclusion of different weights for the concepts does not seem to be sufficient for describing the human aggregation process adequately. Consequently it is not surprising that the γ-model, comprising different weights

Table 6-3: Average prognostic error s_p^2($^* = \alpha \leq 0.05$, $^{**} = \alpha \leq 0.01$).

	Min	*Max*	*Geom. mean*	*γ-model*	*γ*	*smooth. weights* *γ-model*	*γ*
CW-I	0.00092**	0.00209**	0.00101**	0.00087**	0.592	0.00083**	0.588
CW-II	0.00576	0.00917	0.00122**	0.00107**	0.782	0.00111**	0.782
CW-III	0.12631	0.00907	0.00349	0.00244**	0.903	0.00233**	0.901
FB-II	0.00761	0.00679	0.00182**	0.00160**	0.616	0.00157**	0.617
FB-III	0.12691	0.00510	0.00685	0.00117**	0.839	0.00108**	0.837
PE-II	0.00112**	0.00127**	0.00068**	0.00069**	0.597	0.00070**	0.597
PE-III	0.00467	0.00366	0.00133**	0.00137**	0.763	0.00134**	0.761
SE-III	0.12310	0.00260**	0.08228	0.00298*	0.978	0.00352	0.981
LI-III	0.00123**	0.00122**	0.00066**	0.00051**	0.574	0.00057**	0.574
AP-III	0.00046**	0.00083**	0.00039**	0.00039**	0.551	0.00040**	0.548
BB-III	0.00340	0.00285**	0.00190**	0.00205**	0.547	0.00194**	0.547

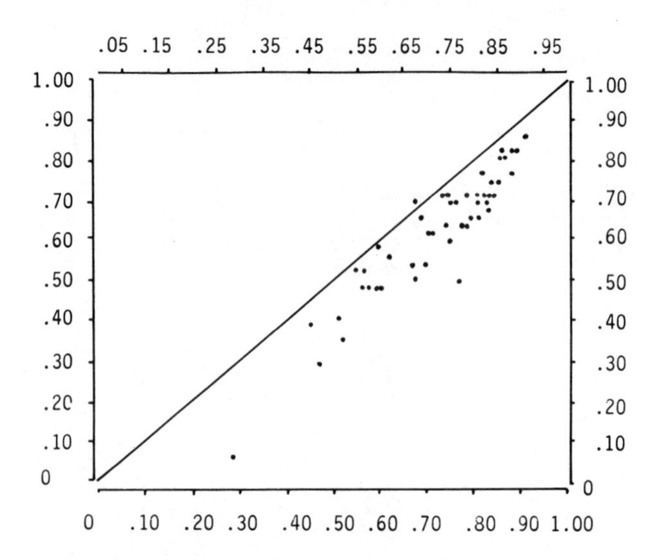

Figure 6-22: CW-II Min-operator.

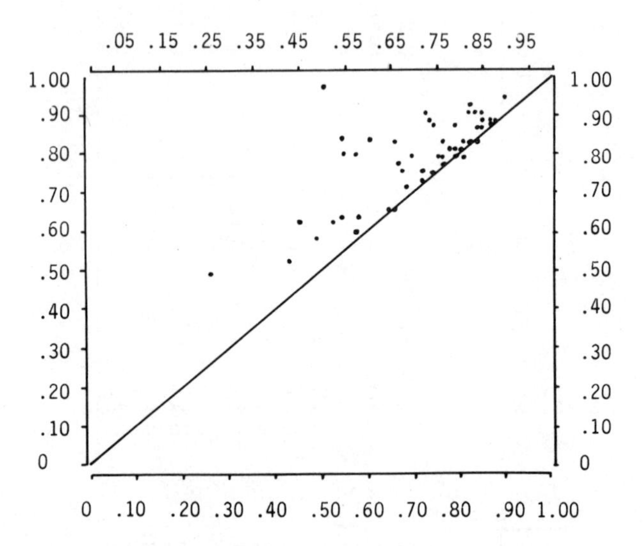

Figure 6-23: CW-II Max-operator.

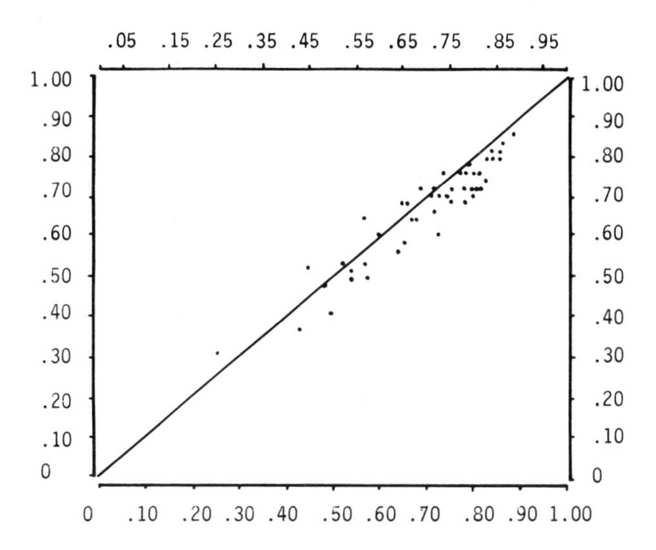

Figure 6-24: CW-II Geometric Mean-operator.

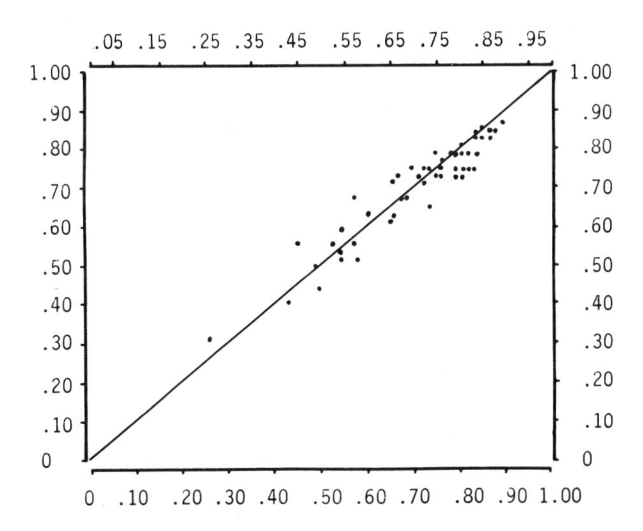

Figure 6-25: CW-II γ-operator.

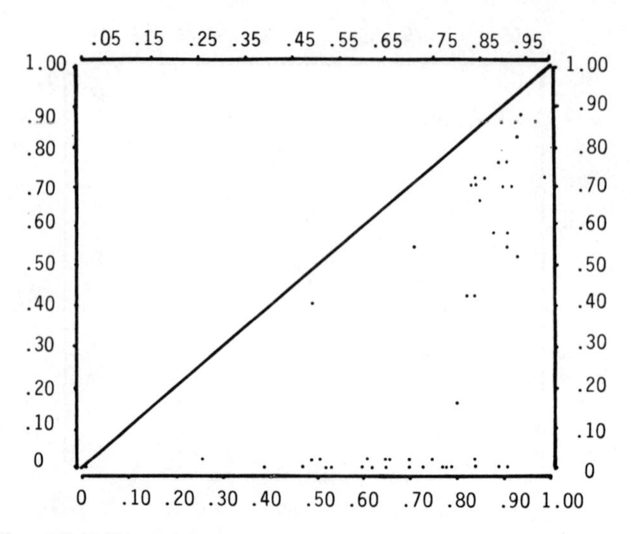

Figure 6-26: SE-II Min-operator.

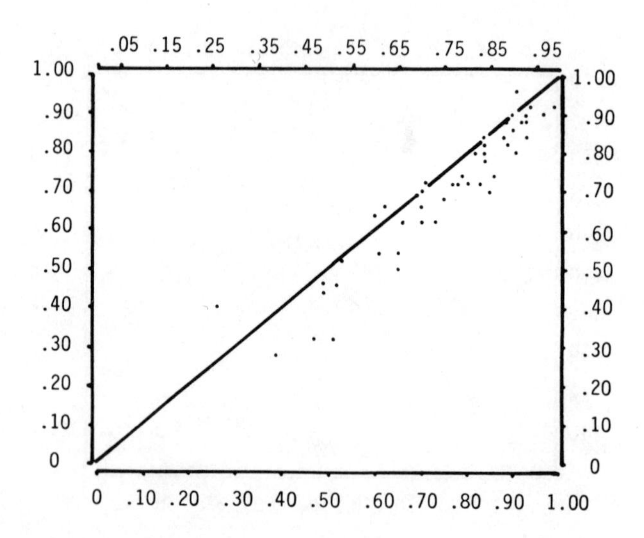

Figure 6-27: SE-III Max-operator.

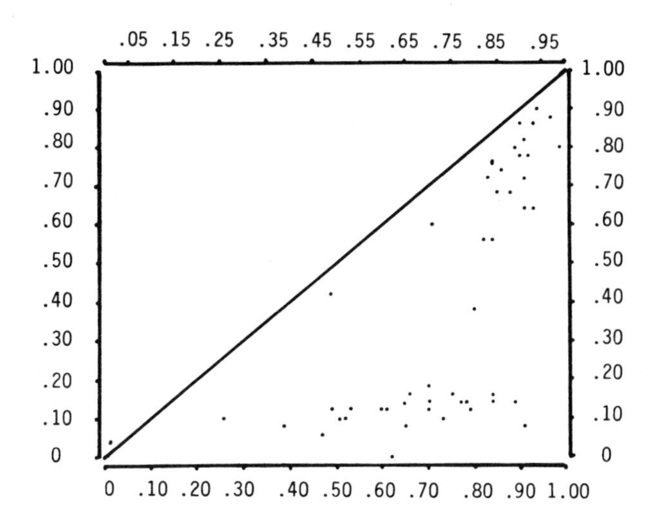

Figure 6-28: SE-III Geometric Mean-operator.

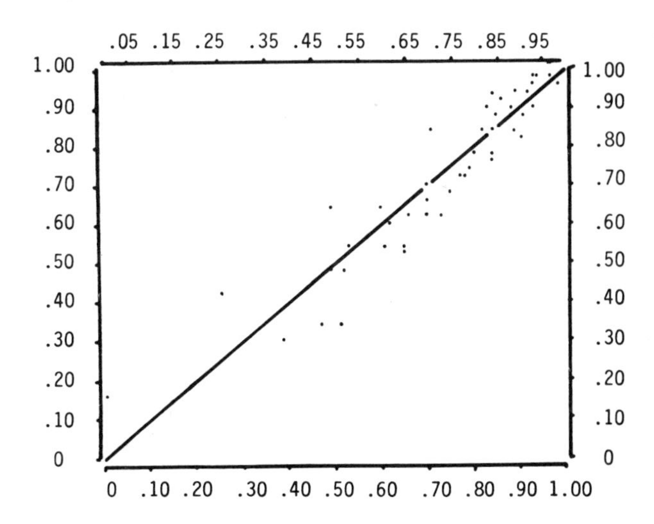

Figure 6-29: SE-III γ-operator.

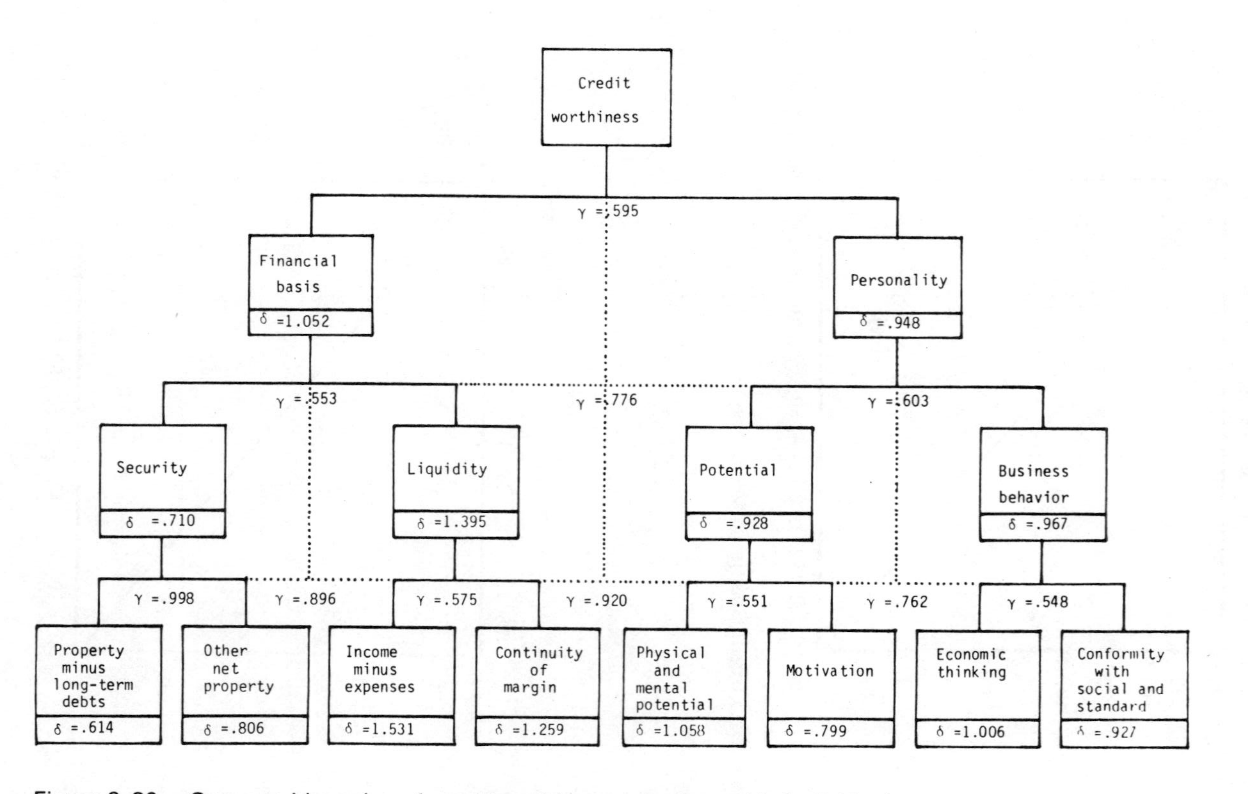

Figure 6-30: Concept hierarchy of creditworthiness together with individual weights δ and γ-values for each level of aggregation.

as well as different grades of compensation, yields the best results.

It should be kept in mind, however, that γ has not been determined empirically. This would have required a further experimental study, based on a theory describing the dependence of γ-values between higher and lower levels. For the present we are content with estimations derived from the data, as proposed by Zimmermann and Zysno [1980]. At least it has been shown that the judgmental behavior of credit clerks can be described quite well if this parameter is taken into account.

Finally, the complete hierarchy of creditworthiness is presented together with the elaborated weighting system and the γ-values for each level of aggregation in figure 6-30.

In summary, we have suggested and tested empirically a number of models for the aggregation—in the sense of the "linguistic and"—of fuzzy sets representing concepts.

The essential difference between these models and normative models of classical utility theory and multicriteria analysis is that the former are more realistic than the latter. The evaluative system can be built with regard to verbal and practical requirements and is empirically testable.

The judgments are classificatory in nature, so the approach is not restricted to preference—or indifference—data. Restrictions and objective functions are modelled equally by fuzzy sets [Bellman, Zadeh 1970].

Our exemplary analysis of the process of rating creditworthiness yields a structure of criteria that is concept-oriented and self-explanatory. The γ-model, which was from the beginning, designed to satisfy mathematical requirements as well as to describe human aggregation behavior proved most adequate with respect to prognostic power. This class of operators is continuous, monotonic, injective, commutative, and in accordance with classical truth tables, all of which manifests their relationship to formal logic and set theory. These operators aggregate partial judgements in such a way that the formal result of the aggregation ought to make them attractive for empirically working scientists and useful for the practitioner.

Banking managers not only evaluate, they also decide. In order to complete the description of a decision process we therefore asked to arrive at a decision for each fictitious credit application. If the creditworthiness was an attribute of the all-or-none type and all credit managers followed the same decision-making process then two homogeneous blocks of credit decisions (one block with 100% yes decisions and one block with 100% no decisions) would result. The number of positive decisions, however, varied over the entire range from 45 to 0. Obviously there existed a considerable individual decision space.

However, when selecting operators for decision models, "empirical fit" is only one of the relevant criteria. In this respect we refer to the eight pragmatic rules mentioned at the end of this chapter's first section.

7 DECISION SUPPORTING SYSTEMS

Knowledge-Based vs. Data-Based Systems

It has long been established [e.g., Newell, Simon 1972] that electronic data processing (EDP) and human decision makers complement each other in the sense that EDP is by far superior or more powerful in terms of data processing—in particular simultaneous and parallel processing—and the human is more capable, for instance, of communicating on the basis of incomplete data, in making judgments etc. The human decision maker needs the help of EDP in terms of information processing capacity and easy-access storage. But if EDP equipment is to be used for this purpose, decision problems must be modelled properly so that the models really represent the decision maker's problems and can be understood by the machine. This normally implies that the decision maker himself knows how to solve the problem and that the solution algorithm can be modelled well enough to be programmed for the machine. In this case the solution procedure—like the information processing process called "decision"—is well defined on the machine and the data input into the program will fully determine the result of the process. We shall call such an EDP program or system *Data-Based* Decision *Support System* or, for short, DSS. Of course there are still problems for the decision maker, and the case in which all algorithmic features are well defined is only a limiting case. The decision maker still has problems with obtaining all the data and feeding them into the computer in the correct format. And, if he does not feel completely sure about the correctness of the data, he might be interested in some type of sensitivity analysis. The DSS can help him in this respect also by supplying a comfortable data-input device such as, for example, a matrix generator. Even if the decision maker is not quite sure in advance about, for instance, what operators to use for aggregation in a fuzzy linear programming code, or if in any other way he can interactively change parameters or procedures in the system we shall still call it a DSS.

There are cases, however, in which the model—or program builder, let us call him analyst—does not know in advance which solution procedure will be best for solving a problem, either because the problem is too ill-structured or because even the best algorithms available are too inefficient to solve it. (Many combinatorial problems are of that kind!) Surprisingly, many such problems, which are too complex even for very modern and powerful algorithms, have been solved by human experts in the past. These experts were supported by their experience, they used heuristics and common knowledge which they had accumulated and applied successfully to a specific problem. EDP systems that use as an input this type of knowledge in addition to data are generally called *knowledge-based* systems. An Expert System (ES) uses this expert knowledge and combines it with computer processing power in order to arrive at good solutions which are not necessarily optimal.

If the expert is conscious of the algorithmic rules he has been applying in order to obtain the solution, these rules can, of course, be included in the program. Often he will not be able, however, to explain clearly why he chooses a certain action in a specific situation. Then the expert system, by applying certain techniques of artificial intelligence, tries to discover the expert's logic and store it for future use. This, in general, is a very difficult task and the techniques currently available are not yet too well advanced. Expert systems can be and are used for quite different purposes. They can be primarily diagnostic, for instance, in medicine, repair and maintenance, failure deduction in computer systems, etc. They can also be used for decision support or for teaching and training purposes.

When fuzzy set theory is applied to either DSS or ES it very often is as a source of linguistic variables or through the use of fuzzy logic or approximate reasoning. In order to make this book self-contained we will describe these terms briefly. (For further details the reader is referred to Zimmermann [1985b, ch. 9].) After which we shall describe the use of fuzzy set theory in an interactive decision support system. The final section of this chapter will be devoted to the use of fuzzy sets in expert systems.

Linguistic Variables, Fuzzy Logic, Appropimate Reasoning

Linguistic Variables

A *variable* is normally thought of as a notion that can be specified by assigning to it certain numerical values. If we define the variable A to mean "age" and specify $0 \leq A \leq 100$, we know that the variable A (whatever it might mean) can have all numbers between 0 and 100 assigned to it.

A *stochastic variable* is characterized by the results of a stochastic experiment. It is generally represented by a distribution function.

The easiest way to understand the notion of a *linguistic variable* is to regard it either as a variable whose numerical values are fuzzy numbers or as a variable the range of which is not defined by numerical values but by linguistic terms. Zadeh called a linguistic variable a "variable of higher order" [Zadeh 1973, p. 75]. The justification for this will become obvious after we have defined it properly.

Definition 7.1

A *linguistic variable* is characterized by a quintupe $(x, T(x), U, G, \tilde{M})$ in which x is the name of the variable; $T(x)$ (or simply T) denotes the term set of x, that is, the set of names of linguistic values of x, with each value being a fuzzy variable denoted generically by x and ranging over a universe of discourse U which is associated with the base variable u; G is a syntactic rule (which usually has a grammatical form) for generating the name, X, of values of x; and $\tilde{M}$ is a semantic rule for associating with each X its meaning, $\tilde{M}(X)$, which is a fuzzy subset of U. A particular X—that is, a name generated by G—is called a term. It should be noted that the base variable u can also be vector-valued.

Often the name of the variable (its label) and the generic name of the elements of the variable are denoted by the same symbol. The same holds for X and $\tilde{M}(X)$.

Example 7.1 [Zadeh 1973a, p. 77]

Let X be a linguistic variable with the label "age" (i.e., the label of this variable is "age" and the values of it will also be called "age"), with $U = [0,100]$. Terms of this linguistic variable, which are again fuzzy sets, could be called "old," "young," "very old," and so on. The base variable U is the age in years of life.

$\tilde{M}(X)$ is the rule that assigns a meaning—that is, a fuzzy set—to the terms:

$$\tilde{M}(\text{old}) = \{(u, \mu_{\text{old}}(u)) \quad u \in [0,100]\}$$

where

$$\mu_{\text{old}}(u) = \begin{cases} 0 & u \in [0,50] \\ \left(1 + \left(\frac{u-50}{5}\right)^{-2}\right)^{-1} & u \in [50,100] \end{cases}$$

$T(x)$ will define the term set of the variable x; for instance, in this case,

$$T(\text{age}) = \{\text{old, very old, not so old, more or less young, quite young, very young}\}$$

where $G(x)$ is a rule which generates the (labels of) terms in the term set. Figure 7-1 sketches these relationships.

A linguistic variable does not necessarily have a numerical base variable. It depends on whether the terms have membership functions of type A or B (see chapter 6).

Definition 7.2

A linguistic variable x is called *structured* if the term set $T(x)$ and the meaning $\tilde{M}(x)$ can be characterized algorithmically. For a structured linguistic variable, $\tilde{M}(x)$ and $T(x)$ can be regarded as algorithms, which generate the terms of the term set and associate meanings with them.

Definition 7.3

A *linguistic hedge*, or a *modifier*, is an operation that modifies the meaning of a term or, more generally, of a fuzzy set. If $\tilde{A}$ is a fuzzy set then the modifier m generates the (composite) term $\tilde{B} = m(\tilde{A})$.

Mathematical models frequently used for modifiers include

Concentration: $\mu_{\text{con}(\tilde{A})}(u) = (\mu_{\tilde{A}}(u))^2$

Dilation: $\mu_{\text{dil}(\tilde{A})}(u) = (\mu_{\tilde{A}}(u))^{1/2}$

Contrast intensification:

$$\mu_{\text{int}(\tilde{A})}(u) = \begin{cases} 2(\mu_{\tilde{A}}(u))^2 & \text{for } \mu_{\tilde{A}}(u) \in [0,.5] \\ 1 - 2(1 - \mu_{\tilde{A}}(u))^2 & \text{otherwise} \end{cases}$$

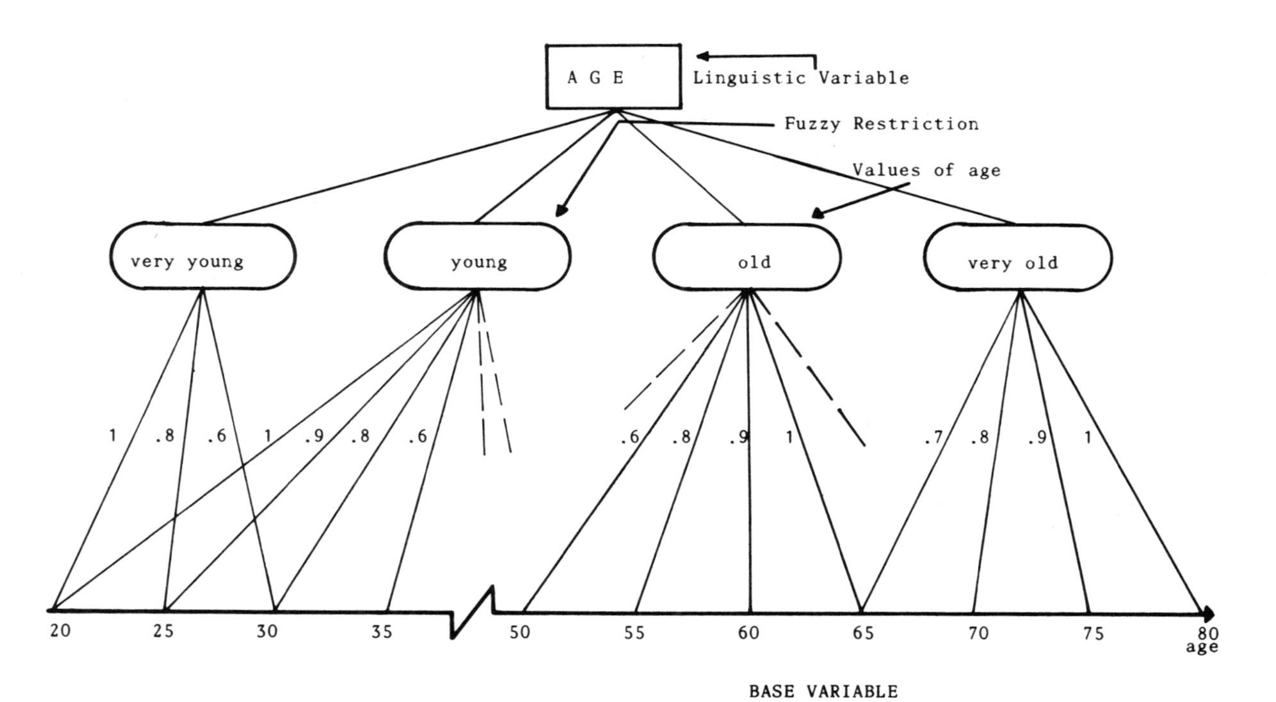

Figure 7-1: Linguistic Variable "Age".

Generally the following linguistic hedges (modifiers) are associated with these mathematical operators.

If $\tilde{A}$ is a term (a fuzzy set) then

$$\text{very } \tilde{A} = \text{con}(\tilde{A})$$

$$\text{more or less } \tilde{A} = \text{dil}(\tilde{A})$$

$$\text{plus } \tilde{A} = (\tilde{A})^{1.25}$$

$$\text{slightly } \tilde{A} = \text{int}\,[\text{plus } \tilde{A} \text{ and not (very } \tilde{A})]$$

where 'and" is interpreted possibilistically (see definition 1.7).

***Example** 7.2* [Zadeh 1973a, p. 83]

Let us reconsider the linguistic variable "age" in example 7.1. The term set shall be assumed to be

$$T(\text{age}) = \{\text{old, very old, very very old,} \ldots\}$$

The term set can now be generated recursively by using the following rule (algorithm) with $R \in T^i_\infty$

$$T^{i+1} = \{\text{old}\} \cup \text{very } T^i$$

where

$$\text{very } T^i := \bigcup_{R \in T^i} \{\text{very } R\}$$

that is

$$T^0 = \emptyset$$

$$T^1 = \{\text{old}\}$$

$$T^2 = \{\text{old, very old}\}$$

$$T^3 = \{\text{old, very old, very very old}\}$$

For the semantic rule we only need to know the meaning of "old" and the meaning of the modifier "very" in order to determine the meaning of an arbitrary term of the term set. If one defines "very" as the concentration, then the terms of the term set of the structured linguistic variable "age" can be determined, given that the membership function of the term "old" is known.

Fuzzy Logic

"Fuzzy logic" and "approximate reasoning" form the core of the so-called "inference engines" in expert systems when fuzzy set theory is used. Fuzzy logic and even more approximate reasoning try to adapt the systems of dual and multi-valued logic, which in a sense are rather limited (see, for instance, the discussion of the "logical and" in chapter 6), to the way in which humans usually argue. It is, therefore, useful to reconsider dual logic briefly.

Logic as basis for reasoning can be distinguished essentially by three topic-neutral (context-independent) items—truth values, vocabulary (operators), and reasoning procedure (tautologies, syllogisms). In Boolean logic truth values can be 0 (false) or 1 (true), and by means of these truth values the operators (vocabulary) are defined via truth tables.

Let us consider two statements, A and B, either of which can be true or false—that is, either can have the truth value 1 or 0. We can construct the following truth tables:

A	B	$\wedge$	$\vee$	$(x)\nabla$	$\Rightarrow$	$\Leftrightarrow$	?	
1	1	1	1	0	1	1	1	
1	0	0	1	1	0	0	1	
0	1	0	1	1	1	0	0	....
0	0	0	0	0	1	1	0	

There are $2^{2^2} = 16$ truth tables, each defining an operator. It is not difficult to assign meaning (words) to these operators for the first four or five columns: the first obviously characterizes the "and," the second the "inclusive or," the third the "exclusive or," and the fourth and fifth the implication and the equivalence. We will have difficulties, however, interpreting the remaining nine columns in terms of our language. If we have three statements rather than two, the task of assigning meanings to truth tables becomes even more difficult.

So far it has been assumed that each statement, A and B, could clearly be classified as true or false. If this is no longer true then additional truth values, such as "undecided" or something similar, can and must be introduced. This leads to the many existing systems of multi-valued logic. It is not difficult to see how the above problems in "labelling" truth tables or operators with two-valued logic increase as we move to multi-valued logic. For only two statements and three possible truth values there are already $3^{3^2} = 729$ truth tables! The uniqueness of interpretation of truth tables, which is so convenient in Boolean logic, disappears immediately because many truth tables in three-valued logic look very much alike.

The third topic-neutral item of logical systems is the reasoning procedure itself, which is generally based on tautologies such as

modus ponens:	$(A \wedge (A \Rightarrow B)) \Rightarrow B$
modus tollens:	$((A \Rightarrow B) \wedge \neg B) \Rightarrow \neg A$
syllogism:	$((A \Rightarrow B) \wedge (B \Rightarrow C)) \Rightarrow (A \Rightarrow C)$
contraposition:	$(A \Rightarrow B) \Rightarrow (\neg B \Rightarrow \neg A)$

Let us consider the modus ponens, which could be interpreted as "if A is true and if the statement 'if A is true then B is true' is also true, then B is true." The foregoing tautologies obviously depend on the character of the statements, the type of permissible truth values, and the definition of the operators; and they assume that, for example, all A's contained in one tautology are identical. The respective assumptions made in dual logic are gradually relaxed in fuzzy logic, approximate reasoning, and plausible reasoning.

Fuzzy logic [Zadeh 1973a, p. 101] is an extension of set theoretic multi-valued logic in which the truth values are linguistic variables (or terms of the linguistic variable "truth"). Since operators, like $\vee$, $\wedge$, $\neg$, and $\Rightarrow$ in fuzzy logic are also defined by using truth tables, the extension principle can be applied to derive definitions of the operators. So far, possibility theory has primarily been used in order to define operators in fuzzy logic, even though other operators have also been investigated [e.g., Mizumoto, Zimmermann 1982] and could also be used. In this book we will limit considerations to possibilistic interpretations of linguistic variables and we will also stick to the original proposals of Zadeh [1973a]. We suggest that the interested reader also study alternative approaches such as [Baldwin 1987; Baldwin, Pilsworth 1980; Giles 1979, 1980], and others.

As already mentioned, in the truth tables of fuzzy logic the truth values (in dual logic 0 or 1) are terms of the linguistic variable "truth." This variable has been defined differently by different authors. Figures 7-2 and 7-3 show graphically the definitions of Baldwin [Baldwin 1979, p. 316] and Zadeh [1973a, p. 9].

Both figures show on the horizontal axis the truth value $v(A)$ of statement A, where $v(A)$ is a point in $V = [0,1]$. One could, for instance, define the truth value $v(\text{not } A)$ as

$$\tilde{v}(\text{not } A) = \{(1 - v_i, \mu_i) | i = 1, \ldots, n, v_i \in [0,1]\}$$

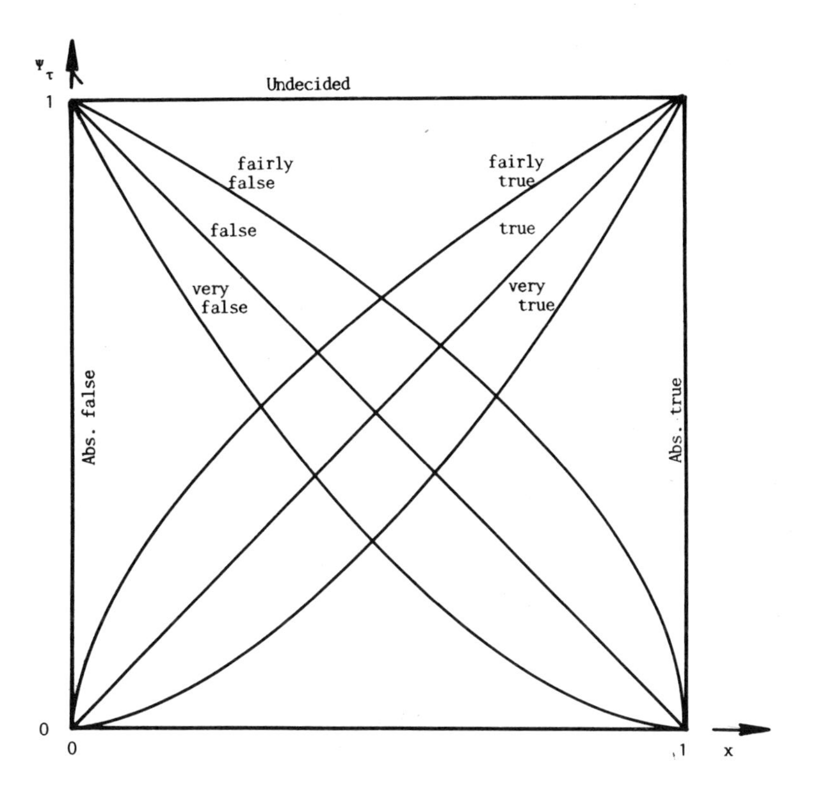

Figure 7-2: Linguistic Variable "Truth", Baldwin.

If one then interpretes 'false" as "not true," then

$$\tilde{v}(\text{false}) = \{(1 - v_i, \mu_i) | i = 1, \ldots, n, v_i \in [0,1]\}$$

Example 7.3 indicates how the membership functions of terms of the linguistic variable "truth" can be generated using modifiers (hedges) and the above agreement about the interpretation of "false."

Example 7.3

If the terms true and false are defined by the following possibility distributions,

$$\text{true} = \{(.5,.6),(.6,.7),(.7,.8),(.8,.9),(.9,1),(1,1)\}$$

$$\text{false} = \tilde{v}(\text{not true}) = \{(.5,.6),(.4,.7),(.3,.8),(.2,.9),(.1,1),(0,1)\}$$

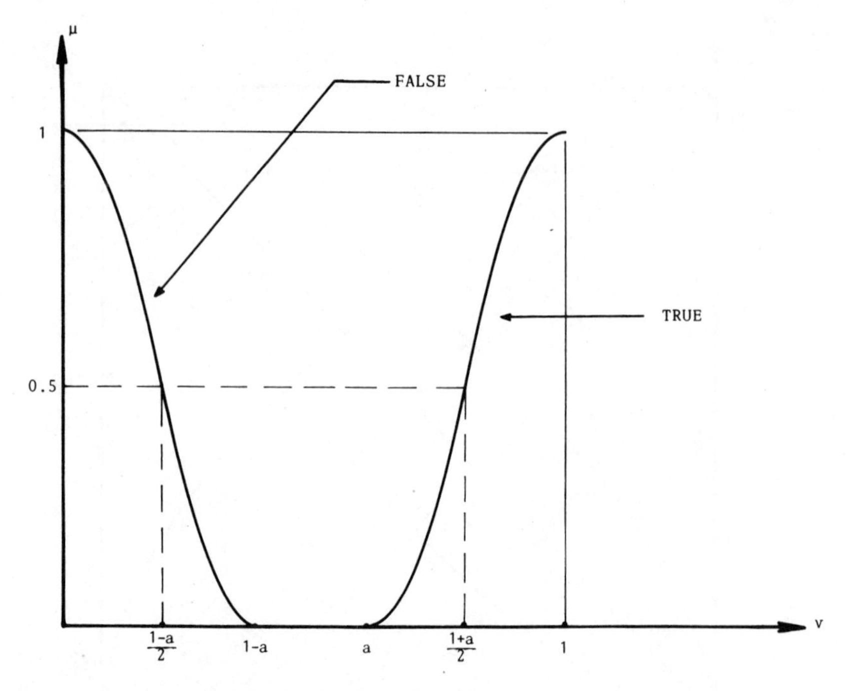

Figure 7-3: Linguistic Variable "Truth", Zadeh.

then

$$\text{very true} = \{(.5,.36),(.6,.49),(.7,.64),(.8,.81),(.9,1),(1,1)\}$$

$$\text{very false} = \{(.5,.36),(.4,.49),(.3,.64),(.2,.81),(.1,1),(0,1)\}$$

Since fuzzy logic is essentially considered to be an application of possibility theory to logic, the logical operators "and," "or," and "not" are defined accordingly.

In classical two- and multi-valued logics, binary connectives (operators) are normally defined by the tabulation of truth values in truth tables. But in fuzzy logic, the number of truth values is, in general, infinite, and tabulation of truth values for operators is, therefore, not possible. We can, however, tabulate truth values, that is, terms of the linguistic variable "truth," for a finite number of terms, such as true, not true, very true, false, more or less true, and so on.

Zadeh [1973a, p. 109] suggests truth tables for the determination of truth values for operators using a four-valued logic including the truth values true, false, undecided, and unknown. "Unknown" is then interpreted as "true or false" ($T + F$) and "undecided" is denoted by $\ominus$.

Extending the normal Boolean logic with truth values true (1) and false (0) to a (fuzzy) three-valued logic (true = T, false = F, unknown = $T + F$), with a universe of truth values being two-valued (true and false), we obtain the following [Zadeh 1973a, p. 116]:

Truth table for "and":

∧	T	F	T + F
T	T	F	T + F
F	F	F	F
T + F	T + F	F	T + F

Truth table for "or":

∨	T	F	T + F
T	T	T	T
F	T	F	T + F
T + F	T	T + F	T

Truth table for "not":

	¬
T	F
F	T
T + F	T + F

In the above truth tables the first row and column give the truth values of the statements A and B, respectively. Thus the truth table for the connective $\wedge$ (and) corresponds to the respective column of the truth table of dual logic shown on page 240.

We have already mentioned that in traditional logic the main tools of reasoning are tautologies such as, for instance, the modus ponens; that is, $(A \wedge (A \Rightarrow B)) \Rightarrow B$ or

Premise:	A is true
Implication:	If A then B
Conclusion:	B is true

A and B are statements or propositions (crisply defined) and the B in the conditional statement is identical to the B of the conclusion.

Approximate Reasoning and Plausible Reasoning

Approximate and plausible reasoning are ways of drawing conclusions from hypotheses; they relax even more assumptions of dual logic than does fuzzy logic. For example, on the basis of what has been said so far two quite obvious generalizations of the modus ponens are

1. to allow statements that are characterized by fuzzy sets (Appr. Reas.),
2. to relax (slightly) the identity of the A's and B's in the implication and the conclusion (Plaus. Reas.).

Example 7.4

Let $\tilde{A}$, $\tilde{A}'$, $\tilde{B}$, $\tilde{B}'$ be fuzzy statements, then the generalized modus ponens reads:

Premise:	x is $\tilde{A}'$
Implication:	If x is $\tilde{A}$ then y is $\tilde{B}$
Conclusion:	y is $\tilde{B}'$

For instance [Mizumoto, Zimmermann 1982]:

Premise:	This tomato is very red
Implication:	If a tomato is red then the tomato is ripe
Conclusion:	This tomato is very ripe

It should be mentioned, however, that the generalized modus ponens alone, which characterizes "plausible reasoning," does not allow obtaining conclusions from unequal premises. Such an inference presupposes or necessitates knowledge about modifications of the premises and their consequences. (For example, knowledge that increase in "redness" indicates an increase in "ripeness" [Dubois, Prade 1984b, p. 325].

In 1973 Zadeh suggested the compositional rule of inference for the above-mentioned type of fuzzy conditional inference. In the meantime other authors [e.g., Baldwin 1979; Baldwin, Pilsworth 1980; Baldwin, Guild 1980, Mizumoto et al. 1979; Mizumoto, Zimmermann 1982; Tsukamoto 1979] have suggested different methods and investigated also the modus tollens, syllogism, and contraposition. In this book, however, we shall restrict considerations to Zadeh's compositional rule of inference.

***Definition** 7.4* [see Zadeh 1973a, p. 37]

Let $\tilde{R}(x)$ and $\tilde{R}(y)$, $x \in X$, $y \in Y$, be fuzzy sets in X, Y, and $\tilde{R}(x,y)$ be a fuzzy relation in $X \times Y$. $\tilde{A}$ and $\tilde{B}$ denote particular fuzzy sets in X and $X \times Y$. The *compositional rules of inference* assert that the solution of the systems $\tilde{R}(x) = \tilde{A}$ and $\tilde{R}(x,y) = \tilde{B}$ is given by $\tilde{R}(y) = \tilde{A} \circ \tilde{B}$, where $\tilde{A} \circ \tilde{B}$ is the composition of $\tilde{A}$ and $\tilde{B}$.

***Example** 7.5*

Let the universe be $X = \{1,2,3,4\}$,
$\tilde{A}$ = little = $\{(1,1),(2,.6),(3,.2),(4,0)\}$, and
$\tilde{R}$ = "approximately equal" be a fuzzy relation in $X \times Y$ defined by

$\tilde{R}(x,y)$:

	1	2	3	4
1	1	.5	0	0
2	.5	1	.5	0
3	0	.5	1	.5
4	0	0	.5	1

For the formal inference, denote

$$\tilde{R}(x) = \tilde{A}, \quad \tilde{R}(x,y) = \tilde{B} \quad \text{and} \quad \tilde{R}(y) = \tilde{A} \circ \tilde{B}$$

Applying the max-min-composition for computing $\tilde{R}(y) = \tilde{A} \circ \tilde{B}$ yields

$$\begin{aligned} \tilde{R}(y) &= \max_x \min \{\mu_{\tilde{A}}(x), \mu_{\tilde{R}}(x,y)\} \\ &= \{(1,1),(2,.6),(3,.5),(4,.2)\} \end{aligned}$$

A possible interpretation of the inference may be

x is little
x and y are approximately equal

---

y is more or less little

A direct application of approximate reasoning are fuzzy algorithms (an ordered sequence of instructions in which some of the instructions may contain labels of fuzzy sets) and fuzzy flow charts. We shall not consider them in more detail in this book.

Fuzzy languages have been developed on the basis of fuzzy logic and approximate reasoning, which we have only very briefly touched here. They are based on LP1, FORTRAN, LISP, and other programming languages. Fuzzy languages differ in their content as well as their aims. The interested reader is referred to either Zimmermann [1985b, p. 139] or other references for more details. For the scope of this chapter they are not absolutely necessary.

An Interactive Decision Support System for Fuzzy and Semi-Fuzzy Multi-Objective Problems

The area of DSS is very large and not as well defined as that of expert systems. In order not to exceed the scope of this book we shall discuss DSS only exemplarily in the following section.

Basic Considerations

The basic motivations for developing the DSS described here were to provide an efficient computer-based and interactive DSS for problems of the mathematical programming type. The objectives were to have a DSS that

1. can cope with multiple (fuzzy) objective functions and crisp and fuzzy constraints;
2. uses realistic and empirically tested membership functions, and
3. provides adequate connectives that can be chosen by the user context-dependently.

If a DSS is to be of practical use there must be concern for more than the scientific considerations—for example, best empirical fit, membership functions, and operators—the requirement of efficiency—that is, computing time, storage space, and user orientation must also be considered. In the following we will describe some compromises between empirical fit and efficiency, which had to be made in order to keep the overall system practically useful.

Membership Functions. We have mentioned four basic types of membership functions: linear and hyperbolic functions in chapter 4 and spline and logistic functions in chapter 6. Theorem 4.1 and example 4.8 showed how hyperbolic functions can be transformed into equivalent linear membership functions. It can also be shown that hyperbolic membership functions and logistic membership functions are isomorphic mathematical models; if appropriate parameters are chosen, these membership functions will be equal. Determining a cubic spline function, however, requires the determination of quite a number of parameters, which might not be at all feasible for a decision maker. The DSS was, therefore, restricted to accommodate only three types of membership functions—linear, hyperbolic, and logistic.

For linear membership functions $\mu_i(c_i^t x_i)$ of the (4.6) type, the equivalent linear programming model (4.8) can be written as

$$\begin{aligned} &\text{maximize} && \lambda \\ &\text{such that} && \lambda \leq \mu_i(c_i^t x_i) \qquad i = 1,\ldots,m \\ & && x \in X \end{aligned} \tag{7.1}$$

If μ_i is linear for all i then (7.1) is a linear programming model and can be solved by any available LP code. For the logistic membership function

$$\mu_{L_i} = \frac{1}{1 + e^{-a(x-b)}} \tag{7.2}$$

(7.1) becomes

$$\begin{aligned} &\text{maximize} && \lambda \\ &\text{such that} && \lambda \leq [1 + \exp(-a_i(c_i^t x - b_i))]^{-1} \qquad i = 1,\ldots,m \\ & && x \in X \end{aligned} \tag{7.3}$$

If (λ^o, x^o) is an optimal solution of (7.3) then λ^o is the degree of membership of x^o in the fuzzy set "decision." (7.3) can not efficiently be solved directly. For

$$\lambda' = \ln\left(\frac{\lambda}{1 - \lambda}\right) \tag{7.4}$$

however, an equivalent formulation is

$$\begin{aligned} &\text{maximize} && \lambda' \\ &\text{such that} && \lambda' \leq a_i(c_i^t x - b_i) \qquad i = 1,\ldots,m \\ & && x \in X \end{aligned}$$

or

$$\begin{aligned} &\text{maximize} && \lambda' \\ &\text{such that} && \frac{1}{a_i}\lambda' - c_i^t x \leq -b_i \qquad i = 1,\ldots,m \\ & && x \in X \end{aligned} \tag{7.5}$$

This again is a standard LP and can be solved easily. Of course the solution has to be retransformed afterwards.

Operators. In chapter 6 evidence was provided for the fact that in decision models the min-operator is very often not a good mathematical model for the "and" aggregation. The γ-operator on the other hand shows a very good performance. Unluckily, if used in LP models the resulting equivalent models turn out to be nonlinear, nonconvex models, which is certainly not very desirable. An alternative is to use the operator

$$\mu_\theta = (1-\gamma) \min_{i=1}^{m} \{\mu_i\} + \gamma \max_{i=1}^{m} \{\mu_i\} \qquad \gamma \in [0,1] \tag{7.6}$$

Here the "min" stands for the "logical and" and the "max" for the "inclusive or." This operator turns out to be a rather good model for aggregation, although the γ-operator performs better.

The advantage of (7.6) is certainly its computational simplicity. A slight disadvantage could be seen in the fact that extreme values get a higher weight and that dominated solutions may not be recognized after aggregation. This is shown in the following example.

Example 7.6

Consider three alternatives, x_1, x_2, x_3. The following matrix shows the ratings of these alternatives with respect to three goals, G_1, G_2, and G_3.

	x_1	x_2	x_3
G_1	.7	.8	.8
G_2	.3	.7	.4
G_3	.1	.4	.4

Obviously x_3 is dominated by x_2. This is not obvious after an aggregation using (7.6) because the min and the max of x_2 and x_3 are equal.

To avoid this effect and to give higher weight to middle values, new operators are proposed by Werners [1984]. The idea is to differentiate between the terms "and" and "or," to allow compensation, and to get the

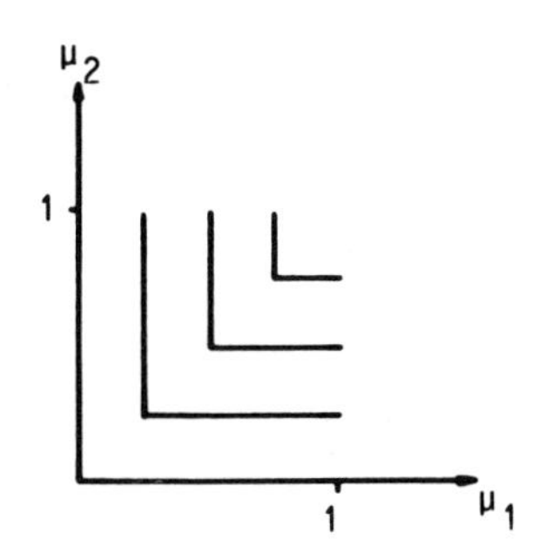

Figure 7-4: "$\widetilde{\text{and}}$", $\gamma = 1$.

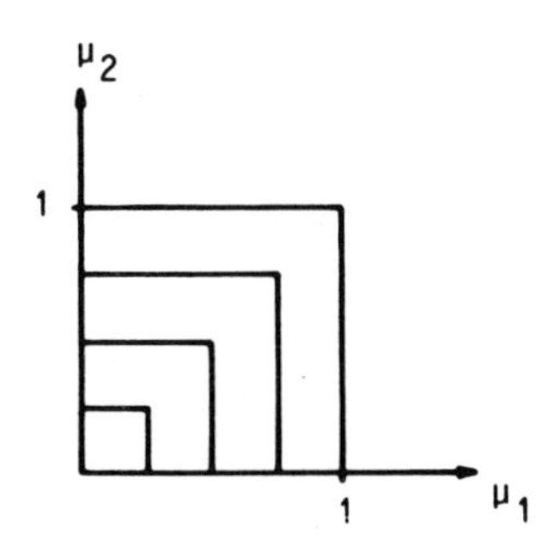

Figure 7-7: "$\widetilde{\text{or}}$", $\gamma = 1$.

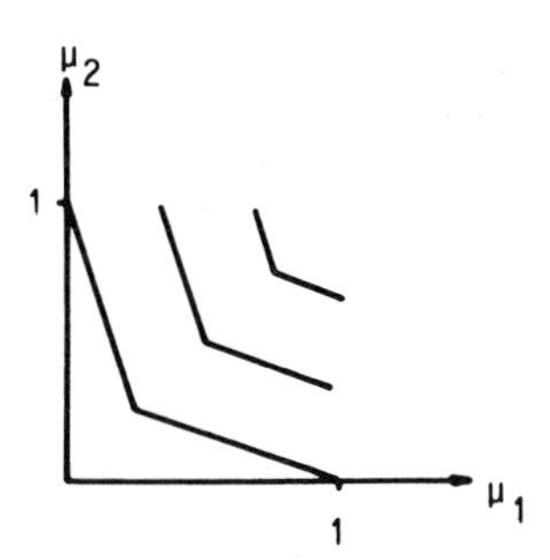

Figure 7-5: "$\widetilde{\text{and}}$", $\gamma = \frac{1}{2}$.

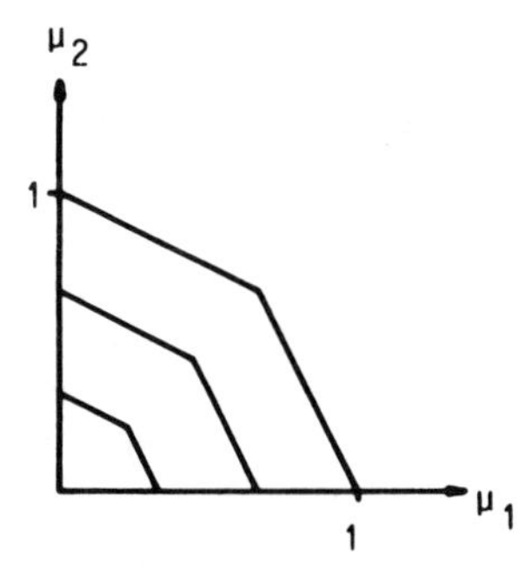

Figure 7-8: "$\widetilde{\text{or}}$", $\gamma = \frac{1}{2}$.

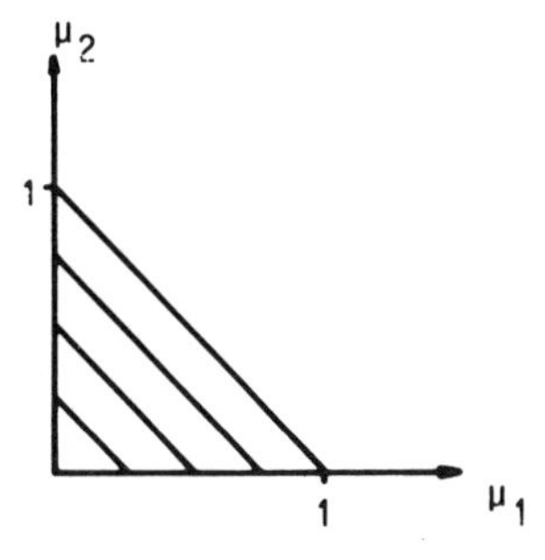

Figure 7-6: "$\widetilde{\text{and}}$", $\gamma = 0$.

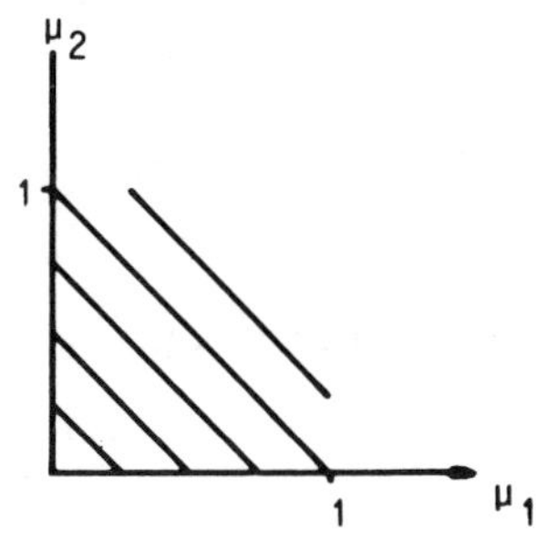

Figure 7-9: "$\widetilde{\text{or}}$", $\gamma = 0$.

minimum when expressing the logical "and" and maximum when intending the logical "or":

$$\mu_{\text{and}} = \gamma \min_{i=1}^{m} \mu_i + (1-\gamma)\frac{1}{m}\sum_{i=1}^{m} \mu_i \qquad \gamma \in [0,1] \tag{7.7}$$

$$\mu_{\text{or}} = \gamma \max_{i=1}^{m} \mu_i + (1-\gamma)\frac{1}{m}\sum_{i=1}^{m} \mu_i \qquad \gamma \in [0,1] \tag{7.8}$$

Here γ is the degree of approximating the logical meaning of "and" and "or," respectively. Use of the arithmetic mean has a compensatory effect. $\gamma = 1$ yields $\mu_{\text{and}} = \min$ and $\mu_{\text{or}} = \max$. The combination of these two operators leads to very good results with respect to the empirical data of Zimmermann and Zysno [1983]. The mathematical structure seems to be rather easy and efficient to handle. Both operators are communative; idempotent; monotonous; continuous; compensatory; and, respectively, generalizations of the logical "and" and "or" [Werners 1984]. These operators are illustrated by figures 7-4 through 7-9.

The computational efficiency of the DSS depends primarily on the type of the resulting "equivalent model," such as (4.9), (7.5), etc. This, however, depends not only on the membership function chosen or the operator used for aggregation, but a combination of both. We shall show this for two operators and different membership functions.

Let us first consider (7.6) and linear membership functions of the type $\mu_i(c_i^t x)$ as used before. The problem is now

$$\max_{x \in X} \left(\gamma \min_{i=1}^{m} \{\mu_i(c_i^t x)\} + (1-\gamma) \max_{i=1}^{m} \{\mu_i(c_i^t x)\} \right) \tag{7.9}$$

Equivalent to (7.9) is the model

$$\begin{aligned} \text{maximize} \quad & \gamma\lambda_1 + (1-\gamma)\lambda_2 \\ \text{such that} \quad & \lambda_1 \le \mu_i(c_i^t x) \qquad i = 1,\ldots,m \\ & \lambda_2 \le \mu_i(c_i^t x) \qquad \text{for at least one } i \in \{1,\ldots,m\} \end{aligned} \tag{7.10}$$

The last set of constraints in (7.10) can be replaced by

$$\lambda_2 \le \mu_i(c_i^t x) + My_i \qquad i = 1,\ldots,m$$

$$\sum_{i=1}^{m} y_i \le m - 1$$

where y_i are binary variables and M is a very large constant. Hence (7.10) becomes

$$
\begin{aligned}
\text{maximize} \quad & \lambda_1 + (1-\gamma)\lambda_2 \\
\text{such that} \quad & \lambda_1 \le \mu_i(c_i^t x) \\
& \lambda_2 \le \mu_i(c_i^t x) + M y_i \qquad i = 1,\dots,m \\
& \sum_i y_i \le m - 1 \\
& y_i \in \{0,1\} \qquad x \in X
\end{aligned}
\tag{7.11}
$$

If the membership functions are linear then (7.11) is a mixed-integer linear program (MILP) which can be solved with available efficient software such as APEX, MPSX etc. This is not true if we use the logistic function as a membership function: then (7.11) becomes

$$
\begin{aligned}
\text{maximize} \quad & [\gamma(1 + \exp(-\lambda_i')^{-1} + (1-\gamma)(1 + \exp(-\lambda_2')^{-1}] \\
\text{such that} \quad & \lambda_1' \le a_i(c_i^t x - b\,) \qquad i = 1,\dots,m \\
& \lambda_2' \le a_i(c_i^t x - b_i) \qquad \text{for at least one } i \in \{1,\dots,m\} \\
& x \in X
\end{aligned}
\tag{7.12}
$$

This is obviously a nonlinear model by contrast to (7.5), in which even logistic membership functions lead to linear equivalent models. Similar results can be obtained for the "fuzzy and" operator.

The problem then becomes

$$
\max_{x \in X} \left[\gamma \min_{i=1}^{m} \{\mu_i(c_i^t x)\} + (1-\gamma)\frac{1}{m}\sum_{i=1}^{m} \mu_i(c_i^t x) \right] \tag{7.13}
$$

An equivalent model for (7.13) is

$$
\begin{aligned}
\text{maximize} \quad & \lambda + (1-\gamma)\frac{1}{m}\sum_{i=1}^{m} \lambda_i \\
\text{such that} \quad & \lambda + \lambda_i \le \mu_i(c_i^t x) \qquad i = 1,\dots,m \\
& \lambda + \lambda_i \le 1 \\
& x \in X \\
& \lambda, \lambda_i \ge 0
\end{aligned}
\tag{7.14}
$$

For linear membership functions, (7.14) is again an LP. This is not the case for the logistic membership function. By appropriate substitutions the constraints can be rendered linear but the objective function will always stay nonlinear.

Table 7-1 summarizes some operator-membership function combinations and their resulting equivalent models. For the DSS, only combinations were

Table 7-1: Resulting Equivalent Models

Membership Function	*Operator*	*Model*
Linear	Min	LP
Logistic	Min	LP
Hyperbolic	Min	LP
Linear	min + $(1 - \gamma)$max	MILP
Linear/Nonlinear	Product	nonconvex NLP
Linear/Nonlinear	γ-Operator	nonconvex NLP
Linear	$\widetilde{\text{and}}$	LP
Linear	$\widetilde{\text{or}}$	MILP
Logistic	$\widetilde{\text{and}}$	NLP with lin. constraints

with: $\widetilde{\text{and}} \triangleq \gamma\min(x,y) + (1 - \gamma)\frac{1}{2}(x + y)$
$\text{or} \triangleq \gamma\max(x,y) + (1 - \gamma)\frac{1}{2}(x + y)$

Table 7-2: M.-F.-Operator Combinations included in DSS

Operator / *M.-Function*	*Min*	*Min/Max*	*Alg. Mean*	*and*
Linear	LP	MILP	LP	LP
Logistic	LP			

included that lead to linear equivalent models. They are mentioned again in table 7-2.

EDP Implementation

DSS supports the decision maker in solving multi-criteria problems with crisp and flexible restrictions. The system has three components:

1. Man/machine communication—
   This part has the following tasks:
   - to guide the decision maker through the system directed by a menu,
   - to present the processed data to the decision maker, and
   - to facilitate the change of the data and of the decision variables by the decision maker.

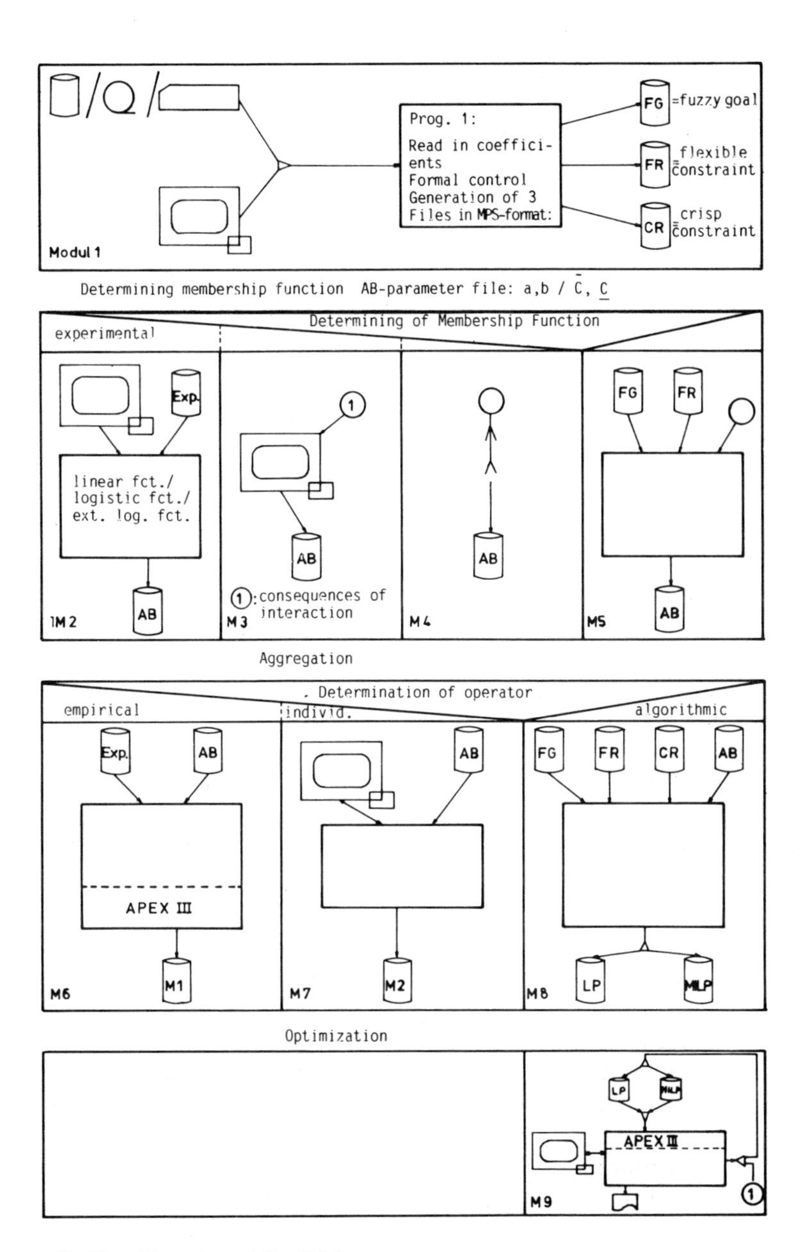

Figure 7-10: Modules of the DSS.

2. Data management—
   This section contains the activities
   - data processing and
   - data update.
3. System/machine communication—
   This part is the interface to other software systems used by DSS. This section
   - generates the interface files and
   - supervises and controls execution of the software system in use.

The nine modules of DSS are shown in figure 7-10.

Working with the DSS

When using the decision support system the decision maker must first specify his goals and constraints for a fuzzy programming model. Goals and constraints are not treated equally as in the fuzzy decision model of Zadeh mentioned earlier. Instead, the DSS user holds that there is a difference between a fuzzy goal and a fuzzy constraint in that the decision maker is able to give more information about a constraint than about a goal. In a way similar to using crisp programming models, where he distinguishes only between 0 and 1 degree of membership for satisfying a constraint, the decision maker a priori provides a membership function for each constraint. The membership function of a fuzzy maximization goal cannot be given in advance but depends on what is possible when satisfying the constraints. So additional information has to be acquired about the dependencies of the model. This can be done by the system. Here extreme solutions are determined by optimizing one goal over two crisp feasable regions: one with a degree of membership of one, the other with a positive degree of membership until zero. The results are used to determine membership functions of the goals.

For solving a crisp vector-maximum model it has been suggested (chapter 5) that we deduce membership functions dependent on the ideal and the pessimistic solutions. The concept used in the DSS is a generalization that is necessary for handling fuzzy goals under crisp and fuzzy constraints. Aggregating all membership values (i.e., of all goals and constraints) a compromise solution is determined. Interactively, the decision maker can now change the proposed membership functions until he is satisfied with the compromise solution.

The interactive fuzzy programming system supports a decision maker, especially in two different ways:

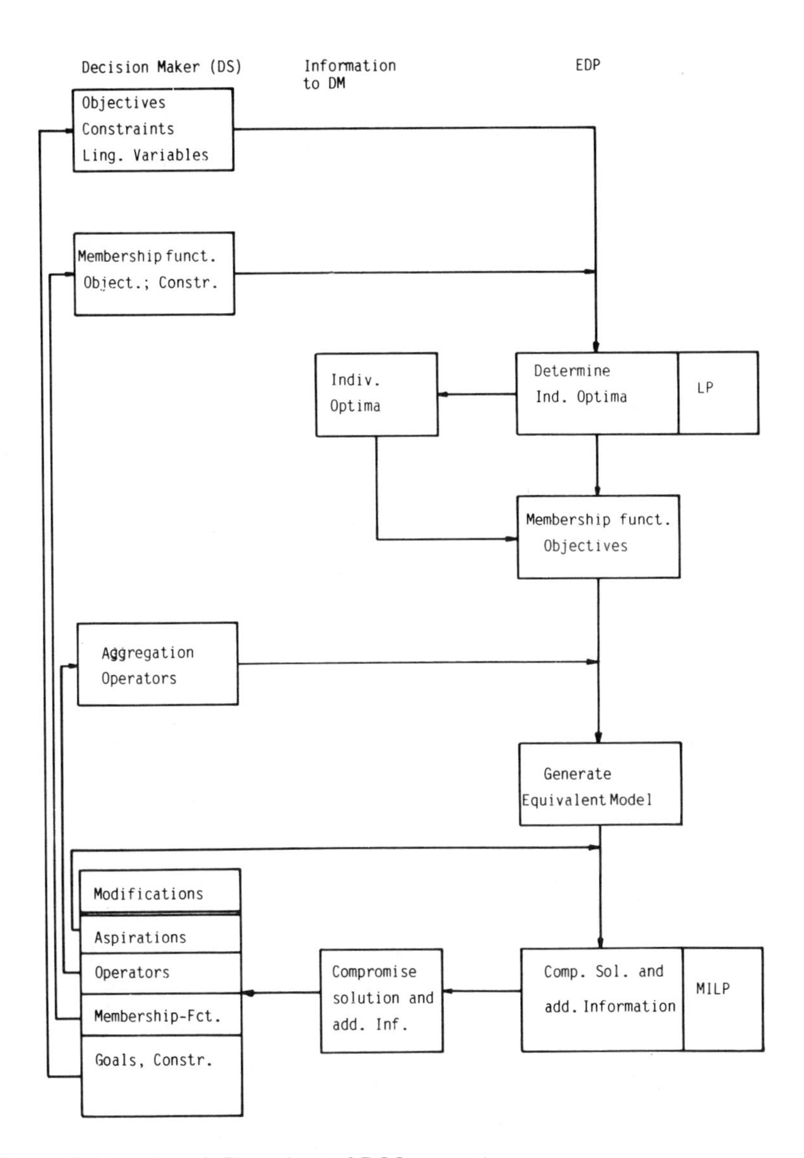

Figure 7-11: Rough Flowchart of DSS-operations.

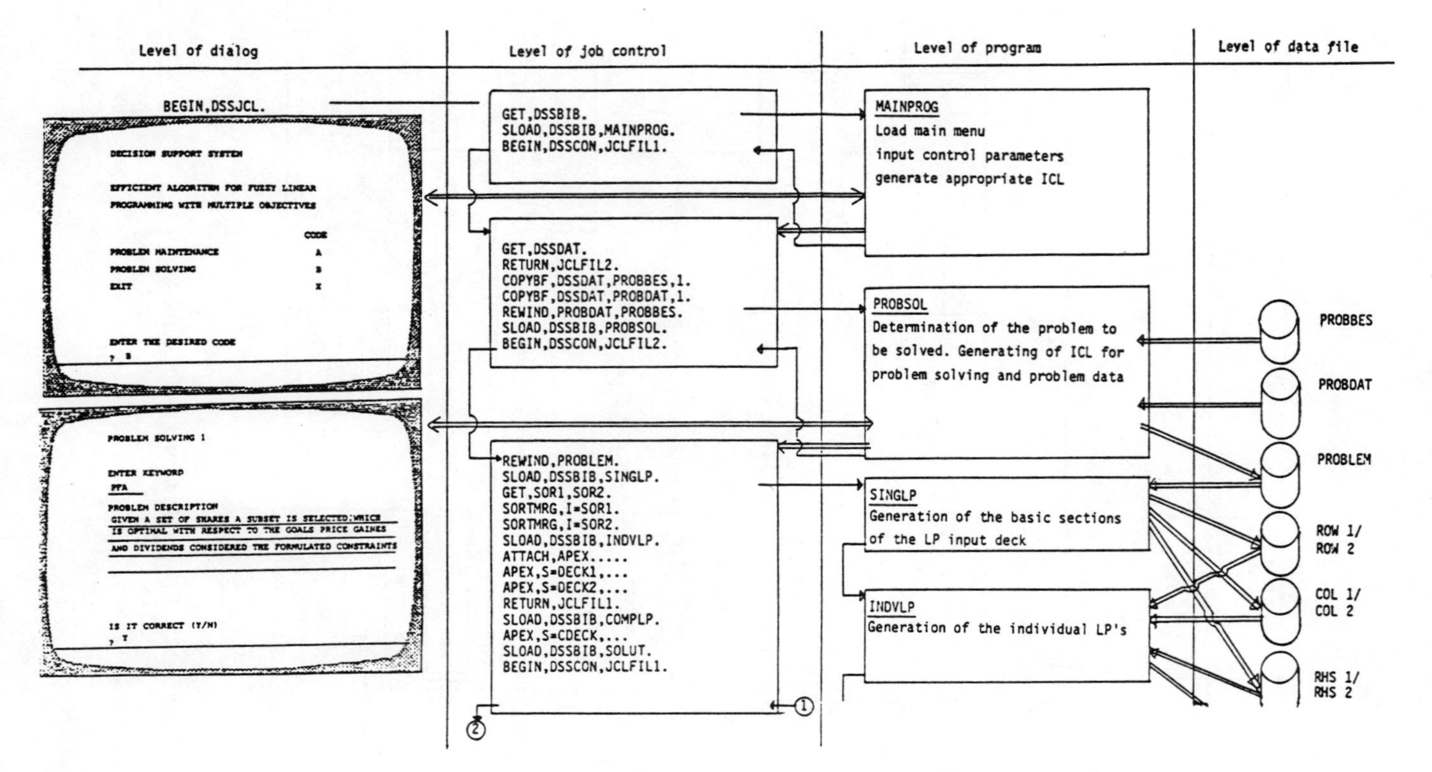
Level of dialog
Level of job control
Level of program
Level of data file
BEGIN,DSSJCL.
DECISION SUPPORT SYSTEM
EFFICIENT ALGORITHM FOR FUZZY LINEAR PROGRAMMING WITH MULTIPLE OBJECTIVES
CODE
PROBLEM MAINTENANCE A
PROBLEM SOLVING B
EXIT X
ENTER THE DESIRED CODE
? B
PROBLEM SOLVING 1
ENTER KEYWORD
PFA
PROBLEM DESCRIPTION
GIVEN A SET OF SHARES A SUBSET IS SELECTED WHICH IS OPTIMAL WITH RESPECT TO THE GOALS PRICE GAINES AND DIVIDENDS CONSIDERED THE FORMULATED CONSTRAINTS
IS IT CORRECT (Y/N)
? Y
GET,DSSBIB.
SLOAD,DSSBIB,MAINPROG.
BEGIN,DSSCON,JCLFIL1.
GET,DSSDAT.
RETURN,JCLFIL2.
COPYBF,DSSDAT,PROBBES,1.
COPYBF,DSSDAT,PROBDAT,1.
REWIND,PROBDAT,PROBBES.
SLOAD,DSSBIB,PROBSOL.
BEGIN,DSSCON,JCLFIL2.
REWIND,PROBLEM.
SLOAD,DSSBIB,SINGLP.
GET,SOR1,SOR2.
SORTMRG,I=SOR1.
SORTMRG,I=SOR2.
SLOAD,DSSBIB,INDVLP.
ATTACH,APEX.....
APEX,S=DECK1,....
APEX,S=DECK2,....
RETURN,JCLFIL1.
SLOAD,DSSBIB,COMPLP.
APEX,S=CDECK,....
SLOAD,DSSBIB,SOLUT.
BEGIN,DSSCON,JCLFIL1.
1
2
MAINPROG
Load main menu
input control parameters
generate appropriate ICL
PROBSOL
Determination of the problem to be solved. Generating of ICL for problem solving and problem data
SINGLP
Generation of the basic sections of the LP input deck
INDVLP
Generation of the individual LP's
PROBBES
PROBDAT
PROBLEM
ROW 1/ ROW 2
COL 1/ COL 2
RHS 1/ RHS 2

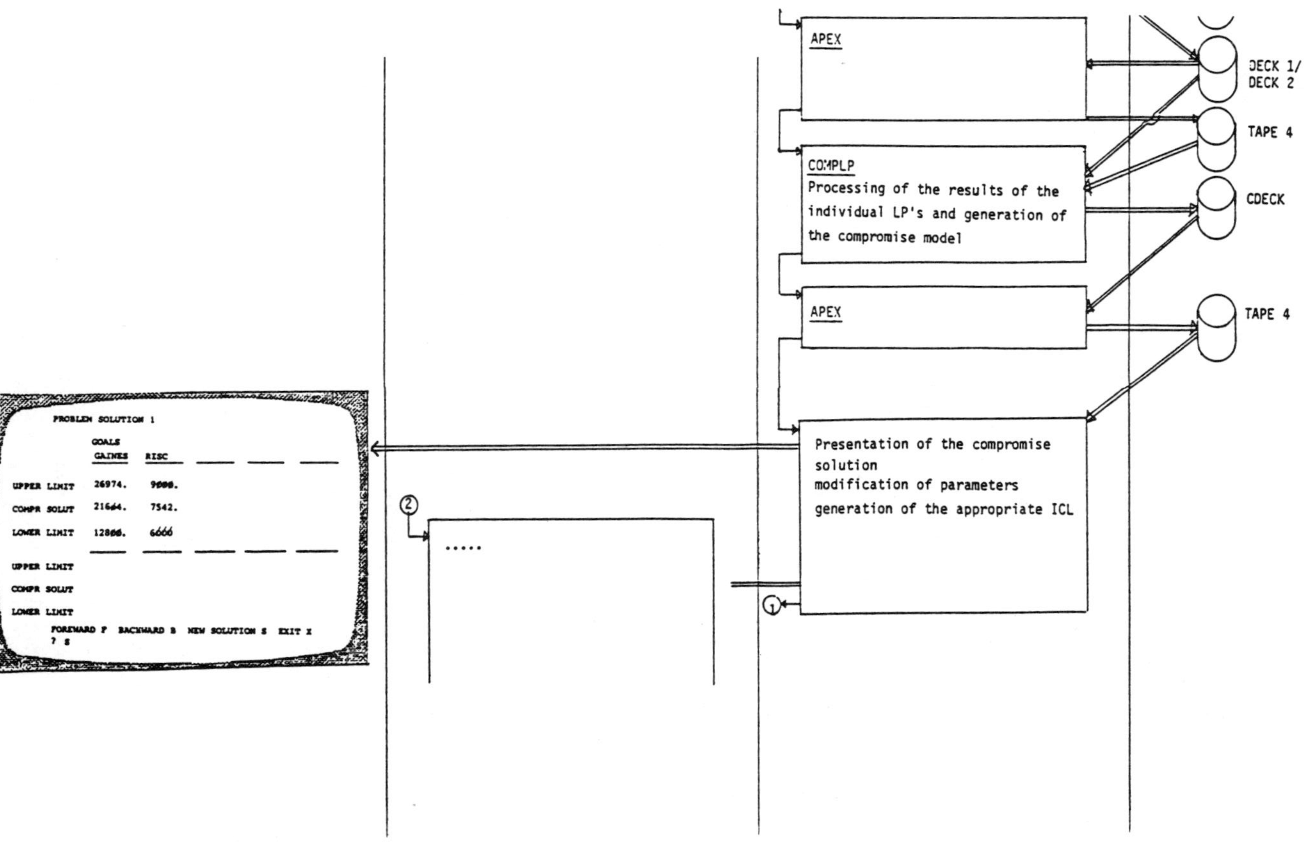

Figure 7-12: OPERATIONS OF DSS.

- First, it determines extreme solutions and proposes membership functions describing the goals.
- Second, it evaluates efficient compromise solutions with additional local informations.

After each presented compromise the decision maker gets progressively more insight into the model and can articulate further preference information: *local*, by modifying membership functions, and *global*, by modifying the model.

DSS is a menu-oriented dialog system for solving multi-criteria problems with crisp and fuzzy restrictions. The rough flow chart in figure 7-11 sketches how the DSS works. A static description of the structure shall be omitted, because the structure of the system is highly dependent on the wishes of the decision maker. Instead we shall try to clarify the structure by describing a typical terminal session. The session will be represented on four levels:

1. Level of dialog
2. Level of job control
3. Level of data files
4. Level of programs

We shall represent the input of a new problem and the solution of this problem. We will omit the complete representation of all masks for reasons of space. In figure 7-12 a single arrow denotes a flow of control, a double one a flow of data.

Expert Systems and Fuzzy Sets

The Structure of Expert Systems

As mentioned at the beginning of this chapter, expert systems are knowledge-based systems; that is they rely not only on data as an input, but also on (expert) knowledge.

Even though the work on (general problem solving) knowledge-based systems started in the sixties, the definitions of what an expert system really is still vary widely. The "Alvey Report," for example, defines "Intelligent Knowledge-Based Systems" as

> Semi intelligent systems for carrying out single complex tasks. This implies working with a large, incomplete, uncertain and rapidly changing knowledge store, use of inferential procedures for applying this knowledge in reacting to variated and

> inreliable inputs in changing environment and the use of sophisticated and flexible control mechanisms. (SERC-DOI, 1982, Vol. 1, Annexes p. 16).

A much narrower view is adopted by the Expert Systems Group of the British Computer Society:

> An expert systems is regarded as the embodiment within a computer of a knowledge-based component from an expert still in such a form that the system can offer intelligent advice or take an intelligent decision about a processing function. A desirable additional characteristic, which many would consider fundamental, is the capability of the system, on demand, to justify its own line of reasoning in a manner directly intelligible by the inquirer. The style adopted to attain these characteristics is rule-based programming." [Holroyd et al. 1985]
> One can also find definitions as broad as Expert systems are problem-solving programs that solve substantial problems generally conceded as being difficult and requiring expertise. [Stefik et al. 1982, p. 135]
> An expert system is one which, as far as the users are concerned, displays expertise in some aspects of problem solving which is useful to them. [Holroyd et al., 1985, p. 5]

Other definitions can be found in Zimmermann [1985b, pp. 152, 153]. Since it is *not* our aim to discuss subtleties of expert systems design, but rather to show how fuzzy sets relate to expert systems, we shall mention just a few features of expert systems that might be accepted by most designers and users of expert systems and seem to be of relevance with respect to fuzzy sets:

1. The intended area of application is restricted in scope, ill-structured, and uncertain. Therefore no well-defined algorithms are available nor are there any efficient enough to solve the problem.
2. The system is—at least in part—based on expert knowledge which is either embodied in the system or can be obtained from an expert and be analyzed, stored, and used by the system.
3. The system has some inference capability and can use the knowledge—in whatever way it is stored—to draw conclusions.
4. The interfaces to the user on one side and the expert on the other side should be such that the expert system can be used directly and that no "knowledge engineer" is needed between the system and the expert.
5. Since heuristic elements are contained in an expert system, no guarantee of optimality or correctness is provided. Therefore and in order to increase user acceptance, it is considered to be at least desirable that the system contains a "justification" or "explaining" module.

The structure of a system that satisfies the above mentioned requirements could be as shown in figure 7-13. Of course, some of the modules may

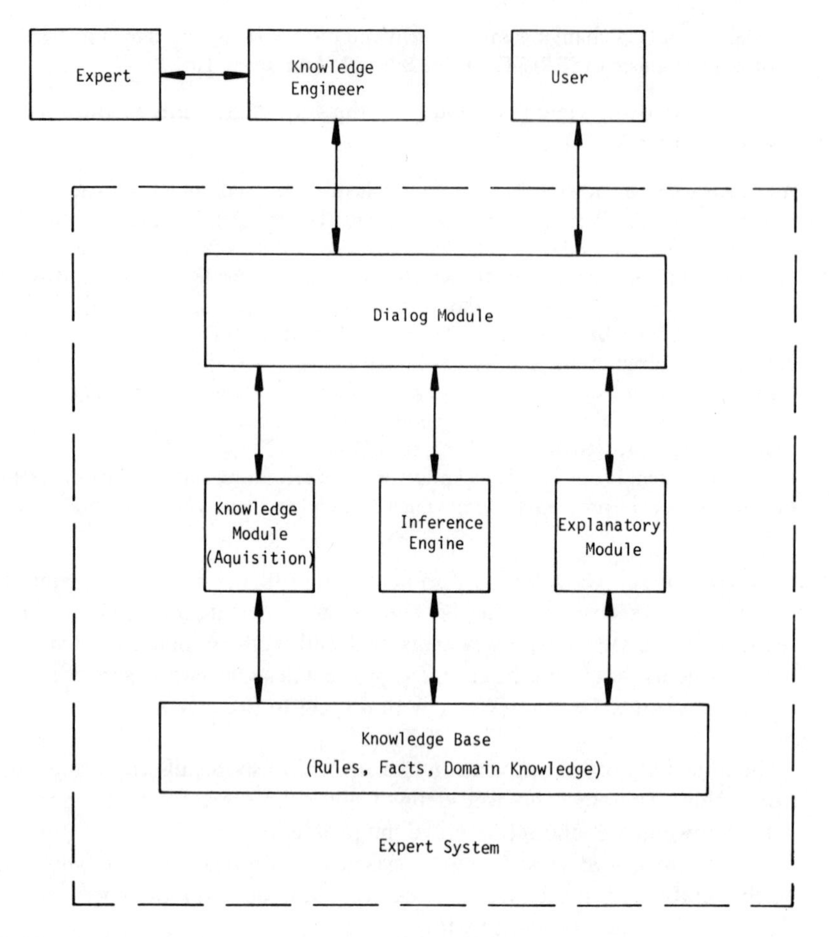

Figure 7-13: Possible structure of an Expert System.

be missing or some other modules may have to be added. The knowledge engineer, for instance, might not be needed; or some special modules for checking for consistency, or for fuzzifying or defuzzifying information might have to be added. To a certain extent this will depend on the specific task of the expert system. The scope of tasks and areas of application of expert systems are as wide as the variety of their definitions.

Table 7-3 shows some functions for which expert systems have been used. In what follows we briefly sketch some examples for each of the categories mentioned in table 7-3. We have not included "Monitoring and Control of

Table 7-3: Functional Areas of Expert Systems

Category	*Problem description*
1. Classification	Evaluation, interpretation or diagnosis of system or object characteristics
2. Debugging and Repair	Prescribing remedies for malfunctions and/or executing plans to administer them
3. Design	Configuring objects and systems under constraints
4. Instruction and Training	Diagnosing, debugging and repairing strident behaviour
5. Planning and Decision Support	Designing actions and supplying aids for better decision making
6. Prediction	Inferring likely consequences of given situations or scenarios.

Systems," because this area is normally treated separately under "Fuzzy Logic Control (FLC)" whenever the application of fuzzy sets is involved [see, for instance, Zimmermann 1985b, ch. 10].

Classification. As used in table 7-3, *evaluation* means judging alternatives with respect to certain criteria, for instance, the determination of the degree of creditworthiness of a customer on the basis of some of his (fuzzily described) characteristics, such as "financial basis," 'personality," "security," etc. An expert system "credit" [Zimmermann, Zysno 1983] for this purpose has been developed and is being tested in German banks. Similar tasks are performed by "Speril I and II" in the area of earthquake engineering [Ishizuka et al. 1983].

Interpretation refers to inferring situation descriptions from sensor data. Examples are DENDRAL [Buchanan, Feigenbaum 1978], which infers a compound's molecular structure from mass spectral and molecular response data; RTC, which classifies ships by interpreting radar images; and VM, which monitors intensive-care patients by interpreting data from ICU test equipment [Fagan 1978].

By *diagnosis* we mean the determination of malfunctions or other system characteristics from observable indicators. The best known example of that type of expert systems is probably PROSPECTOR, which helps geologists to evaluate the mineral potential of a region [Waterman 1986, 49–60], and MYCIN, which helps diagnose and treat bacterial infections [Buchanan, Shortliffe 1984].

Debugging and Repair. Debugging and repair are often combined with fault detection. ACE (Automated Cable Expert), for example was developed by Bell Laboratories in order to identify trouble spots in telephone networks and to recommend appropriate repair activities. It has reached the stage of a commercial expert system and operates without human intervention [Waterman 1986, p. 253].

Design. Design problems are often very complex (due to combinatorial problems). They are not yet solvable algorithmically, therefore, heuristic approaches and human experience are generally necessary to solve them. XCON is successfully used to handle design problems for VAX 11/780 computer-system configurations. XCON, starting from a customer's order, suggests what components must be added to produce a complete operational system [McDermott 1982].

Instruction and Training. Teachers are normally experts in a specific area. Since experts are scarce, expert systems can be used to train humans to become experts in specific activities. Examples of such expert systems are SOPHIE and ATTENDING. The former teaches fault diagnosis in electrical circuits [Brown et al. 1975] and the latter teaches methods of anesthetic management [Miller 1983].

Planning and Decision Support. For this book this is certainly the most relevant class of expert systems. Strictly speaking and using the term *decision* in a broad sense most of the expert systems mentioned so far are to some extent decision supporting. "Planning" as well as "decision" in the context of expert system's use is generally used in the sense of managerial planning or decision making either in a business or in a military context.

The number of existing expert systems in this area is still very small, but this by no means should be considered as an indication of a lack of need for these tools. The reasons are rather the high degree of uncertainty involved in managerial decisions, the need for very efficient data-bank management to supplement the expert system, and probably some reasons linked to attitudes of managers. We shall discuss expert systems such as REVEAL in more detail later in the chapter.

Prediction. Prediction is to varying degrees involved in expert systems of the classes mentioned above. There are, however, expert systems in which prediction is the main task. One example is PTRANS, which helps control the manufacture and distributions of Digital Equipment Corporation's computer systems. In particular it predicts possible impending shortages or surpluses of materials [Haley et al. 1983]. Of quite different nature is fINDex which suggests appropriate forecasting techniques for sales predictions [Whalen, Schott 1985].

Before we discuss more technical matters let us turn to the questions "Why should expert systems be used rather than human experts?" and "Why should human experts still be involved when using expert systems?"

The first question is of interest since expert systems are expensive and their area of application is generally very limited. Teknowledge estimated recently that the cost for building larger custom-made expert systems is in the range of \$1–2 million per system [Pollitzer, Jenkins 1985, p. 413]. For smaller systems and with better tools this cost can certainly be decreased considerably. It is still high compared to the training of a human expert!

The main advantages of expert systems over human experts are that they can be reproduced much more easily and cheaply than human experts, that they do not have to practice in order to stay expert, that they are permanent (i.e., they do not become sick, retire, or die), and that they are much easier to document than human experts. Hence one of the main advantages is their reproducability! On the other hand, expert systems are not creative, they lack common-sense knowledge, and they have a very narrow focus.

Let us now turn to more technical aspects of building expert systems. These are of prime importance and the reader should be familiar with them in order to appreciate the role of fuzzy sets in expert systems:

Knowledge Representation and Expert-System Tools

In data-based systems the algorithms process data (input) and arrive at solutions. In knowledge-based (expert) systems both data and knowledge are the basis for conclusions (output). As mentioned above expert systems very often are organized such that knowledge about the problem (*knowledge base*) is separated from general knowledge about how to solve problems or how to use the knowledge in the knowledge base. This latter part of the knowledge is called the *inference engine*. While the knowledge base contains facts (data) and knowledge about those facts, the inference engine contains knowledge on how to use the former knowledge to infer new knowledge.

There is no simple way to describe in general terms the inference engine. Its structure depends on the type of problem and on the way in which knowledge is represented and organized in the expert system. Now-a-days the building of an expert system is often facilitated by using expert-system shells or tools which, essentially, are expert-systems-building languages. High-level languages, such as EMYCIN [van Melle 1979], have the inference engine in some way built in as part of the language; low-level languages, such as LISP or PROLOG, require the builder of expert system to design and implement the inference engine. In any case the knowledge in the expert system has to be represented formally in order to be useful for the inference process. Quite a number of techniques for *knowledge representation* have been developed in Artificial Intelligence (AI); still others are possible and are used in existing expert systems. For the standard techniques the reader is referred to Barr and Feigenbaum [vol. 1, 1981, ch. III]. There he will find excellent descriptions of ways to represent knowledge formally.

Here we shall briefly describe the four techniques most frequently used in expert systems: predicate calculus, rules, semantic nets, and frames. (In order to keep redundency as low as possible we shall postpone discussion of tools to the next section.)

Predicate Calculus. The predicate calculus, which is the classical form of knowledge representation in Artificial Intelligence, contains statements translated into *well-formed formulas* (wffs) [Nilsson 1980, p. 132] or axioms. These axioms may use the quantifiers "all" and "there exists." The elementary components of the predicate calculus syntax are

P: predicate symbols
V: variable symbols
F: function symbols
C: constant symbols

Predicates are applied to one or more components thus forming a wff. A wff can be interpreted by assigning a correspondence between the elements of, for instance, the English language and the relations, utilities, and functions in the domain of discourse. After an interpretation of a wff has been defined, the formula has value T (true) if the corresponding statement about the domain is true and value F (false) if the statement is false. There exists considerable freedom in translating language statements into predicate calculus. The reader can find a very good and sufficiently detailed description in Nilsson [1980, ch. 4].

***Example** 7.7*

We show "translations" of some statements into wffs:

Statement		*wff*
John is student	→	is (John, student) (*P*) (*C*) (*V*)
Dick buys a car	→	buys (Dick, car) (*P*) (*C*) (*C*)
The parents of Maria are married	→	married (father(Maria), mother(Maria) (*P*) (*F*) (*C*) (*F*) (*C*)

Simple statements (so-called *atomic formulas*) are the elementary building blocks of the predicate calculus language. They can be combined by the use of *connectives*, such as $\wedge$ (and), $\vee$ (or), and $\Rightarrow$ (implies) to form more complex wffs. The *universal quantifier* $(\forall x)$ and the *existential quantifier* $(\exists x)$ in front of a formula render the value of that formula T if it is true for all assignments or if there exists at least one assignment in the domain for which it is true, respectively.

Example 7.8

The statement "Dick rides a red bike" might be represented by

rides (Dick, bike − 1) ∧ color (bike − 1, red)
(*P*) (*C*) (*V*) (*P*) (*V*) (*C*)

The statement "Mary goes to the cinema or to the theatre" can be written as

$$\text{goes (Mary, cinema)} \vee \text{goes (Mary, theatre)}$$

The statement "If the car belongs to Hans, it is red" might be represented by

$$\text{owns (Hans, car} - 1) \Rightarrow \text{color (car} - 1, \text{red)}$$

"All leaves are green" can be written as

$$(\forall x)\,[\text{leaves}\,(x) \Rightarrow \text{color}\,(x, \text{green})]$$

and "There is a person who owns a car" as

$$(\exists x)\ \text{owns}\,(x, \text{person}, \text{car})$$

Predicate calculus uses rules of inference already known from logic—namely, the *modus ponens*, the *universal specialization*, etc.

If a wff consists of a disjunction of literals (an atomic formula and its negation) it is called a *clause*. For these clauses a very important rule of inference is the *resolution*. The resolution rule was introduced by Robinson [1965, p. 23]. In order to decide whether a statement is true or false, it is first translated into a wff and then its negation is added to the set of wffs. Then, using Skolem functions [Nilsson 1980, pp. 146], the existential quantifiers are eliminated and one tries to arrive at an inconsistency by using Robinson's resolution algorithm. A danger of this approach, the "combinatorial explosion," can be counteracted by using certain search strategies (such as breadth-first, set-of-support, etc., see [Nilsson 1980, pp. 164]).

Predicate calculus has certainly some important advantages. It has a well-defined syntax, clear semantic rules of inference, and the property of monotony (i.e., the introduction of new axioms does not influence the set of conclusions that could be inferred before). It does not, however, allow the inclusion of probabilistic elements or the use of other quantifiers, and offers no principles for the design of a knowledge base. Procedural or heuristic knowledge is hardly representable. Some extensions are possible when moving to modal logic in which notions like "will," "can," etc. can be expressed. PROLOG, is one of the very well known AI languages based on predicate calculus.

Semantic Nets. Semantic nets or *semantic networks* are directed graphs in which the *nodes* represent concepts (objects, situations, notions) and the labelled *arcs* represent binary relations between these nodes. Figure 7-14 represents the statement "Maria is blond and lives in New York." Figure 7-15 represents a hierarchy of concepts by using the (transitive) "is-a" relation. The

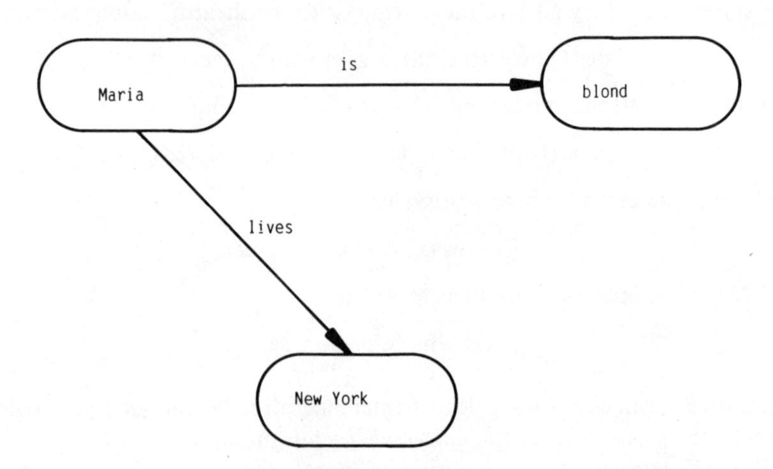

Figure 7-14: A simple semantic net.

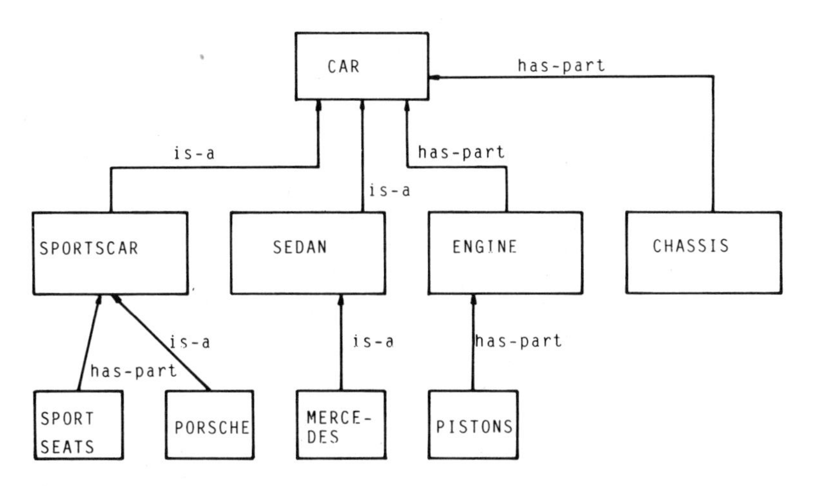

Figure 7-15: Inheritance hierarchy.

is-a relation (like the has-part relation) establishes a property-*inheritance* hierarchy in which we can infer a third statement from two known statements. We can, for instance, infer from "Porsche is a sports car" and "sports cars are fast cars" that "Porsche is a fast car."

Almost all semantic nets have the following types of arcs:

Generalization	(arc connects a concept of object with a more general concept)
Individualization	(arc connects an individual with classes of individuals)
Aggregation	(arc connects objects with attributes)

Of course, arcs can also represent causation, associations, and assertions. Uncertainty can also be represented by assigning probabilities to arcs. PROSPEKTOR, for example, contains such probabilities. Given knowledge about the presence or absence of a fact (node), other facts can be inferred with varying degrees of certainty. In PROSPECTOR this type of propagation is based on Bayes rule. Figure 7-16 shows a simple PROSPECTOR inference net in which each arc corresponds to one if-then rule. (Only seven of more than 1000 rules are represented in the figure!). The two numbers at most of the arcs in figure 7-16 represent two uncertainty factors.

It is possible to use the quantifiers "all" and "there exists" in semantic nets after they have been partitioned. Fuzzy quantifiers cannot be used.

Frames. Frame representation is very similar to a semantic net. A *frame* is a

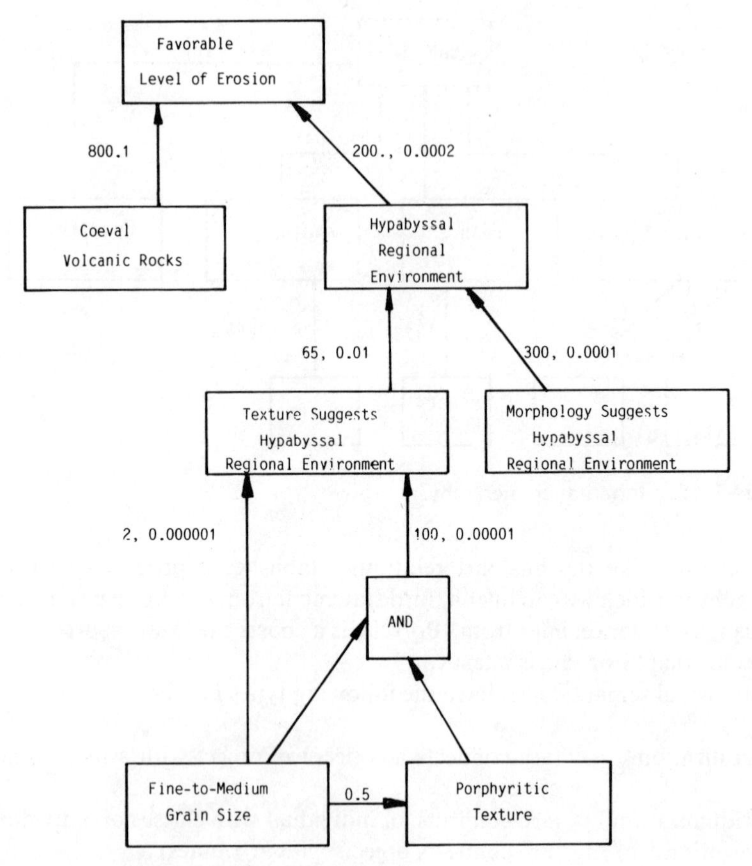

Figure 7-16: Inference Net (PROSPEKTOR).

network of nodes and relations organized in a hierarchy—the topmost nodes representing general concepts and the lower nodes more specific instances of these concepts. Minsky, who originated the frame idea, gives the following description:

> A frame is a data-structure for representing a stereotyped situation, like being in a certain kind of living room, or going to a child's birthday party. Attached to each frame are several kinds of information. Some of this information is about how to use the frame. Some is about what one can expect to happen next. Some is about what to do if these expectations are not confirmed! [Minsky 1975]

The *slots* in frames correspond to the nodes in networks. They are "drawers"

	Concept	
	Data	Procedure
Slot 1	Author	
Slot 2	Topic	
Slot 3	Due Date	
Slot 4	Length	

Figure 7-17: Information in a Typical Frame.

for information that either has to be provided or may be supplied. Slots may themselves be frames.

While frames in general serve to represent object knowledge, *scripts* answer the question of how processes normally proceed. Scripts describe expectations or norms for processes such as a visit to a restaurant, the purchase of a ticket, a telephone conversation, etc.

Frames provide modularity and uniformity to the representation of knowledge. A new concept can often be represented by merely adding a frame. Missing information is readily apparent: the slot for that information is empty. Default information can be provided easily by prior filling of some slots.

Slots not only contain descriptive information, they also contain sets of rules for inferring information for that frame. By connecting frames, by using slots to explicitly point to other frames, one can represent causation, hierarchies of abstraction, and other paths of association.

To "understand" a certain notion, process, or situation the appropriate frame has to be found, located, or activated. This is achieved by comparing the externally provided information with the contents of so-called frame *terminals*. These terminals are slots that contain data that do not refer to other frames.

An example of a language using frames is FRL (frame representation language) [Roberts, Goldstein 1977].

***Example** 7.9* [Abbreviated from Waterman 1986, p. 74]

A program manager has organized his reporting system in a frame system of which figure 7-18 shows a small part as a semantic net. Each node is represented by a frame such as that in figure 7-19. Default information contained in the frames could be:

Progress Report:	Author: Project leader
	Length: 2 pages
Technical Report:	Author: Project members
	Lenght: 30 pages.

An empty frame of the type "Progress Report Number ..." could look as shown in figure 7-19. The procedures mentioned in the slots could be:

Slot 1: *If added*: Notify person in this slot that a report on the subject mentioned in slot 2 of the number of pages mentioned in slot 4 is due by the date mentioned in slot 3.
If removed: Notify person that report with topic from slot 2 has been cancelled.

Slot 2: *If added*: Insert in slot 1 the name of the project leader of the project of slot 2.

Slot 3: *If needed*: Put either "March 31," "June 30," "Sept. 30," or "Dec. 30" in slot 3, depending on which is closer to, but not greater than, to-day's date.

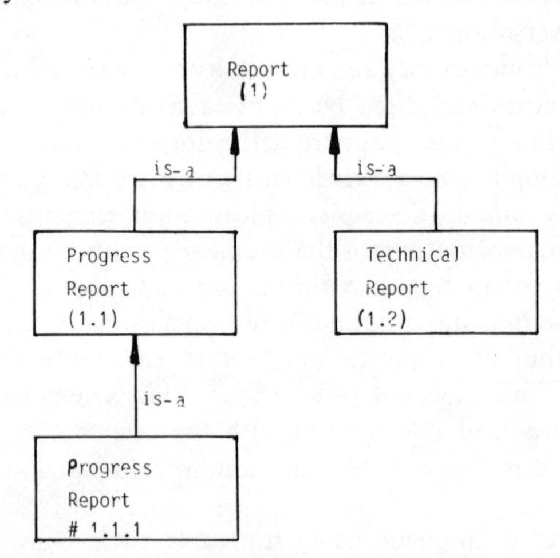

Figure 7-18: Part of a Reporting System.

Progress Report Nr. 111

Slot	Data	Procedure
1		If added If removed
2		If added
3		If needed
4		

Figure 7-19: Empty Frame.

Let us now assume the program manager types into his terminal: "I need a progress report on the Gasification Project." The interface program would then analyze this request and insert into slot 2 of the next empty progress report frame (in this case number 1.1.1) "Gasification Project."

Since something has been added in slot 2 the if-added procedure would be activated—the name of the project leader, M. Smith, would be retrieved from an associated data base and inserted in slot 1. This would activate the if-added procedure of slot 1, which however, can be executed only after the information of slots 3 and 4 is available. Therefore, the if-needed procedure of slot 3 would first be activated. Slot 4 would then be filled by referring to slot 4 of the frame for Progress Reports. Then the if-added procedure of slot 1 could be completed.

Rules. By far the most frequently used method of representing knowledge is by means of *production rules.* These are usually of the form "If a set of conditions is satisfied then a set of consequences can be produced." Production rules are used to capture the expert's rule of thumb or heuristic relations among the facts in the domain. These if-then rules provide the bulk of the domain-dependent knowledge in rule-based expert systems and a separate control strategy is used to manipulate the rules.

If the car won't start and

the car lights are dim

then the battery may be dead

Many experts have found rules a convenient way to express their domain knowledge. Also, rule-bases are easily augmented by simply adding more rules. "The ability to incrementally develop an expert system's expertise is a major advantage of rule-based schemes" [Kastner, Hong 1984].

Different control strategies have been used to direct input and output and select the rules to be evaluated. Two very popular strategies are *forward chaining* and *backward chaining*. In the former, data-driven rules for which the conditional parts are satisfied are evaluated. The latter strategy (goal-driven) selects a special rule for evaluation. The "goal" is to satisfy the conditional part of this rule. If that can not be achieved directly then subgoals are established on the basis of which a chain of rules can be established, such that eventually the conditional part of the first rule can be satisfied.

Hence the inference engine in a system using production rules consists primarily of strategies to evaluate the rules in the knowledge base. If these strategies are also expressed as rules they are called *meta-rules*. Often the result of the inference depends on the sequence in which the rules are evaluated. Nilsson calls production systems commutative if this is not the case and he speaks of decomposable systems if the knowledge base can be decomposed in order to avoid inefficient search paths.

The most important advantage of production systems is their modularity. New rules can be added to an existing knowledge base or inference engine. Since the rules are to a very high degree independent of each other they can be changed rather easily. The uniformity of the knowledge representation facilitates the understanding, and the "natural" way of knowledge representation has lead to a high degree of acceptance of this method.

Fuzzy Sets as a Modelling Device

The expert knowledge used to build a knowledge base is normally available in the form of verbal statements in a natural language. In order to facilitate interaction of the system with the expert on one side and the user of the expert system on the other side, the communication should occur as far as possible in the language of the human being. Allowance must be made for the vagueness or fuzziness of many natural-language expressions. The same holds for the storage and representation of knowledge in the knowledge base.

Human reasoning differs to varying degrees from reasoning methods used in dual logic and other similar areas. If an expert system is to model the (human) expert's reasoning, methods will have to be used that reason like humans do and not like machines.

Experts' opinions very often express views that are uncertain as to their future realization. This uncertainty is not always of stochastic nature but is due to and expresses degrees of belief, conflicting evidence, etc. It is, therefore, not quite appropriate to express this uncertainty of a conclusion by an "uncertainty factor" computed by using Bayesian statistics. Ways of expressing uncertainty in a more differentiated manner are desirable, such as the theory of evidence (see "Management of Uncertainty" later in the chapter. In the following we shall discuss the possible contribution and the possible use of fuzzy set theory

- for the interface between man and machine,
- for the formal storage and representation of vague knowledge,
- in the inference engine,
- for the appropriate expressions of different kinds of uncertainty.

Finally, we will survey existing fuzzy expert systems, expert-system building tools (shell), and high-level fuzzy programming languages.

Man-Machine Interface. Three of the most important reasons for choosing a dialogue language as similar as possible to natural language are (particularly in ill-structured situations)

1. *Written* knowledge, which might be used to start a knowledge base, is normally expressed in a "kind of natural language." This does not mean that it is the language used for our daily conversation—it is the language that experts use and understand. As illustration, consider some of the textbook information that is knowledge available to doctors [Adlassnig, Kolarz 1982, p. 220]:

    Acute pancreatitis is almost always connected with sickness and vomiting.

    Typically, acute pancreatitis begins with sudden aches in the abdomen.

    The case history frequently reports about ulcus ventriculi and duodendi.

Bilirubinurie excludes the meholytic icterus but bilirubin is detectable with hepatocellular or cholestatic icterus."

2. Human experts that try to transfer their expertise to the system in a dialog can do this more effectively if they can use their own language.
3. The chances of gaining a potential user's acceptance of an expert system are greater if the user can communicate with the system in his language than if he first has to learn an artificial language.
4. If we expect the expert to translate his expertise into another (formal) language to accomodate the system, we might loose or falsify a good part of the expert's knowledge.

If the above arguments are valid we should really try to use at least quasi natural language for the dialog between the system and the expert and user. Looking at the methods of knowledge representation described in the last section one could get the impression that they are already geared to natural language. But the fact that semantic nets as well as frames and production rules use words and phrases from natural language does not necessarily mean that they are well suited to represent fuzzy knowledge. The problem is the *semantic representation* of knowledge.

If the *meaning* of a word or notion cannot be defined uniquely—that is, if the boundary of a class of objects is not sharp—then there exists the danger that the vagueness of a notion, even though that notion exists, is not visible by looking at its definition. The reader may want to look at the medical knowledge cited above in order to realize such complications. Representation of fuzzy knowledge is adequate only if the system can make the same deductions from it that a human being could from the natural language statements.

One way to achieve this is the use of linguistic variables as defined earlier. Although the effort, in terms of information processing and computation, will generally be greater than for a formalized artificial dialog language, the advantages of using linguistic variables may well compensate this disadvantage.

Knowledge Representation and Inference. Since, as we have mentioned, the kind of knowledge representation and the method of inference are not independent of each other, we shall discuss these two areas together. Principally, the methods of knowledge representation described in the last section can all also be used for the representation of fuzzy knowledge, if they are modified or extended accordingly. Three of their main weaknesses in this respect are:

1. Words are considered to be sufficiently well defined semantically.
2. Only the universal and the existential quantifiers can be used.

3. The number of connectives is very limited and their definitions may not coincide with the possibly context-dependent meaning they have for human experts.

All three shortfalls can be cured by using fuzzy set theory appropriately:

1. Linguistic variables can be used whenever possible and necessary to define notions, categories, or words properly. This means, of course, that membership *functions* of the appropriate fuzzy sets will have to be stored and processed rather than words or data.
2. A considerable number of fuzzy quantifiers (few, many, frequently, often, very, etc.) have been defined and can enlarge the available classical two quantifiers. (The empirical testing of their—possibly context-dependent—mathematical models might, however, require still more research.)
3. Selection of appropriate connectives (operators) was discussed in detail in chapter 6. More empirical research is certainly needed in this respect. A similar problem, which could be discussed in the context of operators as well as together with quantifiers or membership functions, is that of expressing the possible importance, weight, or urgency of one statement compared to others. Some approaches have been described in chapter 5. A fuzzy satisfactory solution has still not yet been found.

If allowance is made for fuzziness in the knowledge representation, the classical methods for inference (in a broad sense) will have to be modified because

1. they are not designed to infer from fuzzy statements,
2. one may want to model human reasoning better than classical dual logic or predicate calculus does, and
3. one may want to express the result of the inference procedures in quasi natural language.

Toward these ends, the following contributions can be made by fuzzy set theory:

1. The transition from dual logic or, better, from Lukasiewicz logic to fuzzy logic—briefly described earlier in this chapter and in more detail in chapter 9 of [Zimmermann 1985b]. This translation enables us to process statements with fuzzy contents, to use linguistic variables for the truth values of truth tables, and to use fuzzy quantifiers.
2. The use of approximate reasoning methods—which is another step in the direction of modelling human reasoning.

3. The development of computationally efficient methods for fuzzy logic and approximate reasoning—particularly important for practical use of these methods, because the increase of the volume of information that has to be processed in fuzzy logic compared to dual logic is too large to be handled efficiently in a straightforward manner.
4. The use of linguistic approximation (see chapter 5)—in order to find the labels of linguistic variables the membership functions of which have been computed during the inference process.

How and to what extent these possibilities have already been used in practice will be discussed in more detail when describing some of the existing expert systems, shells, and fuzzy languages. First we want to turn to a very crucial point in expert systems: the treatment of uncertainty.

Management of Uncertainty

Before we discuss ways to model and manage uncertainty properly we shall briefly discuss the sources or origins of uncertainty in expert systems. As a point of departure let us consider crisp knowledge representation by rules; similar observations would hold for other methods of knowledge representation.

In an expert system, knowledge and facts enter as

If X then Y (knowledge)
X is true (facts)

Therefore Y is true (conclusion)

The following assumptions are normally made in classical knowledge representation and inference methods:

1. X and Y are crisp statements of the type:

   The piece of furniture has four legs.
   Eve is 15 years old.
   Paul is the father of Eve.
   (Description)

2. The statements are deterministic in character; that is, they are certain, either true or false, and either fully supported or refuted by evidence. (Qualification)
3. If the statements include quantifiers, only two quantifiers are used: the

existential quantifier ("There exists at least one") and the universal quantifier ("all").
(Quantification)
4. The X in the "facts" are fully identical with the X in the "knowledge-statement."
(Matching)
5. The if-then relationship is deterministic (true, reliable, correct, and certain) (Inference),

Points 1 through 4 concern the modelling of facts and knowledge (representation), point 5 models the inference process. We shall discuss points 1–4 first and then turn to point 5.

Description. After what has been discussed in this book so far it would be like carrying coal to Newcastle to explain why facts cannot be assumed to be always crisply describable or to describe what can be done when they are not. The use of fuzzy sets, possibility distributions, fuzzy numbers, and linguistic variables will certainly help to model vague phenomena and relations. In chapter 6, some hints on how to determine membership functions have been given. Here we shall only point to one distinction between the general notion of a fuzzy set and notions such as possibility distributions, fuzzy numbers, and linguistic variables. This distinction is semantically important:

A fuzzy set has been defined as a set to which all elements contained in the support belong to different degrees. A possibility distribution expresses the uncertainty about the exact value of one realization of a possibilistic variable. An example of the former is the fuzzy set "Good friends of Lotfi"; an example of the latter is "The result is approximately seven."

Qualification. We shall distinguish three kinds of qualifications: *truth qualification, probability qualification,* and *possibility qualification.* Qualifications of statements are possible or even necessary, independent of whether the statement or phenomenon is crisp or fuzzy. The kind of modelling, however, will have to be different.

There is a difference between the *truth* of a part of a statement, a fact, or an antecedent and the *truth* of a compound statement. While the former depends on the antecedent's conformity or compatibility with reality, the latter depends, in addition, on the type of connectives used to build the compound statement from its parts. We will discuss the former under "matching"; the latter will be considered when discussing uncertainty in the process of inference. The reader is referred to the first part of this chapter with respect to truth qualification in fuzzy logic and approximate reasoning, and also to the section about possibility qualification further on.

Probability Qualification. It is not surprising that probability qualifications are still the most common way to characterize uncertainty with respect to the occurrence of an event (which might be the real occurrence of the predicted—"true"—outcome of a conclusion). Probability theory has long been the only way to model uncertainty and therefore is still the most accepted method. Of course, probability has often been abused to model all kinds of uncertainty! In the following we shall briefly discuss probability qualifications as point estimates, intervals, and (possibility) distributions. These approaches assume crisply defined events. For models of the probability of fuzzy events, the reader is referred to Zimmermann [1985b, ch. 8], Dubois, Prade [1980, pp. 141–144], and Yager [1984, pp. 273–283].

Let us consider the rule

If A then C
A is true (antecedant)

Then C is true (conclusion)

In the most frequently applied Bayesian approach, the Bayes inversion theorem is used:

$$\Pr(C/A) = \frac{\Pr(C)}{\Pr(A)} \Pr(A/C) \tag{7.15}$$

Hence $\Pr(C/A)$ is the probability of C given A, $\Pr(C)$ the probability of C, etc. If the antecedent has the possible states A_i and the conclusion has the possible states C_j then (7.15) becomes

$$\Pr(C_j/A_i) = \frac{\Pr(C_j)}{\Pr(A_i)} \Pr(A_i/C_j) \tag{7.16}$$

(Determination of probabilities of conclusions in larger inference systems shall not be discussed here, because textbooks on probability theory exist in abundance.)

Objections against this approach are, first of all, that aspects of uncertainty that are nonprobabilistic in nature may be included. Computationally this approach becomes prohibitive if the events (antecedent, conclusion) are considered to be fuzzy—represented as fuzzy sets. A second criticism is the need to identify point values for the probabilities of events that may by far be overstatements of our actual knowledge of the likelihood of occurrence of that particular event.

This criticism has lead Dempster [1967] to suggest the concept of upper and lower probabilities and Shafer [1976] to present his *theory of evidence.* The basic concept of this theory is that instead of representing the probability of an event A by a point value, $\Pr(A)$, it may be bounded by the subinterval $[\underline{\Pr}(A), \overline{\Pr}(A)]$ of $[0,1]$. This theory has some connections to the theory of fuzzy sets and shall, therefore, be discussed in some more detail. Rather than following a purely probabilistic line of argument [see, e.g., Dubois, Prade 1982, p. 171; Goodman, Nguyen 1985] we shall follow Zadeh's line of argument [Zadeh 1984], which seems easier to comprehend and closer to "fuzzy thinking." After an introduction to the basic ideas of Dempster and Shafer, we will return to the more common representation of their theory.

Let us consider the following introductionary example:

Example 7.10

Let us assume we have a data base in which the (atomic) elements are related to each other by first-order relations. One of these may be as shown in table 7-4. In a simple range query of the type "what portion of the employees in the data base have between 1 and 3 children?" we would get, from table 7-4, the answer 3/5, which may be interpreted as the probability of an employee (contained in the data base) having between 1 and 3 children.

Let us now assume that our knowledge is less precise and that we only know the second-order relation shown in table 7-5. We now put the query: "What portion of the employees has between 3 and 5 children?" This is obviously possible for employees 3 and 4. It is not possible for employees 1, 2, and 5! Therefore, the statement "He has between 4 and 5 children" is certainly true for employee 3; it is possibly true for employee 4; and it is certainly not true for employees 1, 2, and 5.

Table 7-4

Emp 1	*Name*	*No. of children*
	1	1
	2	3
	3	5
	4	2
	5	4

Table 7-5

Emp 2	*Name*	*No. of children*	*Between 3 and 5 children?*
	1	1,2	impossible
	2	1	impossible
	3	4,5	certain
	4	5,6	possible
	5	6	impossible

In the Dempster-Shafer theory the portion of the intervals for which the statement is certainly true is called *lower probability*. In our example this is 1/5. As the *upper probability* they consider the portion of the elements (intervals) for which the statement can (possibly) be true (i.e. 1 minus the portion for which the statement cannot be true). In example 7.10 this is $(1 - 3/5 = 2/5)$. The lower probability is also called *measure of belief* and the upper probability is called *measure of plausibility*. It should be noted that in our example the employees were considered as atomic elements (all equal probabilities!). If this is not the case the different probabilities of the intervals will have to be taken into consideration when determining lower and upper probabilities. Shafer calls the sets of attributes (number of children) assigned to the elements *focal elements* and their probabilities of occurrence *basic probability assignment*. In example 7.10 the answer to the question "What is the probability of an employee having between 3 and 5 children?" would be: The lower probability (degree of belief) is 1/5 and the upper probability (plausibility) (degree of belief) is 2/5.

Example 7.10 was a rather intuitive example. Let us now define the uncertainty measures of the theory of evidence properly.

***Definition** 7.5* [see Dubois, Prade 1982, 1985b; Prade 1985; Goodman, Nguyen 1985, p. 32]

Let X be a finite set equipped with a probability measure Pr defined on the set $P(X)$ of subsets of X. Consider a point-to-set mapping Γ from X to some set S. That is, $\forall x \in X$, $\Gamma(x)$ is a subset of S. Let $f \subseteq S$ ($f =$ focal element) and the mapping m from $P(S)$ to $[0,1]$ (basic probability assignment) be defined as follows:

$$m(\varnothing) = 0$$

$$m(f) = \frac{\Pr(\{x \in X, \Gamma(x) = f\})}{1 - \Pr(\{x \in X, \Gamma(x) = \varnothing\})} \qquad \forall f \subseteq S, f \neq \varnothing$$

Let the set $F = \{f \subseteq SX'm(f) > 0\}$ contain at most n elements. Then the *upper probability* or *plausibility measure* is defined as

$$\Pr^*(Q) = PL(Q) = \sum_{f \cap Q \neq \varnothing} m(f) \tag{7.17}$$

The *lower probability, belief function,* or *credibility measure* (Dubois and Prade) is defined as

$$\Pr^*(Q) = \mathrm{Bel}(Q) = \mathrm{Cr}(Q) \sum_{f \subseteq Q} m(f) \tag{7.18}$$

In analogy to these measures of uncertainty, doubt or commonality measures and disbelief or incredibility measures have been defined [Goodman, Nguyen 1985, p. 321]).

Remark: Plausibility and belief are, of course, not unrelated. The following properties hold:

$$PL(Q) = \mathrm{Bel}(Q) = 1 \tag{7.19}$$

$$PL(Q) = \mathrm{Bel}(Q) = 0 \tag{7.20}$$

$$PL(Q) = 1 - \mathrm{Bel}(\neg Q) \tag{7.21}$$

$$PL(A \cap B) \leq \mathrm{PL}(A) + PL(B) - PL(A \cup B) \tag{7.22}$$

$$\mathrm{Bel}(A \cup B) \geq \mathrm{Bel}(A) + \mathrm{Bel}(B) - \mathrm{Bel}(A \cap B) \tag{7.23}$$

(7.19) relates to the normalization condition

$$\sum_{f \in F} m(f) = 1 \tag{7.24}$$

which may lead to some problems [see Zadeh 1984, pp. 6–10].

While Bel (Q) obviously considers evidence supporting Q, PL (Q) focusses on the evidence supporting the contrary. If F contains only singletons then $PL(Q) = \mathrm{Bel}(Q)$; that is, these measures reduce to normal probabilities. So far we have looked at scalar measures (probabilities) and interval measures (belief, plausibility). If we consider probability as a linguistic variable, then a measure for the probability of an event is a term of the linguistic variable "probability" —a fuzzy set characterized by its membership function. The notions of plausibility and belief have also been extended from crisp event (as considered here) to fuzzy event. The reader is referred to [Dubois, Prade 1985a, p. 553; Smets 1981].

Possibility Qualification. We now return to example 7.10 and assume that in table 7-5 the number of children of the various employees are described by possibility distributions [see, e.g., Zadeh 1983b; Zimmermann 1985b, ch. 8].

To review, a possibility distribution can formally be described by a fuzzy set. One difference between a possibility distribution and a fuzzy set, however, is that in a fuzzy set the elements of the support belong to the fuzzy set to various degrees while in a possibility distribution the possibilities indicate the degree of possibility with which a variable can adopt various values. A discrete possibility distribution shall be denoted by

$$\Pi = \{(x_i, \Pi_i)\}$$

Then (7.17) and (7.18) respectively, satisfy the following axioms [Shafer 1976]:

$$PL(A \cup B) = \max\{PL(A), PL(B)\} \tag{7.25}$$

$$\mathrm{Bel}(A \cap B) = \min\{\mathrm{Bel}(A), \mathrm{Bel}(B)\} \tag{7.26}$$

A plausibility measure which satisfies (7.25) is called a *possibility measure* (Π), and a belief measure which satisfies (7.26) is called a *necessity measure* (N) [Prade 1985; Zadeh 1984]. (The latter is called a "consonant belief function" by Shafter.) In contrast to (7.19) through (7.24), possibility measures (Π) and necessity measures (N) have the following properties:

$$\min(N(Q), N(\neg Q)\} = 0 \tag{7.27}$$

$$\max\{\Pi(Q), \Pi(\neg Q)\} = 1 \tag{7.28}$$

$$\Pi(Q) < 1 \Rightarrow N(Q) = 0 \tag{7.29}$$

$$N(Q) > 0 \Rightarrow \Pi(Q) = 1 \tag{7.30}$$

Example 7.11

Let us now assume that the information available concerning the number of children of our employees is not as in table 7-5, but as in table 7-6. Let us now ask "How possible is it that an employees has 3 or 4 children?"

If we consider the possibility of 3 or 4 children as

$$\Pi = \max_{Q \cap f \neq \varnothing} (\Pi_i) = \max\{.6\} = .6$$

the necessity as

$$N = \min_{Q \cap f = \varnothing} (1 - \Pi_i) = \min\{.2,0,0,0,.2,0,0\} = 0$$

then our answer would have to be:

"The possibility of an employee having 3 or 4 children is .6, the necessity is 0."

Table 7-6

Empl 3	*Name*	*Poss. of having × children*
	1	{(1,.8),(2,1)}
	2	{(1,1)}
	3	{(4,.6),(5,1)}
	4	{(5,.8),(6,1)}
	5	{(6,1)}

It should be noted that other interpretations and definitions of "necessity" and "possibility" measures exist [see, e.g., Dubois, Prade 1985a; Prade 1985].

Quantification. In human communication and therefore also in knowledge transfer, statements include quantifiers other than the two quantifiers available in dual logic or classical mathematics. Often these quantifiers are implicit rather than explicit. An assertion of the type "Frenchmen are very charming" often really means "Most (or almost all) Frenchmen are charming." Likewise the proposition "Hans is never late" would normally be interpreted as "Hans is late very rarely."

To model this and other types of quantifiers, fuzzy set theory includes *fuzzy quantifiers*. We shall view a fuzzy quantifier as "a fuzzy number which provides a fuzzy characterization of the absolute or relative cardinality of one or more fuzzy or nonfuzzy sets" [Zadeh 1982, p. 5]. Zadeh distinguishes between fuzzy quantifiers of the first kind (referring to absolute counts), and quantifiers of the second kind (referring to relative counts). Examples of the former are: several, few, many, etc. Examples of the latter kind are most, many, often, a large fraction, etc. Quantifiers of the third kind are ratios of quantifiers of the second kind.

Scalar quantifiers are normally modelled using their cardinality or sigma count (see definition 1.6). Let us consider the proposition "Vickie has several close friends" [Zadeh 1982, p. 11]. The fuzzy set "close friends of Vickie" may be represented by

$$\tilde{F} = \{(\text{Enrique}, 1),(\text{Ramon}, .8),(\text{Elie}, .7),(\text{Sergei}, .8),(\text{Ron}, .7)\}$$

Then the sigma count (cardinality) of

$$\tilde{F} = (1 + .8 + .7 + .8 + .7) = 4$$

If "several" plays the role of a specified subset of integers $1, \ldots, 10$, in which 4 is assumed to be compatible with the meaning of "several" to the degree .8, the above proposition may be modelled as

$$\text{Poss}\{\text{Count (close friends (Vickie))} = 4\} = .8$$

In some cases it might not be appropiate or desirable to express the cardinality of a fuzzy set as a number, rather as a fuzzy set. Zadeh proposed three notions of fuzzy counts based on the concept of α-level cuts:

***Definition** 7.6* [Zadeh 1982, p. 15]

Let $\tilde{F}$ be a (discrete) fuzzy set and F_α an α-level cut of fuzzy set $\tilde{F}$. Card_α represents the cardinality (count) of the elements of an α-level cut.
The *FG-count* is then defined to be the fuzzy set

$$\widetilde{FG} = (\text{Card}_{\alpha_i}, \sup_\alpha \{\alpha \mid \text{Card}_\alpha \geq i\}) \qquad i = 0,\ldots,n$$

The *FL-Count* is defined as

$$\widetilde{FL} = \{(\text{Card}_{\alpha_i}, \sup_\alpha \{\alpha\} \text{Card}_\alpha \geq n - i\}) \qquad i = 1,\ldots,n\}$$

The *FE-Count* is the fuzzy set

$$\widetilde{FE} = \{(\text{Card}_{\alpha_i}, \min \{\mu_{FG}(\alpha_i), \mu_{FL}(\alpha_i)\}\}) \qquad i = 1,\ldots,n\}$$

The counts of definition 7.6 may be interpreted as follows: The *FG*-count is the truth value of the proposition "$\tilde{F}$ contains at least *i* elements", $\widetilde{FL}$ the truth of "$\tilde{F}$ contains at most *i* elements" and the $\widetilde{FE}$-count of "$\tilde{F}$ contains exactly *i* elements."

***Example** 7.12* [Zadeh 1982, pp. 15–16]

Let

$$\tilde{F} = \{(X_1,.6),(x_2,.9),(x_3,1)(x_4,.7)(x_5,.3)\}$$

The α-level sets are listed in table 7–7. The various counts are

$$\widetilde{FG}(\tilde{F}) = \{(0,1),(1,1)(2,.9),(3,.7),(4,.6),(5,.3)\}$$

$$\widetilde{FL}(\tilde{F}) = \{[(2,.1),(3,.3),(4,.4),(5,.7),(6,1)] - 1\}$$

$$= \{(1,.1),(2,.3),(3,.4),(4,.7),(5,1)\}$$

$$\widetilde{FE}(\tilde{F}) = \{(1,.1),(2,.3),(3,.4),(4,.6),(5,.3)\}$$

The normal sigma count would be

$$|\tilde{F}| = \Sigma\,\text{count}(\tilde{F}) = \sum_i \mu_i(\alpha) = 3.5$$

Table 7-7

α	F_1
1	$\{x_3\}$
.9	$\{x_2,x_3\}$
.7	$\{x_2,x_3,x_4\}$
.6	$\{x_1,x_2,x_3,x_4\}$
.3	$\{x_1,x_2,x_3,x_4,x_5\}$

Matching. By *matching problem* we mean the approximation of real evidence by assumed structures or of computational results by communication languages. In expert systems this problem occurs twice: whenever knowledge (relations between facts) contained in the knowledge base has to be used on the basis of observed facts that do not quite coincide with the "models of facts" in the knowledge base, or when it cannot be decided whether it coincides or not.

The first case is represented by example 7.4 in which the knowledge base contains only the "fact" red tomatos while the observed fact is "very red tomato." For the second case, consider the rule "If the rod is hot, stop the heating process." The observed fact could be "The rod has a temperature of 150°C." The question then is "Is that rod hot or not hot?"

Let us call these two types of problems *input matching* and discuss methods for their solution further down. Another matching problem occurs when the result of the inference process has been obtained—e.g., as the membership function of a fuzzy set. The user of the system, however, does not want the answer as a function but in a language close to his own. The problem is then to search for a term of a linguistic variable whose membership function is very close to the one obtained by the system. This is, of course, a problem of output interpretation and we shall call it *output matching.*

The input-matching problem is obviously already reduced if the knowledge base contains descriptions in the form of fuzzy sets rather than only crisp models. Also, it has been suggested that in addition to using similarity relations, truth and certainty values be used to model the degree of compatibility of reality and model and to introduce it into the inference process. Another promising approach is the suggestion by Cayrol, Farrency, and Prade [1982] to use pattern matching where possibility measures and necessity measures are employed, in order to evaluate the semantic similarities between patterns (models) and data.

Output matching is more a psycholinguistic problem. It occurs primarily if approximate or plausible reasoning methods or other fuzzy approaches are used in which membership functions (of linguistic variables, for instance) are used. Even if at the input level the semantic meaning of data and formal knowledge representation coincides satisfactorily, the process of inference may yield membership functions that do not fit the membership functions of linguistic variables or their terms, as defined beforehand, well enough to communicate the results effectively to the user of an expert system.

Certainty factors or degrees of truth do not relay a missing correspondence well enough. Another approach, which seems to be promising but not yet well enough developed to be used efficiently, is the linguistic approximation mentioned in example 5.8.

Inference. Uncertainty can enter inference schemes in three ways: through

1. uncertainty qualifications of the premises (antecedents) (Truth, Probability, etc.) that influence the conclusions;
2. vagueness of the antecedents, which may be, for example, modelled as a possibility distribution or fuzzy set, and which influences the type of inference and the character of the conclusions; and
3. uncertainty of the inference process itself. In general, this uncertainty should probably better be called ambiguity. It is due to the fact that the mathematical models of the connectives (and, or, implication, etc.) are no longer uniquely determined when departing from dual logic or predicate calculus. The choice of the connectives determines the conclusion, given a set of antecedents.

The probabilistic treatment of uncertainty (such as is used in MYCIN) has been well described by several authors [see, e.g., Lagomasino, Sage, 1985; Goodman, Nguyen 1985, pp. 480–485; Prade 1985]. The other two approaches will be discussed in the next section when describing some of the existing expert system tools.

Existing Expert Systems and Tools Using Fuzzy Sets

Expert Systems. While expert systems such as MYCIN [Buchanan, Shortliffe 1985] PROSPECTOR, and SPERIL are dedicated to specific problem areas, expert system *tools* are used to develop such expert systems. They can be categorized either as skeletal systems, general purpose systems, or languages. A skeletal knowledge-engineering language [Waterman 1986, p. 83] or an expert-system shell is simply a stripped-down expert system. It is an expert system with its domain-specific knowledge removed, leaving only the inference engine and support facilities. The designers of PROSPECTOR, for instance, stripped it of knowledge about geology and thus got the shell KAS; MYCIN was the basis for the shell EMYCIN (empty MYCIN); and CASNET, a system for glaucoma consultation, became the shell EXPERT.

In the area of fuzzy set application the other approach has usually been adopted. Languages have been developed to handle fuzzy sets, possibility distributions, fuzzy logic, different types of uncertainty measures, and can now be used to build more problem-specific expert systems. Apart from these tools expert systems containing fuzzy components have been built directly. We shall first briefly discuss some of the expert systems and then turn to the tools.

Examples of expert systems using concepts of fuzzy set theory are, for instance, CADIAC, SPERIL-II, fINDex, SPHINX, EMERGE, etc. Most of them use linguistic variables, fuzzy numbers, approximate reasoning methods, and measures of truth or uncertainty. It would exceed the scope of this book to describe all of them. We shall, however, discuss in some detail the two first-mentioned systems as examples. Table 7-8 at the end of this chapter tries to characterize the other systems without claiming to be in any way complete.

CADIAC

> The medical expert system *CADIAC-2* is intended to function as the physician's active partner in diagnostic situations. It makes a man/machine partnership possible in order to combine the experience, creativeness and intuition of a physician with the knowledge-based power of a computer." [Adlassnig et al. 1985]

CADIAC is a rule-based system. It now available for a variety of medical areas (such as rheuma, pancreas). The following symbols will be used to sketch the system.

$S = \{\tilde{S}_1,\ldots,\tilde{S}_m\}$: Set of fuzzy sets describing the symptoms with their respective apparances

$D = \{\tilde{D}_1,\ldots,\tilde{D}_n\}$: Set of fuzzy sets indicating the degree to which a patient has a specific disease

$P = \{\tilde{P}_1,\ldots,\tilde{P}_q\}$: Set of fuzzy sets indicating to which degree a diagnosis is true for a specific patient

All $\tilde{S}_1$, $\tilde{D}_j$, and $\tilde{P}_k$ are fuzzy sets characterized by their respective membership functions.

$\mu_{\tilde{S}_i}$ expresses the intensity of symptom i,

$\mu_{\tilde{D}_j}$ expresses the degree of membership of a patient to $\tilde{D}_j$, and

$\mu_{\tilde{P}_k}$ assigns to each patient a degree of membership for each different diagnosis.

Two aspects of symptom $\tilde{S}_i$ with respect to disease $\tilde{D}_j$ are of particular interest and are modelled as fuzzy relations:

$$\tilde{R}_O(\tilde{S}_i, \tilde{D}_j): \quad \text{occurence of } \tilde{S}_i \text{ in case of } \tilde{D}_j$$

and

$$\tilde{R}_C(\tilde{S}_i, \tilde{D}_j): \quad \text{confirmability of } \tilde{S}_i \text{ for } \tilde{D}_j$$

The $\tilde{S}_i\tilde{D}_j$ occurrence and confirmability relationships are acquired empirically from medical experts and expressed as the terms of the respective linguistic variables. Figure 7-20 depicts the membership functions of the terms of these linguistic variables. The membership functions of $\tilde{R}_O$ and $\tilde{R}_C$ are arrived at by applying modifiers to "never" and "always." For details of the data acquisition process see Adlassnig and Kolarz [1982, p. 226].

Other relationships such as symptom–symptom, disease–disease, and symptom–disease are also defined as fuzzy sets (fuzzy relations). Possibilistic

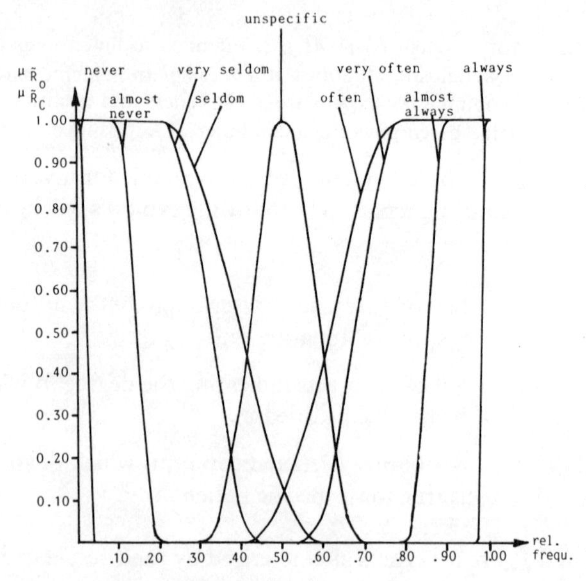

Figure 7-20: Terms of linguistic variables.

interpretations of relations (min-max) are used. Given a patient's symptom pattern, the symptom–disease relationships, the symptom-combination–disease relationships, and the disease–disease relationships yield fuzzy diagnostic indications that are the basis for establishing confirmed and excluded diagnoses as well as diagnostic hypotheses.

Four different fuzzy indications are calculated by means of fuzzy-relation compositions [Adlassnig, Kolarz 1982, p. 237]. The symptom relation, $\tilde{R}_S$, is determined on the basis of the symptom patterns, $\tilde{S}_i$, of the patients, p.

1. $\tilde{S}_i\tilde{D}_j$ occurrence indication $\tilde{R}_1 = \tilde{R}_S \circ \tilde{R}_O$

$$\mu_{\tilde{R}_1}(p,\tilde{D}_j) = \max_{\tilde{S}_i} \min \{\mu_{\tilde{R}_S}(p,\tilde{S}_i), \mu_{\tilde{R}_O}(\tilde{S}_i,\tilde{D}_j)\}$$

2. $\tilde{S}_i\tilde{D}_j$ confirmability indication $\tilde{R}_2 = \tilde{R}_S \circ \tilde{R}_C$

$$\mu_{\tilde{R}_2}(p,\tilde{D}_j) = \max_{\tilde{S}_i} \min \{\mu_{\tilde{R}_S}(p,\tilde{S}_i), \mu_{\tilde{R}_C}(\tilde{S}_i,\tilde{D}_j)\}$$

3. $\tilde{S}_j\tilde{D}_j$ nonoccurrence indication $\tilde{R}_3 = \tilde{R}_S \circ (1 - \tilde{R}_O)$

$$\mu_{\tilde{R}_3}(p,\tilde{D}_j) = \max_{\tilde{S}_i} \min \{\mu_{\tilde{R}_S}(p,\tilde{S}_i), 1 - \mu_{\tilde{R}_O}(\tilde{S}_i,\tilde{D}_j)\}$$

4. $\tilde{S}_i\tilde{D}_j$ nonsymptom indication $\tilde{R}_4 = (1 - \tilde{R}_S) \circ \tilde{R}_O$

$$\mu_{\tilde{R}_4}(p,\tilde{D}_j) = \max_{\tilde{S}_i} \min \{1 - \mu_{\tilde{R}_S}(p,\tilde{D}_{S_i}), \mu_{\tilde{R}_O}(\tilde{S}_i,\tilde{D}_j)\}$$

Similar indications are determined for symptoms–disease relationships, arriving at 12 fuzzy relationships $\tilde{R}_j$. Three categories of diagnostic relationships are distinguished:

1. Confirmed diagnoses
2. Excluded diagnoses
3. Diagnostic hypotheses

SPERIL-II

SPERIL-II is an expert system for damage assessment of existing structures. Fuzzy sets for imprecise data and Dempster and Shafer's theory for combining fuzzy sets with certainty factors are used in an inexact inference. Because the process of the damage assessment is very complex, meta rules are used to control the inference in order to improve the effectiveness and reliability of results. The meta rules in SPERIL-II are represented in logic form with emphasis on the explicit representation of the selection of the rule group and the suitable inference method. [Ogawa et al. 1985, p. 731]

SPERIL-II is a rule-based damage assessment system in which there are three steps in the assessment process:

1. Evaluation of local damageability—which describes the various characteristics and the damage of members of the structure after the diagnosis of damage causes from input data.
2. Evaluation of global damageability—which shows the damages of a local nature, global nature, and cumulative nature.
3. Estimation of the safety or damage state of the whole structure.

Rules for SPERIL-II are of the type:

If *antecedent* THEN *consequence* WITH *certainty factor*

The *antecedent* is represented in the form of a logical statement. The *consequence* is in the form of a descriptive statement. The certainty of the *consequence* is obtained by multiplying the *certainty factor* and the certainty of the *antecedent*, which is calculated using the maximum (minimum) of the certainty values in an AND (OR) relation.

To infer the consequences from independent rules requires a COMB relation [Dempster, 1967]. When at least one node is satisfied in a COMB relation, the ancestor node is satisfied as in an OR relation. The evaluated values of all satisfied nodes are, however, combined to obtain a more precise estimation of the ancestor in a COMB relation, while only one node is used in an OR node. A combination method for this relation has to have the following properties [Ogawa et al. 1985]

1. It increases the certainty factor of the consequence when there are high certainties in all the knowledge sources.
2. The results must not depend on the order of combining the knowledge sources.

The Dempster-Shafer theory of evidence is used to achieve these properties.

To combine two fuzzy sets with certainty factors by applying Dempster's combination rule, a primitive fuzzy set is used—this set has only one element and its membership is 1. The probability of each primitive fuzzy set for the given fuzzy set is calculated using their intersection and the probability of a fuzzy event [Zadeh 1968] as follows: For fuzzy set

$$\tilde{S} = \{(x_i, \mu(x_i))\} \qquad \text{with certainly } \alpha$$

the probability $P(\tilde{A}_j)$ of the primitive fuzzy set $A_j = \{x_j, 1)\}$ is obtained by

$$\sum_{i=1}^{n} \mu_{\tilde{S} \cap \tilde{A}_j} \Pi_i$$

where Π_i is the possibility for each x_i. In this case,

$$\Pi_i = \frac{\alpha}{\mu_{\tilde{S}}(x_j)} \qquad (i = 1, \ldots, n) \tag{7.31}$$

because Π_i depends on the possibilities and the certainty factor. Then, the basic probability mass $m(\tilde{A}_j)$ corresponding to the probability of A' is obtained by

$$\frac{\alpha \mu_{\tilde{S}}(x_j)}{\Sigma \mu_{\tilde{S}}(x_i)}.$$

After $m(\tilde{B}_j)$ has been obtained for $\tilde{B}_j$ in the same way, $m(\tilde{C}_k)(k = 1, \ldots, n)$ are calculated using Dempster's rule of combination:

$$m(\tilde{C}_k) = \frac{\sum_{\tilde{A}_i \cap \tilde{B}_j = \tilde{C}_k} m(\tilde{A}_i) m(\tilde{B}_j)}{1 - \sum_{\tilde{A}_i \cap \tilde{B}_j = \varnothing} m(\tilde{A}_i) m(\tilde{B}_j)} \tag{7.32}$$

The basic probability mass $m(\tilde{C}_k)$ also corresponds to the probability $P_r(\tilde{C}_i)$ of the primitive fuzzy set $\tilde{C}_i\{(x,.1)\}$, which is used to obtain a new fuzzy set. The membership function of the new fuzzy set is obtained by

$$\mu_{\tilde{C}_i}(x_i) = \frac{P_r(\tilde{C}_i)}{\max_j [p_r(\tilde{C}_j)]} \tag{7.33}$$

SPERIL-II is experimentally implemented using the knowledge and the metaknowledge obtained from several case studies. With regard to four cases described by Ogawa et al. [1985], SPERIL-II has produced the same results as the experts. The knowledge in SPERIL-II is currently being modified for practical use by experienced structural engineers including Prof. Yao of Purdue University and Dr. Hanson and other experts at Wiss, Janney, Elstner and Associates, Inc. (WJE).

Tools, Shells, and Languages. In recent years a number of expert-system tools that either concentrate on the use of fuzzy set theory or at least facilitate its use have been developed. These tools vary with respect to generality and scope. Some are a kind of planning language—for example, they do not provide a real, specified inference engine, but rather provide facilities to build one. Normally these tools provide user-oriented I/O-facilities and are easy to use. They do not require special expertise in fuzzy set theory from the user. Some default models—for example, models for quantifiers, operators, and modifiers (hedges)—are normally provided. If the user is not proficient in fuzzy set theory or approximate reasoning, however, he will certainly not be in a position to design sophisticated models and inference schemes.

Other languages concentrate on sophisticated inference engines, on appropriate and possible multidimensional treatment of uncertainty, provide alternative ways of inferences, etc. In general, however, these languages, do not particularly care for a very user-friendly interface. To show the scope of the numerous tools available we will describe three in more detail. Table 7-9 gives information and references for those languages not discussed here.

REVEAL

REVEAL [Jones 1986; Small 1984] is one of the very few commercially available languages for which training seminars are offered and which accomodates the use of fuzzy set theory in expert—or decision support—systems. Originally developed by Decision Products Inc. in California it is now marketed and serviced by Tymshare in the U.K. REVEAL is intended to model and analyze complex problems primarily in the area of management. The steps in development of an elementary REVEAL model are normally as follows:

1. Define the problem to be analyzed.
2. Assemble a list of data elements.
3. Organize the data elements into a logical sequence and define the logical relationships among them.
4. Call up the REVEAL Editor to enter the model program.
5. Execute the model and generate output (graphs, tables, and/or reports).

REVEAL programming language can be used to create conventional algorithmic operations using procedural programming techniques and the standard arithmetic, Boolean, and character-string operations, loops, conditionals, and other manipulative statements. It enables complex programs to be modelled using few statements and provides a wide variety of special functions including:

1. DATA HANDLING including the manipulation of specific rows and columns in a table.

2. MATHEMATICAL FUNCTIONS operating on simple variables and on the rows and columns of REVEAL tables.
3. STRING VARIABLE FUNCTIONS for the manipulation of character data and for the manipulation of user-defined data objects.
4. FINANCIAL FUNCTIONS including mortgage payment calculation, depreciation, and compound interest calculations.
5. SPECIAL FUNCTIONS including the ability to set a portion of an array to a given value, query various workspace parameters, and generate random numbers.

REVEAL also includes facilities for the linguistic representation of imprecise data and approximate enquiries. A REVEAL model may contain a set of linguistic statements written in a declarative form (without any order of execution being implied). This form of statement is known as a REVEAL *policy* and might take the following forms:

Our price should be quite low.

Our price should be near that of our competitors' price.

Our price should be about 2 times our direct costs.

Policy statements for REVEAL include:

1. *Linguistic variables*, for example, price, direct costs, competitors' price. Each linguistic variable has a name and a domain of applicability (for example, from Ŀ 100 to Ŀ 99.99 9).
2. *Qualifiers* are an expression of concept which applies to a linguistic variable (e.g., "low"). Each qualifier is represented by a truth function indicating the extent to which any price is to be considered low, medium, or high, for example. This representation is on a numerical scale from 0 to 1.
   These qualifying linguistic variables can be further qualified by *hedges*, for example, "quite" and "about," which strengthen or weaken the force of the qualifier and consequently its truth function.
3. *Noise words*, for example, "should be," "our." "that," "of." These simply improve the readability of the statements without affecting their logical meanings.

Several types of model analysis are possible in REVEAL: among these are:

1. GOAL SEEKING. The user defines his target and the REVEAL model

seeks the given target using specified criteria.

2. STABILITY. A particular target is set and the model is then used to ascertain the value of a particular variable which maintains the target value in respone to the fluctuations in other variables.
3. SENSITIVITY. A model can be executed repeatedly, using different policy guidelines to determine its sensitivity to different factors. Post-processing logic may be applied to select a number of situations that fulfill the conditions specified to the system.
4. AGGREGATION. Individual sets of tables can be established with the same general format but representing particular sets of data. Specific sections of these tables can then be aggregated in order to reveal one particular aspect of interest.

To use the approximate-reasoning facilities of REVEAL it is first necessary to install a vocabulary, that is, a file holding the definitions of the concepts, applicable to a particular set of problems. The user is free to define linguistic variables via a fuzzy set, qualifiers, hedges, etc. For most of the latter concepts default definitions are available. Hedges (modifiers) such as "very" or "quite" are defined as power functions applied to the membership function of the respective fuzzy set ("very" is modelled as the squaring operation and "quite" as the square root). Similar models are available for "about," "near," "around," "more," "less," etc. It should be pointed out, however, that the justification for these models is heuristic (see chapter 6) and that the user should be careful to avoid use of these default definitions without considering their appropriateness in given contexts. The same holds for the definitions of "and" and "or," which are purely possibilistic (min/max).

Programs are written to express the rules for determining the value to be assigned to a set of variables in terms of the concepts defined in a vocabulary. These programs are called POLICIES.

A policy may contain both conditional and unconditional statements, although they are treated slightly differently.

The COMPOSITION RULE defines the method by which the values of variables resulting from policies are worked out from their truth function.

The REVEAL system provides two composition rules to be selected by the user using the FRULES mode:

1. COMPOSIT MAXIMUM. This is the default rule whereby the value assigned to a variable corresponds to the maximum value of the truth function. If the maximum value is a plateau with two corners, the value corresponding to the center of the plateau is taken. If the maximum value is a plateau with two corners, the value corresponding to the center of the

plateau is taken. If the maximum value is a plateau with one corner, the value corresponding to the corner is taken.

2. COMPOSIT MOMENTS. This rule assigns to the variable a value corresponding to the center of gravity of the truth function.

FLOPS

FLOPS [Buckley et al 1986] is a much younger expert system tool. It is, however, already available commercially (Kemp-Carraway Heert Institute, Birmingham). As was EMYCIN, FLOPS was first developed for a special application —to process echocardiogram images of the heart by computer. Since its inception, it has become a shell which can be used for other applications as well.

FLOPS is based on the AI language OPS 5, uses production rules for knowledge representation, and is particularly suitable for managing the processing of imprecise numerical data bases and runs on PC's such as IBM-XT or AT. The input to this system can contain fuzzy numbers and discrete fuzzy sets, the rules are designed to process the fuzzy data and the output is a fuzzy set. Fuzzy numbers in this system are defined to be fuzzy sets, the membership functions of which are continuous and monotonically increasing, constant, or monotonically decreasing in different intervals, such that applying basic operations to fuzzy numbers yields fuzzy numbers. Crisp numbers or relations are treated as special cases of fuzzy notions. Standard fuzzy arithmetic [see Zimmermann 1985b, ch. 5.3; Dubois, Prade 1980] is used. Rules are of the type

$$\text{If } [\ ] * [\ ] * \ldots * [\ ], \text{ then } D \tag{7.34}$$

where [ ] is called a "pattern" and has the form

$$[\ ] = \text{operand } \{, \text{relative operator, operand}\}$$

{ } being optional. An operand is an attribute of an object together with its "degree of confidence" (*cf*). *cf* is in [0, 1] and the default value is 1. The * are logical operators such as "and," "or," "not," modelled so far as min, max, or $(1 - \mu)$. The rules R_i are considered to be members of the fuzzy set $\tilde{R}$. Their degree of membership to this set $\tilde{R}$ is interpreted as "the a priori degree of belief in R_i." A "relative operator" can be a fuzzy relation, $\tilde{F}$. In this case a pattern has the form

$$(\tilde{P}_1 cf_1)\tilde{F}(\tilde{P}_2 cf_2)$$

Here $\tilde{P}_1$ and $\tilde{P}_2$ are attributes and the *cf* their respective degrees of confidence. The rules are evaluated as to their degrees of confidence as follows.

If the pattern has only one operand then its value is the attribute's *cf*. If the pattern contains relative operators then the value of that pattern is

$$K = \min(cf_1, cf_2, \widetilde{P_1 FP_2}) \tag{7.35}$$

Hence the posterior "confidence level" of a rule is obtained by determining the minimum of the membership values of the attributes, those of the predicates that relate the attributes, and those of the rule itself.

FLOPS includes some checks for illogical or inconsistent patterns and hedges. So far, these checks are different from the linguistic hedges (modifiers) one is normally accustomed to in fuzzy set theory ("very," "quite," etc.) and as they are used in REVEAL. In FLOPS a hedge operates on fuzzy relations and, in a sense, calibrates their membership functions. More details can be found in [Buckley et al. 1986]. FLOPS uses backtracking with a weakly monotonic logic which allows replacement of knowledge by newer facts if their "degree of confidence" is higher than that for the one stored. The use of non-possibilistic operators, dual measures of uncertainty, linguistic hedges, etc. is considered but not yet implemented.

SPII-1

In contrast to the tools described so far, *SPII-1* [Martin-Clouaire, Prade 1986]is a language containing an inference engine that has not been arrived at by stripping down an expert system. It focusses particularly on the treatment of uncertainty and on the combination of evidence from different sources. The framework of SPII-1 is possibility theory and the use of dual uncertainty measures. The authors define the difference between imprecision and uncertainty as follows:

> A proposition is imprecise if the value of some implicitly or explicitly involved parameters is (only) partially or roughly specified; a proposition is uncertain if one cannot be absolutely sure it is true or false given the available information. [Martin-Clouaire, Prade 1986, p. 117]

Statements of the form "*X* is *A*" are called *facts* and are represented by a possibility distribution Π_x, represented by the membership function of the fuzzy set $\{\tilde{A}, \mu_{\tilde{A}}(u)\}, \forall u \in U_x$. Complete absence of information about the value of x in U_x is represented by

$$\Pi_x(u) = 1$$

Composite information of the type "*X* is *A* and *X* is *B*" is represented as "*X* is *A* and *B*," that is

$$\Pi_x = \mu_{\tilde{A} \cap \tilde{B}}$$

where $\mu_{\tilde{A} \cap \tilde{B}} = \min(\mu_{\tilde{A}}, \mu_{\tilde{B}})$.

Uncertainty (lack of confidence) of the fact "X is A" interpreted as doubt about whether x belongs to the support of $\tilde{A}$, and it is estimated by $(1 - \beta)$. Hence the combination of uncertainty and imprecision is modelled as:

$$\Pi_x(u) = \max(\mu_{\tilde{A}}(u), \beta) \qquad \forall u \in U_x \tag{7.36}$$

This is illustrated in figure 7-21.

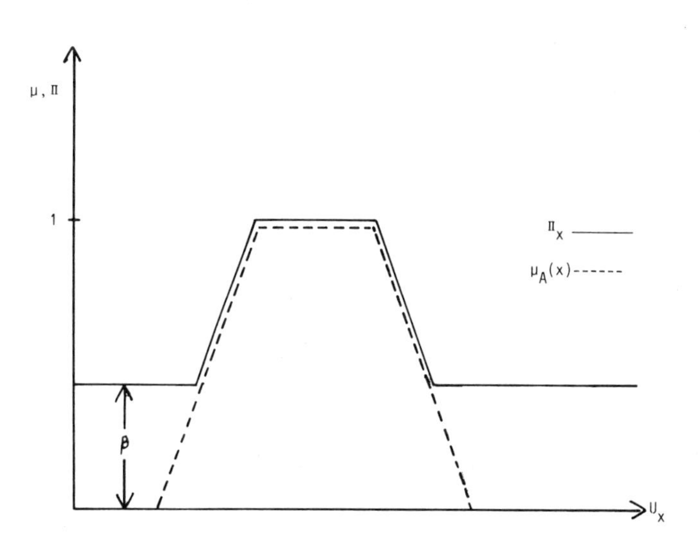

Figure 7-21: Combination of imprecision and uncertainty.

Equation (7.36) says that there is a possibility equal to β that the value of x lies outside the support of $\tilde{A}$. (The reader is referred to definition 7.5 and to example 7.11.) On this basis, the above could also be expressed as: The certainty (necessity) of "X is A" is taken to be the impossibility of the opposite alternative, which is $(1 - \beta)$.

Let us now turn to *rules*: An if-then rule is called *imprecise* if it includes fuzzy sets. "If x is A then y is B" is either interpreted as a relation between the value of x and the value of y and is modelled as a conditional possibility distribution or it is considered as a conjunction of several elementary conditions. This rule is called *uncertain* if one is not completely sure that "y is B" is true whenever "x is A" is true. The authors of SPII-1 follow the basic ideas described earlier under the heading of "Qualification" and use dual uncertainty measures as follows.

Assuming that A and B are crisp one could evaluate first the degree to which "X is A" has to be true in order that "Y is B" can be considered true, and second the necessity that "X is A" be true for "Y is B" to be true also. This corresponds to determining the degree to which the first statement has to be false in order to render the second false also.

If one casts this information into the form

$$N(\text{"If } x \text{ is } A \text{ then } y \text{ is } B\text{"}) \geq a \qquad a \in [0,1]$$

and

$$N(\text{"If } x \text{ is not } A \text{ then } y \text{ is not } B\text{"}) \geq a' \qquad a' \in [0,1]$$

N stands for necessity—see (7.27)–(7.30), then the rule "If x is A then y is B" can be expressed by the conditional possibility distribution:

$$\Pi_{x|y}(v,u) = \begin{cases} 1 & \text{if } u \in A,\ v \in B \\ 1 - a & \text{if } u \in A,\ v \notin B \\ 1 - a' & \text{if } u \notin A,\ v \in B \\ 1 & \text{if } u \in A,\ v \notin B \end{cases} \qquad \text{for } u \in U,\ v \in V \qquad (7.37)$$

Let p stand for "x is A" and q for "y is B," $(p \rightarrow q)$ stands for "if p then q."

Then the following reasoning pattern can be established [Martin-Clouaire, Prade 1986, p. 123]:

$$\begin{array}{l} N(p \rightarrow q) \geq a \\ N(p \rightarrow q) \geq a' \\ N(p) \geq b, \operatorname{Pos}(p) \leq b' \quad \text{with} \quad \max(1-b,b') = 1 \\ \hline N(q) \geq \min(a,b), \operatorname{Pos}(q) \leq \max(1-a',b') \end{array} \tag{7.38}$$

The generalized modus ponens (still for crisp p and q!) yields a possibility distribution for $\tilde{B}'$:

$$\mu_{\tilde{B}'}(v) = \begin{cases} \max(1-a',b') & \text{if } v \in B \\ 1-\min(a,b) & \text{if } v \notin B \end{cases}$$

If A and B are fuzzy sets rather than crisp sets the generalized modus ponens (see example 7.4) is used and the membership function of $\tilde{B}'$ is computed from those of $\tilde{A}$, $\tilde{A}'$, and $\tilde{B}$ by

$$\mu_{\tilde{B}'}(v) = \sup_{u \in U} \min(\mu_{\tilde{A}'}(u), \Pi_{y|x}(v,u)) \qquad \text{for } v \in V \tag{7.39}$$

For these computations, an especially efficient technique is used [Martin-Clouaire 1984]. Uncertainty in this case is also expressed as dual measures.

The inference engine of SPII-1, which runs on a Bull-DPS8 computer, is controlled by a backward-chaining mechanism and uses three kinds of rules:

1. rules to handle imprecision expressed as possibility distributions,
2. rules that focus on uncertainty of crisp constituents of the rules and which determine dual measures of uncertainty, and
3. hybrid rules which have some imprecise (fuzzy) components in their condition part, but only crisp (precise) components in the conclusion part.

In the hybrid rules the b_k and b'_k being the b's of the kth condition in (7.38) are computed as the necessity and possibility that the condition is satisfied by the fact against which it is matched. According to [Zadeh 1978] and [Dubois, Prade 1980] this is done via

$$\begin{aligned} N(\tilde{A};\tilde{A}') &= \inf_{u \in U} \max(\mu_{\tilde{A}}(u) \qquad 1-\mu_{\tilde{A}'}(u)) =: b_k \\ \operatorname{Pos}(\tilde{A},\tilde{A}') &= \sup_{u \in U} \min(\mu_{\tilde{A}}(u), \mu_{\tilde{A}'}(u) =: b'_k \end{aligned} \tag{7.40}$$

Uncertainty of combined results q_i with $N(q)_i$ and $\operatorname{Pos}(q)_i$ is computed by applying (7.39) to the rules of type 2 or 3, which yields

$$N = 1 - \frac{1 - \max_i N(q)_i}{\max\left\{\min_i (1 - N(q)_i), \min_i \operatorname{Pos}(q)_i\right\}}$$

$$\operatorname{Pos} = \frac{\min_i \operatorname{Pos}(q)_i}{\max\left\{\min_i (1 - N(q)_i), \min_i \operatorname{Pos}(q)_i\right\}} \tag{7.41}$$

Obviously SPII-1 cannot yet handle all possible combinations of imprecision and uncertainty, but the treatment of cases that are manageable is quite satisfactory. To illustrate the power of the system we present an abbreviated and slightly modified example from Martin-Clouaire, Prade [1986]:

Example 7.13

In hiring personell, the suitability of applicants for certain jobs has to be evaluated. Table 7-8 lists the rules of SPII-1 type in a small fictitious knowledge base. Of these rules, rule 1 is of type 3 (hybrid), rules 6 through 11 are of type 2 (uncertain), and the others are of type 1 (fuzzy). All italicized expressions are represented by possibility distributions with the support [0,20] corresponding to the grading scale. Rules of type 2 and 3 include in brackets the dual uncertainty measures.

Figure 7-22 shows the hierarchy modelling the relationships between the various evaluation criteria. The arcs correspond to rules, and the nodes to resulting subcriteria (subjective categorise). Whether a conjunctive or disjunctive combination of rules is requested is shown for each node.

Consider a candidate with the following characteristics [see Martin-Clouaire, Prade 1986, p. 127]:

- It is almost certain (.8) that his education is ok.
- He has achieved a score approximately between 11 and 14 in the intelligence test.
- His spoken language is rated rather good.
- His written language is rather poor.
- His working experience is definitely (1,1) ok.
- It seems possible (0,.6) that he is prepared to adapt himself to the working conditions.
- He is certainly (1,1) sportive.
- He has almost no (0,.2) artistic skills.

Table 7-8: Rules in knowledge base

r1	If she/he has received an appropriate education and her/his tests result is *acceptable* then she/he definitely has the general aptitudes to the job (1.,1.)
r2	If her/his score in the intelligence test is *approximately between 10 and 14* and her/his score in the language test is *approximately between 6 and 9* then her/his tests result is considered as *rather poor*
r3	If her/his score in the intelligence test is *approximately greather than 14* and her/his score in the language test is *approximately between 6 and 9* then her/his test result is considered as *good*
r4	If her/his score in the intelligence test is *approximately between 10 and 14* and her/his score in the language test is *approximately greater than 9* then her/his test result is considered as *satisfactory*
r5	If her/his score in the intelligence test is *approximately greater than 14* and her/his score in the language test is *approximately greater than 9* then her/his tests result is considered as *excellent*
r6	If her/his work experience is OK and her/his adaptability is OK then she/he has the fundamental aptitudes (0.2,0.7)
r7	If she/he has the fundamental aptitudes then she/he has the required quality for the job (1,1)
r8	If she/he has manual skills then she/he has some special aptitudes
r9	If she/he is sportive then she/he has some special aptitudes (0.7,0.5)
r10	If she/he has artistic skills then she/he has some special aptitudes (0.8,0.0)
r11	If she/he has some special aptitudes then she/he has the required quality for the job (0.7,0.0)
r12	If her/his score in the spoken language test is *approximately between 6 and 9* and her/his score in the written language test is *acceptable* then her/his score in the language test is considered as *rather poor*
r13	If her/his score in the spoken language test is *acceptable* and her/his score in the written language test is *acceptable* then her/his score in the language test is considered as *good*
r14	If her/his score in the spoken language test is *acceptable* and her/his score in the written language test is *approximately between 6 and 9* then her/his score in the language test is considered as *satisfactory*.

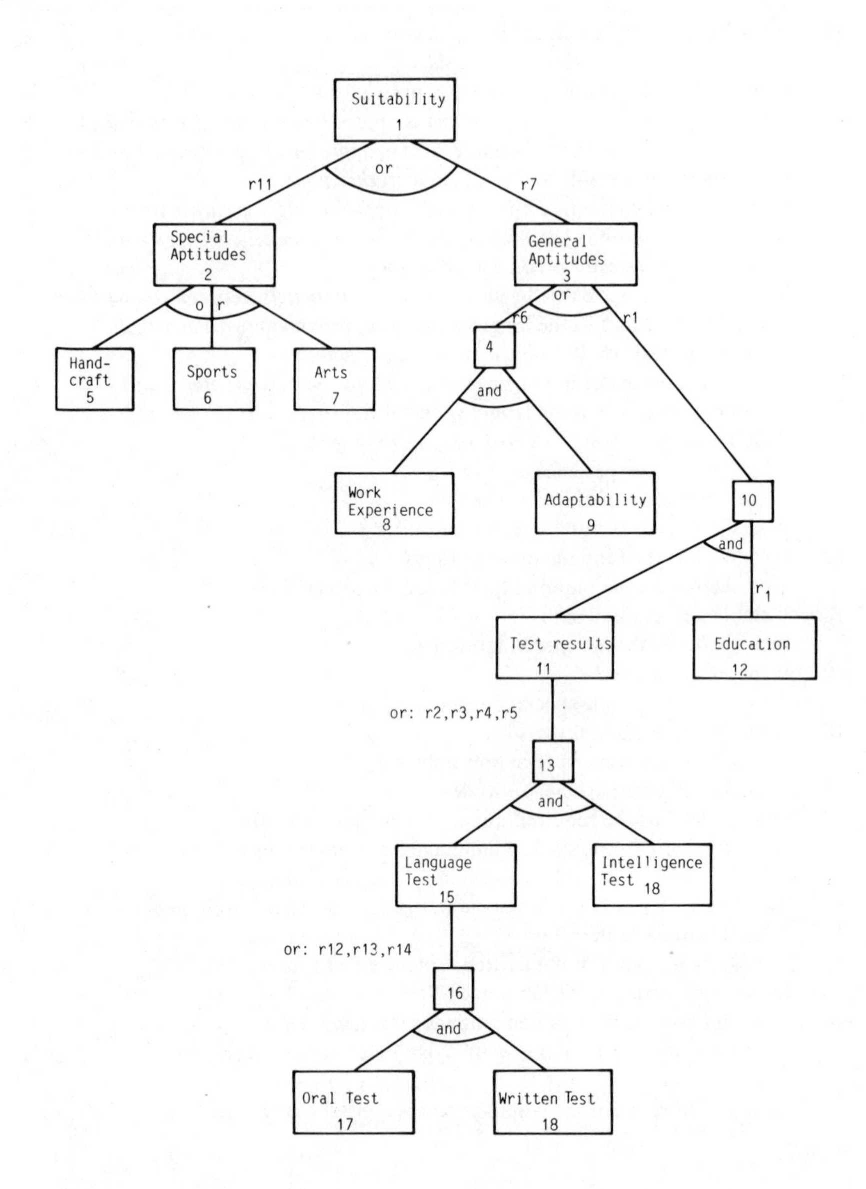

Figure 7-22: Evaluation Hierarchy.

SPII-1 would then, for instance, argue as follows:

Node 15: The grade in the language test is approximately between 10 and 14 (obtained by combining the outcomes from r12, r13, r14).

Node 11: The grade in the test results (summary of language and intelligence test results) is approximately between 10 and 14 (obtained by combining the outcomes from r2, r3, r4, r5).

Node 3: There is suggestive evidence (.5 1) that the candidate has the fundamental aptitudes (this conclusion is obtained by combining the uncertainties (.6 1) and (0 .8) coming from r1 and r6 respectively).

Node 2: There is rather strong evidence (.7 1) that the candidate has some special aptitudes (this conclusion is obtained by combining the uncertainties (0 1) and (.7 1) coming from r10 and r9 respectively).

Node 1: There is rather strong evidence (.7 1) that the global quality of the candidate is ok (this conclusion is obtained by combining the uncertainties (.7 1) and (.5 1) coming from r11 and r7 respectively).

The reader should realize the similarity and the difference between figure 7-20 and figure 6-30. While the former represents a purely possibilistic aggregation (min/max) including measures of uncertainty, the latter shows the aggregation using the nonpossibilistic "compensatory-and" and assuming full credibility of input data and rules.

SLOP

The system *SLOP*, like SPII-1, has been developed as a tool for designing expert systems and shells in which uncertainty plays an important part. Support logic programming generalizes logic programming so that various forms of uncertainty can be included. In this system a conclusion does not logically follow from some axioms but is supported to a certain degree by evidence. The negation of the conclusions is also supported to a certain degree, and the two supports do not necessarily add up to one. Thus, as in SPII-1, dual measures of uncertainty are used in SLOP. They are interpreted in a different way and the uncertainty calculus differs from the one described above for SPII-1.

Baldwin [1986] calls his dual measures the "support pair" of which the first number provides "a necessary support" and the second number a "possible support" for a statement to be true.

A support logic program is a set of program clauses. A clause is of the form

$$A\ :\ -B1, B2, \ldots, Bn\ :\ [Sn,Sp]$$

where A is an atom and $B1, \ldots, Bn$ are literals. A literal is a positive or negative atom. An atom is of the form ⟨predicate_name⟩(⟨argument⟩*). This should be understood as a Prolog clause with the addition of the support pair $[Sn,Sp]$. It can be given the following interpretation. For each assignment of each variable occuring in the clause "if $B1, B2, \ldots, Bn$ are all true," A is necessarily supported to degree Sn and NOT A is necessarily supported to degree $(1 - Sp)$. Sn and Sp are called the necessary and possible supports respectively of A given $B1, \ldots, Bn$ true. They are thus conditional supports and satisfy the constraint

$$Sn + (1 - Sp) \leq 1$$

$(Sp - Sn)$ measures the unsureness in support of the rule pair

$$\{A\ :\ -B1, \ldots, Bn;\ \text{NOT}\ A\ :\ -B1, \ldots, Bn\}$$

A is known as the rule head and $(B1, B2, \ldots, Bn)$ as the body of the clause. In the case when the support pair is [1,1], the clause is an ordinary Prolog clause and is interpreted as follows. In order to prove A, the conjunction $(B1, B2, \ldots, Bn)$ must be proved.

If the body of the clause is empty we have a unit clause, represented as

$$A\ :\ [Sn,Sp]$$

This has the following procedural interpretation. For each assignment of each variable A is necessarily supported to degree Sn and NOT A is necessarily supported to degree $(1 - Sp)$. Again the constraint

$$Sn + (1 - Sp) \leq 1$$

is satisfied and $(Sp - Sn)$ measures the unsureness associated with the support for the pair

$$\{A;\ \text{NOT}\ A\}$$

In probabilistic terms, if $Sn = Sp$ then the support can be interpreted as a probability. Furthermore, if we assume that the probability of a fact lies somewhere in the interval $[a,b]$, then we can put $Sn = a$ and $Sp = b$.

SLOP also allows disjunctions of atoms in the body of the evidence. For example the body of the clause

$$A\ :\ -B1;\ B2\ :\ [Sn,Sp]$$

is interpreted as $B1$ OR $B2$ and $B1$, $B2$ can be a conjunction, disjunction, or mixture of atoms. Thus this clause is interpreted as providing a necessary support to A of Sn and a necessary support to NOT A of $(1 - Sp)$ if $B1$ or $B2$ is true.

It should be observed that the sum of the necessary supports for an atom and its negation do not necessarily add up to 1. The necessary support for the negation of an atom is not determined from the necessary support of the atom. Instead, the necessary support for NOT A is (1 − the possible support for A) and the possible support for NOT A is (1 − the necessary support for A). We thus have

IF

$$P : -Q : [Sn, Sp]$$

THEN

$$\text{nec\_sup}(P|Q) = Sn; \ \text{pos\_sup}(P|Q) = Sp$$

$$\text{nec\_sup}(\text{NOT } P|Q) = 1 - Sp; \ \text{pos\_sup}(P|Q) = 1 - Sn$$

where Q is the conjunction, disjunction, or mixture of atomic formulae and

IF

$$P : [Sn, Sp]$$

THEN

$$\text{nec\_sup}(P) = Sn; \ \text{pos\_sup}(P) = Sp$$

$$\text{nec\_sup}(\text{NOT } P) = 1 - Sp; \ \text{pos\_sup}(\text{NOT } P) = 1 - Sn$$

We can further state that

$$\text{nec\_sup}(P \text{ OR NOT } P) = 1; \ \text{nec\_sup}(P \text{ AND NOT } P) = 0$$

A further form of knowledge representation is allowed in the support logic programming system. A pair of statements of the form

$$P : -Q : [S1n, S1p]$$

is allowed and these statements are processed together by the system. This is analogous to providing the conditional probabilities $\Pr(P|Q)$ and $\Pr(P|\text{NOT } Q)$ for use in the equation

$$\Pr(P) = \Pr(P|Q) \cdot \Pr(Q) + \Pr(P|\text{NOT } Q) \cdot \Pr(\text{NOT } Q)$$

The determination of the support pairs for conjunctions and disjunctions of statements as well as the determination of those pairs when combining supports from different proof paths is achieved in a very efficient way using a method that ressembles the stepping-stone algorithm commonly employed when solving transportation models. The results are then cast into rules for support logic programming. Regrettably the scope of this book does not allow detailed presentation of the interesting methods of SLOP. The reader is referred in this respect to Baldwin [1986] or Baldwin and Monk [1986]. We do, however, include the following features as useful in characterizing SLOP.

1. Any clause that does not contain a pair of supports is understood by the system to have a support pair [1,1]. Likewise, any fact not in the knowledge base is understood by the system to have a support pair [0,1], and is treated accordingly.

2. It is assumed that the same calculus is applicable whether the uncertainty in the support for a given conclusion arises from fuzzy imprecision or from stochastic uncertainty due to a lack of information. The algorithm for determining the support pairs will be different for these two cases. Once the measures of uncertainty are given, their source is considered to be irrelevant. They are both regarded as inducing an uncertainty in the truth of a proposition. SLOP can cope with nonmonotonic logic.

3. SLOP consists of an interpreter and a translator. The interpreter runs support logic programs; the translator compiles these programs into pure Prolog programs which can then be run directly by Prolog. The translated programs are much faster so that the interpreter should be used for program development and the working version then translated. Any Prolog statement can be used with the SLOP interpreter, including the cut, negation by failure, disjunction, etc. The SLOP negation and disjunction are different from those of Prolog. For example, the negation in SLOP is not negation by failure. In SLOP if a fact is not in the knowledge base, a support pair [0,1] representing uncertainty is returned to the system. A closed world is therefore not assumed.

4. The system is part of the FRIL system [Baldwin 1985] which contains support logic in addition to PROLOG and a fuzzy relational inference mechanism. FRIL is very flexible system and is written in C for easy portability.

Hybrid Systems

The term *hybrid systems* in the context of expert systems has been used in a number of ways. Some authors talk of hybrid systems whenever several techniques for knowledge representation are used. Since, however, rules can easily be combined into nets, and frames can as well be associated with nodes of nets as be the "host" for rules, this view is certainly legitimate but rather limited. It might be more relevant from the point of view of the developer of expert systems than from a users viewpoint. We shall use the term hybrid system whenever the ideas of classical decision support systems are merged with those of "classical" expert systems.

It should be realized that expert systems have primarily been developed in the area of artificial intelligence. This area was mainly concerned with rather ill-structured problem-solving areas and studies of the problem-solving process of human beings in the sense of a "General Problem Solver" (GPS). Let us quote from Newell and Simon:

> GPS is a problem solving program developed initially by the authors and J.C. Shaw in 1957. It grew out of the work on LT. GPS's first task environment was the Moore-Anderson logic task, just as we have described it. GPS obtained its name of "general problem solver" because it was the first problem solving program to separate in a clean way a task-independent part of the system containing general problem solving mechanisms from a part of the system containing knowledge of the task environment. It has since been applied to a number of different tasks (Ernst and Newell, 1969) and other programs essentially similar in structure have worked on yet other problems (Quinlan and Hunt, 1968). However, our concern in this chapter is with logic. We will describe GPS in a task-independent way (indeed that is the natural way to describe it), but we will not assess its suitability to other task environments.
>
> GPS operates on problems that can be formulated in term of objects and operators. An operator is something that can be applied to certain objects to produce different objects (as a saw applied to logs produces boards). The objects can be characterized by the features they possess, and by the differences that can be observed between pairs of objects. Operators for a given task may be restricted to apply only to certain kinds of objects; and there may exist operators that apply to several objects as inputs, producing one or more objects as outputs (as the operation of adding two numbers produces a third number, their sum). [Newell, Simon 1972, p. 414]

Operations research, on the other hand, has focused its attention primarily on problems that are well structured; and has developed in the last 40 years very efficient algorithms for well-defined types of problems, such as linear and nonlinear programming, netflow algorithms, combinatorial methods, etc. Ill-structured problems were generally considered to be not solvable by OR methods.

One of the largest areas of potential applications of OR techniques—as well as of AI techniques, since well-structured and ill-structured problems can be found there in abundance—has been to "management information systems" (MIS) as decision aids. Unluckily the communication between the three areas mentioned above has not been very intensive, resulting in a situation in which none of the areas is aware of the potentials of the others. In the recent past this has been recognized by a few authors:

Table 7-9: Expert Systems and—tools using fuzzy set theory

Name	*Application Area*	*Knowledge Repres.; Inference*	*Uncertainty*	*Ref.*
ARIES	Tool	Rules, nets	Multiple truth qualification	[Appelbaum, Ruspini 1985]
CADIAC-2	Medical Diagnosis	Rules	Degrees of Confidence	[Adlassnig et al. 1985]
DIABETO	Treatment of Diabetes	Rules	Poss. Distr.	[Buisson et al. 1985]
EMERGE	Chest Pain Analysis	Rules	Certainty factors (prob.)	[Hudson et al. 1985]
FAGOL	Tool	Fuzzy algorithms	Fuzzy Probabilities	[Alexeyev 1985]
fINDex	Forecasting	Rules Ling. Variables	Ling. Variables	[Whalen, Schott 1985]
FLIP	Tool	Fuzzy Logic	Degree of Belief, weights	[Giles 1980]
FLOPS	Tool Mgt. of imprec. databases	Rules Weakly nonmonotonic	Truth qualific. Ling. Variables	[Buckley et al. 1986]
FRDB	Tool	Fuzzy relations	Qualific. Ling. Var.	[Zemankova Kandel 1985]

FRIL	Tool	Fuzzy relations	Truth Qualific.	[Baldwin 1985 1979]
FUZZY	Tool			[Le Faire 1974]
Fuzzy Planner	Tool	Fuzzy Logic	Truth Qualific.	[Kling 1973]
LPL	Tool	Fuzzy Logic	Truth Qualific.	[Adamo 1980]
METABOL	Tool	PROLOG-Clauses Relations	Plausibility Credibility	[Ernst 1985]
PROSPECTOR 2	Mineral Exploration	Semantic + Inference Networks	Bayes Fuzzy Logic	[Benson 1986]
PRUF	Tool	Poss. Theory App. Reasoning; Rules	Truth, prob., Poss. Qualific.	[Zadeh 1981]
REVEAL	Tool (Mgmt., Planning)	Rules	Poss. Qual.	[Jones 1985]
SAGE	Tool	Rules, others	Fuzzy Logic, Bayes	[Williams 1986]
SLOP	Tool	Support Logic Programming	"Support Pairs"	[Baldwin 1986]
SPERIL-II	Damage assessment	Rules	Dempster, Shafer	[Ogawa et al. 1985]
SPHINX	Medical Diagnosis	Trees, rules	Similarity Index, Uncertainty Interval	[Fieschi et al. 1982]
SPII-1	Tool	Rules	Necessity, Possibility	[Martin-Clouaire Prade 1986]
TAIGER	Tool	Rules	Necessity, Possibility	[Farreny et al. 1986]
VLSI	Hardware Tool	Fuzzy Logic, Rules	Certainty factors	[Togai, Watanabe 1986]

The needs of managers require two main features of expert systems: a sophisticated data base management system (D.B.M.S.) and a knowledge base as an expert model of decision policies. The design of expert systems, if meant to be useful for managers, has to overlap four fields of investigation:

— relational D.B.M.S., with regard to inferential capabilities of relational data models;
— approximate reasoning, in order to handle the fuzzy environment of decision making in the firms by means of a knowledge model;
— relational deductive data base systems, in order to describe data definition rules with the same inferential formalism as that of the decision rules described in the knowledge base;
— management decision systems, in order to handle the complexity of coordination and control processes in the firm, particularly at top decision levels. [Ernst 1982, p. 197]

Recently, several expert systems have been developed that use large mathematical packages for a portion of the problem solving task. Several examples of such systems are ELAS (Weiss et al, 1982) which uses mathematical models for oil exploration, RX (Blum, 1983) which uses a statistics package for medical data, and SACON (Bennett and Engelmore, 1979) which uses mathematical models for structural analysis. By combining mathematical techniques with the AI heuristics, these expert systems are able to efficiently represent the various aspects of their problem domains. In addition, they can make use of the highly developed mathematical packages already developed.

These hybrid expert systems use heuristics to focus control, set default values, and provide interpretation and explanation of their numerical results. The mathematical techniques are used to efficiently simulate complex phenomena, correlate facts, and analyze numerical data. Such expert systems can benefit from the many years of research and development of mathematical models for their problem domains. One of the most obvious first applications of expert systems to OR would be in this spirit. [Kastner, Hong 1984, p. 291]

From this point of view the design of large relational data bases that can effectively handle uncertainty [e.g., Zemankova-Leech, Kandel 1984; Buckles, Petry 1982], the development of respective retrieval systems [Buell 1982; Chang, Ke 1978], and the integration of these with efficient OR techniques and AI approaches to attack ill-structured problems in a flexible way seem to be most appropriate and desirable. These are what we call "hybrid systems."

We will conclude this chapter by citing the opinion of two practitioners:

Although the field of expert systems research is only a few years old, already a surprisingly large number of high quality performance systems have been developed. There are now available several domain independent expert system frameworks so that the time and effort to develop a new application has been greatly reduced.

Expert systems are becoming a potent new thrust in AI and major efforts are underway by universities, industry, and government to capitalize on its potentials. Expert systems are seen as an important cornerstone of a new generation in computer technology allowing one to provide computer problem solvers in areas that have resisted traditional automation. Expert systems are achieving high quality performance in problem solving areas too vague, ill-structured, or too complex for complete formal mathematical modelling.

There are still largely unexplored applications for expert systems in management and operational research. The combination of new AI techniques with more traditional mathematics will probably produce a new generation of high quality performance expert systems. The area of operational research is still largely untapped and it is only a matter of time before expert systems will be developed for traditional OR application areas. [Kastner, Hong 1984, p. 291]

Table 7-9: indicates the present state of developments in this area. It is restricted to expert systems using fuzzy sets and it does not claim to be exhaustive.

Bibliography

Ackoff, R. [1962]. Scientific Method: Optimizing Applied Research Decisions. New York.

Adamo, J.M. [1980]. Fuzzy decision trees. *FSS* 4, 207–219.

Adlassnig, K.-P. [1982]. A survey on medical diagnosis and fuzzy subsets in: Gupta, Sanchez (eds.) 1982, 203–277.

Adlassnig, K.P., Kolarz, G. [1982]. CADIAG-2: Computer-assisted medical diagnosis using fuzzy subsets in: Gupta, Sanchez (eds.) 1982, 219–248.

Adlassnig, K.-P., Kolarz, G., Scheithauer, W. [1985]. Present state of the medical expert system CADIAG-2. *Med. Inform.* 24, 13–20.

Ackoff, R.L. [1978]. *The Art of Problem Solving.* New York.

Alexeyev, A.V. [1985]. Fuzzy algorithms execution software: The FAGOL-System in: Kacprzyk, Yager (eds.) 1985, 289–300.

Alsina, C. [1985]. On a family of connectives for fuzzy sets. *FSS* 16, 231–235.

Anderson, J., Bandler, W., Kohout, L.J., Trayner, C. [1985]. The design of a fuzzy medical expert system in: Gupta et al. (eds.) 1985, 689–704.

Appelbaum, L., Ruspini, E.H. [1985]. ARIES: An approximate reasoning inference engine in: Gupta et al. (eds.) 1985, 745–755.

Arrow, K.J. [1951]. *Social Choice and Individual Values.* New York.

Asai, K., Tanaka, H., Okuda, T. [1975]. Decision-making and its goal in a fuzzy environment in: Zadeh et al. (eds.) 1975, 257–277.

Aubin, J.-P. [1981]. Cooperative fuzzy games *Math. Op. Res.* 6, 1–13.

Aubin, J.-P. [1984]. Cooperative fuzzy games: The static and the dynamic point of view in: Zimmermann, H.-J., et al. 1984, 407–428.

Baas, M.S., Kwakernaak, H. [1977]. Rating and ranking of multiple-aspects alternatives using fuzzy sets. *Automatica* 13, 47–58.

Backer, E. [1978]. Cluster analysis formalized as a process of fuzzy identification based on fuzzy relations. Rep. IT-78-15, Delft University.

Baldwin, J.F. [1979]. A new approach to approximate reasoning using a fuzzy logic. *FSS* 2, 309–325.

Baldwin, J.F. [1982]. An automated fuzzy reasoning algorithm in: Yager (ed.) 1982, 169–195.

Baldwin, J.F. [1985]. A knowledge engineering fuzzy inference language—FRIL in: Kacprzyk, Yager (eds.) 1985, 253–269.

Baldwin, J.F. [1986]. Support logic programming. *Int. J. Gen. Systems* 1, 73–104.

Baldwin, J.F. [1987]. Evidential support logic programming. *FSS*, forthcoming.

Baldwin, J.F., Baldwin, P., Brown, S. [1985]. A natural language interface for FRIL in: Kacprzyk, Yager (eds.) 1985, 270–279.

Baldwin, J.F., Guild, N.C.F. [1979]. Comparison of fuzzy sets on the same decision space. *FSS* 2, 213–232.

Baldwin, J.F., Guild, N.C.F. [1980]. Feasible algorithms for approximate reasoning using fuzzy logic. *FSS* 3, 225–251.

Baldwin, J.F., Monk, M.R.M. [1986]. SLOP—a system for support logic programming. ITRC research report, University of Bristol.

Baldwin, J.F., Pilsworth, B.W. [1980]. Axiomatic approach to implications for approximate reasoning with fuzzy logic. *FSS* 3, 193–219.

Baldwin, J.F., Pilsworth, B.W. [1982]. Dynamic programming for fuzzy systems with fuzzy environment. *JMAA* 85, 1–23.

Baldwin, J.F., Whiter, A.M. [1982]. *PI-Fuzzy: Fuzzy Logic Based on Possibility Measures.* Bristol.

Barr, A., Feigenbaum, E.A., eds. [1981–1982]. *The Handbook of Artificial Intelligence.* Los Altos (Calif.), 1981 (vol. 1), 1982 (vols. 2 and 3).

Beckmann, M.J. [1968]. *Dynamic Programming of Economic Decisions.* Berlin, Heidelberg, New York.

Behringer, F.A. [1977]. Lexicographic quasiconcave multiobjective programming. *Zeitschr. f. Op. Res.* 21, 103–116.

Behringer, F.A. [1981]. A simplex based algorithm for the lexicographically extended linear maxmin problem. *EJOR* 7, 274–283.

Bellman, R.E. [1957]. *Dynamic Programming.* Princeton.

Bellman, R., Giertz, M. [1973]. On the analytic formalism of the theory of fuzzy sets. *Inf. Sciences* 5, 149–156.

Bellman, R.E., Zadeh, L.A. [1970]. Decision-making in a fuzzy environment. *Manag. Sci.* 17, B141–164.

Bennett, J.S., Engelmore, R.S. [1979]. SACON: A knowledge based consultant for structural analysis. *Proc. 6th Int. Conf. on AI*, Tokyo 1979, 47–49.

Benson, I. [1986]. Prospector: An expert system for mineral exploration in: Mitra, G. (ed.) 1986, 17–26.

Bezdek, J.C., Spillman, B., Spillman, R. [1978–1979]. A fuzzy relation space for group decision theory. *FSS* 1 (1978), 255–268; *FSS* 2 (1979), 5–14.

Bhat, K.V.S. [1982]. On the notion of fuzzy consensus. *FSS* 8, 285–289.

Blin, J.M. [1974]. Fuzzy relations in group decision theory. *Cyb.* 4, 17–22.

Blum, R.L. [1983]. Representation of empirically derived causal relationships. *Proc. 8th Int. Conf. on AI* 1983, 268–271.

Bonissone, P.P. [1979a]. A pattern recognition approach to the problem of linguistic analysis in systems analysis. *Proc. IEEE, Int. Conf. Cyb. and Soc.*, Denver 1979.

Bonissone, P.P. [1979b]. The problem of linguistic approximation in systems analysis. Ph.D. thesis, DEECS, UCB, Berkeley.
Borisov, A., Krumberg, O. [1983]. A theory of possibility for decision making. *FSS* 9, 13–23.
Bortolan, G., Degani, R. [1985]. A review of some methods for ranking fuzzy subsets. *FSS* 15, 1–21.
Bouchon, B. [1985]. On the forms of reasoning in expert systems in: Gupta et al. (eds.) 1985, 341–354.
Brown, J.S., Burton, R.R., Bell, A.G. [1975]. SOPHIE: a step toward creating a reactive learning environment. *IJMMS* 7, 675–696.
Buchanan, B.G., Feigenbaum, E.A. [1978]. Dendral and meta-dendral. *Artificial Int.* 11, 5–24.
Buchanan, B., Shortliffe, E. [1984]. Use of MYCIN inference engine in: Buchanan, Shortliffe (eds.), 1st printing, 295–301.
Buchanan, B., Shortliffe, E., eds. [1985]. *Rule-based Expert Systems*, 2nd printing (1st printing 1984). Reading, MA.
Buckles, B.P., Petry, F.E. [1982]. A fuzzy representation of data for relational data bases. *FSS* 7, 213–266.
Buckles, B.P., Petry, F.E. [1985]. Query languages for fuzzy databases in: Kacprzyk, Yager (eds.) 1985, 241–252.
Buckley, J.J. [1983]. Fuzzy programming and the Pareto optimal set. *FSS* 10, 57–63.
Buckley, J.J. [1984a]. The multiple judge multiple criteria ranking problem: A fuzzy set approach. *FSS* 13, 25–37.
Buckley, J.J. [1984b]. Multiple goal non-cooperative conflicts under uncertainty: A fuzzy set approach. *FSS* 13, 107–124.
Buckley, J.J. [1985]. Ranking alternatives using fuzzy numbers. FSS, 15, 21–31.
Buckley, J.J., Siler, W., Tucker, D. [1986]. A fuzzy expert system. *FSS* 20, 1–16.
Buell, D.A. [1982]. An analysis of some fuzzy subset applications to information retrieval system. *FSS* 7, 35–42.
Butnariu, D. [1978]. Fuzzy games: a description of the concept. *FSS* 1, 181–192.
Butnariu, D. [1979]. Solution concepts for n-person fuzzy games in: Gupta, Ragade, Yager (eds.) 1979, 339–360.
Butnariu, D. [1980]. Stability and shapley value for an n-persons fuzzy game. *FSS* 4, 63–72.
Carnap, R. [1946]. *Introduction to Semantics*. Cambridge, MA.
Cayrol, M., Farreny, H., Prade, H. [1982]. Fuzzy pattern matching. *Kybernetes* 11, 103–116.
Chanas, S. [1983]. The use of parametric programming in fuzzy linear programming. *FSS* 11, 243–251.
Chanas, S., Kolodziejczyk, W., Machzj, A. [1984]. A fuzzy approach to the transportation problem. *FSS* 13, 211–222.
Chang, C.L. [1975]. Interpretation and execution of fuzzy programs in: Zadeh et al. (eds.) 1975, 191–218.
Chang, S.K., Ke, J.S. [1978]. Database skeleton and its application to fuzzy query translations. *IEEE Trans. on Softw. Eng. SE-4*, 31–43.

Chang, S.S.L. [1975]. On risk and decision making in a fuzzy environment in: Zadeh et al. (eds.) 1975, 219–226.

Chankong, V., Haimes, Y.Y. [1983]. *Multiobjective Decision Making.* New York, Amsterdam, Oxford.

Charnes, A., Cooper, W.W. [1961]. *Management Models and Industrial Applications of Linear Programming.* New York.

Chen, Shan-Huo [1985]. Ranking fuzzy numbers with maximizing set and minimizing set. *FSS* 17, 113–130.

Cheng, Y.Y.M., McInnis, B. [1980]. An algorithm for multiple attribute, multiple alternative decision problems based on fuzzy sets with application to medical diagnosis. *IEEE Trans. SMC* 10, 645–650.

Cronbach, L.J. [1950]. Further evidence on response sets and test designs. *Educ. Psychol. Meas.* 10, 3–31.

Churchman, C.W. [1961]. *Prediction and Optimal Decision.* Englewood Cliffs, NJ.

Czogala, E., Gottwald, S., Pedrycz, W. [1983]. Logical connectives of probabilistic sets. *FSS* 10, 299–308.

Dempster, A.P. [1967]. Upper and lower probabilities induced by a multi-valued mapping. *Ann. Math. Stat.* 38, 325–339.

Diederich, G.W., Messick, S.J., Tucker, L.R. [1957]. A general least squares solution for successive intervals. *Psychometrika* 22, 159–173.

Dimitrov, V. [1983]. Group choice under fuzzy information. *FSS* 9, 25–39.

Di Nola, A., Pedrycz, W., Sessa, S. [1985]. Fuzzy relation equations and algorithms of inference mechanism in expert systems in: Gupta et al. (eds.) 1985, 355–367.

Dombi, J. [1982]. Basic concepts for a theory of evaluation: The aggregative operator. *EJOR* 10, 282–293.

Dompere, K.K. [1982]. The theory of fuzzy decisions. in: Gupta, Sanchez (eds.) 1982, 365–380.

Dresher, M. [1961]. *Games of Strategy.* Englewood Cliffs, NJ.

Dubois, D., Prade, H. [1979]. Decision making under fuzziness in: Gupta, Ragade, Yager (eds.) 1979, 279–303.

Dubois, D., Prade, H. [1980]. *Fuzzy Sets and Systems.* New York.

Dubois, D., Prade, H. [1982]. On several representations of an uncertain body of evidence in: Gupta, Sanchez (eds.) 1982, 167–182.

Dubois, D., Prade, H. [1983]. Ranking of fuzzy numbers in the setting of possibility theory in: *Inf. Science* 30, 183–224.

Dubois, D., Prade, H. [1984a]. Criteria aggregation and ranking of alternatives in the frame of fuzzy set theory in: Zimmermann et al. 1984, 209–240.

Dubois, D., Prade, H. [1984b]. Fuzzy logics and the generalized modus ponens revisited. *Cybern. Syst. ISL* 293–331.

Dubois, D., Prade, H. [1985a]. Evidence measures based on fuzzy information. *Automatica* 21, 547–562.

Dubois, D., Prade, H. [1985b]. A survey of set-functions for the assessment of evidence in: Kacprzyk, Yager (eds.) 1985, 176–188.

Dyer, J.S. [1972/73]. Interactive goal programming. *Manag. Sci.* 19, 62–70.

Ebert, R.J., Mitchell, T.R. [1975]. *Organizational Decision Processes.* New York.

Efstathiou, J. [1984]. Practical multi-attribute decision-making and fuzzy set theory in: Zimmermann et al. 1984, 307–322.

Efstathiou, J., Rajkovic, V. [1979]. Multiattribute decision making using a fuzzy heuristic approach *IEEE Transactions SMC* 9, 326–333.

Efstathiou, J., Tong, R.M. [1982]. Ranking fuzzy sets: A decision theoretic approach. *IEEE Trans. SMC* 12, 655–659.

Enta, Y. [1982]. Fuzzy decision theory in: Yager (ed.) 1982, 439–450.

Ernst, C.J. [1982]. An approach to management expert systems using fuzzy logic in: Yager (ed.) 1982, 196–203.

Ernst, C.J. [1985]. A logic programming metalanguage for expert systems in: Kacprzyk, Yager (eds.) 1985, 280–288.

Ernst, E. [1982]. *Fahrplanerstellung und Umlaufdisposition im Containerschiffsverkehr* (Diss. Aachen). Frankfurt/M., Bern.

Ernst, G.W., Newell, A. [1969]. GPS: A Case Study in Generality and Problem Solving. New York.

Eshrag, F., Mamdani, E.H. [1981]. A general approach to linguistic approximation in: Mamdani, Gaines (eds.) 1981, 187–196.

Esogbue, A.O., Bellman, R.E. [1984]. Fuzzy dynamic programming and its extensions in: Zimmermann et al. 1984, 147–167.

Fabian, C.; Stoica, M. [1984]. Fuzzy integer programming in: Zimmermann et al. (eds.) 1984, 123–132.

Fagan, L. [1978]. Ventilator manager: a program to provide on-line consultative advice in the intensive care unit. Rep. HPP 78-16, Comp. Sc. Dept. Stanford, Sept.

Farkas, J. [1902]. Über die Theorie der einfachen Ungleichungen. *J. f. reine u. ang. Mathematik* 124, 1–27.

Farreny, H., Prade, H., Wyss, E. [1986]. Approximate reasoning in a rule-based expert system using possibility theory: a case study. *Proc. 10th IFIP World Congr.*, Dublin 1986.

Feng, Y.J. [1983]. A method using fuzzy mathematics to solve the vectormaximum problem. *FSS* 9 129–136.

Fieschi, M., Joubert, M., Fieschi, D., Soula, G., Roux, M. [1982]. Sphinx: An interactive system for medical diagnoses aids in: Gupta, Sanchez (eds.) 1982, 269–282.

Fishburn, P.C. [1964]. *Decision and Value Theory*. New York, London, Sydney.

Freeling, A.N.S. [1980]. Fuzzy sets and decision analysis. *IEEE Trans. SMC* 10, 341–354.

Fu, K.S., Ishizuka, M., Yao, J.T.P. [1982]. Application of fuzzy sets in earthquake engineering in: Yager (eds.) 1982, 504–518.

Fung, L.W., Fu, K.S. [1975]. An axiomatic approach to rational decision making in a fuzzy environment in: Zadeh et al. 1975, 227–256.

Gaines, B.R., Shaw, M.L.G. [1985]. Systemic foundations for reasoning in expert systems in: Gupta et al. (eds.) 1985, 271–282.

Gass, S.I. [1964]. *Linear Programming*. New York.

Giles, R. [1979]. A formal system for fuzzy reasoning. *FSS* 2, 233–257.

Giles, R. [1980]. A computer program for fuzzy reasoning *FSS* 4, 221–234.

Gillett, E. [1976]. *Introduction to Operations Research*. New York.

Goglio, S., Miniciardi, R., Puliafuto, P.P., Spinelli, G. [1984]. Multiexpert systems: An application of fuzzy logic. *Int. Symp. on Fuzzy Inf. Proc. and OR*. Cambridge.

Goguen, J.A. [1967]. L-fuzzy sets. *JMAA* 18, 145–174.

Goguen, J.A. [1969]. The logic of inexact concepts. *Synthese* 19, 325–373.

Goodman, I.R., Nguyen, H.T. [1985]. *Uncertainty Models for Knowledge-based Systems*. Amsterdam, New York, Oxford.

Gupta, M.M., Sanchez, E. [1982]. Approximate reasoning in decision analysis Amsterdam, New York, Oxford.

Gupta, M.M., Sanchez, E., eds. [1982]. *Fuzzy Information and Decision Processes*. Amsterdam, New York.

Gupta, M.M., Kandel, A., Bandler, W., Kiszka, J.B. (eds.) [1985]. *Approximate Reasoning in Expert Systems*. Amsterdam, New York, Oxford.

Gupta, M.M., Ragade, R.K., Yager, R.E., eds. [1979]. *Advances in Fuzzy Set Theory and Applications*. Amsterdam, New York.

Haley, P., Kowalski, J., McDermott, J., McWhorter, R. [1983]. PTRANS: A rule-based management assistant. Tech. Rep., Comp. Sc. Dept. Carnegie-Mellon-Univ. Pittsburgh.

Hamacher, H. [1978]. *Über logische Aggregationen nicht binär expliziter Entscheidungskriterien*. Frankfurt/Main.

Hamacher, H., Leberling, H., Zimmermann, H.-J. [1978]. Sensitivity analysis in fuzzy linear programming. *FSS* 1, 269–281.

Hannan, E.L. [1981]. Linear programming with multiple fuzzy goals. *FSS* 6, 235–248.

Harré, R. [1967]. *An Introduction to the Logic of Sciences*. London, Melbourne, Toronto.

Harré, R. [1972]. *The Philosophies of Sciences*. London, Oxford, New York.

Helson, H. [1964]. *Adaption-level Theory*. New York: Harper & Row.

Hirota, K. [1981]. Concepts of probabilistic sets. *FSS* 5, 31–46.

Holroyd, P., et al. [1985]. Developing expert systems for management applications. *Omega* 13, 1–11.

Howard, R.A. [1960]. *Dynamic Programming and Markov Processes*. New York.

Hudson, D.L., Cohen, M.E., Deedwania, P.C. [1985]. Emerge—An expert system for chest pain analysis in: Gupta et al. (eds.) 1985, 705–718.

Hwang, Ch.-L., Masud, A.S. [1979]. *Multiple objective decision making*. Berlin, Heidelberg, New York.

Hwang, Ch.-L., Yoon, K. [1981]. *Multiple Attribute Decision Making*. Berlin, Heidelberg, New York.

Ignizio, J.P., Daniels, S.C. [1983]. Fuzzy multicriteria integer programming via fuzzy generalized. networks *FSS* 10, 261–270.

Ishizuka, M., Fu, K.S., Yao, J.T.P. [1983]. Rule-based damage assessment system for existing structures. *SM-Archives* 8, 99–118.

Jain, R. [1976]. Decision making in the presence of fuzzy variables. *IEEE Trans. SMC*, 698–703.

Jain, R. [1977]. Procedure for multi-aspect decision making using fuzzy sets. *Int. J. Syst. Sci.* 8, 1–7.

Jones, A., Kaufmann, A., Zimmermann, H.-J., eds. [1986]. *Fuzzy Set Theory and*

Applications. Dordrecht, Boston, Lancaster.
Jones, P.L.K. [1986]. REVEAL: Addressing DSS and expert systems in: Mitra (ed.) 1986, 49–58.
Kabbara, G. [1982]. New utilization of fuzzy optimization method in: Gupta, Sanchez (eds.) 1982, 239–246.
Kacprzyk, J. [1978]. Decision making in a fuzzy environment with fuzzy termination time. *FSS* 1, 169–179.
Kacprzyk, J. [1979]. A branch and bound algorithm for the multistage control of a fuzzy system in a fuzzy environment. *Kybernetes* 8, 139–147.
Kacprzyk, J. [1982]. Multistage decision processes in a fuzzy environment: A survey in: Gupta, Sanchez (eds.) 1982, 251–263.
Kacprzyk, J. [1983]. *Multistage Decision-Making Under Fuzziness*. Köln.
Kacprzyk, J., Staniewski, P. [1982]. Long-term inventory policy-making through decision-making models. *FSS* 8, 117–132.
Kacprzyk, J., Yager, R.R., eds. [1985]. *Management Decision Support Systems Using Fuzzy Sets and Posibility Theory*. Köln.
Kahne, S. [1975]. A procedure for optimizing development decisions. *Automatica* 11, 261–269.
Kastner, J.K., Hong, S.J. [1984]. A review of expert systems. *EJOR* 18, 285–292.
Kaufmann, A. [1975]. *Introduction to the Theory of Fuzzy Subsets*. New York, San Francisco, London.
Keeney, R.L., Raiffa, H. [1976]. *Decisions with Multiple Objectives*. New York, Santa Barbara, London.
Kickert, W.J.M. [1978]. *Fuzzy Theories on Decision Making*. Leiden, Boston, London.
Kim, J.B. [1983]. Fuzzy rational choice functions. *FSS* 10, 37–43.
Kling, R. [1973]. Fuzzy planner: Reasoning with inexact concepts in procedural problem solving language. *Cybern*. 4, 105–122.
Kuhn, H.W., Tucker, A.W. [1951]. Nonlinear programming in: J. Neymen (ed.), *Proc. of the 2nd Berkeley Symp. on Math. Stat. and Prob*. 1951.
Kuz'min, V.B., Orchinnikov, S.V. [1980]. Group decisions I: In arbitrary spaces of fuzzy binary relations. *FSS* 4, 53–82. Design of group decisions II: In spaces of partial order fuzzy relations. *FSS* 4, 153–165.
Laarhoven, van, P.J.M., Pedrycz, W. [1983]. A fuzzy extension of Saaty's priority theory. *FSS* 11, 229–241.
Lagomasino, A., Sage, A.P. [1985]. Imprecise knowledge representation in inferential activities in: Gupta et al. (eds.) 1985, 473–498.
Lasker, G.E. (ed.) [1981]. *Applied Systems and Cybernetics*. New York, Oxford, Toronto.
Leberling, H. [1981]. On finding compromise solutions in multicriteria problems using the fuzzy min-operator. *FSS* 6, 105–118.
Leberling, H. [1983]. Entscheidungsfindung bei divergierenden Faktorinteressen und relaxierten Kapazitätsrestriktionen mittels eines unscharfen Lösungsansatzes. *Zeitschr. f. betriebsw. Forschung* 35, 398–419.
Le Faivre, R. [1974]. Fuzzy: a programming language for fuzzy problem solving. Tech. Report 202, Madison, Wisc., Univ. of Wisc. Comp. Sci. Dpt.

Lesmo, L., Saitta, L., Torasso, P. [1982]. Learning of fuzzy production rules for medical diagnosis in: Gupta, Sanchez (eds.), 1982, 249–260.

Little, J.D.C. [1970]. Models and managers: the concept of a decision calculus. *Manag. Sci.* 16, 446–458.

Luce, R.D., Raiffa, H. [1957]. *Games and Decisions.* New York, London, Sydney.

Luce, R.D., Suppes, D. [1965]. Preferences, utility and subjective probability in: R.D. Luce, et al. (eds.) *Handbook of Mathematical Psychology*, vol. III. New York.

Luhandjula, M.K. [1983]. Linear programming under randomness and fuzziness. *FSS* 10, 45–55.

Luhandjula, M.K. [1984]. Fuzzy approaches for multiple objective linear fractional optimization. *FSS* 13, 11–24.

Lusk, E.J. [1982]. Priority assignment: A conditioned sets approach. *FSS* 7, 43–55.

MacCrimmon, K.R. [1974]. Descriptive Aspects of Team Theory; Observation, Communication and Decision Heuristics in Information Systems. Management Science 20, 1323–1334.

Mamdani, E.H., Gaines, B.R., eds. [1981]. *Fuzzy Reasoning and Its Applications.* New York.

Marschak, J., Radner, R. [1972]. Economic Theory of Teams. New Haven.

Martel, J.M., d'Avignon, R., Couillard, J. [1986]. A Fuzzy Outranking Relation in Multicriteria Decision Making. EJOR 25, 258–267.

Martin-Clouaire, R. [1984]. A Fast Generalized Modus Ponens. BUSEFAL 18, 75–82.

Martin-Clouaire, R., Prade, H. [1986]. SPII: A Simple Inference Engine Capable of Accommodating Both Imprecision and Uncertainty in: Mitra (ed.) 1986, 117–131.

McDermott, J. [1982]. A Rule-based Configurer of Computer Systems. Artificial Intelligence 19. Miller, P.L. [1983]. Medical Plan-analysis: The Attending System. Proceedings IJCAI-83, 239–241.

Minsky, M. [1975]. A Framework for Representing Knowledge in: Winston (ed.), 1975.

Mitra, G. (ed.) [1986]. Computer Assisted Decision Making. Amsterdam, New York, Oxford.

Mizumoto, M., Fukami, S., Tanaka, K. [1979]. Some Methods of Fuzzy Reasoning, in Gupta et al. (eds.) 1979, 117–136.

Mizumoto, M., Zimmermann, H.-J. [1982]. Comparison of fuzzy reasoning methods. *FSS* 8, 253–283.

Moscarola, J. [1978]. Multicriteria Decision Aid: Two Applications in Education Management in: Zionts (ed.), 402–423.

Nagel, E. [1969]. *The Structure of Science.* London.

Nakamura, K. [1982]. Quantification of social utilities for multi-aspect decision making. *Policy Inf.* 6, 59–69.

Nakamura, K. [1984]. Some extensions of fuzzy linear programming. *FSS* 14, 211–229.

Negoita, C.V. [1985]. *Expert Systems and Fuzzy Sets.* Menlo Park, CA.

Negoita, C.V., Stefanescu, A.C. [1982]. On fuzzy optimization in: Gupta, Sanchez (eds.) 1982, 247–250.

Nemhauser, G.L. [1966]. *Introduction to Dynamic Programming.* New York, London, Sydney.

Neumann, J. von, Morgenstein, O. [1970]. *Theory of Gamees and Economic Behavior.*

Princeton.
Newell, A., Simon, H.A. [1972]. *Human Problem Solving*. Englewood Cliffs, NJ.
Nilsson, N.J. [1980]. *Principles of Artificial Intelligence*. Palo Alto, CA.
Nojiri, H. [1979]. A model of fuzzy team decision. *FSS* 2, 201–212.
Norman, J.M. [1975]. *Elementary Dynamic Programming*. Southampton.
Norwich, A.M., Turksen, I.B. [1981]. Measurement and scaling of membership functions in: Lasker (ed.) 1981, 2851–2858.
Nurmi, H. [1981a]. A fuzzy solution to a majority voting game. *FSS* 5, 187–198.
Nurmi, H. [1981b]. Approaches to collective decision making with fuzzy preference relations. *FSS* 6, 249–259.
Nurmi, H. [1982]. Imprecise notions in individual and group decision theory. *Stochastica* 6, 283–303.
Oden, G.C. [1977]. Integration of fuzzy logical information. *J. Exp. Psychol.* 106, 565–575.
Ogawa, H., Fu, K.S., Yao, J.T.P. [1985]. SPERIL-II: An expert system for damage assessment of existing structure in: Gupta et al. (eds.) 1985, 731–744.
Orlovsky, S.A. [1977]. On programming with fuzzy constraint sets. *Kybernetes* 6, 197–201.
Orlovsky, S.A. [1978]. Decision making with a fuzzy preference relation. *FSS* 1, 155–167.
Orlovsky, S.A. [1980]. On formulization of a general fuzzy mathematical problem. *FSS* 3, 311–321.
Ostasiewicz, W. [1982]. A new approach to fuzzy programming. *FSS* 7, 139–152.
Owen, G. [1969]. *Game Theory*. Philadelphi, London, Toronto.
Pollitzer, E., Jenkins, J. [1985]. Expert knowledge, expert systems and commercial interests. *Omega* 5, 407–418.
Ponsard, C. [1981]. An application of fuzzy subset theory to the analysis of the consumer's spatial preferences. *FSS* 5, 235–244.
Popper, K. [1959]. *The Logic of Scientific Discovery*. London.
Prade, H. [1982]. Degree of truth: matching statement against reality. *Busefal* 9, 88–92.
Prade, H. [1985]. A computational approach to approximate and plausible reasoning with applications to expert systems. *IEEE Trans. on Patt. An. and Mach. Int.* 7, 260–282.
Quinlain, J.R.; Hunt, E.B. [1968]. A Formal Deductive Problem Solving System. Journal of the ACM 15, 625–646.
Radford, K.J. [1977]. *Complex Decision Problems*. Reston, VA.
Rappaport, A., ed. [1970]. *Information for Decision Making*. Englewood Cliffs, NJ.
Rieger, B.B., ed. [1981]. *Empirical Semantics*. Bochum.
Roberts, R.B., Goldstein, I.P. [1977]. The FRL Manual Memo 409, MIT Artificial Intelligence Laboratory, Cambridge MA.
Robinson, J.A. [1965]. A machine oriented logic based on the resolution principle. *J. ACM* 12, 23–41.
Rödder, W., Zimmermann, H.-J. [1977]. Analyse, Beschreibung und Optimierung von unscharf formulierten Problemen. *Zeitschr. f. Op. Res.* 21, 1–18.
Rödder, W., Zimmermann, H.-J. [1980]. Duality in fuzzy linear programming in: A.V.

Fiacco, K.O. Kortanek (eds.), *Extremal Methods and Systems* Analyses. Berlin, Heidelberg, New York, 415–429.

Rommelfanger, H. [1984]. Entscheidungsmodelle mit Fuzzy-Nutzen. *OR-Proceedings* 1983, Berlin, Heidelberg, 559–567.

Roy, B. [1971]. Problems and methods with multiple objective functions. *Math. Progr.* 1, 239–266.

Roy, B. [1975a]. From optimization to multi-criteria decision aid. Three main operational attitudes in: H. Thiriez, S. Zionts (eds.): *Multiple Criteria Decision Making.* Heidelberg, New York, 1–34.

Roy, B. [1975b]. Why multicriteria decision aid may not fit in with the assessment of unique criterion in: M. Zeleney (ed.), *Multiple Criteria Decision Making.* Heidelberg, New York, 283–286.

Roy, B. [1976]. Partial preference analysis and decision-aid: the fuzzy outranking relation concept in: *SEMA.* Paris.

Roy, B. [1977a]. A conceptual framework for a prescriptive theory of "decision aid." *TIMS Stud. Manage. Sci.* 6, 179–210.

Roy, B. [1977b]. Partial preference analysis and decision aid: The fuzzy outranking relation concept in: O.E. Bell, R.L. Keeney, H. Raiffaa, *Conflicting Objectives in Decisions,* Chichester.

Roy, B. [1980]. Selektieren, Sortieren und Ordnen mit Hilfe von Prävalenzrelationen. *Zeitschr. f. betriebsw. Forschung* 32, 465–496.

Roy, B., Vincke, Ph. [1981]. Multicriteria analysis: survey and new directions. *EJOR* 8, 207–218.

Rubin, P.A., Narasimhan, R. [1984]. Fuzzy goal programming with nested priorities. *FSS* 14, 115–130.

Saaty, T.L. [1978]. Exploring the interface between hierarchies, multiple objectives and fuzzy sets. *FSS* 1, 57–68.

Saaty, T.L. [1980]. *The Analytic Hierarchy Process.* New York.

Saaty, T.L., Vargas, L.G. [1982]. *The Logic of Priorities.* Boston, The Hague, London.

Sakawa, M. [1984]. Interactive multiobjective decision making by the fuzzy sequential proxy optimization technique—FSPOT in: Zimmermann et al. 1984, 241–260.

Sanchez, E., Gouvernet, J., Bartolin, R., Voran, L. [1982]. Linguistic approach in fuzzy logic of W.H.O. classification of dyslipoproteinemias in: Yager (ed.) 1982, 522–588.

Schwab, K.-D. [1983]. *Ein auf dem Konzept der unscharfen Mengen basierendes Entscheidungs-modell bei mehrfacher Zielsetzung.* Frankfurt, Bern, New York.

Shafer, G. [1976]. *A mathematical Theory of Evidence.* Princeton, NJ.

Simon, H.A. [1955]. A behavioral model of rational choice. *Q. J. Econ.* 69, 99–118.

Simon, H.A. [1956]. Rational choice and the structure of the environment. *Psych. Rev.* 63, 129–138.

Simon, H.A. [1957]. *Models of Man.* New York, London.

Siskos, J., Lochard, J., Lombard, J. [1984]. A multicriteria decision-making methodology under fuzziness: Application to the evaluation of radiological protection in nuclear power plant in: Zimmermann et al. 1984, 261–284.

Sixtl. F. [1967]. *Messmethoden der Psychologie.* Beltz, Weinheim.

Small, M., ed. [1984]. *Knowledge Engineering and Decision Support.* Tymeshare UK,

London.
Smets, Ph. [1981]. The degree of belief in a fuzzy event. *Inf. Sci.* 25.
Smets, Ph. [1982]. Probability of a fuzzy event; an axiomatic approach. *FSS* 7, 153–164.
Spillman, B., Spillman, R., Bezdek, J. [1982]. A dynamic perspective on leadership: development of a fuzzy measurement procedure. *FSS* 7, 19–33.
Stefik, M., et al. [1982]. The organization of expert systems. *Artif. Intell.* 18, 135–175.
Stein, W.E. [1980]. Optimal stopping in a fuzzy environment. *FSS* 3, 253–259.
Steuer, R.E. [1986]. *Multiple Criteria Optimization.* New York, Chichester, Brisbane, Toronto.
Sticha, P.J., Weiss, J.J., Donnell, M.L. [1979]. Evaluation and Integration of Imprecise Information. Final Technical Report PR 79-21-90, Decisions & Designs, McLean.
Suppes, P. [1961]. Meaning and use of methods in: H. Freudenthal, (ed.): *The Concept and the Role of the Model in Mathematics and Natural and Social Sciences.* Dordrecht.
Takeda, E. [1982]. Interactive identification of fuzzy outranking relations in a multicriteria decision problem in: Gupta, Sanchez (eds.) 1982, 301–307.
Takeda, E., Nishida, T. [1980]. Multiple criteria decision problems with fuzzy domination structures. *FSS* 3, 123–136.
Tanaka, H., Asai, K. [1984]. Fuzzy linear programming problems with fuzzy numbers. *FSS* 13, 1–10.
Tanaka, K., Mizumoto, M. [1975]. Fuzzy programs and their execution in: Zadeh et. al. (eds.) 1975, 41–76.
Tanaka, H., Okuda, T., Asai, K. [1974]. On fuzzy mathematical programming. *J. Cybern.* 3, 37–46.
Tanaka, H., Okuda, T., Asai, K. [1979]. Fuzzy information and decision in statistical model in: Gupta, Ragade, Yager (eds.) 1979, 303–320.
Tanino, T. [1984]. Fuzzy preference orderings in group decision making. *FSS* 12, 117–131.
Tarski, A. [1953]. A general method in proofs of undecidability in: Tarski et al. (eds.): *Undecidable Theories.* North Holland, Amsterdam, 11.
Thole, U., Zimmermann, H.-J., Zysno, P. [1979]. On the suitability of minimum and product operators for the intersection of fuzzy sets. *FSS* 2, 167–180.
Thurstone, L.L. [1927]. A law of comparative judgment. *Psychol. Rev.* 34, 273–286.
Togai, M., Watanabe, H. [1986]. A VLSI implementation of a fuzzy-inference engine: Toward an expert system on a chip. *Inf. Science* 38, 147–163.
Tong, R.M., Bonissone, P.P. [1979]. Linguistic decision analysis using fuzzy sets Memo UCB/ERL M79/72, Berkeley.
Tong, R.M., Bonissone, P.P. [1984]. Linguistic solutions to fuzzy decision problems in: Zimmermann et al. 1984, 323–334.
Tsukamoto, Y. [1979]. An approach to fuzzy reasoning method in Gupta et al. (eds.) 1979, 137–149.
van Melle, W. [1979]. A Domain-independent Production-rule System for Consultation Programs. Proceedings IJCAI-79, 923–925.
Verdegay, J.L. [1982]. Fuzzy mathematical programming in: Gupta, Sanchez (eds.) 1982, 231–238.

Verdegay, J.L. [1984]. A dual approach to solve the fuzzy linear programming problem. *FSS* 14, 131–141.

Vincke, Ph. [1986]. Analysis of Multicriteria Decision Aid in Europe. EJOR 25, 160–168.

Wagenknecht, M., Hartmann, K. [1983]. On fuzzy rank-ordering in polyoptimization. *FSS* 11, 253–264.

Wang, P.P., ed. [1983]. *Advances in Fuzzy Sets, Possibility Theory and Application.* New York, London.

Wang, P.P., Chang, S.K. (eds.) [1980]. *Fuzzy Sets.* New York, London.

Watada, J. [1983]. Theory of fuzzy multivariate analysis and its application Diss. University of Osaka, Feb.

Watada, J., Fu, K.S., Yao, J.T.P. [1984]. Linguistic assessment of structural damage CE-STR-84-30, Purdue.

Waterman, D.A. [1986]. *A Guide to Expert Systems.* Reading, MA.

Weber, S. [1983]. A general concept of fuzzy connectives, negations and implications based on t-norms and t-conorms. *FSS* 11, 115–134.

Weiss, S., et al. [1982]. Building expert systems for controlling complex programs. *Proc. 2nd Ann. Nat. Conf. on AI*, Pittsburgh, 1982, 322–326.

Wenstop, F. [1980]. Quantitative analysis with linguistic values. *FSS* 4, 99–115.

Wenstop, F. [1981]. Deductive verbal models of organisations in: Mamdani, Gaines (eds.) 1981, 149–167.

Werners, B. [1984]. *Interaktive Entscheidungsunterstützung durch ein flexibles mathematischees Programmierungssystem.* München.

Whalen, Th., Schott, B. [1983]. Decision support with fuzzy production systems in: Wang (ed.) 1983, 199–217.

Whalen, Th., Schott, B. [1985]. Goal-directed approximate reasoning in a fuzzy production system in: Gupta et al. (eds.) 1985, 505–518.

White, D.J. [1969]. *Dynamic Programming.* San Francisco.

White, D.J. [1975]. Decision Methodology. London, New York.

White, D.J., Bowen, K.C. [1975]. *The Role and Effectiveness of Theories of Decision in Practice.* London.

Whiter, A. [1984]. *PI-QL: Nearer to the Ideals of Logic Programming via Fuzzy Logic.* Farnborough.

Wiedey, G., Zimmermannn, H.-J. [1978]. Media selection and fuzzy linear programming. *J. Op. Res. Soc.* 29, 1071–1084.

Witte, E. [1968]. Phasen-Theorem und Organisation komplexer Entscheidungen. *Zeitschr. f. betriebsw. Forschung* 20, 625.

Wong, F.S., Ross, T.J., Boissonade, A.C. [1984]. Fuzzy sets and survivability analysis of protective structures RP 8411, FSW, Feb.

Yager, R.R. [1978]. Fuzzy decision making including unequal objectives. *FSS* 1, 87–95.

Yager, R.R. [1980]. On a general class of fuzzy connectives. *FSS* 4, 235–242.

Yager, R.R. [1981]. A procedure for ordering fuzzy subsets of the unit interval *Inf. Science* 24, 143–161.

Yager, R.R., ed. [1982]. *Fuzzy Set and Possibility Theory.* New York, Oxford, Toronto.

Yager, R.R. [1984]. A representation of the probability of fuzzy subset. *FSS* 13, 273–283.

Yager, R.R. [1985]. Knowledge trees in complex knowledge bases. *FSS* 15, 45–64.

Yeh, R., Bang, S. [1975]. Fuzzy relations, fuzzy graphs and their applications to clustering analysis in: Zadeh et al. 1975, 125–150.

Ying, C.C. [1969]. A model of adaptive team decision. *Oper. Res.* 17, 800–811.

Yu, P.L. [1984]. Dissolution of fuzziness for better decisions—perspectives and techniques in: Zimmermann et. al. 1984, 171–208.

Yu, Yandong [1985]. Triangular norms and TNF-sigma-algebras. *FSS* 16, 251–264.

Zadeh, L.A. [1965]. Fuzzy sets. *Inf. Control* 8, 338–353.

Zadeh, L.A. [1968]. Probability Measures of Fuzzy Events. J. Math. Anal. Appl. 23, 421–427.

Zadeh, L.A. [1971]. Similarity relations and fuzzy orderings. *Inf. Sciences* 3, 177–200.

Zadeh, L.A. [1972]. On fuzzy algorithms Memo ERL-M 325, UCB, Berkeley.

Zadeh, L.A. [1973b]. Outline of a new approach to the analysis of complex systems and decision processes. *IEEE Trans. SMC* 3, 28–44.

Zadeh, L.A. [1977]. Linguistic characterization of preference relations as a basis for choice in social systems Memo UCB/ERL M 77/24, Berkeley.

Zadeh, L.A. [1976]. A Fuzzy-algorithmic Approach to the Definition of Complex or Imprecise Concepts. Int. J. Man-Machine Studies 8, 249–291.

Zadeh, L.A. [1978]. Fuzzy Sets as a Basis for a Theory of Possibility. FSS 1, 3–28.

Zadeh, L.A. [1979]. Fuzzy sets and information granularity in: Gupta et al. (eds.) 1979, 3–18.

Zadeh, L.A. [1981]. Test-score semantics for natural languages and meaning-representation via PRUF in: Rieger 1981, 281–349.

Zadeh, L.A. [1982]. A computational approach and fuzzy quantifiers in natural languages Memo UCB/ERL M 82/38, May/Nov.

Zadeh, L.A. [1983a]. A computational approach to fuzzy quantifiers in natural languages. *Comp. & Maths. with Appl.* 9, 149–184.

Zadeh, L.A. [1983b]. The role of fuzzy logic in the management of uncertainty in expert systems. *FSS* 11, 199–227.

Zadeh, L.A. [1983c]. A theory of commonsense knowledge Memo UCB/ERL M 83/26.

Zadeh, L.A. [1984]. A simple view of the Dempster-Shafer theory of evidence. Cognitive Science Progr., Berkeley, October.

Zadeh, L.A., Fu, K.S., Tanaka, K., Shimura, M., eds. [1975]. Fuzzy sets and their applications to cognitive and decision processes. New York, San Francisco, London.

Zangwill, W.I. [1969]. *Nonlinear Programming.* Englewood Cliffs, NJ.

Zeleny, M. [1975]. Games with multiple payoffs. *Int. J. Game Theory* 4, 179–191.

Zemankova-Leech, M., Kandel, A. [1984]. *Fuzzy Relational Data Bases—A Key to Expert Systems.* Köln.

Zemankova-Leech, M., Kandel, A. [1985]. Uncertainty propagation to expert systems in: Gupta et al. (eds.) 1985, 529–548.

Zimmermann, H.-J. [1976]. Description and optimization of fuzzy systems. *Int. J. Gen. Syst.* 2, 209–215.

Zimmermann, H.-J. [1978]. Fuzzy programming and linear programming with several objective functions. *FSS* 1, 45–55.

Zimmermann, H.-J. [1980]. Testability and meaning of mathematical models in social sciences. *Math. Model.* 1, 123–139.

Zimmermann, H.-J. [1983a]. Fuzzy mathematical programming. *Comput. Oper. Res.* 10, 291–298.

Zimmermann, H.-J. [1983b]. Using fuzzy sets in operational research. *EJOR* 13, 201–216.

Zimmermann, H.-J. [1985a]. The applications of fuzzy set theory to mathematical programming. *Inf. & Control* 36, 29–58.

Zimmermann, H.-J. [1985b]. *Fuzzy Set Theory and Its Applications.* Boston: Kluwer-Nijhoff.

Zimmermann, H.-J. [1986a]. Fuzzy set theory and mathematical programming in: Jones et al. (eds.) 1986, 99–114.

Zimmermann, H.-J. [1986b]. Multi criteria decision making in crisp and fuzzy environments in: Jones et al. (eds.) 1986, 233–256.

Zimmermann, H.-J., Pollatschek, M.A. [1984]. Fuzzy 0-1 Programming in: Zimmermann et al. 1984, 133–146.

Zimmermann, H.-J., Zysno, P. [1980]. Latent connectives in human decision making. *FSS* 4, 37–51.

Zimmermann, H.-J., Zysno, P. [1982]. *Zugehörigkeitsfunktionen unscharfer Mengen.* DFG-Forschungsbericht.

Zimmermann, H.-J., Zysno, P. [1983]. Decisions and evaluations by hierarchical aggregation of information. *FSS* 10, 243–266.

Zimmermann, H.-J., Zysno, P. [1985]. Quantifying vagueness in decision models. *EJOR* 22, 148–158.

Zimmermann, H.-J., Zadeh, L.A., Gaines, B.R. (eds.) [1984]. *Fuzzy Sets and Decision Analysis.* Amsterdam, New York, Oxford.

Zysno, P. [1982]. The Integration of Concepts within Judgmental and Evaluative Processes in: Trappl et al. (eds.), 509–516.

Index